The Illustrated Reference Book of Science

Picture Credits

The Joy of Knowledge
GENERAL EDITOR: JAMES MITCHELL

The Illustrated Reference Book of Science

WINDWARD

Preface

How to use this book

Science is a vital section of the *Joy of Knowledge*. It contains all the general knowledge my editors and I think most interesting about the physical sciences. It deals with the history of those subjects – mathematics, physics and chemistry – and goes on to explain the basic scientific laws and theories in non-specialist language.

The spread system

Every topic in the *Joy of Knowledge* takes the form of an article that occupies two facing pages of text and pictures; what we call a "spread". Each two-page spread in the book is organized in the same way. It is the heart of our approach to explaining things.

The spread system is a strict discipline but once you get used to it we hope you'll find the structure to be systematic and reassuring. You should start to feel at home in all sorts of unlikely areas of knowledge with the spread system to guide you. It works like this.

Each spread in this volume, as throughout the *Joy of Knowledge,* tells a self-contained story. It explains all the essential facts you need to know about its subject in as efficient a manner as possible. We believe that the discipline of having to get in all the essential and relevant facts in this comparatively small space actually makes for better results than a rambling essay could achieve – text that has to get straight to the point, pictures and diagrams that illustrate the salient points in a clear and comprehensible fashion, and captions that really work and explain the point of the pictures.

The spreads are, in a sense, the building blocks of knowledge. Like the various circuits and components that go to make up a computer, they are also systematically "programmed" to help the reader find out things more easily and remember them better. Each spread, for example, has a main article of about 850 words summarising the subject. This article is illustrated by an average of ten pictures and diagrams, the captions of which both complement and supplement the basic information in the main article. Each spread, too, has a "key" picture or diagram in the top right-hand corner. The purpose of this picture is twofold: it summarises the story of the spread visually and it is intended to act as a memory stimulator to help you recall all the integrated facts and pictures on a given subject.

Where to start

A good way to begin acquiring knowledge from this particular part of the *Joy of Knowledge* series is initially to read the Introduction. The Introduction provides a useful framework for the information contained in the following pages. If, however, you prefer to plunge straight into the book (but don't have much basic general knowledge on the subject) I suggest you look first at the spreads "Mathematics and civilization" beginning on page 8 and "What is an atom?" on page 44, "The nature of energy" on page 50 and "What is chemistry?" on page 114. Once you have absorbed the information on these spreads you can build up a more comprehensive general knowledge by exploring the rest of the book.

Science is a book all about discovery, about man's search for those laws of nature that govern the world he lives in. I hope you will find it both stimulating and helpful.

Contents

The Illustrated Reference Book of Science

Editor's Introduction

Today's scientists owe much of the development of modern science to the efforts of the early thinkers – men such as Aristarchus, Aristotle and Democritus. They were "natural philosophers" – experts on matters of their day. Their ceaseless questioning of every aspect of their world forms the basis of what we now call science. But it was not until the age of the experimenters, when men such as Tycho Brahe, Galileo Galilei and Isaac Newton started their inquiries into the ways of the world, that true science was born. For, rather than just postulating (as the first thinkers did), they saw the need to test their theories by experiment. As a result, they modified their theories using experiment, and thus the scientific method was established.

This wide-ranging book documents the organization of man's scientific knowledge, from prehistoric and ancient sciences through to the modern science of giant molecules and the chemistry of life. The book divides naturally into four general subjects: the history of science, mathematics, physics and chemistry.

The history of science

As often happens today, scientific principles do not always precede their technological applications, so prehistoric and ancient science must be seen in the light of the technology of the times. In the spread on Asian and medieval science, we see the unmistakable evidence of an organized scientific method and in the spread on Alchemy and the Age of Reason, the struggle between established custom and the introduction of new ideas is evident. This battle has affected the development of science even to this day.

Mathematics

Science leads us logically through the first principles of mathematics and illustrates the subject's natural development, in particular, man's need to use measurements in his everyday activities. The book progresses through the development of our number system and its use in finding unknown quantities by arithmetic and algebraic manipulations. Working with lines and angles is probably one of the earliest of scientific developments. The theorems of plane geometry were developed by the Greek thinkers, but many of the problems encountered in the modern world were unknown to early scientists and, without calculus, our understanding of the world would be even more limited. Altogether thirty-four instructive pages are devoted to setting out the principles upon which much of the rest of the book depends.

Physics

The first suggestion that matter might consist of separate minute particles – atoms – was made in the 5th century BC, probably by Leucippus of Miletus. A whole new branch of learning (particle physics) is now devoted to devising a single theory that will fully explain the behaviour of the even smaller particles that make up atoms. Starting with the principles of atomic theory, the book examines the scientific advances that have led to the atomic bomb and nuclear power.

Newton's laws of motion describe how mass and force are related, and how forces acting against each other can produce a state of equilibrium. The study of the forces that affect a stationary object is known as statics. When an object moves, different forces act upon it, and the study of moving forces is known as dynamics. *Science* explains all these topics as well as speed, acceleration and hydraulics and also examines how the natural forces of gravity, magnetism and electricity obey similar laws.

In the part of the book that deals with sound, two-page spreads explain noise, loudness, pitch and frequency. The reasons why various musical instruments – woodwind, brass or strings, for example – sound different are discussed. The book goes on to describe the different states of matter – gases, liquids and solids – and the ways these are affected by temperature and pressure. There is also an explanation of what happens to matter at extremely high and extremely low temperatures, and how energy transfer during changes in temperature is governed by the laws of thermodynamics.

An important and fascinating section on light discusses colour and the visible spectrum; mirrors and lenses and their use in instruments such as microscopes and periscopes; relativity and the speed of light; light waves and refraction; the energy in light and ways it can be used and measured; and the nature of lasers and the ways in which these high-energy light beams can be used.

Few aspects of twentieth-century life are unaffected by electricity, and so the book devotes twenty pages to the subject, explaining exactly what electricity and electric currents are; the history of magnetism and how it works; how magnetism is used in industry, transport and in everyday life; how transformers, motors and dynamos use and generate electricity; and the principles behind AC and DC circuits, semiconductors and general electronics.

Chemistry

Finally, this absorbing book describes the chemical elements that make up everything on earth. It begins with the history of their discovery and classification and then considers simple and complex chemicals and their structures. The nature of chemical reactions, electro-chemistry and chemical analysis are thoroughly explained, and the section ends with an account of the principles of biochemistry, the study of the chemistry of living things.

Prehistoric and ancient science

Nearly two million years ago the ancestors of man used stones as weapons and tools. The need to master the environment and develop tools for the purpose involved a primitive knowledge of science [Key]. Ever since that time the development of science, technology and civilization have been interrelated.

Science of prehistoric man

After perhaps half a million years, the descendants of these first tool-users had become more selective, concentrating on flint, with its useful cutting edges [1, 2]. They discovered how to make fires.

Cave paintings of 15,000 years ago indicate a primitive knowledge of animal anatomy. Some, which show prehistoric elephants with the position of the animal's heart indicated by arrows, may be a record of hunting prowess, or a form of sympathetic magic attempting to influence the hunt.

About 10,000 years ago, men began to adopt a more settled way of life. They invented a repetitive system of food production that involved the domestication of animals and the cultivation of plants. Life in such

settled communities stimulated invention in various building materials, used to provide better shelter and protection. Fires were kept burning continuously for warmth and cooking and frightening off marauders, and it is possible that the women who tended the fires were the first to notice that when clay is left near a fire it hardens into pottery. When certain stones and earths were roasted in a fire, heavy liquids sometimes ran out which, when cool, hardened into useful metals.

Egypt and Mesopotamia

The people who settled in the Nile valley found themselves in an area that was exceptionally safe and fertile. They noticed that the silt brought down by the yearly floods renewed the fertility of the soil so they dug channels and built embankments to divert the fertile silt-laden flood waters onto their fields. These flood-control operations marked the invention of large-scale engineering. The Nile valley dwellers later applied engineering techniques in the construction of the pyramids [5].

It is probable that the science of geometry

arose from the need to fix positions where landmarks had been washed out by annual flooding. Arithmetic was developed to calculate quantities of crops so that they could be shared among the people. Egyptian arithmetic depended on a method of doubling, much as in the operations of a modern computer. Geometrical surveying led the Egyptians to a good method of calculating the area of a circle; they assumed the circumference of a circle to be the square of eight-ninths times its diameter. They also needed to determine the seasons and the times of the Nile floods and so devised a calendar of 365 days.

The people of Mesopotamia, in the double valley of the rivers Tigris and the Euphrates, were developing in a similar way but under rather different conditions. There was little stone in their land, so they recorded information by making marks on soft clay tablets, which were then baked. The Mesopotamians introduced the idea that the value of a digit depends on its position in a number and they even solved algebraic equations. The Egyptians were primarily concerned with simple, practical calculations

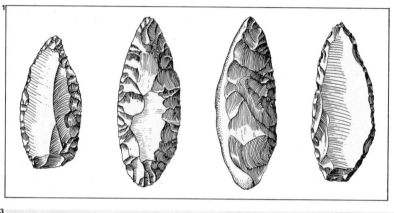

1 Tools of the middle Palaeolithic or Mousterian stage in France date from 70,000 to 32,000 years ago. There were various human groups living in Europe in this period. They left many traces of their culture in shelters and entrances to caves. Tools are found dating from the beginning of the last period of glaciation and the scrapers and knives shown here illustrate fine stone tool technology.

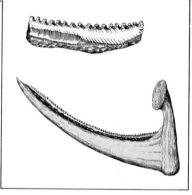

2 Bones, antlers and wood were used by early men as raw materials for tools and weapons. A wooden tool could be given an efficient cutting edge by adding a row of suitably shaped flint slivers, as in this early Egyptian wooden sickle from about 3000–2500 BC. Pointed wooden implements could also be hardened by charring the point in a fire. Antlers were shaped by carving or heating.

3 The Neolithic people who occupied the region of Stoney Littleton, England in about 3000 BC, constructed large barrows for the burial of their dead [A]. A barrow is a long structure with an entrance passage crossed by transept chambers; this barrow has three pairs. The passage [B] contains a vault with corbels or projections from the walls to carry "capstones", in a manner similar to those in vaults found on islands lying off the coast of Scotland.

whereas the Babylonians were much more sophisticated, especially in connection with the science of astronomy.

One of the first Greeks to visit and study other civilizations was Thales of Miletus, who was born in about 630 BC. He returned from Egypt well versed in the techniques of Egyptian geometry. From experience in building, the Egyptians had learned that if a triangle has two sides of equal length, then the angles at its base are also equal. Thales looked for a way of proving this fact. He made two identical triangles, each with two equal sides, and found that when one was picked up and turned over, it could be laid on top of the other and fitted exactly. In this way, a mathematical proof was developed.

Famous Greek scientists

To Pythagoras, born about 60 years after Thales, is attributed a proof of the famous theorem that the square on the longest side of a right-angled triangle is equal to the sum of the squares on the other two sides. Pythagoras sought to explain the properties of matter in terms of numbers.

Another Greek, Euclid (born 330 BC), provided the basic principles for the teaching of classical geometry that have been used ever since. Less than 50 years later, in 287 BC, Archimedes was born in Sicily. He applied the new mathematics with extraordinary power and logic and made many inventions. He established the principle that, when a body is weighed in a liquid, its apparent loss in weight is equal to the weight of the liquid displaced; he is credited with inventing a screw for raising water [7] from one level to another; and he succeeded in launching a large ship using levers.

Astronomy was first placed on an adequate scientific basis by Eudoxus, who was born in about 408 BC. He showed that the motions of the Sun and planets could be explained by assuming that they moved with uniform motion in perfect circles, the centres of which are near, but not exactly at, the centre of the Earth. Later Greek astronomers arranged far more complex systems of circular motions, equalling in accuracy the work of Nicolas Copernicus (1473–1543), nearly 2,000 years later.

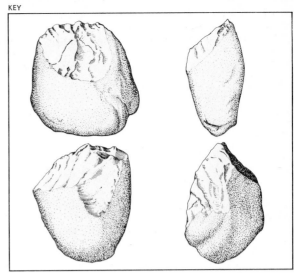

These Oldowan tools were first discovered by Louis Leakey (1903–72) in 1931 in the Olduvai Gorge in northern Tanzania, East Africa. They range from simple broken pebbles to chopping tools, and are 1.2 million years to 1.8 million years old.

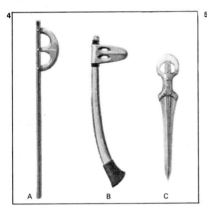

4 The introduction of metals gave early toolmakers much more manageable raw materials – first soft metals such as gold and copper, later bronze and finally iron. Shown here are an Egyptian eye axe [A] from Megiddo (*c*. 1900 BC), an Egyptian duck-bill axe [B] from Ugarit (*c*. 1800 BC) and an Egyptian bronze dagger [C] of the Hyksos period (*c*. 1650 BC). But iron made the best cutting edge.

5 The Great Pyramid in Egypt was erected by command of the pharaoh Khufu (in Greek, Cheops) of the 4th Dynasty, about 3000 BC. It contains 6.5 million tonnes of limestone. A primary purpose of the pyramids was to provide grand tombs. They may also have had other purposes. The whole group of the major Egyptian pyramids was built within little more than a century. They involved an enormous concentration of labour and it has been suggested that their construction may have provided a convenient means of organizing the whole population of Egypt, creating a centralized state – hence the short building period.

6 The Mesopotamians, lacking the Egyptians' papyrus for writing, made records on clay tablets. Characters were formed by pressing the wedge-shaped end of a stylus into the soft clay and a permanent record could be obtained by baking the clay in a fire until it became hard. From its wedge shape, the writing is known as cuneiform. The associated number system used strokes that, to our eyes, faintly resemble the Roman numerals of 30 centuries later. A numeral's position determined its value.

7 An Archimedean screw is used for raising water. Archimedes (287–212 BC) was a master both of the most refined mathematics and of practical invention. It is said that he invented the screw for raising water to assist irrigation in Egypt. It consists, in principle, of a wedge that can exert sustained pressure in a particular direction by being continuously revolved. In the machine shown in this illustration the water is raised from the sink on the left. When the curved pipe is rotated by pulling the rope, the water is pushed up inside it and delivered into the tank at the top on the right. Screws were not known before Archimedes: those for fastening objects probably arose from his device.

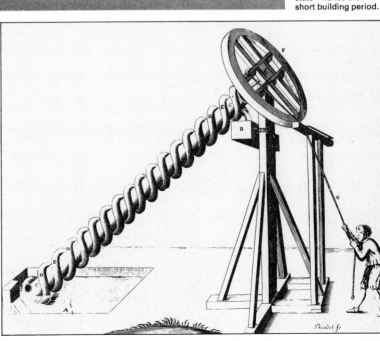

Asian and medieval science

By the fifth century AD the long-ailing Roman Empire lost control of Western Europe. It was overcome by its excessive size, by the "softness" of its citizens, and by a population explosion in Asia that propelled vigorous new peoples against Rome's extended frontiers. At the same time the Eastern Roman Empire, whose capital was at Byzantium (later Constantinople and now Istanbul), flourished until a new attack from the east in the seventh century.

International influences

The Arabs emerged from Arabia as the followers of the new prophet Mohammed (AD c. 570–632), a trader from Mecca. Within about 100 years they captured much of the Middle East and North Africa and invaded Spain and even France [2]. These new conquerors had no culture of their own, but they borrowed learning from Syriac, Greek, Indian and other peoples whom they encountered through their conquests and travels. They became the founders of the internationalism that is one of the most striking features of science. They aimed at all-embracing knowledge and perhaps Avicenna (980–1037) came nearest to attaining it.

The Muslims had a strong trading tradition. Like other peoples, they were interested in the exact calculation of shares in goods and the allocation of family inheritances. They assessed the declining value of female slaves in much the same way as cars are depreciated today. When they invaded India, they discovered Indian mathematics.

The Indians introduced the number system now universally in use, together with the zero symbol and decimals. Their work became known to Al-Khwarizmi (780–c. 850), the greatest of the Arab mathematicians. He was librarian to the caliph Al-Mamun (786–833) in Baghdad and published in 830 his treatise on *Al-jabr wa'l muqabala*, from which the word algebra is derived. He studied various classes of quadratic (second order) equations and called the unknown quantity to be calculated "the root". Knowledge of mathematics in medieval Europe was based mainly on Latin translations of his works. One of his most famous successors was the Persian poet Omar Khayyám (c. 1048–1122), who dealt with special classes of cubic equations.

The Arabs devoted much attention to pharmacy [5] and to astronomy. They calculated elaborate trigonometrical tables, which were used to determine the exact times of prayers and to navigate the Indian Ocean. Córdoba in Spain became the most advanced intellectual centre in Europe. The dependence of medieval Europe on Arab knowledge is illustrated by the example of Adelard of Bath, who went to Córdoba disguised as a Muslim student in 1120. He returned to England with a copy of Euclid's book, which served as a mathematical text for feudal Europe for the next four centuries.

Chinese science and technology

The Arabs also brought knowledge of Chinese inventions and discoveries to Europe, including gunpowder, the magnetic compass, printing with movable type and an efficient horse harness.

The Chinese invented an escapement mechanism for a water clock [1], generally credited to Yi Hoing, in 725. It enabled them

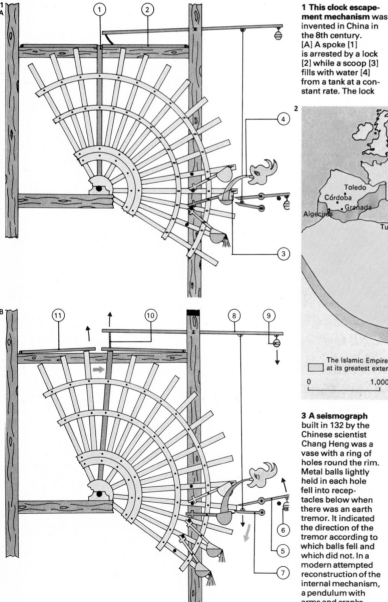

1 This clock escapement mechanism was invented in China in the 8th century. [A] A spoke [1] is arrested by a lock [2] while a scoop [3] fills with water [4] from a tank at a constant rate. The lock is released [B] when the filling scoop trips a checking fork [5], overcomes its counterweight [6] and trips a coupling tongue [7], which pulls down an upper lever [8] with its own counterweight [9]. This jerks a chain [10], freeing the lock and allowing the wheel to swing clockwise until the lock drops again, arresting the following spoke which is also held steady by a ratchet lock [11].

2 The Islamic Empire, by the 8th century, stretched from India to the Pyrenees, making major contributions to mathematics and chemistry and laying the basis for the international spread of learning.

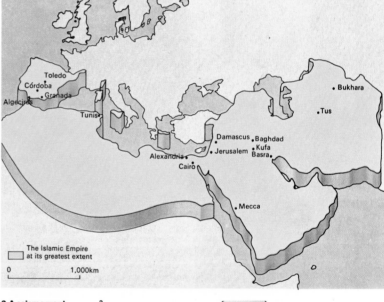

The Islamic Empire at its greatest extent

0   1,000km

Toledo · Córdoba · Granada · Algeciras · Tunis · Bukhara · Tus · Damascus · Baghdad · Kufa · Basra · Alexandria · Jerusalem · Cairo · Mecca

3 A seismograph built in 132 by the Chinese scientist Chang Heng was a vase with a ring of holes round the rim. Metal balls lightly held in each hole fell into receptacles below when there was an earth tremor. It indicated the direction of the tremor according to which balls fell and which did not. In a modern attempted reconstruction of the internal mechanism, a pendulum with arms and cranks governs the motion of the balls.

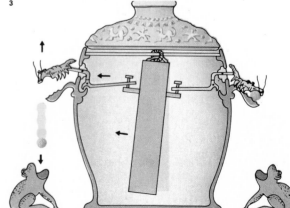

to build the first accurate mechanical clocks. Chinese science also produced the first seismograph, for detecting earthquakes [3], built by Chang Heng in 132. In 1054 they observed the great new star – a nova, the parent of the Crab Nebula – later to become one of the most important objects in the development of modern radio astronomy.

The Arabs performed a unique service as world informants on ancient and contemporary science. They introduced the ideas of India and China to the Western world. But they were not the founders of modern science, for this arose in Europe.

Medieval science

The Roman Empire in Europe disintegrated into a multitude of individual strongholds of local military chieftains. Slaves became bandits, or peasants tied to the land, but no longer slaves. So the feudal period began. People who settled around the strong-points came to be known as the bourgeoisie, because they lived outside the castle or burg. Many of them were craftsmen. They were dependent on what they could learn from the

Arab encyclopaedists but they looked at the old knowledge in a more individual way. One such man who played a significant role in the advance of medieval science was Leonardo Fibonacci of Pisa (c. 1180–1250). His father was employed on the Barbary coast and there Leonardo learned the Arabic language and arithmetic. On his return to Pisa he introduced Arabic numerals into Europe.

The most eminent of English medieval scientists was Roger Bacon (1214–94). He proposed combinations of lenses for telescopes and microscopes and may have been the first to suggest spectacles [4].

Roger Bacon said that the only man he knew who was to be praised for his experimental science was Petrus Peregrinus of Maricourt, who published a treatise on magnetism in 1269. He explicitly pointed out the importance of manual skill in science. He was one of the forerunners of modern science, in which experiment and theory are equally balanced. This became possible only through the emancipation of the craftsman in medieval Europe, a change that was to lead to the Renaissance.

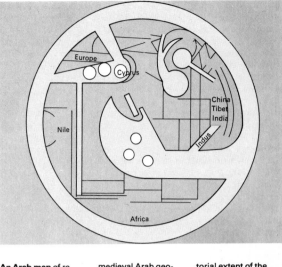

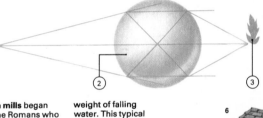

An Arab map of remarkably modern graphic style shows the seas and land masses known to medieval Arab geographers. The concept of a round world with an encircling ocean and the terri- torial extent of the map indicates the importance of the Arab contribution to man's knowledge.

4 Roger Bacon [A] was not personally an experimenter or mathematician but he realized the importance of experiment and mathematics for the advancement of science. His imagination enabled him to make a remarkable collection of scientific suggestions, culled from many sources and ranging from vague hints to clear diagrams. He gave substantially correct optical explanations of [B] why a spherical flask of water [2] acts as a burning glass [3] to concentrate the rays of the sun [1] and [C] how a convex lens [4] produces a magnified image [5] of an object [6] beneath it.

5 A typical pharmacy shop of the Middle Ages was based on Arab traditions. The Arabs brought knowledge of Persian and Indian drugs and spices such as camphor, cloves, cassia, nutmeg and senna. Their influence on European pharmacy was exerted chiefly through Benedictine monks. In the 14th century pharmacy, medicine, chemistry and the grocery business were combined and apothecaries and grocers organized themselves in guilds.

6 Corn mills began with the Romans who spread techniques that helped them to exploit their empire. They built undershot and overshot water mills, one driven by the momentum of flowing water and the other by the weight of falling water. This typical modern example has an undershot drive [6] with a hopper [1] for the corn and a chute [2] conveying it to grindstones [3]. The flour produced fell into a chute [4] and then poured into a bag [5].

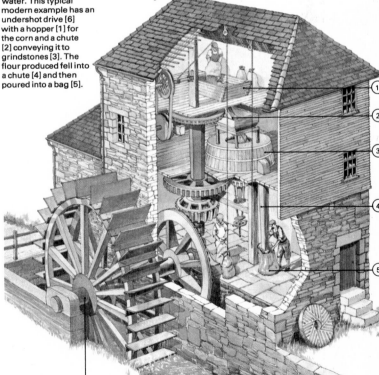

Alchemy and the age of reason

Men gained some practical knowledge of the working of materials in early times but work in the crafts (what is now called technology) was regarded as a lowly pursuit. One reason for this attitude was the disagreeable working conditions associated with them. An Egyptian scribe of 1500 BC noted that the metalworker "stinks like fish-spawn"

Alchemy and the Renaissance
In the second century AD, Diocletian (245–313) ordered that all books on the working of gold, silver and copper should be destroyed to prevent counterfeiting and inflation. The effect was to reduce rational research on practical problems and to increase interest in magic as a method of transmuting base metals into gold. The centre of the development was Alexandria and the Arabs called the new science *alchemy* after Khem, or "black", the name given to Egypt because of its black earth.

The Alexandrians invented apparatus for heating, melting, filtering and distilling substances. They introduced the glass flasks and retorts still typical of chemical laboratories.

The Arabs [1] adopted, extended and transmitted these advances. Their greatest chemist was Jabir ibn Haijan, or Gebir (*c.* AD 721–817), who worked on the transmutation of metals and propounded a theory of their constitution that was not completely superseded until the eighteenth century. Besides being familiar with chemical operations such as crystallization, solution and reduction, he attempted to explain them. His most useful discovery was nitric acid.

Modern science was founded during the Renaissance in the urban society of Italian cities where craftsmen became emancipated and even famous. The supreme example was Leonardo da Vinci (1452–1519) who knew little Latin and no Greek but analysed technical processes scientifically.

Copernicus and Galileo
Nicolas Copernicus (1473–1543) was a Polish–German scholar who studied at Cracow and Bologna in the 1490s. He noted from astronomical references in Latin and Greek literature that Heraclides (388–315 BC) had assigned a motion to the earth "after the manner of a wheel being carried on its own axis". Copernicus found "by much and long observation" that a consistent account of the movements of the planets could be given on the basis that the earth revolves around the sun. The account of this in Copernicus' treatise *De Revolutionibus Orbium Caelestium* was published in 1543 when he was on his deathbed. The Copernican theory [Key] is perhaps the most important scientific theory in history for it changed man's conception of his place in the universe. Formerly man had believed that the universe revolved around the earth and himself; now he realized that man was but a minute incidental speck in a universe of almost inconceivable vastness.

The Renaissance effort in science was completed by Galileo Galilei [2] who cleared the way for modern science. Copernicus discovered how the Solar System works but Galileo gained the first precise knowledge of how things on the earth move. He was born in Pisa in 1564, the same year as Shakespeare, and died in 1642, the year in which Isaac Newton was born. He went to the local

1 Alchemical processes are represented by the figures on this Arab manuscript reflecting cross-cultural influences. The Arabs gained their main introduction to alchemy through Alexandria and spread it to Western Europe in about the eleventh century. Although they improved on the experimental techniques of the Alexandrians they did not escape the influence of their mystical theorizing which was based on animistic beliefs in objects possessing souls.

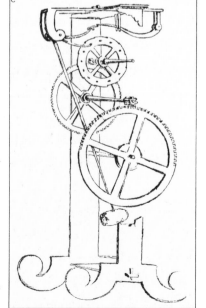

2 Galileo [A] discovered the constancy of the swing of a pendulum, which he later adopted into a pendulum clock [C]. His development of the telescope led to original observations on the planets, including the discovery of the satellites of Jupiter, first described in a pamphlet of 1610, a page of which [B] is shown here. The Church imprisoned him for refuting its divine knowledge.

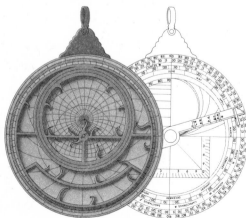

3 The astrolabe, invented by the Greek Hipparchus around 150 BC and developed by Arab scholars and astronomers, was introduced to Europe in about the tenth century. Two metal discs bore projections of the celestial and terrestrial spheres. A rotating arm on the back enabled the user to set the inclination of an object from the horizon and to calculate various angles. A forerunner to the sextant, it was a navigational aid whose uses included finding angles of latitude and the time.

university. According to legend, a swinging lamp in the cathedral attracted his attention. He noticed that the time of the swing was independent of the size of the swing (its amplitude). When he arrived home he checked the fact with a bullet and a piece of string. He later used this fundamental property of a pendulum in designing a pendulum clock.

When Galileo was appointed professor he was obliged to teach Aristotelian science. This caused him to make a careful study of Aristotle's ideas, especially those on the motion of objects. Aristotle (384–322 BC) based his theory on the assumption that objects fall with a speed proportional to their weight. Galileo devised experiments to measure exactly how fast objects do fall and found that all that fall freely do so at the same speed. He made many other discoveries. The results of his application of the telescope to astronomical observation were particularly spectacular evidence that Aristotle's picture of the universe was incomplete and mistaken. Galileo did not fully grasp the theological implications of this.

Galileo's demonstration that the move-ment of objects could be exactly determined by a combination of experiment and mathematical reasoning was extended by Isaac Newton (1642–1727). Newton [5] showed that all the then known physical aspects of the universe and nature could be completely described by mathematical theory utilizing laws consistent with experience. Newton's account, in his *Philosophiae Naturalis Principia Mathematica* (1687), is possibly the greatest single intellectual effort yet made.

The Age of Reason
Newton's achievements increased confidence in the power of human reasoning. They had a particularly striking effect in France where Pierre Laplace (1749–1827) and Joseph Lagrange (1736–1813) extended the Newtonian theory and its supporting mathematics. The new confidence in experiment and calculation developed also in other sciences. Antoine Lavoisier (1743–94) revolutionized chemistry, dispatching the magical and mystical remnants from it and in doing so laying the foundations of modern chemistry [6].

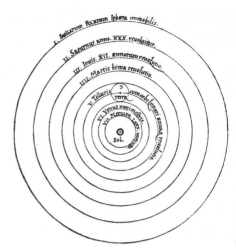

Copernicus pictured the planets as revolving around the sun in a complicated pattern of circular motions, the basis of which is shown here. His theory did not give more accurate planetary predictions than Ptolemy's of AD 140, but it was a triumph of ideas that showed man in his true place in nature. Proof that the planets revolve in ellipses came in 1609 from the German astronomer Johannes Kepler (1571–1630).

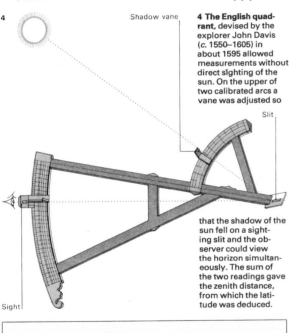

4 The English quadrant, devised by the explorer John Davis (*c.* 1550–1605) in about 1595 allowed measurements without direct sighting of the sun. On the upper of two calibrated arcs a vane was adjusted so that the shadow of the sun fell on a sighting slit and the observer could view the horizon simultaneously. The sum of the two readings gave the zenith distance, from which the latitude was deduced.

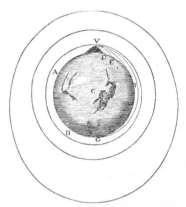

5 Isaac Newton [A] calculated the speed at which a body projected horizontally from the top of a mountain would leave the earth and begin revolving around it. His diagram of the path of an artificial satellite [B] was published in 1728, the year after his death. Newton's genius emerged while he was at Cambridge University. Within a few years he had laid the basis of differential and integral calculus, elucidated the nature of light and colour and had begun to explore the usefulness of mathematical analysis to physical theories. His main achievements in physical science were expressed in his *Principia* (1687) and *Opticks* (1704).

6 Antoine Lavoisier [B] founded modern chemistry by means of experiments leading to his theory about the nature of combustion. This had previously been ascribed to the transfer of a substance called phlogiston, the main agent of chemical change sometimes released as fire. Lavoisier heated mercury and air in a flask with a curved neck, which enabled him to measure exactly the decrease in volume of gas and gain in weight of mercury during 12 days' heating. By means of this apparatus (illustrated here from Lavoisier's own diagram [A]) he showed that the changes could be explained completely in terms of the active constituent of the air discovered by Joseph Priestley (1733–1804), to which Lavoisier gave the name oxygen. The idea of phlogiston was superfluous and chemistry could develop as a rational science based entirely on quantitative measurements. Experiments gave rise to theories that were then tested by other experiments.

Mathematics and civilization

Mathematics is a continuously expanding system of organized thought. It is employed in science, technology, art, music, architecture, economics, sociology, sport – in fact, in almost every aspect of human activity – and has influenced, and often determined, the direction of philosophical thought concerned with man and his universe. Throughout history mathematics has not only reflected developments in civilization but also made a major contribution to those developments.

Algebra, geometry and calculus

There are three major aspects of mathematics. The assembling and combining of sets of objects led to concepts of number [1], computation and algebra. Concern with the measurement of time and space led to geometry, astronomy and chronology. The struggle to understand ideas of continuity and limit led to mathematical analysis and the invention of calculus in the seventeenth century. These three aspects of mathematics overlap considerably. There are now, for example, algebras of sets, vector algebra and algebraic geometry, and a host of specialities

that employ the concepts of other fields of study.

Everything natural or man-made has a structure comprising elements that are related in some special way [Key]. A rock crystal, a plant [6], a spaceship and a political system each has a structure, the study of which is mathematical. Mathematics is the result of the thought process known as abstraction, in which activities related to a physical structure can be organized in such a way that the physical structure is replaced by a mental one, an abstract mathematical model. The power of mathematics is further demonstrated when abstract concepts, such as those of number and space, can be represented by concrete symbols, which may be algebraic, geometric or graphical [3].

Mathematics can be described as a form of inquiry made according to defined rules for drawing conclusions from accepted mathematical truths. History shows, however, that mathematics is also a field of creative activity employing great flights of intuition and imagination [7]. The driving force for the creativity is usually the need man has

to solve the problems of his society. But the motivation may also simply be the challenge of intellectual activity for its own sake.

The first mathematicians

All primitive civilizations developed concepts of number and measure as soon as trade progressed beyond the process of barter. Almost 6,000 years ago the Sumerians were using a numeration system based on 10 (denary system) as well as one based on 60 (sexagesimal system). The sexagesimal system still survives in the measure of time and rotation, reflecting the Babylonian preoccupation with the motion of the Sun, Moon and other planets and their influence on man.

The knowledge acquired became not only a religious force but also solved basic problems of agriculture and social organization. The flooding in Babylon and Egypt demanded seasonal surveys of land, the techniques of which led to geometry. Political, commercial and religious pressures to build palaces, ships, temples and tombs stimulated the further development of

1 **The concept of number** is fundamental to mathematics. It probably developed originally out of the need for farmers to count their animals and produce. Numbers also led to money systems, making buying and selling possible.

2 **Stonehenge** was built in the Bronze Age as a sort of calendar, which probably also had a religious significance.

The positions of the stone blocks can be used to measure the movements of the Sun and Moon and to "predict" eclipses.

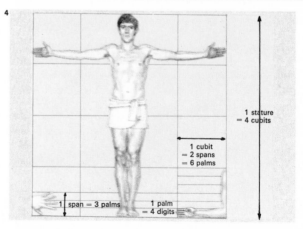

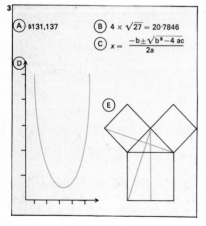

3 **Mathematics** has generated its own "language". Numbers are themselves short-hand forms of words and, linked with units, define exact amounts or measurements [A]. Other symbols stand for operations such as multiplication and square roots [B]. In algebra letters often stand for unknown quantities, as in this formula [C] for finding the solutions to a quadratic equation. A graph [D] can "draw" algebraic functions. Pythagoras created his own geometrical conventions [E].

(A) $131,137

(B) $4 \times \sqrt{27} = 20 \cdot 7846$

(C) $x = \dfrac{-b \pm \sqrt{b^2 - 4\,ac}}{2a}$

(D)

(E)

4 **Man probably first counted on his fingers** and sized objects in terms of his own body. This diagram shows some of the ancient units of length. "Body units" are still used in some countries today. A hand, equal to 4in (about 10cm), is a standard unit for measuring the height of horses and in North America and Britain a foot – 12in (30.5cm) – is still used in measurement as a unit of length. The metric system is now the most widely accepted system of measurement.

1 stature = 4 cubits

1 cubit = 2 spans = 6 palms

1 span = 3 palms

1 palm = 4 digits

geometry. At the same time, astronomy regulated social and religious events and thus served the political ends of ruling priests.

The Greeks established mathematics as a rigid study, placing mathematical argument on a logical basis so that propositions, previously not self-evident, could be deduced from basic assumptions. Euclid's *Elements*, produced in about 300 BC, was a prime example of this approach and dominated geometric thinking for 2,000 years. The Greeks saw beauty in number and shape and their excitement with the Golden Ratio [5] manifested itself in their art and architecture and has been echoed by later civilizations in such places as Notre-Dame in Paris, the architecture of Le Corbusier and the United Nations building in New York.

Every civilization has demanded systems for measuring and each new method has borrowed ideas from previous ones. As civilizations expanded, their influences and trade spread, and the need for standardized units increased. The earlier systems were all based on convenience, so that parts of the body were used for measuring length [4], the working capacity of oxen for area, stones for weight, skins for volume. Each society learned to standardize; in 1791 the French devised the metric system based on the metre, one ten-millionth of the Earth's quadrant (a quarter of the circumference), a distance calculated from an actual survey. International trade has now forced most of the Western world to adopt the metric system of measurement.

The heritage of numbers

Mathematics resembles a living organism in that its growth is affected by the environment in which it lives. The golden age of Greece produced mathematical beauty that afterwards lay dormant for centuries. The Romans used earlier mathematics but solved no new problems. Not until the sixteenth century was there another great advance. Today the whole world is experiencing change at a pace unequalled in the past. This is mirrored in the development of new mathematics and its applications in solving the problems of science, technology, industry and commerce [8] peculiar to the late twentieth century.

Everything on earth, from the atoms in this crystal to the leaves on a tree, consists of individual components. Mathematics seeks to establish the relationships existing between such components.

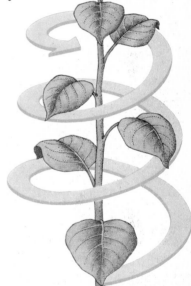

5 Greek mathematicians extended their logical thinking into the arts, establishing mathematical relationships in music and art. The Golden Ratio (approximately 1.618) was to the Greeks a pleasing proportion, incorporated here in the Parthenon (built 447–432 BC).

6 Fibonacci ratios are elements in the series 1/1, 2/1, 3/2, 5/3, 8/5, 13/8 and so on. These values approach the Greek Golden Ratio. Both the numerators and the denominators in the series are formed by adding consecutive members of the series. These ratios occur in nature; a spiral following leaves on this stalk has gaps and turns in the ratio of 5/3.

8 An electronic calculator is a modern machine for "doing sums". It and the much more complex digital computer have replaced earlier calculating devices such as the mechanical calculator, the slide rule and, oldest of all, the abacus.

7 The Grand Canal at Venice was a favourite subject of the Venetian painter Canaletto, whose real name was Giovanni Canal (1697–1768). Renaissance painters studied perspective and so laid the foundations of projective geometry in mathematics, map-making and the draughtsmanship used in architecture and engineering, enabling a three-dimensional object to be represented in two dimensions.

The grammar of numbers

People use arithmetic so frequently in everyday life that they hardly ever think about it. Yet every time a woman buys something and counts her change [Key] she uses the basic concepts of addition and equality, ideas in use since trading began.

Basic rules of arithmetic

The four main types of calculations are addition, subtraction, multiplication and division. They are carried out following basic laws – most of which are merely statements of common sense. The commutative law holds for both addition and multiplication. It simply states that the sum of seven and two $(7+2)$, for example, is the same as the sum of two and seven $(2+7)$. In other words, the order in which numbers are added does not matter. The same is true of multiplication: $4\times3 = 3\times4$ or, in general terms, $a\times b = b\times a$.

The associative law is an extension of this idea and states that, in adding or multiplying a series of numbers, the order of addition or multiplication does not matter [1]. Using symbols to stand for any numbers, $(a+b)+c = a+(b+c)$, or $(a\times b)\times c = a\times(b\times c)$.

The distributive law states that if two numbers are to be added together and the sum multiplied by a third number, the same result is obtained if each of the first two is first multiplied by the third and the two products added. This law is easier to state using symbols: $(a+b)\times c = (a\times c)+(b\times c)$, and is made clear by an example: $(5+7)\times3 = (5\times3)+(7\times3) = 36$.

Multiplication is equivalent to repeated addition. For instance 7×5, is a shorthand way of writing $7+7+7+7+7$. People learn multiplication tables because it is quicker to apply them than to add columns of figures. Electronic calculators and computers, renowned for their speed and accuracy, cannot multiply; they work by successive addition, but do so extremely quickly.

Just as subtraction is the reverse of addition, so division can be regarded as the reverse of multiplication – a repeated subtraction [3]. This is the method employed in doing "long division" sums. Often it is not possible to subtract successively one number from another an exact number of times – there is generally something "left over",

called the remainder. For example, 380 divided by 70, is 5, and the remainder is 30.

Squares and square roots

When a number is squared, it is multiplied by itself (the area of a square is the length of one side multiplied by itself). Three squared (written 3^2) equals 9. The reverse operation is called taking the square root: what number multiplied by itself makes a given number? Squaring a whole number (integer) gives an integer result, but taking the square root of a whole number often does not. And, as the Greek mathematician Pythagoras and his co-workers discovered, there is not always a rational number (expressible as the ratio of two integers) that when squared will equal a particular integer. The square root of 4 is 2 (both integers), but the square root of 2 is somewhere between 1.4142 and 1.4143. The square root of 2 cannot be computed exactly and is called an irrational number.

Fractions, proportions and ratios

Three-sevenths is written as 3/7, meaning 3 divided by 7. It is a fraction (from the Latin

1 Addition is associative – that is, a series of additions can be carried out in any order without affecting the result. This diagram shows the effects of successively weighing [A] 3, 4 and then 5 units of a substance on a spring balance and [B] weighing 4, 5 and then 3 units. In both cases the total weight – the sum or the additions – is 12 units. As in many other mathematical laws, this is applied common sense.

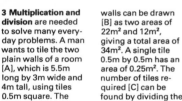

$$3 + 4 = 7$$
$$+ 5 = 12$$
i.e. $3 + 4 + 5 = 12$

$$4 + 5 = 9$$
$$+ 3 = 12$$
i.e. $4 + 5 + 3 = 12$

2 A series of subtractions can also be carried out in any order. Starting with a piece of wood 10 units long [A], we can cut off first 2 units and then remove a further 3 units from the 8 remaining (so completing the sum $10-2-3 = 5$). Or [B] we can remove first 3 units and then cut off another 2 units from the original 10. This time the subtraction sum is $10-3-2 = 5$ but the result is exactly the same.

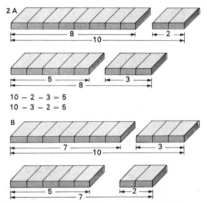

$$10 - 2 - 3 = 5$$
$$10 - 3 - 2 = 5$$

3 Multiplication and division are needed to solve many everyday problems. A man wants to tile the two plain walls of a room [A], which is 5.5m long by 3m wide and 4m tall, using tiles 0.5m square. The walls can be drawn [B] as two areas of 22m² and 12m², giving a total area of 34m². A single tile 0.5m by 0.5m has an area of 0.25m². The number of tiles required [C] can be found by dividing the area of one tile (0.25m²) into the total area to be covered (34m²), giving the result 136 tiles. The same problem can be tackled another way [D]. If the whole area to be tiled is considered, it measures 8.5m by 4m. The long side will accommodate 17 half-metre tiles and the short side only 8 tiles. The total number of tiles required is therefore 17 ×8 = 136, the same result as before but without calculating areas.

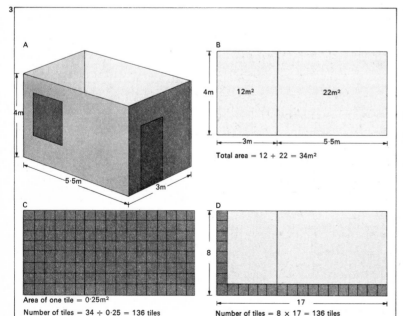

Area of one tile = 0·25m²
Number of tiles = 34 ÷ 0·25 = 136 tiles

Total area = 12 + 22 = 34m²

Number of tiles = 8 × 17 = 136 tiles

4 Dividing quantities into equal parts is a method of forming them into fractions. An athlete such as a pole-vaulter intuitively judges his run-up by dividing it into an equal number of paces so that the pole is in exactly the correct place for the jump – he cannot make half a pace. The same is true when we speak of a bottle being half full or say that we have read a third of a book. In a fraction such as three-quarters, written 3/4, 3 is called the numerator and 4 is the denominator, if the numerator is smaller than the denominator, the fraction is termed "proper"; in an improper fraction the numerator is larger than the denominator, although it can be simplified to a whole number and a fraction.

word *fractus* meaning broken). In books, a fraction may be printed as $\frac{1}{3}$ or 1/3. The number below or to the right of the line is called the denominator and is the number of parts that a unit quantity has been "broken" into. The number above or to the left of the line is the numerator and represents the number of such parts being considered. Two pieces of wood 3m and 7m long have lengths in the proportion of 3 to 7, or in the ratio 3 to 7 (often written 3:7). The shorter piece is 3/7 the length of the longer.

There are two types of fractions, called proper and improper. In a proper fraction, the numerator is less than the denominator: 3/7, 7/8 and 29/54 are examples. An improper fraction has a larger numerator than denominator, as in 5/4 and 22/7. Generally these are simplified by dividing out and expressing the remainder as a fraction, as in 1 1/4 and 3 1/7.

The laws of arithmetic also apply to fractions, but special techniques are sometimes needed in manipulating them. Multiplication is simple – the numerators are multiplied together and the denominators multiplied together, and the result expressed as a new fraction. Thus $2/3 \times 7/11 = 14/33$. To divide, invert the second fraction (the divisor) and multiply: $2/3 \div 7/11 = 2/3 \times 11/7 = 22/21$. Here the result is an improper fraction that can be simplified to 1 1/21 (that is, one and one-twenty first).

Addition and subtraction of fractions is more complicated. They must first be written in terms of the same denominator and for simplicity the smallest possible one is chosen (called the lowest common denominator or LCD). Then the numerators can be added or subtracted as necessary, the result expressed in terms of the LCD and simplified if possible [5, 6, 7].

Decimals are a way of writing fractions whose denominators are powers of ten. For example, 1 9/10, is the fraction 19/10 and is written in decimals as 1.9. The decimal point separates the whole number part (the argument) from the fractional part. Every fraction can be expressed as the sum of a series of such fractions (tenths, hundredths, thousandths, and so on) and can be represented in decimal form.

A cash register at a modern supermarket adds together the cost of each purchase. Some machines will also calculate and even issue the correct change and print a ticket.

5 Before fractions can be added they must all be expressed in terms of the same denominator. To add 1/2, 1/3 and 1/4 they must all be stated in twelfths (in this example, 12 is the lowest common denominator) as 6/12, 4/12 and 3/12. They can then be added to give 13/12, an improper fraction that simplifies to 1 1/12. This sum explains why it is impossible to divide anything into "shares" of 1/2, 1/3 and 1/4 – their sum is larger than 1.

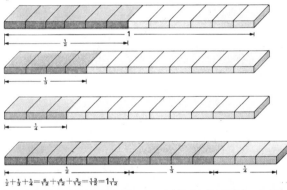

$$\tfrac{1}{2}+\tfrac{1}{3}+\tfrac{1}{4}=\tfrac{6}{12}+\tfrac{4}{12}+\tfrac{3}{12}=\tfrac{13}{12}=1\tfrac{1}{12}$$

6 To multiply fractions merely multiply the numerators and then multiply the denominators. A third of a half is $1/3 \times 1/2 = 1/6$ (the same as a half of a third – order does not matter).

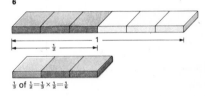

$\tfrac{1}{3}$ of $\tfrac{1}{2}=\tfrac{1}{3}\times\tfrac{1}{2}=\tfrac{1}{6}$

7 To divide fractions invert the divisor and multiply. For example, 5/6 divided by 5 is $5/6 \times 1/5 = 1/6$, which is exactly the same as the quantity described as a third of a half, as shown in illustration 6.

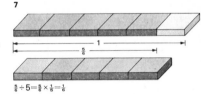

$\tfrac{5}{6}\div 5=\tfrac{5}{6}\times\tfrac{1}{5}=\tfrac{1}{6}$

8 At a public meeting a vote is often decided by "a show of hands" – those in favour of a motion raise their hands and are counted. But the way in which the results are announced or reported – as fractions or percentages – can convey different shades of meaning. At such a meeting, with 580 people present, 348 voted for the motion and 232 voted against. This basic fact can be expressed in various ways: "Three out of five people voted in favour"; "40 per cent of the voters were against the motion"; and "The motion was carried with a 20 per cent majority" are all true statements based on these figures. Fractions, proportions and ratios (often expressed as percentages) are merely different ways of presenting the same information. But if 200 of the people present did not vote (abstained), a figure of "60 per cent voting in favour" means that of the 580 present only 228 people were in favour of the motion – less than half the people present.

9 Proportions are also used to define slopes – for example, gradients on roads. "A slope of one in nine" means, mathematically, that a slope rises one unit of length for every nine horizontal units. In practice distances are measured along the road's surface and a one-in-nine hill climbs one metre (or one yard) for every nine metres (yards) travelled along the road. Mathematically this hill has a slope of 1 in 8.944m – near enough for a road sign. But proportions can best be compared as percentages. Thus the ratios 7 to 13 and 28 to 53 (corresponding to fractions 7/13 and 28/53) are difficult to compare. But as the percentages 53.85% and 52.83%, the former is obviously larger than the latter.

The language of numbers

The idea of number is a basic concept. The distinction between one and many is probably the easiest for a child to understand. A boy on a beach can pick up one pebble although he can see many more. If he picks up a handful, he obviously has more than one pebble but far less than the total number he can see. To obtain a precise idea of how many he has, he can count the number of pebbles in his hand and find, for example, that there are 12. "Twelve" is the name given to that number of pebbles. It is a property possessed by all collections of 12 objects: 12 cows, 12 seagulls and 12 encyclopaedias.

Positive and negative integers
Whole numbers such as 1, 5 and 212 are called positive integers and have been used ever since men began to count. In the Middle Ages the Hindus developed the concept of negative integers to deal with amounts owing in a trading transaction. A man might own five (+5) sheep and owe three (−3), so that he really owned only 5−3 = 2 sheep.

As long as mathematical operations are limited to counting, integers are sufficient as numbers. But as soon as men started to measure they found that nature is not organized into integer lengths and areas. A farmer could make a measuring stick (a ruler) by marking off a piece of wood into similar lengths equal to, say, the length of his foot. He might find that one of his animals was 5 "feet" long, whereas its offspring was only 2 "feet" long. Then he might find an animal that was 3½ "feet" and another of 2⅓ "feet". He would thus discover a whole new family of numbers, called rational numbers. Any number that can be written in such a form as 8/3 – as a fraction (the ratio of two integers) – is a rational number. Such numbers can be positive or negative and all integers are rational [1A].

In the sixth century BC Greek mathematicians discovered that a square with sides one unit long has a diagonal whose length cannot be measured exactly. No matter what scale of length is used, and no matter how finely it is subdivided into fractions, such a length cannot be measured with precision nor can it be written as a fraction. The system had to be extended again to include this new class of numbers, which are now called irrational numbers [3A].

Today we use zero (0) to denote the absence of a number, but this has not always been so. The Roman numeral system, for instance, had no zero. It was introduced for its present role in about 600 BC by Hindu mathematicians who formulated rules for calculating with it: multiplying by zero always gives a zero result and addition or subtraction of zero leaves a number unaltered. Hindu mathematicians also recognized that dividing by zero does not produce a result that can be defined by the number system.

Infinite and imaginary numbers
The concept that there are infinitely large numbers was first discussed by the Greek mathematician Archimedes. Starting with the largest number in the Greek number system, "a myriad myriads" (a hundred million), he constructed even larger numbers. He then estimated the number of grains of sand in the universe and showed that this was less than his largest number.

Archimedes (c. 287–212 BC) showed

1 Three types of numbers are the real, imaginary and complex numbers. Real numbers [A] can be represented as points along a line extending from minus infinity to plus infinity. They include all negative and positive numbers. Imaginary numbers [B] are based on i, the square root of −1, and can also be positive or negative. Complex numbers [C] each have a real and an imaginary part. They can be pictured as points defined by a distance along the real number axis and a distance along the imaginary number axis. Complex number P, for example is 4+3i, and Q is −3−5i. Complex numbers are much used by scientists.

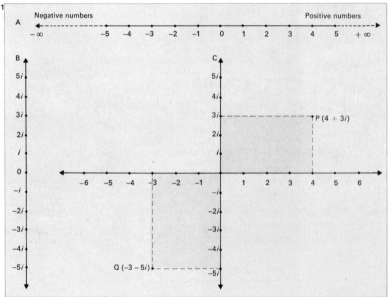

2 Five oranges, five hens' eggs and five bottles full of wine all possess the identical property of "fiveness". The number 5, fifth along the positive real number scale shown in illustration 1A, can be applied to any such group of five objects. The bottles do not all have the same shape, but this obviously does not affect their number. Only adding or removing some bottles would do that.

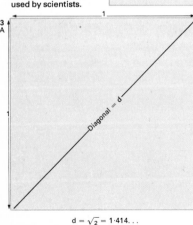

$$d = \sqrt{2} = 1\cdot414\ldots$$

$$\frac{C}{D} = \pi = 3\cdot1415\ldots$$

3 An irrational number cannot be expressed as a fraction using integers (whole numbers). A square with sides each one unit long [A] has a diagonal equal in length to the square root of 2. This is approximately equal to 1.414..., with a never-ending series of numbers after the decimal point. Another irrational number is the ratio of the circumference of a circle to its diameter [B], represented by the Greek letter π. It is equal to 3.1415..., again with a never-ending series of numbers after the decimal point. A rough approximation to π is given by the fraction (rational number) 22/7, which is equal to 3.1428.... Irrational numbers were discovered by the Greek mathematician Pythagoras.

4 Keeping a tally was one of the earliest forms of counting. In this old English game called shove ha'penny the players slide coins along a board into marked-off sections. They keep their scores with chalk tally marks at the edges of the board. Ancient farmers probably counted their animals using a tally-stick, a piece of wood carved with a series of notches. In some European beer halls today, the waiter gives a customer a new beer mat with each drink and keeps the old mats as a tally of the total drunk.

that there is no upper limit to a number system. Infinity, unlike zero, is not a number. No matter how large a number is there is still an indefinite number larger than it. Infinity can never be reached.

With the concepts of zero and infinity, men had a complete number system that could be pictured as every real number along a line stretching from minus infinity to plus infinity. But with the development of squares (the square of a number is that number multiplied by itself) and square roots (the square root of a number is another number which, when multiplied by itself, equals the original number), mathematicians encountered such problems as: what is the square root of -5? At first such problems were thought to be impossible to solve because there is no real number which, when squared, gives a negative result. Then in the sixteenth century Italian mathematicians introduced the "imaginary" quantity i which, when squared, gives the result -1. Numbers involving i are called imaginary numbers.

Complex numbers consist of a real part and an imaginary part, such as $5+3i$. They can be manipulated in the same way as purely real numbers. Many branches of modern engineering and electronics use them.

The system of numbers commonly used today was adapted from the Arabic numbering system [5] which, in turn, was based on Hindu ideas. In this system the position of a digit (numeral) in a number is significant. Using the basic digits 0 and 1 to 9 it is possible to construct any number. This base-10 or decimal system was introduced into Europe by Adelard of Bath in about 1100 and by 1600 was in almost universal use.

What is the base?

The base, or radix, is the number of digits in a number system. Position is important because in a number such as 333, the first 3 stands for 300 (three hundreds), the second for 30 (three tens) and the third for 3 units. But any convenient base can be used. Modern digital computers, for example, "count" using the base of 2 – the binary system of numbers – because its only digits, 1 and 0, can easily be represented by "on" or "off" pulses of electricity [9B].

An abacus is an ancient type of calculating machine still used in China and Japan. It has a number of beads on wires, generally divided into two sections with two beads (each standing for 5) and five beads (each of which stands for 1). Numbers are added or subtracted by moving the beads.

5 Various numeral systems have been used through the ages. The earliest, such as the Egyptian, used a simple pen stroke or a mark in clay to represent 1; other numbers up to 9 were formed by repeating the 1 symbol. The Romans and Mayans had an additional symbol for 5. Modern Arabic and Chinese have different symbols for each number, although 1 to 3 are formed by adding successive stokes.

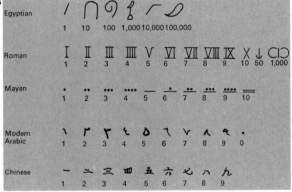

Egyptian	𓏺	𓎆	𓍢	𓆼	𓂭	𓁨
	1	10	100	1,000	10,000	100,000

Roman	I	II	III	IIII	V	VI	VII	VIII	IX	X	L	C
	1	2	3	4	5	6	7	8	9	10	50	1,000

Mayan	•	••	•••	••••	—	•̄	••̄	•••̄	••••̄	═
	1	2	3	4	5	6	7	8	9	10

Modern Arabic	١	٢	٣	٤	٥	٦	٧	٨	٩	٠
	1	2	3	4	5	6	7	8	9	0

Chinese	一	二	三	四	五	六	七	八	九
	1	2	3	4	5	6	7	8	9

6 Clockfaces may have Arabic numerals [A], Roman numerals [B] or no numerals at all [C], because in a clock the numbers have come to stand merely for positions.

	English	French	Italian	German	Dutch	Spanish
1	One	Un	Uno	Ein	Een	Uno
2	Two	Deux	Due	Zwei	Twee	Dos
3	Three	Trois	Tre	Drei	Drie	Tres
4	Four	Quatre	Quattro	Vier	Vier	Cuatro
5	Five	Cinq	Cinque	Funf	Vijf	Cinco
6	Six	Six	Sei	Sechs	Zes	Seis
7	Seven	Sept	Sette	Sieben	Zeven	Siete
8	Eight	Huit	Otte	Acht	Acht	Ocho
9	Nine	Neuf	Nove	Neun	Negen	Nueve
10	Ten	Dix	Dieci	Zehn	Tien	Diez

7 The names of numbers in various European languages reveal common word origins. But all these countries use the same number symbols, originally based on early Arabic numerals.

8 Large numbers are awkward to write and have different names even among English-speaking countries. American and British names are different. The scientific use of powers of 10 is unambiguous.

Number	British name	American name	Powers of ten
100	Hundred	Hundred	10^2
1,000	Thousand	Thousand	10^3
1,000,000	Million	Million	10^6
1,000,000,000	(Milliard)	Billion	10^9
1,000,000,000,000	Billion	Trillion	10^{12}
1,000,000,000,000,000	—	Quadrillion	10^{15}
1,000,000,000,000,000,000	Trillion	Quintillion	10^{18}

9 High-speed calculations are needed to deal with a changing situation in which numerical quantities vary continually, as at the tote on a racecourse [A], which computes winning odds for individual runners (horses or dogs) in accordance with the amount of money bet on them. For more complicated varying situations, a computer [B] is needed in order to complete the calculation in "real time" – that is in time for the information to be of use.

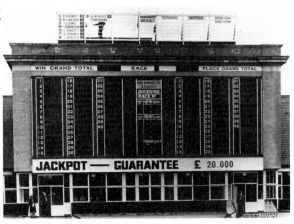

Measurement and dimensions

Four students – a chemist, a physicist, a mathematician and a humanities graduate – were each given a barometer and told to measure the height of a church tower. The chemist knew all about gases. He measured the air pressures at the top and bottom of the tower with his barometer and from the barely perceptible difference produced an answer of "anywhere between 0 and 60m" (0–200ft). The physicist was used to handling expensive equipment casually. He dropped his barometer off the tower and timed its fall, calculating the height as 27–33m (90–110ft). The mathematician compared the length of the tower's shadow with that of the barometer, arriving at a height of 30–30.5m (99–101ft). The humanities graduate sold the barometer, bought the verger a few drinks with the money, and soon found out that the tower was 30.4m (100ft) tall exactly.

Putting numbers on things
This apocryphal story illustrates the variety of ways of "putting numbers on things" and the different results that can be obtained. Life in the modern world depends greatly on man's ability to make accurate measurements, and laboratories throughout the world maintain standards of length, time, mass and voltage to ensure uniformity. Every large factory has a set of reference gauges that have been calibrated against a substandard that, in turn, has been checked against a national copy of the standard metre. As a result, a replacement bearing made in Japan can exactly fit a motor shaft made five years previously in West Germany.

Behind the practice of measurement lies theory. There is the physical theory of the process and also mathematical principles such as dimensional analysis. This derives the "dimensions" of measured quantities in terms of the fundamentals length [L], mass [M] and time [T]. Area, for example (square metres, square yards, acres or hectares), has dimensions [L²]; volume (cubic metres, cubic yards and so on) has dimensions [L³]. If the volume of a paraboloid were stated to be $\pi H^2/8D$, with H as its height and D its base diameter, then without making any calculations at all a student can be sure that the formula is wrong. It involves the product of two lengths divided by a length and so has dimensions [L²/L] = [L]. It must therefore represent a length – it cannot possibly represent a volume. (The correct formula is $\pi H^2 D/8$.)

Similarly, given that the time-of-swing t of a pendulum might depend on its length l, the mass of its bob m and the acceleration imparted by gravity g, any formula for t based on a relationship between l, m and g must yield a number with the dimensions of time. Acceleration is measured in metres per second per second and has dimensions [L/T²]. So
$$t \equiv T = \sqrt{T^2} = \sqrt{L/\tfrac{L}{T^2}} \equiv \sqrt{l/g}$$
($\equiv$ is the sign for "is equivalent to".)

In fact the formula is $t = 2\pi\sqrt{l/g}$ (dimensional analysis can never deduce numerical factors such as 2π). Dimensional analysis is often helpful when checking calculations for errors, but one cannot derive physical laws from mathematics alone. Only by experiments can we prove that the period of swing of the pendulum is independent of its mass.

The length in metres and acceleration in metres per second per second must give an answer in seconds. "Coherent" systems of

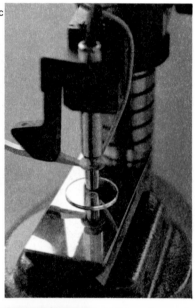

1 Different techniques of measurement have different degrees of precision. The chart-recorder [A, bottom] is precise to about 1 in 100; it is hard to read a chart more accurately than that. The chemical balance [B] can reach 1 in 10⁶ and the frequency counter [A, top] 1 in 10⁸. Both these have a numerical display; no meter could be calibrated so finely. An air gauge [C] measures extremely small dimensions by sensing the flow of air through a small gap. Its precision of up to 1 in 10⁹ is near the limits of current technology (at about 1 in 10¹¹ for a laser gauge). The micrometer [Key] is 10 million times less accurate.

2 Two sheets of glass in near-contact show an optical interference pattern between them. This is a contour map scaled in half-wavelengths of light and makes accurate surface measurements possible.

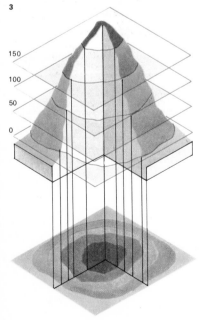

3 Recording a three-dimensional shape on a flat surface is a problem that can be solved by the convention of contour scaling. This is shown when the cross-sections of a hill at 50-, 100- and 150-metre heights are projected onto a map of the hill. The hill can be envisaged fairly well from such a map, although the "coarseness" of the contour intervals loses some finer detail. The steepness of the sides can be judged by the contour lines on the map. "Newton's rings" and similar interference patterns (as in illustration 2) are fine contour maps. Special techniques make it possible to reveal tiny deformations of stressed surfaces by means of such contours.

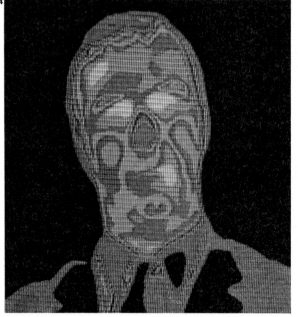

4 A false-colour thermogram, also known as a thermoscan, records the temperatures on the skin of a man's face. The technique allows a doctor to study the extent of skin damage caused by burns and has been adapted to aid in the diagnosis of diseases such as cancer of the breast. An infrared camera has a rotating prism scanner that detects the heat levels in a strip of the picture, and the resulting signal is amplified and displayed on a colour television screen. Blue colours represent low temperatures; the redder the colour, the"hotter" it is. Thermograms can also help architects to design houses for minimum heat loss and aid householders to insulate them.

units such as SI units (the international unit system used throughout science) guarantee an answer in correct units. The speed of a piston multiplied by its area and the pressure it exerts gives its power, for example. With units of feet per second, square inches and atmospheres, the answer would have the dimensions of power $[ML^2/T^3]$ but be in no recognized power units. Using SI units (metres per second, square metres, and newtons per square metre) guarantees an answer in watts. Other common units are the cgs (centimetre-gramme-second) and MKS (metre-kilogramme-second) systems.

Scaling the heights

If a 10-metre (33ft) scale model of a blade of grass were actually made from grass, it would promptly collapse. Similarly a flea the size of an elephant would not be able even to stand, let alone jump. This is because the weight of an object, like its volume, increases as the cube of its height, whereas its strength increases only as its square. Many related properties scale differently so it is quite difficult, for example, to calculate what thrust

will propel an aircraft from the force needed to sustain a scale model in a wind-tunnel. One way out of this difficulty is to think in terms of "dimensionless groups" like Reynold's Number, valuable in many problems of gas and fluid flow. This is LVd/η where L is a length (perhaps of a wing-section), V is a gas velocity, d is its density and η (eta) its viscosity. This combination is a dimensionless ratio – a pure number – having the same value in any units.

Dimensionless ratios

Dimensionless ratios, free from arbitrary units, are fundamental entities. The ratio of the electrical to gravitational force between a proton and an electron, for example, is about 10^{39} (that is, 1 followed by 39 zeros). This is also approximately the ratio of the diameter of the knowable universe to that of the proton and of the estimated age of the universe to the time light takes to traverse a proton. The square of 10^{39}, 10^{78}, is about the number of particles in the knowable universe. Some cosmologists wonder if this ratio is trying to tell us something.

A micrometer can measure a small object with a pre-cision of up to 1 in 10,000. This is adequate for most high-grade engineering, but far higher precision is possible.

5

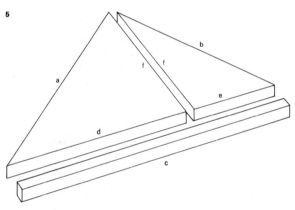

5 With c accurately known, d is found by measuring e and subtracting; error in e is diluted in the longer d. But obtaining e as c−d is inaccurate; it is a small difference between two larger numbers. Obtaining f by Pythagoras as $\sqrt{a^2-d^2}$ is worse; squaring the two similar and large values increases their uncertainty. But e, and f are dissimilar lengths, so that b can be found accurately as $\sqrt{e^2+f^2}$.

6

6 By the surface volume scaling law, fine structures have relatively more surface to their volume. Each die weighs 2g (0.07oz) and has 9cm² (1.4in²) of surface. The sugar lump is made of 0.5mm (0.02in) grains and has about 200cm² (31in²) of total surface. The 2g of "molecular sieve" on the watchglass is porous to the molecular level and has a remarkable 1,500m² (16,150 sq ft) of total effective surface area.

7
A

B

7 If the size of a balloon is doubled, its surface (and therefore weight) goes up four times, but its volume (and therefore lift) goes up eight times. This surface/volume scaling law shows that balloons become more efficient the bigger they are [A]. Conversely, doubling an aircraft's size increases its weight by eight times, but the wing area by only four times [B]. Small aircraft pose fewer design problems.

8

8 Various formulae link the dimensions of plane figures. In a triangle [A] the cosine formula states that $a^2 = b^2+c^2-2bc$. $\cos A$; and the sine formula that $a/\sin A = b/\sin B = c/\sin C$. If $S = \frac{1}{2}(a+b+c)$, the area of the triangle $= \sqrt{s(s-a)(s-b)(s-c)}$. In a circle [B] angle $O = 2B = 2E$ and the circumference of arc ADC is $\pi rO/180$. In a regular n-sided polygon [C] angle $A = 180(1-2/n)$; angle $O = 360/n$; the area of the polygon $= \frac{1}{2}nld$ and the radius $r = d.\sec(180/n)$.

9
A   **B**

9C

9 The volumes and areas of solid figures can be linked by formulae. In a cone [A] the volume of the full cone $= \frac{1}{3}\pi R^2H$; and the area of the curved surface is given as πLR. In the frustrum of the cone (the lower section) the area of the curved surface $= \pi l(R+r)$; and the volume $= \frac{1}{3}\pi h(R^2+Rr+r^2)$. In a sphere and cylinder [B] the surface area of the sphere $= 4\pi r^2$. The curved surface of the cylinder $= 2\pi rh$. The volume of the sphere $= 4\pi r^3/3$; and of a cylinder it is given as πr^2h. The volume of the section of sphere between planes x and y $= V_s = \pi[L^2(r-L/3)-l_1^2(r-l_1/3)]$. In a regular tetrahedron [C] the distance $r = d/\sqrt{3}$; $H = d(\sqrt{2}/\sqrt{3})$; and $R = \frac{1}{2}d(\sqrt{3}/\sqrt{2})$. The height of the centre of gravity is given as $h = H/4$.

Finding unknown quantities: algebra

In arithmetic various quantities such as lengths, areas and sums of money are represented as numbers (and the appropriate units). But some mathematical problems are concerned with *finding* a number – an unknown quantity. If two numbers add up to 10 and one of them is 6, what is the other? The answer to this simple problem is 4 and yet the method of formalizing it is a basic technique of algebra.

To solve this problem by algebra, let the unknown number be x. Then $6 + x = 10$ (this is an algebraic equation). By subtracting 6 from each side of this equation, it simplifies to $x = 10 - 6 = 4$. By making a letter, x, stand for the unknown quantity, the problem can be solved, and this way of using letters is a basic technique of algebra.

Greek and Arab mathematicians
Greek mathematicians such as Diophantus (c. third century AD) used letters in their equations. But the word algebra is derived from the Arabic words *al-jebr*, meaning "bone-setting" (the restoration and reduction of a bone fracture). This formed part of

the title of a book by the Arab mathematician Al-Khwarizmi. By the sixteenth century, mathematical problems were fully formulated in algebraic terms, initially in France by Franciscus Vieta (1540–1603). The normal convention of using the last few letters of the alphabet (x, y and z) to denote unknown quantities and the first few letters to stand for known prescribed numbers was introduced by the French mathematician René Descartes (1596–1650).

Algebraic equations and formulae
Common practical applications of algebraic equations are the various formulae used in science, particularly in mathematics and physics. The volume of a cylinder, for example, is given by the formula $V = \pi r^2 h$, where V is the volume, r is the radius of one end and h is the cylinder's height [1]. The formula provides a shorthand way of saying "the volume of a cylinder equals the area of one end multiplied by the height".

Algebraic equations [2] and formulae can be manipulated according to established rules. The subject (V) of the cylinder equa-

tion can be changed to find the radius or height of a cylinder of known volume. For instance, $h = V/\pi r^2$. Such formulae are perfectly general – they apply to all cylinders, whether they are tall and thin or short and squat. There are similar formulae for the areas and volumes of all common geometrical figures.

Many problems in algebra involve more than one unknown quantity. Consider the problem of finding two positive numbers whose product is 15 and whose difference is 2. Let the two numbers be represented by the letters x and y. Then the "product" information can be stated as the equation $xy = 15$. There are several possible solutions to this equation: 1 and 15, 3 and 5, 7.5 and 2, and so on. To proceed we must use the "difference" information, which generates the equation $y - x = 2$, rearranging to give $y = x + 2$. Substituting this expression for y in the first equation yields $x(x + 2) = 15$, or $x^2 + 2x - 15 = 0$.

Now this third equation contains only one "unknown" quantity: x. The only positive number that satisfies it is 3 (when the equa-

1 The formula for finding the volume of a cylinder is $V = \pi r^2 h$, where r is the radius of one end and h is the height. The two cylinders [A and B] have the same volume, but very different radii and heights. In fact, the diameter of one is almost equal to the height of the other, that is h is about equal to $2r$ and $2R$ is almost the same as H. Another cylinder [C] has volume V. Doubling its height doubles its volume [D] (for C volume $= \pi r^2 h$, for D vol. $= 2\pi r^2 h$). But doubling the radius of the cylinder increases its volume four-fold [E] (for E volume is equal to $\pi(2r)^2 h = 4\pi r^2 h$). These changes are predicted using algebra.

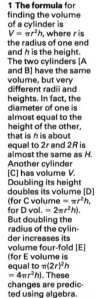

2 An equation in algebra is in a state of balance; the terms on the left-hand side taken together equal those on the right-hand side, just as a collection of objects balances on a pair of scales [A]. In simplifying an equation it is essential that the same operation be carried out on each side. For example, $3x$ is subtracted from each pan of the balance [B] (and from each side of the equation). A further simplification is made [C] by subtracting $2y$ from each side. As a result the original equation $3x + 5y = 4x + 2y$ reduces to $3y = x$. It is also possible to multiply or divide each side by a factor.

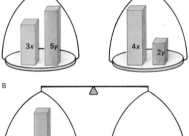

$3x + 5y = 4x + 2y$

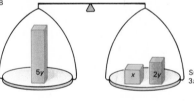

Subtract $3x$ from each side:
$3x - 3x + 5y = 4x - 3x + 2y$
$5y = x + 2y$

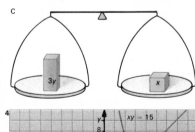

Subtract $2y$ from each side:
$5y - 2y = x + 2y - 2y$
$3y = x$

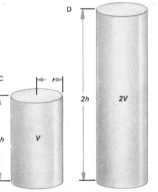

3 Houses in this street are numbered consecutively. A man notices that four times his number is ten more than three times his neighbour's higher up the street. What is his number? Let the house number be x, then the neighbour's is $x + 1$. So $4x = 3(x + 1) + 10 = 3x + 3 + 10$. Subtracting $3x$ from each side of this equation gives $x = 13$. The house number is 13 (and his neighbour's is number 14).

4 Algebraic equations can be plotted as lines on a graph, a technique which is the province of analytic geometry. This graph shows plots of the equations $xy = 15$ and $y = x + 2$. Treated as simultaneous equations, they are both true at the points where the lines cross. When the equation to a straight line is expressed in the form $y = mx + c$, where m and c are numbers, the letter m is a measure of the slope of the line, here equal to 1.

tion becomes $9 + 6 - 15 = 0$). Finally, to find y we substitute this value of x in either of the two original equations. According to the first, $y = 15/x = 15/3 = 5$ and for the second $y = x + 2 = 3 + 2 = 5$. The answer to the problem is therefore 3 and 5. In algebraic terms, we have solved two equations that are both true at the same time – called simultaneous equations.

By considering points in space defined by referring to their distances from a line (the x-axis) and another line (the y-axis), the equations of algebra take on a whole new meaning. The equation $xy = 15$, for example, represents a curve on which all points have the product of their x-distance and y-distance equal to 15. The equation $y = x + 2$ represents a straight line and all points along it satisfy this equation.

If these two curves are drawn [4] (to a mathematician, even a straight line is a "curve"), they intersect at the point whose x-distance is 3 and whose y-distance is 5 – the point defined as (3, 5). The graphic approach to the problem gives exactly the same solution as the purely algebraic approach. It also

reveals another point at which the curves intersect, corresponding to $x = -3$ and $y = -5$. These solutions are, however, disallowed by the original problem, which called for two *positive* numbers.

The whole procedure of plotting algebraic equations as curves is the province of analytic geometry. It is the branch of mathematics in which algebra and geometry come together.

Algebra also supplies an insight into other puzzles and paradoxes. Any three-digit number whose middle digit is the sum of the other two is divisible by 11. Why? The answer can be supplied by using algebra [5].

Maintaining the balance
The examples already described serve to show the power of algebra in solving problems, particularly by manipulating equations. But there are rules about such manipulation. If there are two unknowns, such as x and y, an equation is simplified by having all the terms in x on one side and all the terms in y on the other. This can be achieved by adding or subtracting equal quantities from each side [2].

KEY

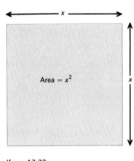

Arithmetic deals with numerical quantities — for example, the number of people in

this crowd. But algebra can tackle problems involving unknown quantites, gen-

erally by allocating to them a letter such as x. Then x might stand for the number of men.

5 The three-digit numbers in this table have two properties in common: the middle digit is the sum of the other two and all of them are divisible by 11. If the first digit is x and the third y, the middle one is $(x + y)$. The whole number has the value $100x + 10(x + y) + y$. This expression can be factorized and simplified to $11(10x + y)$; it is a general formula for all the numbers in the table and has 11 as a factor.

110	220	341	473	671
121	231	352	484	682
132	242	363	495	693
143	253	374	550	770
154	264	385	561	781
165	275	396	572	792
176	286	440	583	880
187	297	451	594	891
198	330	462	660	990

6 Squaring the circle – drawing a square with exactly the same area as a given circle – was a problem that defied ancient mathematicians. But it can be tackled using algebra. The area of a circle of radius r is πr^2 and of a square of side x is x^2. For equal areas $\pi r^2 = x^2$, or $x = r\sqrt{\pi}$. If $r = 10$, $x = \sqrt{314.2}$, which equals 17.72 approximately. A square of side 17.72cm has an area almost exactly the same as a circle of radius 10cm.

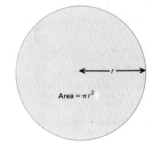

Area = x^2

If $x = 17.72$
Area = 314.2

Area = πr^2

If $r = 10$
Area = 314.2

Minutes	(x)	1·0	2·5	4·0	6·5	7·5	9·0	11·0
Litres	(y)	0·6	1·7	2·3	4·0	4·5	5·5	6·6

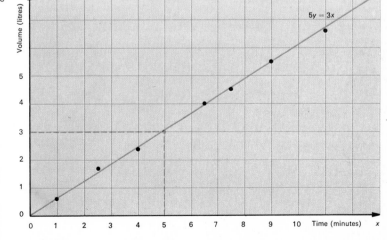

$5y = 3x$

7 A woman uses a photographer's clock to time the rate at which a bucket is filling with liquid [A] (the volume of the bucket is calibrated in litres on a scale inside it). The results of the measurements are shown in the table [B]. How

much liquid flowed into the bucket after five minutes? To solve this problem she can draw a graph showing the rate of flow [C], which plots volume (litres) against time (minutes). The volume discharge in five minutes can be read off the graph as

3 litres. The graph is a straight line, which shows that during the time in which she made the measurement the rate of flow was constant. The line passes through the origin, at which both axes are zero. It therefore has an equation

of the general form $y = mx$, where m is the slope of the line. In this example, the slope is 3/5, so the equation of the line is $y = 3x/5$ or $5y = 3x$. This equation can be used instead of the graph to calculate values of volume or time.

17

Mathematical curves

Anyone who can catch a ball has an intuitive grasp of mathematical curves and their transformations in space. A thrown ball travels in a mathematical curve which is (very nearly) a parabola: and many sportsmen can, with the ball still rising far away, begin to run at once to where it will fall. This is not just a simple matter of "seeing where it will go" by elementary estimation. A ball on a long piece of elastic, as is used in some tennis-trainers, is almost impossible to catch even if it is close and moving slowly. It travels in some curve other than a parabola and parabolically attuned reflexes are baffled by it.

Curves, equations and laws

Gunnery fire-control and ballistic-tracking systems have to predict curves as does the sportsman. Lacking his intuitive reflexes, they need high-speed computers to represent the trajectories mathematically. This is done by deducing a precise and complete "specification" of the trajectory in the form of an equation. Mathematics is the art of making precise statements and a mathematical curve is merely one that has such a specification. It does not have to be put in equation form and indeed an informal statement is sometimes clearer. Thus the statement that a circle is a curve on which every point is the same distance from a given centre is easier to understand than the curve whose mathematical equation is $x^2 + y^2 = R^2$ [2].

A mathematician can always translate the specification into an appropriate equation that is true for every point on the curve or surface but false for all other points. He can work out all the properties of the curve by manipulating algebraic symbols, which is much easier than pictorial geometry. When Thomas Telford (1757–1834) built the suspension bridge over the Menai Strait, Wales, in 1826, he had to determine the curve of the hanging chains by setting up a large model across a dry valley and measuring it – a sad consequence of mathematical ignorance. Nowadays an engineer can derive the equation of a suspension bridge cable and find out all he needs to know about it without even drawing a diagram.

Because the world is governed by simple mathematical laws, mathematical curves are all around us. A stone falls in a straight line if dropped or a parabola if thrown; the Moon and artificial satellites move in (very nearly) ellipses; the Sun and Earth are nearly spherical; and a static liquid surface is (very nearly) flat – all because of the mathematical form of the law of gravity. A rainbow is a circular arc and the bright cusp you sometimes see in a sun-illuminated cup or pan is an epicycloid [9B] because of the laws of optics. Indeed, much of the process of scientific discovery consists of observing such things, or conducting experiments to reveal them and then deducing "laws" that must hold to give rise to them. But most often the scientist finds mathematical curves in his results only when he draws them (plots them as a graph). Then the equation of the graph tells him the "law" revealed by his experiment.

Spheres occur in nature in objects that adopt this shape as the "line of least resistance" to forces affecting them. Small droplets of water and soap bubbles are spherical to minimize their areas under the effect of surface tension. Lead shot was once made by pouring molten lead down inside a tall

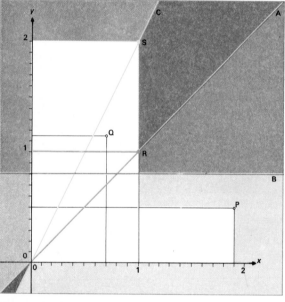

3 An important family of mathematical curves results from sectioning a cone at various angles. A horizontal section [1] gives a circle; an inclined one [2] an ellipse. A section parallel to one side of the cone [3] gives a parabola and still greater inclination [4] a hyperbola. All these have the same general equation: $ax^2 + by^2 + 2hxy + 2gx + 2fy = c$. With h^2 greater than ab, it is a hyperbola; with $h^2 = ab$, a parabola; h^2 less than ab gives an ellipse, of which the circle ($h = 0$, $a = b$) is a special case. The terms a, b, c, h, g and f are chosen constants; with $b = c = h = g = 0$, $a = 1$ and $2f = 1$, the equation becomes $y = -x^2$. As $h^2 = ab$ (both $= 0$) this is the equation of a parabola.

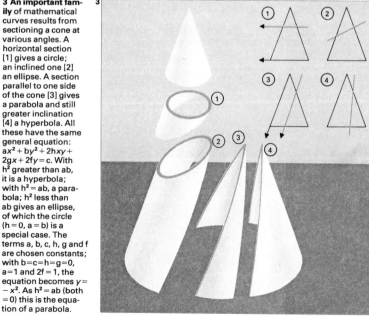

1 To give a mathematical curve an equation, first draw two lines at right-angles: the x axis ([0x] on the diagram) and the y axis [0y]. Then every point on the paper can be defined by its "x distance" and "y distance" along these axes. Thus point Q has $x = 0.7$ and $y = 1.15$; point P has $x = 1.9$ and $y = 0.5$. On the straight line A it is obvious that for every point on it (eg R, with $x = 1$ $y = 1$) the x distance equals the y distance or $x = y$. This then is the equation of line A as a mathematical curve, true for all points on it and false for all others. Line C has equation $y = 2x$ (as point S shows); line B, equation $y = 0.8$.

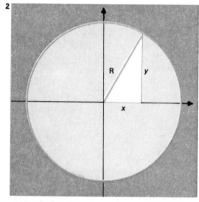

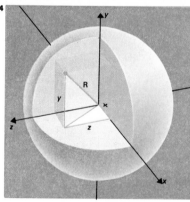

2 To find the equation of a circle, observe that each point on it forms a right-angled triangle whose sides are the x distance and y distance and whose hypotenuse is R. Pythagoras's theorem tells us that $x^2 + y^2 = R^2$. For points outside the circle $x^2 + y^2$ exceeds R^2; inside it $x^2 + y^2$ is less than R^2. Along the intersection of these two regions the equation balances. All mathematical curves divide space in this way.

4 A mathematical surface can be defined like a curve, using three mutually perpendicular axes in space, x, y, z. The equation of the sphere is $x^2 + y^2 + z^2 = R^2$. All points outside it have $x^2 + y^2 + z^2$ greater than R^2; those inside have $x^2 + y^2 + z^2$ less than R^2; the equation balances on the boundary. An equation such as $x^2 + y^2 + z^2 - 2x - 8z + 17 = R^2$ also defines a sphere but its centre is not at the intersection of the three axes.

5 A parabola rotated about its axis of symmetry gives a mathematical surface, the paraboloid. A uniformly rotating liquid acquires a paraboloidal surface from the interaction of gravity and centrifugal force, as can be seen by spinning a pan of liquid on a turntable. This surface is perfect for radio- and optical-telescope mirrors; a mirror surface can be made by spinning plastic resin in a dish while it sets and coating it with metal.

building into a tank of cold water. During their fall down the tower the droplets of lead formed spheres and cooled sufficiently to retain their shape when they hit the water.

From theory into practice

Mathematical curves and surfaces are involved in all sorts of human activities. Lenses, for example, have spherical surfaces not because this is the ideal optical shape (although it is quite good) but because it is so easy to make. A spherical surface is the only one that presents the same form and curvature no matter how it is turned around. Therefore a hard surface and a soft one, rubbed together with back-and-forth and mutual twisting movements, will wear together into mating spherical surfaces as these are the only ones that enable them to fit exactly together every time. As a result, simple grinding processes suffice to produce spherical surfaces; where other surfaces are needed (as in telescope corrector-plates and some zoom lenses), manufacture is much more difficult.

Similarly, cylindrical objects (tubes, rods,

bolts) and holes are so common because this type of surface is readily created by rotating machinery. Boilers and pressure vessels are cylindrical because this shape resists pressure better than others. Cooling towers are hyperboloidal because the two-way "saddle" curvature resists weight and wind loadings well. A trumpet has an exponentially flared horn because this is the mathematically ideal way of launching the intense sound vibrations in its throat into the open atmosphere.

Beauty and the mathematician

The cooling tower, trumpet, bridge arch and radio-telescope dish all derive their forms from pure mathematical physics. Yet they, and other engineering creations, have an aesthetic appeal that is sometimes sadly missing in those architectural and automobile creations whose "styling" lacks any mathematical necessity. It is an appealing flight of fancy to wonder whether the same intuition that enables the ordinary man to recognize and respond to the unity and inevitability of mathematical curves at work, also enables him to catch a moving ball.

These three bridges spanning the River Tyne, are curves at work. The arches are close to parabolas of different forms. The parabola is ideal for an arch whose weight is negligible compared to the even weight of the roadway. For an actual bridge the arch's own weight must be allowed for.

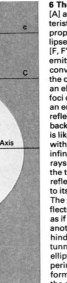

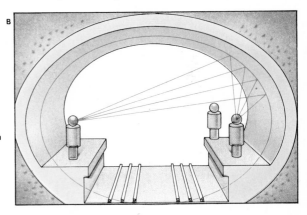

6 The conic sections [A] all have characteristic "reflecting" properties. An ellipse has two foci [F, F'] such that rays emitted from one converge [A, a] on the other. A circle is an ellipse with its foci coincident and an emitted ray is reflected straight back [B, b]. A parabola is like an ellipse with the other focus infinitely far away: rays emitted from the true focus are reflected parallel to its true axis [C, c]. The hyperbola reflects rays from F as if they came from another focus F" behind it. Paris Metro tunnels are almost elliptical and whispering on one platform can be heard on the other by the focusing effect [B].

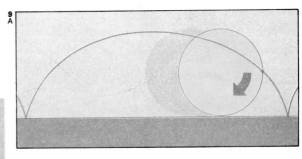

7 Many living creatures grow by compound interest; the bigger they become the faster they grow. The pearly nautilus of the Indian and Pacific oceans extends its shell continuously in spiral fashion as it grows, generating a natural "logarithmic spiral." This mathematical curve is also called the "equi-angular spiral" because a line drawn outwards from the centre intersects the curve at the same angle.

9 A point on the rim of a rolling wheel traces out a cycloid [A]. This famous mathematical curve received attention from Galileo, who suggested it as an arch-form for stone bridges, and Newton, who proved that inverted it was that surface down which a particle slid in the minimum time. A wheel rolling on another wheel generates an epicycloid [B]. To mesh smoothly without "stepping" from tooth to tooth, gear wheels need teeth of defined curves. The rise of an epicycloid from the inner wheel is one ideal curve. The point on the rim of a wheel rolling inside another wheel generates a curve called a hypocycloid, also used in gears.

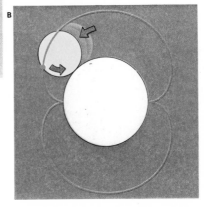

8 An "Archimedean spiral" is traced by a point that travels around a centre, varying in distance from it in proportion to the angle it moves through. Similarly a helix is the curve of a point that moves around a cylinder, travelling along it in proportion to its total angular rotation. Both are created automatically by a lathe whose cutting tool traverses a rotating workpiece. Many cylindrical objects show their machine finishing as a fine helical pattern.

Logarithms and slide rule

As the science of mathematics and its applications progressed, men found themselves having to carry out more and more complicated calculations – especially ones involving multiplication and division. Even a modern computer or electronic calculator takes about ten times as long to multiply two numbers as it does to add them, and this is certainly true of human mathematicians.

Both multiplication and division were simplified in the 1500s by the introduction of decimal notation. Then a Scottish mathematician, John Napier (1550–1617), published his book *Mirifici Logarithmorum Canonis Descriptio* (1614) which announced the discovery of logarithms.

Arithmetic and geometric progressions

A practical form of Napier's ideas about logarithms was a set of numbered rods, or bones, that could be used for carrying out multiplication by merely using the mathematical operation of addition [1]. As with logarithms (and the slide rule) they made use of two types of mathematical series, called arithmetic and geometric.

An arithmetic progression is a series of numbers in which each is obtained by adding a "common difference" to the one before it in the series. The ordinary ordinal sequence of numbers, for example – 1, 2, 3, 4, and so on – is an arithmetic series with a common difference of 1. In a geometric progression, each term is obtained from the previous one by miltuplying it by a "common ratio". In the series 2, 4, 8, 16, and so on, the common ratio is 2.

In the three following series:

$$1 \quad 2 \quad 3 \quad 4 \quad 5 \ldots$$
$$10 \quad 100 \quad 1{,}000 \quad 10{,}000 \quad 100{,}000 \ldots$$
$$10^1 \quad 10^2 \quad 10^3 \quad 10^4 \quad 10^5 \ldots$$

the first is an arithmetic progression and the second a geometric one (with a common ratio of 10). The third row, equivalent to the second, shows how the succeeding powers of 10 in the second (geometric) series are in an arithmetic progression.

The powers (exponents) in the bottom row are called the logarithms of the corresponding terms in the middle row "to the base 10". The logarithm of a given number is the power to which a fixed number (the base) must be raised in order to equal the given number. Thus the logarithm of 100 to the base 10 is 2 (because $10^2 = 100$).

Logarithms, pianos and guitars

Ten is not the only base for logarithms; Napier's original tables were to the base "e" (an irrational number) and are still much used in science, where they are called natural or Naperian logarithms. The pitch of the notes on a piano is in a logarithmic ratio to the base 2, whereas the keys are in a linear sequence of octaves.

The sound wavelength of any note is twice that of the one an octave above it. The pieces of metal called frets across the fingerboard of a guitar also form a logarithmic series (in terms of spacing).

Numbers expressed in terms of powers or exponents are multiplied by adding the exponents. Thus $10^2 \times 10^4 = 10^{2+4} = 10^6$. And since logarithms are also exponents, to multiply two numbers their logarithms are merely added and tables can supply the number whose logarithm is the result. In this way multiplication is reduced to the much easier

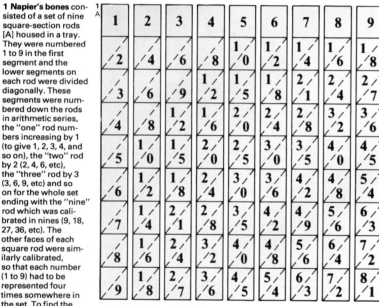
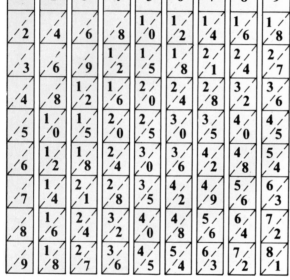

1 Napier's bones consisted of a set of nine square-section rods [A] housed in a tray. They were numbered 1 to 9 in the first segment and the lower segments on each rod were divided diagonally. These segments were numbered down the rods in arithmetic series, the "one" rod numbers increasing by 1 (to give 1, 2, 3, 4, and so on), the "two" rod by 2 (2, 4, 6, etc), the "three" rod by 3 (3, 6, 9, etc) and so on for the whole set ending with the "nine" rod which was calibrated in nines (9, 18, 27, 36, etc). The other faces of each square rod were similarly calibrated, so that each number (1 to 9) had to be represented four times somewhere in the set. To find the multiples of a number – for example 1,572 – the rods numbered 1, 5, 7 and 2 are removed from the tray and laid side by side [B]. To find 3×1,572 the third row of rod segments is used, as at C. The numbers displayed can be added diagonally as shown, to yield 4,716, which is the required product. To find 8×1,572 the segments in the eighth row are used, as at D. When added diagonally, the numbers displayed this time add to 12,576 – again the required product. To multiply by a larger number, say 38, the appropriate products are merely added together (47,160 – a zero is added because we are now multiplying by 30 not 3 – and 12,576) to give 59,736.

1,572×3=4,716

1,572×8=12,576

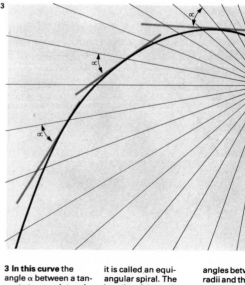

2 The frequency of a note in music is twice that of the one an octave below it. On a keyboard instrument the frequencies of a note and its successive octaves are in the proportions 1:2:4:8:16, etc. This is a logarithmic scale to the base 2. The spacing of the metal frets across the fingerboard of a guitar are also in a logarithmic sequence and by pressing his fingers against each in turn the guitarist is able to play the notes up a chromatic scale. An unfretted instrument such as a violin works on the same principle but the divisions are not marked on the fingerboard.

3 In this curve the angle α between a tangent at any point and the radius drawn from the centre is constant. For this reason it is called an equiangular spiral. The lengths of the radii to the curve are proportional to the logarithms of the angles between the radii and the initial horizontal direction; it is therefore also known as a logarithmic spiral.

task of addition. Similarly, logarithms can be used to perform division by actually carrying out a subtraction.

To calculate in decimal numbers, logarithm tables need be compiled only for the numbers between 0 and 9.999 (in four-figure tables; five-figure tables include 9.9999, and so on to as many figures as required). Larger numbers are expressed by adding a whole number (integer) called the characteristic, which represents in base-10 logs the corresponding power. The four-figure logarithm to the base 10 (written $\log_{10}$) of 2, for example, is 0.3010 [4]. The log of 200 is 2.3010 and of 2,000 is 3.3010 (200 is $10^2 \times 10^{0.3010} = 10^{2.3010}$, and 2,000 is $10^3 \times 10^{0.3010} = 10^{3.3010}$).

The slide rule

A slide rule [5] is a mechanical device for multiplying and dividing numbers to limited accuracy. Logarithmic scales are engraved on rods that can be slid in relation to each other, and numbers on them added or subtracted as needed – added for multiplication and subtracted for division. Because of the log scale,

the numbers become closer together along the slide, just like the frets on a guitar's fingerboard. Unlike an ordinary ruler the scale is geometric rather than arithmetic [6].

In its simplest form a slide rule has only two scales – called the X or D scales on a complicated slide rule. To multiply two numbers, the 1 on the upper scale is set opposite one of these numbers on the lower scale and the required product read off it opposite the second number on the upper scale [6A]. For division the two numbers are lined up and the quotient read off against the 1 [6B]. A transparent sliding "saddle" called a cursor can be moved along to line up the graduations and make them easier to read.

The accuracy of a slide rule is limited mainly by its length. A cylindrical slide rule [7] has scales up to a metre long wound round it like a screw thread. Most ordinary slide rules have additional scales to aid various types of calculations: reciprocal (a scale of all the numbers divided into 1), square (numbers multiplied by themselves), square root and even trigonometrical functions such as sine, cosine, and tangent.

KEY

The curve shown in illustration 3 is a logarithmic spiral. Such curves occur in nature, generally revealing the effects of accelerating growth as in the spiral shells of snails and various other molluscs and in flowers like this one.

4

To calculate 1·113 × 1·456

	0	1	2	3	4	5	6	7	8	9	1	2	3	4	5	6	7	8	9
10	0000	0043	0086	0128	0170	0212	0253	0294	0334	0374	4	8	12	17	21	25	29	33	37
11	0414	0453	0492	0531	0569	0607	0645	0682	0719	0755	4	8	11	15	19	23	26	30	34
12	0792	0828	0864	0899	0934	0969	1004	1038	1072	1106	3	7	10	14	17	21	24	28	31
13	1139	1173	1206	1239	1271	1303	1335	1367	1399	1430	3	6	10	13	16	19	23	26	29
14	1461	1492	1523	1553	1584	1614	1644	1673	1703	1732	3	6	9	12	15	18	21	24	27
15	1761	1790	1818	1847	1875	1903	1931	1959	1987	2014	3	6	8	11	14	17	20	22	25
16	2041	2068	2095	2122	2148	2175	2201	2227	2253	2279	3	5	8	11	13	16	18	21	24
17	2304	2330	2355	2380	2405	2430	2455	2480	2504	2529	2	5	7	10	12	15	17	20	22
18	2553	2577	2601	2625	2648	2672	2695	2718	2742	2765	2	5	7	9	12	14	16	19	21
19	2788	2810	2833	2856	2878	2900	2923	2945	2967	2989	2	4	7	9	11	13	16	18	20
20	3010	3032	3054	3075	3096	3118	3139	3160	3181	3201	2	4	6	8	11	13	15	17	19

Logarithm of 1·113 =
0·0453 + 0·0011 = 0·0464

Logarithm of 1·456 =
0·1614 + 0·0018 = 0·1632

To multiply, add the logarithms :
0·0464
+ 0·1632
= 0·2096 log
i.e. 1·113 × 1·456 = 1·620

4 Log tables can be used to multiply or divide numbers. In this example 1.113 is found by adding the log under 1.11 to that for 0.003, to give 0.0464. Similarly the log of 1.456 is 0.1632. The two logs are then added to give 0.2096 and the required product is the number that has this logarithm – the number 1.620 in the table. In practice, results are found by consulting tables of antilogarithms.

5 A modern slide rule has various scales such as x, x^2, $1/x$, root x and so on. Some also have trig-onometrical and other functions for calculations by navigators, engineers and others who use them.

5

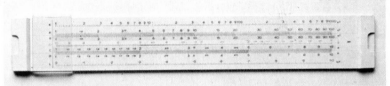

6
A

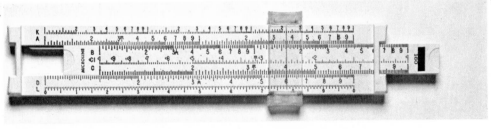

B

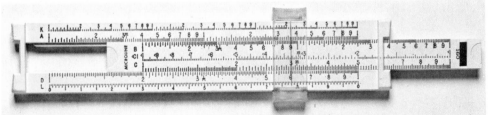

7

6 To multiply using a slide rule [A], for example to find the product of 1.5 and 4, the 1 on the upper scale is lined up with 1.5 on the lower scale. The required product is read off on the low-er scale opposite the 4 on the upper – in this example to give 6. The example of division [B] is 6÷3. The 3 on the upper scale is lined up with the 6 on the lower scale and the answer read off opp-osite the 1 on the upper scale. In this example the re-quired answer is 2.

7 A cylindrical slide rule can be pictured as a set of long scales wound round the cylinder like a screw thread.

Sets and groups

The mathematical theory of sets was first investigated by Georg Cantor (1845–1918) and later systematized by Ernst Zermelo (1871–1956), but the basic concepts were known earlier. Some adults new to these ideas find them difficult; but children have an intuitive grasp of them early in life. The concepts of number and operations on numbers are abstractions from the experience of sorting and combining sets of objects.

Collecting objects together

The idea of a set is the most fundamental concept in mathematics. A set is a collection of objects with a common description or definition, listed in any order or according to a formal law. The set of oceans, for example, is defined as: oceans = {Pacific, Atlantic, Indian, Arctic, Antarctic} or $O = \{x \mid x$ is an ocean}. The letter O labels the set; x is called a variable; { and } are called braces; and the symbol | means "where" or "such that". This kind of set is a finite set because its cardinality (number of elements) is finite – it has a known value, in this case five. The set of counting numbers is an infinite set because we cannot say exactly how many elements it has: counting numbers = {1, 2, 3,...}, or $C = \{x \mid x$ is a counting number}.

The set of natural numbers is $J^+ = \{1, 2, 3, ...\}$, with the same elements as the set of counting numbers. We say that C and J^+ are equal sets. Sets with the same cardinality are called equivalent sets: the set {blue, green, yellow, orange, red} is equivalent to the set of oceans – they each have five elements.

The language of sets can be understood by studying a particular example. A universal set [1], the set of all elements under consideration, can be partitioned into what are called disjoint subsets – that is, non-overlapping sets. If there are only two such sets, one is the complement of the other [2]. The set of elephants living at the North Pole is an example of the empty or null set, since it has no elements. The null set is written as ø. In illustration 2, for example, there is no intersection of sets A and B, or P and C, so the intersection equals ø. The concepts of partition, complement, intersection [3] and union [4] are fundamental to the processes of classification of information.

Networks [5] give rise to the Cartesian product of two sets. This is obtained by finding all possible ordered pairs of elements, taking one from each set. The word Cartesian is derived from René Descartes (1596–1650), who propounded the concept of co-ordinates. If set X is associated with the infinite set of points making one line in a plane and set Y is associated with the infinite set of points making another intersecting line, the Cartesian product of X and Y is associated with the infinite set of points making the plane containing the two lines [6].

Boolean and propositional algebra

The algebra of sets is known as Boolean algebra. It is isomorphic – that is, it has a one-to-one correspondence – with the algebra of propositions or logic. It is named after George Boole (1815–64), who founded the modern study of logic. The two types of algebra use different symbols, with *union* (∪) and *intersection* (∩) corresponding to *or* (∨) and *and* (∧). Propositional algebra analyses the sets of logical possibilities in which various statements and combinations

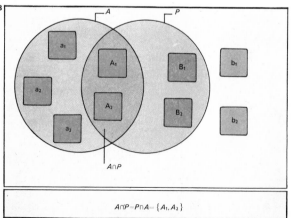

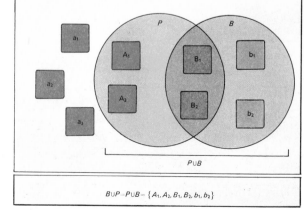

1 Two families – one with three children and one with two – together make up a universal set [A]. It can be represented diagrammatically [B] and letters given to each of the elements in the set. The letters are then sufficient for the mathematical manipulation of the set in what are called Venn diagrams, first introduced by the mathematician John Venn (1834–1923) in 1880. In such diagrams, areas represent sets of things.

2 These Venn diagrams show how the universal set of illustration [1B] can be split into two non-overlapping subsets. Each family can make up a subset [A] or the parents and children can each form subsets [B]. In each case the subsets are complementary to each other because they include between them all the elements of the first universal set. The complementary relationships in [A], for example, are written as $A' = B$ and $B' = A$.

Complementary sets $A' = B$ $B' = A$

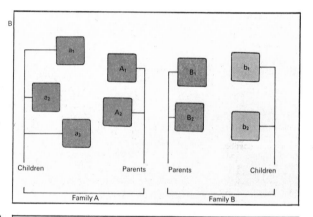

Complementary sets $P' = C$ $C' = P$

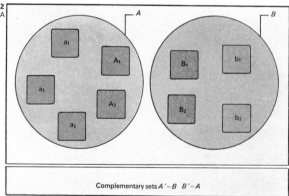

$A \cap P = P \cap A = \{A_1, A_2\}$

3 Intersection of sets generates another subset that contains all the elements common to both. Here the intersection of A and P (written as $A \cap P$) gives a subset containing only A_1 and A_2.

4 Union of sets generates yet another subset that contains all the elements in two original sets, in this example B and P. It is written $B \cup P$ and contains the elements A_1, A_2, B_1, B_2, b_1 and b_2. $B \cup P = P \cup B$ illustrates the commutative law.

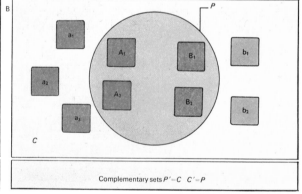

$B \cup P = P \cup B = \{A_1, A_2, B_1, B_2, b_1, b_2\}$

of the statements are either true or false.

A mathematical system is created when one or more binary operations are applied to a set of elements. A binary operation combines two elements into a third of the same set. One of the most valuable systems is the "group", as it occurs in many diverse situations and helps to unify the study of mathematics. The theory was developed by Evariste Galois (1811–32) and later systematized by Arthur Cayley (1821–95). The concept of a group can be illustrated by studying a simple case of formation dancing [8] in which four dancers change their positions (or remain still) to form various patterns. The movements form the set and the operation is a combination of movements called "follows", indicated mathematically by the symbol $\otimes$. Combining any two movements results in one of the four. The identity element is I and each element is its own inverse in this particular example. We have the relationships $(J \otimes K) \otimes L = L \otimes L = I$ and $J \otimes (K \otimes L) = J \otimes J = I$, so that the associative law $(J \otimes K) \otimes L = J \otimes (K \otimes L)$ is valid. In the particular example of dancing

there is another law, the commutative law:
$A \otimes B = B \otimes A$.

From the four possible choices available in moving a rectangle [9], a set of four transformations arises. These can be paired by the operation "follows" to produce a combination of movements that is in a one-to-one correspondence to those in the dancing example. The two types are said to be isomorphic. The search for isomorphisms is essentially the core of mathematical study.

The usefulness of group theory
Group theory is useful in the study of number systems. The set of integers (whole numbers) with 0 included, $\{\ldots -3, -2, -1, 0, +1, +2, +3, \ldots\}$, is a group under addition with 0 as the identity element. The set of rational numbers is a group under addition if 0 is included. It is a group under multiplication if 0 is excluded. The use of group theory in the study of arithmetic not only enriches it but leads to higher concepts such as those of rings and field, sets of elements subject to two binary operations (addition and multiplication) that satisfy certain axioms.

Any collection of objects constitutes a mathematical set – a collection of cans of soup, bottles of vinegar, supermarket trolleys or people in the shop are all definable sets.

5 A map shows the roads connecting two towns A and C. All the roads pass through town B. The two routes from A to B are one set and the three between B and C another set. There are six possible ways of going between A and C. This is known as the Cartesian product of two sets, in this case all possible combinations of paired elements, taking one from each set. The study of networks is one aspect of the subject of topology.

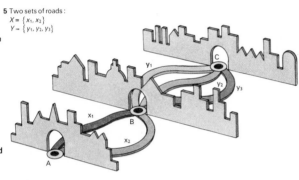

5 Two sets of roads:
$X = \{x_1, x_2\}$
$Y = \{y_1, y_2, y_3\}$

Six possible routes: $X \times Y = \{(x_1, y_1), (x_1, y_2), (x_1, y_3), (x_2, y_1), (x_2, y_2), (x_2, y_3)\}$

6 A plane defined by two lines is related to the Cartesian product of two sets that represent an infinite number of points on the lines. The point at the corner of the plane is defined by the co-ordinates x and y, written (x, y). These are called Cartesian co-ordinates and are used in co-ordinate, or analytic, geometry in which all lines, whether straight or curved, can be expressed in terms of algebraic equations.

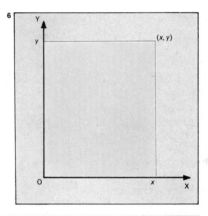

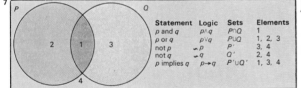

Statement	Logic	Sets	Elements
p and q	$p \wedge q$	$P \cap Q$	1
p or q	$p \vee q$	$P \cup Q$	1, 2, 3
not p	$\sim p$	P'	3, 4
not q	$\sim q$	Q'	2, 4
p implies q	$p \rightarrow q$	$P' \cup Q'$	1, 3, 4

7 Union and intersection in set theory correspond to "or" and "and" in logic. This relationship enables particular elements and combinations of elements from sets to be defined by logical statements.

8 Four dancers [A], starting at the corners of a square, can have various positions [B], represented by the symbols I, J, K and L. Carrying out pairs of movements, one after the other, results in new positions [C] described as J follows I, for example. Sequences of three movements can be analysed as two and the final position predicted. L follows K follows J, for example, reduces to L follows L, equals I.

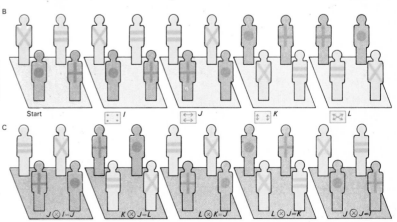

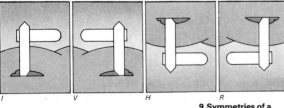

$V \otimes H = R$
$H \otimes R = V$

9 Symmetries of a rectangle involve rotating it in various ways – vertically V, horizontally H or in the plane of the picture R. The letter I represents its original position. Again successive pairs of movements always result in one of the four.

Start I J K L

$J \otimes I = J$ $K \otimes J = L$ $L \otimes K = J$ $L \otimes J = K$ $J \otimes J = I$

Finding changing quantities: calculus

In a "political vocabularly" compiled for the daily newspaper the *Guardian*, the noun "decrease" was cynically defined as: "reduction in rate of increase – as in unemployment, crime, inflation, taxation, etc". This not only exposes official double-talk [2] but also highlights the universality of a central concept of calculus – rate of change.

Rates of change became important in physics in 1638 when Galileo (1564–1642) concluded that a falling or thrown body had a downward velocity that increases steadily – that is, its rate of increase of downward velocity is constant [1]. What then is its trajectory? It took the genius of Isaac Newton (1642–1727) and Gottfried Leibniz (1646–1716) to solve this problem neatly and completely; the tool they created for the job was calculus.

Velocity, said Newton, is rate of change of position with time – 60km/h, for instance. Similarly, acceleration is rate of change of velocity with time. A car that takes three seconds to reach a speed of 60km/h from a standing start has an average acceleration of 20km/h per second. Galileo's law is that the downward acceleration of a falling body is constant. Calculus provides the methods of obtaining velocity from acceleration and position from velocity, and the whole problem is neatly solved. The calculus operation of deriving velocity from position, for example, is called differentiation. Its inverse is called integration.

The simplicity in symbolism

All mathematics is a sort of symbolic machinery for making subtle conceptual deductions without having to think them out – all the thought has been built into symbolism. Long division, for example, enables 431,613 to be divided by 357 by the unthinking application of a few rules; it is not necessary to know why it works, or what division really means. Calculus is perhaps the supreme example of a symbolism whose economical elegance reduces intractably complex and elusive problems to back-of-an-envelope simplicity.

In mechanics, the branch of physics for which calculus was invented, it is omnipresent in Newton's second law of motion: force equals mass multiplied by acceleration. Given any two of these quantities, the equation defines the third. Consider an internal combustion engine. What is the instantaneous acceleration of the piston as the crank passes top dead centre? Calculus provides the answer so that, knowing the piston's mass, it is possible to find the force on it that must be withstood by the connecting-rod. For what speed will this force become excessive? Again, the pressure on the piston during the power stroke is changing every instant with the burning of the charge and the changing volume of the gases in the cylinder as the piston descends. What then is the total energy imparted to the piston by the whole stroke and for what moment of ignition is it a maximum? This and a myriad of other mechanical problems could hardly be formulated, let alone solved, without calculus.

Electronic applications

Analogous applications occur in electrical engineering [Key]. Take, for example, a resistor (across which the voltage is proportional to the current), a capacitor (in which

1 A falling hammer is shown [A] in six exposures 0.03sec apart and the hammer position curve [D in diagram B] follows them [1–6]. Its changing slope is important and diagram C explains how this is measured, like a road gradient, by tangent triangles with so many units vertically for each one horizontally. The slopes at points 7–11 of line 12 are 0:2, 1:2, 2:2, 3:2 and 4:2 respectively – or 0, $\frac{1}{2}$, 1, $1\frac{1}{2}$ and 2. Line 13 plots the increasing slope of line 12. (Obtaining a slope curve from a curve is called differentiation; the reverse is integration.) In [B], the slope of the distance curve for the first exposure is given by a vertical drop of 2.8cm for a time-interval, measured horizontally, of 0.02 sec. So the velocity here is 2.8cm in 0.02sec = 140 cm/sec. Similar slope measurements give the velocity at other points and yield velocity curve V which initially increases downwards, like the distance. The acceleration (the rate of change of velocity with time) is the slope of the velocity curve – constant while the hammer is falling freely (curve A). At exposure 3, the hammer hits the nail at 200 cm/sec and things start to happen. In a milli-second (thousandth of a second) the velocity is braked back to about 40 cm/sec (curve V); this rapid deceleration drives A off-scale upwards to perhaps 100 times its free-fall value. Newton's law then gives a correspondingly large force on the nail, 100 times the weight of the hammer, and this is how the hammer works – driven by the force generated by rapid deceleration of the head. As the wood seizes the nail the shock kicks the hammer upwards; then in free fall again the hammer resumes steadily increasing downward velocity and constant acceleration.

the current is proportional to the rate of change of voltage with time), and an inductor (where the voltage is proportional to the rate of change of current with time). Connect them all together and apply an alternating voltage. What happens? Calculus swiftly expresses this seemingly mind-boggling tangle as a differential equation and solves it to show, among other things, that at a certain frequency the whole affair "resonates" and very large currents can flow for very little applied voltage. Resonance is of fundamental value throughout electronics. The tuning control of a radio selects one station out of many by setting a circuit to resonate at the station's transmission frequency.

One powerful application of calculus is in seeking maxima, minima, and optima generally. A vertically thrown ball is momentarily stationary at the top of its flight: when the height is a maximum, the rate of change of height with time is zero. It can be found by differentiating the expression relating height and time and putting this equal to zero. This is a general rule of great value – for all technology is governed by the search for optima.

What is the optimum speed for a journey, for example? Too slow wastes time, too fast wastes fuel; both of these have an assignable cost. Calculus enables the rate of change of overall cost with speed to be found and the speed for which it is zero. This must then be the speed for minimum cost. Such calculations are essential in making the best use of ships and aircraft and the same principles apply in all searches for the best design or flow-rate or working temperature of almost every industrial system [6].

Universal principle

Many physical laws embody the same principle [3, 4, 5]. Thus light traverses an optical system by a path that takes less time than any other possible path – a principle from which the whole of classical optics can be derived. Indeed Leibniz, possibly carried away by the power of his creation, proposed that the whole universe had been designed in some such mighty self-optimization process and that this was the best of all possible worlds. He seems not to have considered the possibility that it might be the worst.

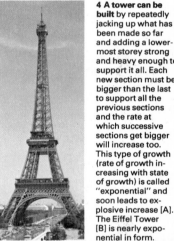

Faraday's "anchor ring" was the first-ever transformer. It revealed the law that the voltage on the output coil depends on the rate of change of voltage on the input coil.

2 Calculus can be used to analyse a headline such as: "Government acts to hold prices; rate of increase of inflation cut back". Suppose curve 1 is the rate of increase of inflation. Inflation itself will be the integral of 1 – curve 2, whose rate of increase at each point is proportional to the height of curve 1. Thus the slopes shown (black) are equal. Inflation is the rate of increase of prices, so prices (curve 3) are the integral of curve 2. It is then obvious that prices are not being "held".

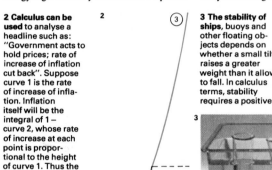

3 The stability of ships, buoys and other floating objects depends on whether a small tilt raises a greater weight than it allows to fall. In calculus terms, stability requires a positive rate of change of height energy with tilt. The picture shows that with more than a critical volume of ballast-liquid, a cylindrical tube floats vertically [1]. Tubes 2 and 3 have too little.

4 A tower can be built by repeatedly jacking up what has been made so far and adding a lowermost storey strong and heavy enough to support it all. Each new section must be bigger than the last to support all the previous sections and the rate at which successive sections get bigger will increase too. This type of growth (rate of growth increasing with state of growth) is called "exponential" and soon leads to explosive increase [A]. The Eiffel Tower [B] is nearly exponential in form.

5 The curvature of a beam at any point depends on its loading. A projecting strip is bent at each point by the weight of the length beyond it and calculus-based beam-theory adds up all these changing curvatures to arrive at the final shape of self-loaded beams. These plastic strips have different thicknesses and their degrees of deflection vary roughly as the inverse square of their thickness. Engineering beams do not sag as much but the same design principles apply.

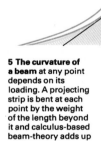

6 The cost benefit of increased insulation on a pipe [A] depends on reduction of heat loss (E on the pale blue) offsetting higher capital costs C. Their sum is least at MI. Increasing diameter reduces pumping costs (E on the dark blue) while raising capital cost (least at MD). The overall minimum cost is (MI¹, MD¹) at X. A chemical plant [B] must minimize cost over hundreds of variables.

Lines and shapes: geometry

Imagine the United Nations decided to encircle the world at the equator with a steel band symbolizing international unity. If the contractor made it too long by one part in ten million – 4m in 40,075km (13ft in 24,900 miles), how high would it stand above the surface all round the globe? The answer is 63.7cm (approximately 25ins).

Lines and shapes working for a living

The foregoing is an example of simple geometry, the mathematics of size and shape. Since all solid objects have size and shape geometry is one of the most practical mathematical studies. If someone wants to know how thick to make a rotating shaft to transmit a certain amount of power, or what contour to give a ship's propeller, or even how much paint is needed to cover a room or concrete to lay a path he uses geometry to provide the solution [5]. Indeed, geometry arose from the surveying needs of the early Egyptians, who had to share out fairly the featureless hectares of fertile mud left by the annual flooding of the River Nile.

The Greeks took geometry over [3] and built an amazing intellectual edifice out of it. Euclid's *Elements of Geometry*, which was written in about 300 BC, develops a complete "axiomatic system" – a web of interlocking proofs all derived from a few basic axioms. "If you can't prove it, you don't know it!" challenged the *Elements* and ever since the admitted business of mathematicians has been the clarifying of basic axioms and the proving or disproving of statements derived from them.

A practical engineer seldom bothers with proofs; he generally accepts the mathematician's formulae and uses them. And almost instinctively, because geometry makes it simple, he designs objects from rigid parts linked at pivot joints. Many mechanisms around us embody the truths of plane geometry. The motions of a typewriter, the pantograph of an electric locomotive [2], the suspension of a car, the linkages in a sewing-machine or an autochange gramophone can all be described as working "models" of a set of geometrical theorems.

Some machines – printing presses and knitting machines for example – appear almost magical in the motions they generate by ingenious geometrical linkages. And most rigid structures use the geometrical fact that a triangle is the only rigid figure. A triangle of rods joined at pivots cannot deform whereas a square, say, can distort to a diamond shape. As a result, girderwork is generally made up of triangles (a big girder bridge is a good example, as is a geodesic dome [Key]).

Pi in the sky, and elsewhere

The circle is a simple geometrical shape but one that is mathematically rich. The Greeks succeeded in proving its circumference to be $2\pi r$ and its area πr^2, where r is its radius and π some number between $3\frac{1}{7}$ and $3\frac{10}{71}$. In fact π cannot be expressed as any whole-number fraction. Expressed in decimals it begins 3.1415926535 . . . and goes on for ever, with a never-ending series of numbers after the decimal point with no numbers repeating. It is a fundamental constant in trigonometry, a numerical branch of geometry invented for mapping the stars and now fundamental to astronomy, navigation, surveying and all kinds of practical measure-

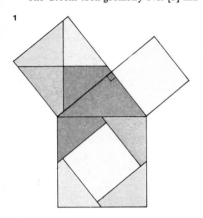

1

5A

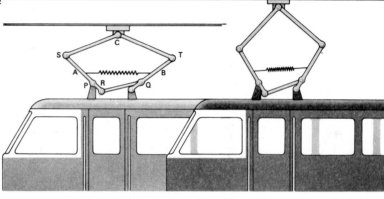

2

1 Pythagoras' theorem is the famous one children learn at school. The square on the hypotenuse (the longest side of a right-angled triangle) is the sum of the squares on the other two sides. The big bottom square (the hypotenuse square) divides into four corner sections, which can be reassembled into the top left square, and the one in the centre, which is the size of the top right square.

3 The ancient Greek Eratosthenes measured the earth's circumference by geometry. He found that when the sun was overhead at Syene it was 7° from the vertical at Alexandria. He knew the distance between them, about 800km (500 miles), and he reasoned that it represented 7° at the earth's centre. The full 360° of circle representing the earth's circumference must be $360 \div 7 \times 800$ (500) = about 41,140km (25,700 miles).

2 An electric locomotive must always maintain contact with the overhead wire, which itself is not perfectly level. The geometry of the pantograph achieves this. A spring system urges points P and Q together, pivoting arms A and B to shorten distance ST. This distortion of triangle STC keeps C against the overhead wire. As arm A pivots linkage RQ makes B pivot too, preserving symmetry.

5 Tiling a floor with identical tiles can be done in various ways. Obviously it can be done with equilateral triangles [A], hexagons [B], squares, or with tiles made by fusing shapes together [C]. But it can-

not be done with pentagons or any tiles with pentagonal symmetry. Geometry proves that there are just 5 basically different tiling patterns – including the most ornate – using identical tiles.

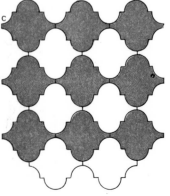

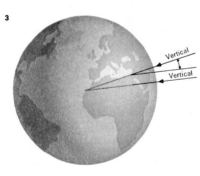

4 A

B

C

B

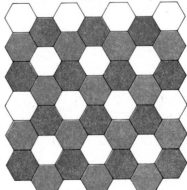

C

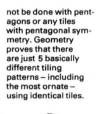

4 Molecules are too small to be visible so chemists use geometry to deduce molecular structures. Dichloromethane (a solvent used in paint-strippers) has one carbon atom, two hydrogen atoms and two chlorine atoms in its molecule. If they

were arranged as a square with the carbon in the middle, two forms of dichloromethane should exist, one with the chlorines adjacent [A] and one with them opposite [B]. But if the atoms are arranged tetrahedrally only one form is poss-

ible [C]. Only one form has ever been obtained so the square structure is wrong. By such reasoning chemists deduced the spatial arrangements of thousands of molecules long before methods such as crystallography provided direct evidence.

ment. In fact π has "escaped" from geometry and pervades all numerical measurements.

Some of the most elaborate geometry based on the circle is used in lens design. Almost all lenses – for cameras, spectacles, telescopes and so on – have circular cross-sections. Tracing the light path through a multi-component lens system is a complex geometrical task now carried out by computers. The computer programs calculate the characteristics of many possible lens designs and select the one with the fewest aberrations (for no lens system can be absolutely perfect). The result is a compromise, but the best that can be reached bearing in mind the practical difficulty of actually grinding the lenses.

Geometries beyond intuition

Euclidean geometry takes a number of intuitive notions for granted – the idea of a straight line, for example. Euclid thought of it as a line of zero curvature, the shortest line that could be drawn between two points. In practical matters, such as sighting and surveying, we assume that light travels in straight lines. But the physicist feels free to question

these suppositions. He considers it possible that light flashed out from the earth might go all round the universe and return to its starting-point, just as a person would who travelled in what he regarded as a "straight line" on the spherical earth. Indeed cosmology, the study of the universe as a whole, currently favours a "closed curved" universe with a finite volume but no boundaries just as the earth's surface has a finite area but is without edges.

Mathematicians see Euclidean geometry as just one of many imaginable geometries, each true of space of a particular curvature [10]. Their theorems may be strange, but provided they can be rigorously derived from the stated axioms (assumed facts), mathematical protocol is satisfied. And which of them is true of our real space is a matter of scientific experiment, not of axiomatic assertion. Fortunately, any curvature must be very small, so that Euclidean geometry works well in the small volumes we can deal with, just as in mapping a small area of the earth it can be assumed to be flat without significant error.

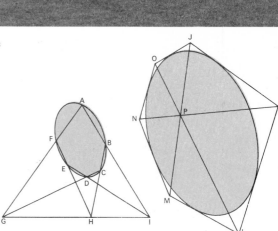

A geodesic dome is a rigid structure made from many triangles and designed for both lightness and strength.

6

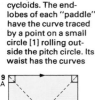

6 An air compressor uses the subtle geometry of interlinked cycloids. The endlobes of each "paddle" have the curve traced by a point on a small circle [1] rolling outside the pitch circle. Its waist has the curves from a similar circle [2] rolling on the inside of the pitch circle. As the paddles mesh like 2-toothed cogwheels, they always touch each other, trapping successive volumes of air and compressing them.

7 This model of Felton and Murray's early steam engine is a geometrical theorem in action. The inner cogwheel rolls around a fixed outer gear of twice its diameter. Geometrically, this implies that one point on it reciprocates in an exact straight line. A piston rod attached at this point is driven from a cylinder; a crank takes the drive from the centre of the rolling wheel, to drive other machines.

7

8

8 The principle of duality in geometry states that any two lines define a point (their intersection) and any two points define a line (the one joining them). If six points [A–F] touch an ellipse, then the lines joining them form three opposite pairs whose points of intersection meet at a single line [GHI]. The dual of the theorem is that if six lines touch an ellipse then the points at which they intersect [J–O] form three opposite pairs whose lines of connection meet at a single point [P]. So points and lines are "duals" of each other and if these words are interchanged in a theorem, a new theorem results.

9

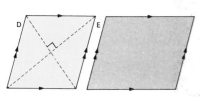

9 Quadrilaterals include a square [A], with right-angles and all its sides equal and parallel; a rectangle [B] with only opposite sides equal; a trapezium [C] with only two opposite sides parallel; a rhombus [D] and a parallelogram [E], both with opposite sides parallel and no right-angles.

10

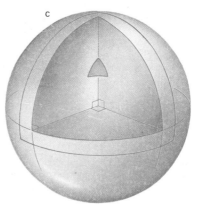

10 Euclidean geometry [A] is not inevitable and may not be true of real space. Mathematicians accept any geometry that is not self-contradictory and recognize many different kinds. In Lobachevskian geometry [B] the angles never reach 180°, like geometry on a trumpet surface. In Riemann geometry [C] angles of a triangle always exceed the Euclidean 180°, like geometry on the surface of a sphere. Extended to three dimensions this is geometry of "curved space".

Lines and angles: trigonometry

The Simplon tunnel, between Italy and Switzerland, is 20km (about 12 miles) long and was bored from both ends through the Alps. When the headings met in the middle, in 1906, they were in exact horizontal alignment and only 10cm (4in) out vertically. The engineers managed to smooth out the discontinuity. Using trigonometry they had set up their machines to cut along the 10km (6 mile) sides of two huge triangles in the mountain.

Sines, cosines and tangents
Trigonometry is the art of calculating the dimensions of triangles. The basic idea [1] is that the ratios between the sides of a right-angled triangle depend on its base angle [A]. The ratios have been named the sine of A (sin A), the cosine of A (cos A), the tangent of A (tan A) and others. They have been tabulated for many values of the angle A. Sin A is the length of the triangle side opposite the angle A divided by the longest side; cos A is the length of the side adjacent to the angle A divided by the longest side; and tan A is the ratio of the length of the opposite and adjacent sides of the triangle.

Armed with trigonometrical tables anyone can determine the dimensions of any triangle with great accuracy. Since nearly any shape can be broken up into a series of triangles this is a powerful method of solving even complex spatial problems. To use it in tunnelling engineers set up a station from which both the ends are visible or (as this may be difficult with mountains all around) a station from which other stations are visible, from which in turn the ends can be seen. They measure the angles between all the stations by optical sighting and thus relate the two ends. Trigonometry then tells them the tunnelling angles that will align the two headings. The required accuracy of a thousandth of a degree implies a certain expertise; but the mathematical principle involved is nevertheless extremely simple.

Trigonometry in everyday life
Trigonometrical ratios have, however, "escaped" from their simple geometrical interpretation and uses in surveying and measuring, and now crop up in all sorts of mathematical problems that do not seem to be at all "angular". Some of their most fruitful applications are in circuit theory, radiation physics and information-handling, in which the angles are not real but introduced merely for convenience.

The sine of 0° is 0 and it increases with increasing angles up to 90°, whose sine is 1. Between 90° and 180° the sine reduces again to 0. From 180° to 270° the sine is negative, decreasing to −1. And from 270° to 360° the sine increases again from −1 to 0. Thus if a trigonometrical angle is regarded as winding up continuously [5], its sine swings between +1 and −1 and back at each revolution of 360°. This periodic behaviour gives mathematicians a framework for handling waves, vibrations, oscillating radiation such as light and radio waves, and alternating current (AC) electricity. In most European countries a power station generator spins at 50 revolutions a second. As a result its output voltage (which depends on the sine of the angle of rotation) swings back and forth between positive and negative at 50 cycles per second (50Hz) to generate mains-frequency AC. Any other source of oscillation, even

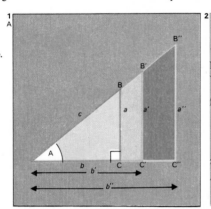

1 Trigonometry (literally, "triangle-measuring") is based on six named ratios in a right-angled triangle. Triangles ABC, AB′C′ and AB″C″ [A] all have base angle A. Clearly they have the same relative proportions so $a/b = a'/b' = a''/b''$. In fact any right-angled triangle of base angle A will have this fixed ratio between those sides. It is called the tangent of A or tan A. Thus when A = 45°, $a = b$, so tan 45° = 1. The other ratios are: b/a, cotangent (cot A); a/c, sine (sin A); b/c, cosine (cos A); c/b, secant (sec A); c/a, cosecant (cosec A). These are tabulated for all angles; nowadays some pocket calculators can work them out. They will give the dimensions of any triangle, not just right-angled ones, via the formulae [B]: $a/\sin A = b/\sin B = c/\sin C$ and $a^2 = b^2 + c^2 - 2bc \cos A$. (Side a is always opposite angle A, side b opposite angle B, etc.)

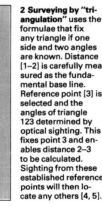

2 Surveying by "triangulation" uses the formulae that fix any triangle if one side and two angles are known. Distance [1–2] is carefully measured as the fundamental base line. Reference point [3] is selected and the angles of triangle 123 determined by optical sighting. This fixes point 3 and enables distance 2–3 to be calculated. Sighting from these established reference points will then locate any others [4, 5].

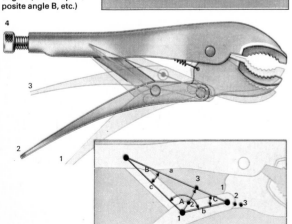

4 In triangle ABC of the self-grip wrench, $a^2 = b^2 + c^2 - 2bc \cos A$. As b and c are constant lengths a^2, and hence a, change only with the cos A term. Reducing A increases cos A and hence a, closing the jaws. When A is large, a small decrease increases cos A substantially. But as A approaches 0°, cos A is near its limit of 1 and changes little. The final closure moves the jaws slightly giving a big leverage ratio with gripping force.

3 On a sphere such as the earth any distance can be represented by the angle it makes at the centre. Thus distance PB may be represented by angle POB. Accordingly positions are defined by angles of latitude (with the equator) and of longitude (north/south line). Point A has longitude x° west, latitude y° south; B has x′° east, y′° north. The "spherical trigonometry" of "spherical triangles" such as PAB tells a navigator the distance AB and the compass bearing (angle A) of the journey. Similarly in mapping the heavens astronomers locate stars on spherical celestial triangles like παβ.

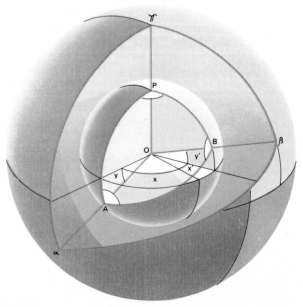

light with a frequency of 600 million million Hz, can be similarly assigned a notional "phase angle" winding up at the appropriate rate of time.

Any vibration, however complicated, can be made up of a set of sine-wave components (or cosine-wave ones which are similar), each with its own frequency. Each frequency is quite independent of the rest. (Two stones thrown into water together generate two sets of spreading ripples which intersect and go right through each other, emerging quite unaffected.) Similarly, the human ear can pick out the notes in a chord although they make a single vibrational pattern in the air or a single groove on a gramophone record.

Angles in a radio beam
Many electronic techniques process these frequency components of vibrations in ways governed by trigonometry. An AM (amplitude modulated) radio transmitter, for example, has to take a sine-wave audio frequency A (say the musical note A, 440Hz) and attach it somehow to a radio sine-wave "carrier" C, being broadcast at perhaps one

million Hz (1MHz, in the medium-wave band). It does this in effect by multiplying the audio voltage at each instant by the carrier voltage at that instant and transmitting the result. Now one of the many trigonometrical formulae for simple angles asserts that $\sin A \times \sin C = \frac{1}{2}\cos(A-C) - \frac{1}{2}\cos(A+C)$. Since A and C are phase-angles of audio and carrier frequencies the result of the multiplication is two cosine-waves (just like sine-waves), one at $(1,000,000 - 440)$ Hz and the other at $(1,000,000 + 440)$ Hz, each of half the intensity of the original carrier.

The splitting of the carrier into two closely spaced "sidebands" is called amplitude modulation, or AM. A transmission generally has many such pairs of sidebands continuously changing in their spacing and intensity with the changing frequency-components of the audio signal. At the receiver the audio signal is recovered by the reverse process of demodulation. It may seem incredible that a mathematical formula first proved for static triangles on paper can be impudently applied to the imaginary rotating angles of an electronic signal.

The quadrant was an early instrument used by astronomers to find the altitude of the heavenly bodies. The surveyor's quadrant developed as a portable version for surveying and artillery ranging. This example was made by Jacob Lusuerg of Rome in 1674. Its most interesting feature is the Vernier scale – invented by Pierre Vernier (c. 1580–1637) in 1631 – for measuring to $1/60°$. This is the lower arc-scale joining the legs of the pivoting V-shaped unit which slides over the static quadrant base plate. Another scale shows the tangent of the measured angle.

5 As a rotating radius sweeps out an ever increasing angle, the angle's sine varies cyclically, repeating itself for every additional 360° of rotation. For a circle of unit radius the sine is the height of the end of the radius above the horizontal. Such sinusoidal waveforms occur in vibrations. The frequency is the number of radius-rotations per second. Two simultaneous sine-waves of different frequency will add together to a complex waveform: thus sine-waves [1] and [2] add to give the waveform [3], which might represent the variation in sound-pressure of two notes sounding together.

6

6 A waveform can be made by combining sine-waves; it can also be broken down into them. This diagram shows the amplitude (intensity) spectra of the waveforms of illustration 5. Waveform 1 has only one component in its spectrum, at the frequency f. Waveform 2 has a single component of frequency 2f but of lower intensity. Their combination [3] has both these lines in its spectrum.

5

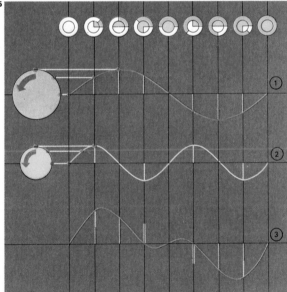

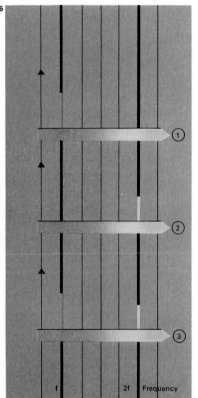

f 2f Frequency

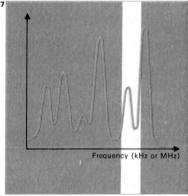

Frequency (kHz or MHz)

7 The complex waveform of all the signals entering the radio receiver's aerial will have many components in its frequency spectrum. Each peak is a broadcast on a specific frequency. Some stations are weak, some strong; tuning the radio moves a narrow frequency-acceptance band along the frequency scale to select just one of them. The small modulation is then decoded to give sound.

8
A

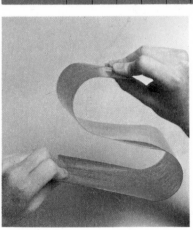

8 A bent steel strip [A] does not adopt a sine-wave form but a related "sine-generated" curve. The direction of the strip from point to point varies sinusoidally with distance along the strip. This minimizes the energy of bending stored in the steel. This curve is created on a grand scale [B] when a slow-moving river winds to the sea. The water has little energy and so seeks the line of least resistance as it cuts its channel.

B

Surface and volumes: solid geometry

In 1826 the German astronomer Heinrich Olbers (1758–1840) asked what may seem to be a silly question: Why is it dark at night? Silly questions are sometimes the most profound and Olbers tackled this one using straightforward solid geometry. He imagined the universe divided into a series of concentric shells around the Earth, like the layers of an onion spreading out to infinity. He supposed that the stars were more or less uniformly distributed. Then, through solid geometry, Olbers calculated that a shell twice as far away is bigger and contains four times as many stars. But, in theory, only a quarter as much of their light should reach the Earth. Each shell therefore contributes the same radiance to the night sky no matter how far away it is. Because there are an infinite number of shells the night sky should be infinitely bright – or at least as bright as the face of the Sun.

So why is the night dark? Even today, astronomers do not agree on the structure of the heavens. The universe might be finite in space, with only a limited number of shells; or finite in time, so that light from the most distant shells has yet to reach here; or it may be expanding, weakening the light from distant shells. Olbers's paradox remains an outstanding example of how simple mathematics can provoke the most surprising conclusions from uncontroversial assumptions.

Sizing things up

Mathematicians and engineers alike have to be able to calculate the areas and volumes of various solid objects. For an object with flat faces the surface area equals the sum of the areas of the faces. Thus for a cube, the surface area is merely six times the area of one face. For a sphere the area is four times π times the square of the radius. The volume of a cube is the length of one side multiplied by itself three times (the length cubed), and the volume of a sphere is 4/3 times π times the cube of the radius.

Pyramids, prisms, cylinders, cones and ellipsoids present more complex problems, but all can be calculated using solid geometry, that is the geometry of shapes in three dimensions. Mathematicians use solid geometry to find the surface areas of such shapes and whether they can be made by forming a flat paper shape (a cylinder, prism, pyramid and cone can be made this way, but not a sphere or ellipsoid). The path that a grinding-wheel of known dimensions must traverse to cut a given shape from a metal blank, or how much earth must be shifted to make a railway embankment of a given height, or what size cylinders can be bored in an engine-block for a given safe spacing between them (and the resulting swept volume) – to determine all these quantities, engineers make use of solid geometry.

Networks of force

The subject-matter of solid geometry includes not just the shapes of objects and assemblies, but the invisible strains and forces that traverse them. The centre of gravity of a cylinder is half-way up it; stood on end and tilted it will not fall over provided that any part of the top surface is still vertically above any part of the bottom surface. But the centre of gravity of a cone is a quarter of the way up it. It can be tilted until its tip is one-and-a-half times as far to one side as the

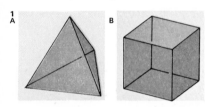 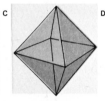 

1 A regular polygon has all its sides and angles equal, as in the equilateral triangle, square and pentagon. Euclid proved that there can be only five regular solids whose faces are all identical regular polygons: the tetrahedron [A], the cube [B], the octahedron [C], the dodecahedron [D] (with 12 faces), and the icosahedron [E] (with 20 faces). These can be found in nature as crystals and viruses.

3 All solids that do not have holes through them, and have flat faces, obey Euler's theorem: $V + F = E + 2$ where V is the number of vertices (corners), F the number of faces and E the number of edges. For the tetrahedron [A] $4 + 4 = 6 + 2$; for the octahedron [B], $6 + 8 = 12 + 2$. The shapes C, D also obey the rules. In fact the shape and size of the solid does not matter at all.

2 Solid geometry controls the perspective appearance of the world because light travels in straight lines. The laws of perspective envisage a picture-plane between the eye and the scene to be represented. Connect each point in the scene to the eye by a straight line: the place where this penetrates the picture-plane is its position in the perspective representation of the scene. From the eye's viewpoint, a perspective picture is seen.

4 A perspective picture has a central "vanishing point" to which parallel lines perpendicular to the picture-plane all converge. Other horizontal lines (such as edges of the cuboid box) converge to other points on the picture's horizon. A circular disc is distorted by perspective representation unless it is directly in front of the eye: the effect is small for most deviations from this position. This picture is the perspective view of illustration 2.

5 Uniform polyhedra can have several different regular polygons contributing to their faces. There are 13 "Archimedean solids", not counting the infinity of simple prisms allowed by this definition – each of which has a regular polygon top and bottom joined by square faces around the middle. If faces are allowed to intersect, 53 additional uniform polyhedra result. This ditrigonal dodecahedron is composed of several dodecagons.

edge of the base extends on the other side.

Such simple results, elaborated for far more complex shapes, determine for example what form a dam must have in order that the water pressure should not push it over; how high in the water a boat of given shape will float, and how far over it will heel if loaded lop-sided; and what overloading of a tower-crane will just topple it.

For forces more complex than gravity still more intricate questions arise. What pressure can a round-ended gas cylinder withstand, and where will it fail if overpressurized? (Answer: on the inner surface, at a point midway between the ends.) What structure must an aircraft wing be given in order that, when loaded by lift and thrust and weight and drag, it will deflect into the desired shape without overstressing any of its parts? Problems such as these can be solved by modelling, or by computing and translating the solid geometry of the model into its numerical equivalents.

There are systems whose geometry reveals the active forces directly. A magnetic-liquid labyrinth [Key] reveals the opposing magnetic forces that mould it. And in nature, a bone or a tree that grows against the forces on it reveals those forces to the intelligent eye by the shape it grows into – the ideal shape for the loads it has to bear.

Molecular architecture

The solid geometry of molecules is surprisingly important in modern chemistry. It determines not only how they pack into crystals, but how they react. It is particularly significant for understanding enzymes, the powerful biological catalysts that bring about reactions which the chemist is often helpless to imitate. An enzyme is a huge molecule with a complicated active surface on which only the right reacting molecules can fit. And having fitted they are then held in the right positions to react. In doing so the reactants' geometry alters and they spring from the surface, leaving it ready to accept more reagents. The double helix of the DNA molecule consists of two interlinked twisting strands. The whole marvellous mechanism of the human body depends on the sub-microscopic solid geometry of the fundamental catalysts of life.

KEY

This mixture of a magnetizable liquid and an immiscible transparent one is in a magnetic field.

Every part of the magnetic liquid then repels every other part, so it seeks to divide into many small sections. But every division uses energy so the liquid compromises to the shape shown here.

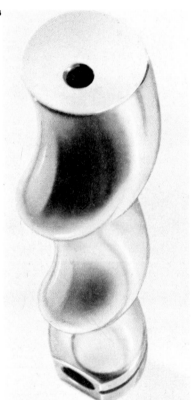

6 The geometrical shapes of engineering objects are often beautiful. This sludge-pump impeller is a stack of discs whose centres are helically disposed around the central axis of the impeller.

C

7 There is no complete mathematical construction to the general problem (given a closed line) of finding a minimum-area surface that has that line as a boundary. A soap film solves it automatically for any closed line. The film is always in tension and shapes itself to minimize its area. Here is one outlining the smooth and elegant minimum-area surface for a three-lobed loop made of copper wire.

8 Optical components have surfaces governed by the laws of optics and the solid geometry of ray paths. The big rectangular outline mirror of this infra-red spectrometer has an ellipsoidal surface. It intercepts a diverging beam of infra-red radiation coming from the left and reflects it so that it all converges on the radiation detector, that is the stalk mounted in front of the mirror.

The mirror [bottom left] has a spherical surface and processes the invisible beam at an earlier stage of its journey through the instrument. The complete instrument has about 20 reflecting surfaces.

9 For maximum volume from a given area of tin-plate, the height should equal the diameter. A standard 425g (15oz) can [D] has a height 1.4 times the diameter because stamping out and forming the ends wastes some tin-plate. This is thus the practical optimum. The polish tins [A, B] are wider than ideal for easy access to the contents; the aerosols [C, E] are narrower to resist internal pressure.

9 A   B

E

D

10

10 The absolute minimum surface area for a given volume container is a sphere. (A soap bubble proves this by minimizing its surface area round an enclosed volume of gas.) This also gives the greatest resistance to internal pressure. Spherical tanks are used to store liquids under pressure. Such tanks are also used for liquids held at low temperatures where the absolute minimum wall area minimizes leakage of heat from outside into the liquid.

Shape and symmetry

If in the same boarding houses there are two rooms of equal aspect and furnishings, then their rents will be equal. For suppose the rents are different: then one tenant will be paying less than he might, which is absurd. This elegant theorem formulated by the Canadian humorist Stephen Leacock (1869–1944) illustrates the mathematical idea of symmetry.

Symmetry is a powerful concept and its workings can be seen in many aspects of the world. The two halves of a bridge span, the wings of a bird or of an aircraft, the blades of a propeller, all have symmetry – for otherwise one of them is worse than it need be, which is also absurd. Mathematicians recognize many different types of symmetry all described by the group of real or imaginable "symmetry operations" which leave the symmetrical entity apparently unchanged. A square, a cube or a four-bladed propeller can all be turned through 90 degrees without apparent change: they are said to have a "fourfold axis of symmetry". An irregular object has the lowest symmetry because any twist or turn is detectable. A sphere has the highest possible symmetry; no twist or turn is detectable. This made it the "perfect" figure to the ancient Greeks and makes it highly useful today. A ballrace is so simple because the balls need no aligning; no matter how they roll they cannot jam the bearing. A roller-bearing of lower symmetry needs guides to keep rollers parallel to the bearing axis; a tapered roller-bearing of lower symmetry has even more geometrical constraints.

Symmetry of nature

A snowflake [Key] shows how the laws of nature give symmetry to their products. It has 120-degree angles between many faces because in the water molecules of which it is comprised two hydrogen atoms form a 120-degree angle with an oxygen atom. The crystal lattice in ice is formed by the regular interpacking of the molecules and reflects this symmetry.

But this does not explain why the whole elaborate structure has a sixfold axis of symmetry. How does one branch of the flake know how its fellows are growing, so as to imitate them exactly? The physicist Samuel Tolansky (1907–73) made the suggestion that a snowflake, as it falls and takes up water vapour from the cold air, is vibrating with the symmetry of its crystal structure. All the branches move and twist together in a complex and changing pattern; the fastest points on each branch intercept the most water vapour and so grow together.

Such symmetries of process are common throughout nature. The radial shatter-pattern of a broken window betrays the symmetrical stresses that radiated outwards from the impact point.

Symmetry in the abstract

Mathematics manages symmetry by "group theory", a fascinating topic which, from a few apparently trivial axioms, develops rapidly into a structure of amazing subtlety and elegance. The oddest thing about it is that, unlike number theory, it allows $a \times b$ not to equal $b \times a$. This lack of symmetry in the mathematics of symmetry may seem like complete nonsense, but in practice the order of events can also be important. Sanding down a door, then painting it, for example,

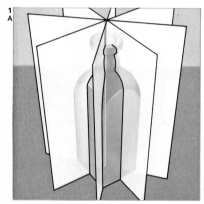
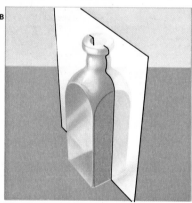
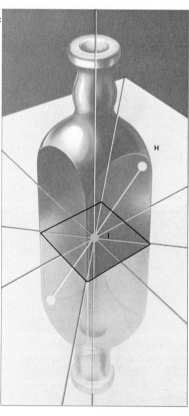
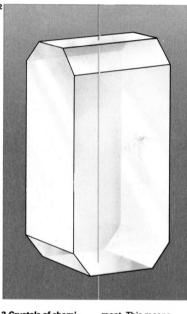
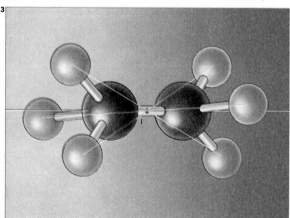

1 An object or mathematical entity has symmetry if some defined "symmetry operation" on it leaves it unchanged. If the bottle [A] is rotated through 90° about its vertical axis it presents its original appearance again. Because this symmetry operation would recur four times in a complete revolution the axis is a "fourfold axis of rotational symmetry". The bottle's other "symmetry elements" are four mirror planes. Reflecting every point on the bottle through such a plane to the corresponding position on the other side is a symmetry operation. A bottle with a blank label [B] has no rotation axis and only one mirror plane as symmetry element. The pseudo-bottle [C] has new symmetry elements: a horizontal mirror-plane H and four twofold axes in it, as well as a centre of inversion [I], about which the bottle can be rotated and remain unchanged.

2 Crystals of chemical substances show symmetry that derives from the lattice of molecules composing them. The urea crystal has a vertical "improper axis of symmetry" for a symmetry element. This means that rotating the crystal through 90° and then reflecting it in a bisecting horizontal plane leaves it apparently unchanged. It also has two mirror planes and two 2-fold axes.

3 Ethane is a gas whose molecules each have two carbon atoms [blue spheres] and six hydrogen atoms [green spheres]. It has the centre of inversion [I] but the two CH_3 groups are not related by a mirror plane between them. These groups can mutually rotate into alignment, giving the molecule such a mirror-plane but destroying the centre of inversion. Molecular symmetry and its alteration with internal motion dominates much of chemical theory.

4 The common starfish (*Asterias rubens*) has five appropriate planes of symmetry and a 5-fold rotation axis. Among animals only a few specialized sea creatures (radiata) have such high symmetry. They probably evolved from ancestors of lower symmetry, as inferred from their larvae, which have the approximate mirror-symmetry of most creatures, including man. The starfish has no horizontal mirror plane; it has a true "top" and a true "bottom".

gives a different result from painting it and then sanding it down.

For an object with symmetry its group consists of the "operations" that can be carried out on it: turning it through 90 degrees, reflecting it in a plane and so on. Take a squat square-shouldered pill bottle without its label, hold it upright and pivot it through a right-angle about its top-left and bottom-right corners. It will then be horizontal with the neck on the left. Turn it clockwise through 90 degrees and it will be upright again. That is a symmetry operation. But if the latter is performed first and then the former the bottle will finish upside down: $a \times b$ does not equal $b \times a$.

The uses of group theory

Group theory is one of the many inventions of nineteenth-century mathematics that later found scientific use. Indeed, the rapid spread of its strange but potent "arithmetic" in twentieth-century physics earned it the title, among an older generation of physicists, of *die Gruppenpest* ("group nuisance"). But its incorporation into modern physics and chemistry, with their need to understand the subtle symmetries of molecules and crystals and their energy states, has made possible the theories which give us such modern marvels as semiconductor electronics.

So much symmetry exists in scientific theories and mathematics that researchers acquire a feeling for it and any "lopsided" features of a theory or experiment make them uneasy. In electromagnetism, for example, the fact that electric charges (positive and negative) can be isolated, whereas magnetic poles (north and south) cannot, seems somehow to be "wrong". Many physicists have sought magnetic monopoles to complete the symmetry of the situation but, so far, attempts to discover such particles have been unsuccessful. But the most daring of all such insights was that of Albert Einstein (1879–1955) when he reasoned that the speed of light (and indeed every phenomenon of physics) must be the same for all observers, no matter how fast they themselves were travelling. Implicit in that mighty assertion of symmetry was nuclear power and the atomic bomb.

The symmetry of a snowflake echoes the symmetry of its molecules but owes its elaborate perfection to the subtle process of crystal growth by vapour-deposition on a vibrating surface.

5

5 Just as an object can have symmetry, so can an infinite repeating lattice. The symmetry operations for objects also apply to lattices. But there are other operations which, applied to an infinite lattice of appropriate symmetry, will leave it apparently unchanged. One is "translation", that is, shifting the lattice sideways. Every lattice can be divided into repeating "unit-cells" and displacement by one unit-cell spacing is a symmetry operation. Another is "gliding", reflection in a line followed by translation along it. This painting, "Angels and Devils" by M. C. Escher (1898–1972), has symmetry elements decreasing in size.

6
A

B

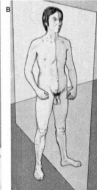

6 Why does a mirror turn an image right-to-left and not upside down? The answer to this confusing question is that the mirror's transformation is neither right-to-left nor up-to-down, but back-to-front. The left side stays on the left and the top stays on top, but the back becomes the front. Because hands [A], like other pairs of body parts related by mirror symmetry, are called "right" and "left", a right hand becomes a left one, starting the confusion. Some lack of symmetry is not obvious: in man [B] the heart and other organs are on the right if he considers his mirror image.

7

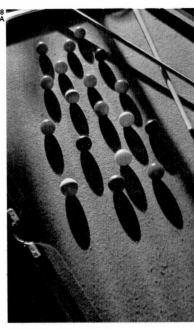

8
A

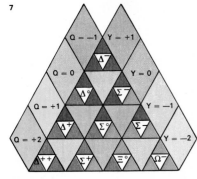

B

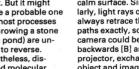

7 Symmetry considerations are basic to nuclear-particle physics. Many fundamental particles are now known, but the laws governing their occurrence and properties are poorly understood. One attractive theory has them composed of "quarks". The diagram shows how the d-quark [blue], the u-quark [red] and the s-quark [green] might combine in threes to form each of 10 particles called hyperons (−, 0, or +). The charge [Q] and "hypercharge" [Y] of each hyperon is correctly predicted by this type of symmetry classification, which also predicted the Ω^- particle before its discovery.

8 One of the most paradoxical of physical laws is that of time symmetry: any process can go backwards. This may seem absurd but in a film of two or more billiard balls colliding [A], it might not be possible to tell if it was run backwards. The reversed film would still show a possible physical event. But it might not be a probable one and most processes (eg throwing a stone into a pond) are unlikely to reverse. Nonetheless, dispersed molecular motions could converge on a stone and eject it spontaneously through a calm surface. Similarly, light rays can always retrace their paths exactly, so a camera could be used backwards [B] as a projector, exchanging object and image, and remain in focus.

The language of space: topology

When the comic film character Monsieur Hulot traces along a tangled hosepipe from a tap and finds it leads back to the tap again, why does the audience laugh? And what is so odd about a household hint from *The Times* of London: "Mending a hole in a tablecloth: lay the cloth on a table with the hole uppermost . . ."? Both items offend our instincts about topology – a branch of mathematics that deals not with shape or size but with much more fundamental properties of objects and of space.

Spheres, nets and knots

It is a topological truth that, regardless of its length or curvature, a hosepipe has two ends. Similarly, we feel sure that no matter what the size of a tablecloth, or the outline of a hole in it, it would be hard to spread the cloth out with the hole underneath. Topology takes such intuitive matters and formalizes them into mathematical logic. It is concerned with all those properties of objects that are unaffected by any change of form, however extreme. For instance, any simple solid object without holes is a "ball" to a

topologist, for if made of deformable clay it could be rounded into a ball without being torn. Thus topology is sometimes called "rubber sheet geometry".

A button with four holes in it is not a topological ball. It is a "quadruply connected solid" because you would have to make four cuts in it, opening out the holes to the edge of the button, to make a shape that is a topological sphere. Small creatures living on the button would find it a different kind of space to the surface of a sphere. Any closed curve on a sphere [1], for example, must fence in and enclose a definite area. On a button this is not so. A closed curve round one of the holes does no such thing. The pure topologist's main concern is to decide whether particular abstract entities (objects or spaces of many forms and dimensions) are or are not topologically equivalent. Human intuition in comprehending the basic topology of even simple figures is relatively limited and sometimes leads to wrong conclusions.

This strange branch of mathematics has links with the real world [7]. An electrical circuit is a topological entity, for example; its

exact layout does not matter because only the pattern of interconnections is electrically significant. Graph theory [3, 4], the branch of topology that handles networks, is fundamental in advanced circuit design. And the age-old crafts of knitting and weaving are really exercises in applied topology. A loop with a knot in it retains that knot however it is deformed and cannot be "undone"; it is topologically different from an unknotted loop. Textile manufacturers practise topology in their efforts to produce garments with specific topological properties: ones that can be knotted in one piece or that will not unravel if a fibre breaks [Key].

A mathematical playground

Most serious topology has, as yet, little to do with the practical world. No branch of it is as closely tied to human affairs as, say, arithmetic is to banking. It is therefore a subject full of potential – for time and time again in the history of mathematics such theorists' playgrounds have become the workshops of a new science or discipline. At present, however, theorems in topology, although proved

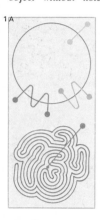

1 **"Any closed curve** divides a surface into an inside and an outside, and a line connecting these crosses the boundary an odd number of times."** This theorem may seem obvious [A] but is not true of all surfaces. A table and statue [B] are topological balls on which the theorem holds. But a chair and man (because of his alimentary canal) have holes through them, like a doughnut [C], which need not obey the theorem.

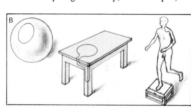

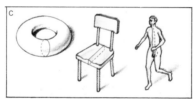

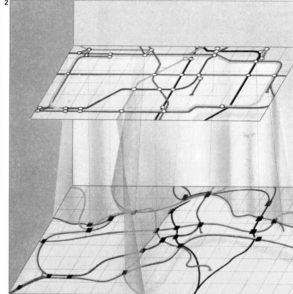

2 **The London Underground map** is a very distorted plan of the lines. But they correspond point-by-point, and two points joined on the map are connected in reality. This fundamental test makes them topologically identical.

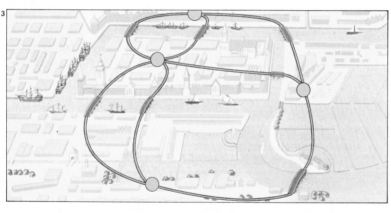

3 **Königsberg,** a Prussian town, posed a teaser that led to topological "graph theory". Could you take a stroll crossing each of its seven bridges only once? In 1734 the Swiss mathematician Leonard Euler analysed the problem to form a theory of the traversability of a network or "graph" (shown superimposed on the city). One bridge has to be crossed twice. The problem depends on connections, not distances.

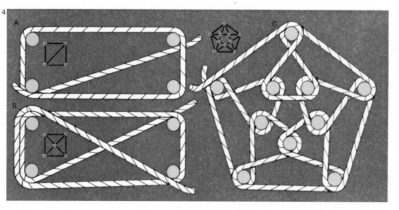

4 **A graph traversable in one pass** must have an even number of lines meeting at each junction. The pentagram C is traversable but the rope makes a double pass on rectangle B and begins and ends at different points on rectangle A.

5 **A flat map** needs no more than four colours to prevent adjacent areas sharing the same colour. This unproved theorem is part of graph theory, for every map can be drawn as a graph with areas as junctions and boundaries as lines.

with full rigour, are less directly-useful than those of a subject like geometry.

A typical topological theorem says that in colouring a flat map no more than five colours are ever needed to ensure that adjacent areas need not share the same colour. The theorem does not state how this can be accomplished for any given case but merely asserts that it can always be done somehow. In fact, four colours may be sufficient [5], although this has not been mathematically proved. Similarly, it is topologically certain that however briskly a cup of tea is stirred, at any instant at least one point in the liquid is not moving. The topologist is not concerned to identify this point; he just proves that it must exist. In different types of space different theorems hold good. There need be no fixed points in a stirred inner-tube full of water; on a doughnut, up to seven colours may be needed for a map without adjacent colours [6]; and on a Möbius strip, up to six colours may be needed.

A Möbius strip is some sort of vindication of Monsieur Hulot for it is a contradiction of the strong human intuition that a piece of

paper must have two sides. It is named after the German astronomer and mathematician August Möbius (1790–1868). His strip can be made simply by cutting out a ribbon of paper, making a half turn in the middle of it and sticking the ends together to form a twisted loop. This loop now has only one side, as you can prove by drawing along it with a pen, never going over the edge until you meet your starting-point again. Cutting along the line creates another surprise.

Twisted space

Topologists study such "twisted spaces" in more dimensions than two, hard though they are to imagine. Indeed it is topologically entirely possible that the universe itself has a Möbius twist in it. One result of this might be that a traveller who went far enough out into space would return reversed in mirror-image fashion with his heart in the right side of his chest. Glove manufacturers might then be able to make only left-handed gloves and ship half their output around the universe from where they would return as matching right-handed ones.

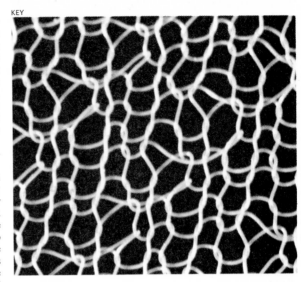

The significance of topology in textile manufacture is shown in the structure of a pair of tights photographed through a microscope. The complex system of knots is designed to avoid a "run" in the garment if a fibre is broken.

6 On a doughnut or torus a map can need up to seven colours to prevent adjacent areas sharing the same colour. The map shown (with its mirrored reflection for completeness) needs all seven because each area touches the other six. The sections form a continuous helix winding round twice before closing on itself.

7 Any structure has many "modes of failure". Engineering disasters such as the collapse of the River Yarra bridge in Melbourne can occur because of modes which the designers have not recognized. As a novel design such as the box girder bridge is refined and made lighter and cheaper, unsuspected modes of failure may be discovered the hard way. Classification of abstract entities by their "spatial" properties can help here. Topological "catastrophe theory" is concerned with the ways shapes can change; its principal application is to morphogenesis, the biological study of the ways in which organs and tissues develop and form.

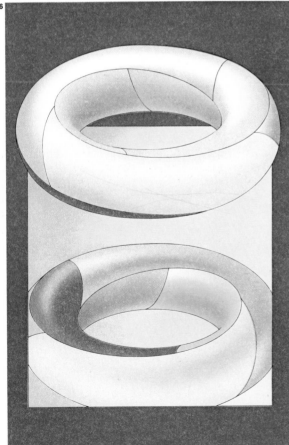

8 A ball covered with fur cannot be smoothed down all over; at least two crowns must remain where the fur radiates from a point or piles up at one, or a set of partings. This "hairy ball" theory governs the way directions, like hairs, can be aligned on a sphere. If they are lines of magnetic flux, it shows that every magnet must have two poles. If they are wind directions on the globe, the theory proves that somewhere in the world the wind is not blowing.

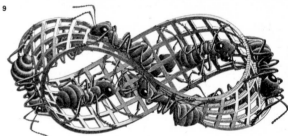

9 These ants, by M. C. Escher (1898–1972), illustrate the counter-intuitive properties of the Möbius strip. All are on the one side but appear to be on opposite sides. A "strip" made with two half twists does have two sides. The number of twists dictates the number of sides and dramatically affects the result produced by cutting along the middle. Topology allows us to explore and describe such spatial relationships.

Maths and mapping

Can you read a map? A blueprint? A circuit diagram? Morse code? Then you are a mathematician because these are all examples of mathematical mappings. The idea is simple: a map is any way of relating one set of objects to another set [1]. In a geographical map [3], every one of the infinite number of points on the earth's surface corresponds to (or is "sent" to) just one of the infinite number on the map. Similarly blueprints and circuit diagrams map certain features of a physical object onto a pattern on paper.

Maps and their meaning
One interesting thing about such maps is what they can and cannot do. It is impossible, for example, to map the whole globe onto flat paper without sacrificing some features to preserve others. True directions on a map are impossible to achieve without some distortions. But even distorted mapping is still mathematically acceptable – like the hidden painting of a skull [Key]. The apparently meaningless set of distorted smears is an anamorphic painting (one that appears in proportion when viewed from a particular angle, generally using a lens or mirror), designed to map to a recognizable image when viewed correctly.

Mathematical maps embrace much more than these simple correspondences of points in space. They deal with anything: points, numbers, sets and abstract entities with no meaning beyond themselves. They even handle the mapping of a set of objects onto itself. This seeming paradox is commonplace, for example, in secret coding. A code is a rule for replacing each letter of a message by another from the same alphabet; it is a complex mapping of the alphabet onto itself. Similarly the two-times table relates a number to its double and (if we include fractions in it too) is a mapping of the set of all real numbers onto itself.

One-to-one maps are not the only kind. The "zero-times table" that takes all numbers to zero is a good mathematical map. But the mapping must specify a definite image for every element in its "domain" of operation. Therefore there is the old puzzle of the village whose barber shaves everyone who does not shave himself. This purports to describe a mapping that sends all the "shavers" to themselves and all the "non-shavers" to the barber. It is not a well-formed mapping because it leaves the barber himself in a paradoxical position. Does he map to himself? (That is, does he shave himself?) If so, he shouldn't, and if not, he should.

By contrast the marriage map between *n* men and *n* women (where *n* is any whole number) is a proper map and defines a possible set of marriages. Assuming that each individual has some order of preferences for his or her *n* possible partners, then it is a wry outcome of mapping theory that of all possible such maps – ways of pairing off the men and women – one and one only is stable. In all others cases will inevitably occur in which a couple, not married to each other, will prefer each other to their own spouses.

Maps between one thing and another
The above mappings are examples of "discrete" instead of "continuous" maps. Unlike those of points on a surface or a set of all real numbers they handle a finite set of elements only. The mapping of telephone subscribers

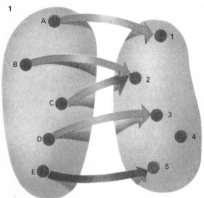

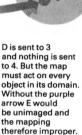

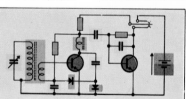

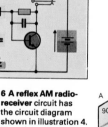

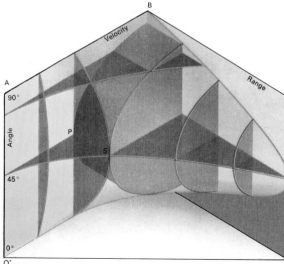

1 A mathematical map relates one set of objects (eg A, B, C, D) to an "image" set (eg 1, 2, 3, 4), symbolized by the arrows. One-to-one correspondence is not necessary; both B and C are sent to 2, D is sent to 3 and nothing is sent to 4. But the map must act on every object in its domain. Without the purple arrow E would be unimaged and the mapping therefore improper.

2 Light is transmitted by a fibre from one point to another; the bundle maps an object into its image [A]; it may be deformed by reduction [B] or by scrambling the fibres [C]. This is called fibre-optic mapping.

3 Each point on the globe is sent to one on the map in this diagram. The "zenithal projection" is mapping the Southern Hemisphere; each point is projected along a line from the North Pole onto a plane touching the South Pole. The Equator becomes a circle, as do other lines of latitude. Lines of longitude become radii. The scale is not constant; it increases dramatically towards the edge of the map.

4 An electronic circuit diagram is a map unconcerned with scale or shape. It shows the connections between components using stylistic conventions – wires, for example, become straight-line segments.

6 A reflex AM radio-receiver circuit has the circuit diagram shown in illustration 4. They do not look alike but are related by a mapping which ensures that the connections to each component are the same in both the physical and schematic layouts. The manufacturer is unconstrained by circuit-diagram conventions and routes the wiring for tight packing of components, for example. But adjacent components may interact, by their electric or magnetic fields, through space.

5 The muzzle velocity and elevation angle of a gun are mapped onto the range of the shell. The plane OAB is a "map" of angle and velocity; the height of a point [P] represents elevation angle and its horizontal distance from OA represents muzzle velocity. The perpendicular distance PS from the surface at P represents the range for those settings. The surface contour shows that range increases with velocity and is greatest at 45° elevation.

onto their telephone numbers is like this too. Each subscriber has his own number, but not all numbers are represented. For example, there is no number 000 0000. A reservoir of possible but unused numbers is held by the telephone companies. This map illustrates a new point too. Our previous examples sent points to points, numbers to numbers, people to people; this one sends people to numbers.

The mapping of one set of entities onto another apparently quite different set is a powerful mathematical technique. For instance, analytical geometry maps geometry onto algebra [11]. Each geometrical curve or line is sent to its corresponding equation; and for each geometrical theorem there is a corresponding algebraic identity. The mapping preserves the relational features of geometry so that geometrical problems of great difficulty (for example, those in many dimensions) can be mapped by easier-to-handle algebra, solved and then mapped back to give the required geometrical truth.

Morse code is another example of such mapping. Letters and numbers are mapped onto combinations of dots and dashes. These

in turn can be transmitted as short and long flashes of light or pulses of electric current. At the receiving end the dots and dashes are mapped back to letters and numbers.

A vast range of scientific and technical enterprise depends on mapping from the real world into symbolic systems that preserve the important features. An astronomer maps the positions of the heavenly bodies into terms of a set of equations. From the ensuing calculations, he can recover terms that map back into future positions of the bodies and perhaps predict an eclipse.

Mapping: theory into practice

It is the business of mathematical science to make sure that mappings work. All scientific theories are maps in this sense and so are the calculations and designs of an engineer who decides on paper that an aircraft as yet unbuilt can fly. Like geographical maps of the globe, these maps sacrifice some features to preserve others and so they are incomplete. They fail totally in some areas of experience and distort so badly in others that they are useless for any practical purposes.

KEY

Anamorphic art is a technique in which an artist draws or paints a familiar shape in a grossly distorted form. It is an example of mapping, just as maps of the earth's curved surface can be drawn on a flat sheet of paper by a suitable choice of projection. In this painting part of "The Ambassadors" by Hans Holbein (1533), the stretched shape at the bottom is a "map" of a skull; it can be seen [below] by viewing from the lower right.

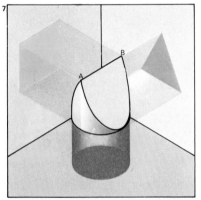

7

7 A draughtsman's projection is a mathematical map in which many points on the object go to the same point on the image. In the blue triangular projection all the points on the line AB are sent to the top vertex of the triangle. They retain their identity in the yellow square projection, but lose it in the circular red one. All projections "compress" information in this way, so draughting makes use of several.

8

9

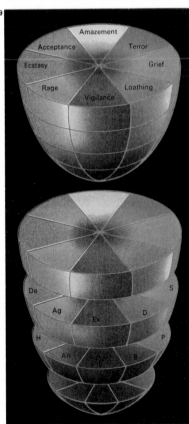

9 The psychologist Plutchik mapped the emotions onto this "emotional solid". The most intense ones map to the top. The next layer shows diluted versions of these (by their initial letters): delight, anger, expectancy, disgust, sadness etc, and the next layer happiness, annoyance, interest, boredom, pensiveness etc. The lower marks neutrality. Any sequence of emotions is a "worm-track" through this solid.

10 A weight suspended by a spring in water [A] and an electrical circuit [B] are mathematical maps of each other. If disturbed, the weight will vibrate with decreasing vigour and an electrical pulse will cause oscillations in the circuit to fade away gradually. Both examples have an energy-storing element (the spring or capacitor), an inertial element (the weight or inductor) and an energy-dissipating element (the water or resistor).

10

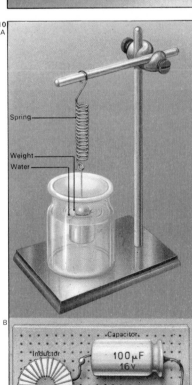

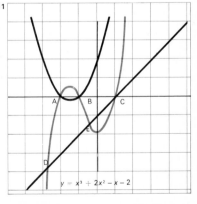

8 The male and female sex organs are both distortions of a primitive system and are mappings of each other in the mathematical sense. The testicles [A] map into the ovaries and the penis and

bladder map into the elaboration of uterus and urogenital tract [C]. This suggests that both systems may have evolved from a common one [B] and that, in nature, different structures can have the same form.

11

$$y = x^3 + 2x^2 - x - 2$$

11 "Mathematics is the art of saying the same thing in different words" (Bertrand Russell). The curves are geometry, their equations algebra. The mapping between these is analytical geometry. The two curves intersect at A and B; their equa-

tions will yield two solutions whose values give the co-ordinates of A and B. Similarly the straight line intersects one of the curves at C, D and E whose co-ordinates are found by solving the equations simultaneously.

Facts and statistics

In the next minute at least 60 and not more than 310 babies will be born. This statistical claim requires no knowledge of any individual women. It just assumes the average world birth-rate of three per second – and it has only one chance in a thousand of turning out to be wrong.

Making reliable statements about chance events is the business of statistics. Think of a tossed penny – the classic uncertainty. An unbiased penny tossed a million times gives, with 99 per cent certainty, between 498,700 and 502,300 heads and the rest tails. Conversely, if bias is suspected, one toss will not confirm it. But a million tosses giving 500,000 heads indicates, again with 99 per cent certainty, that the bias of the coin used is between 0.4987 and 0.5013 (a perfect coin has a bias of 0.5000).

Chance and certainty

Phrases such as "99 per cent certainty" are common to all reliable statistical statements. Certainty is never 100 per cent and for this reason a reputable statistician always states his error and confidence limits. Ninety-nine

times out of 100 he would be right in bracketing the penny's bias between the given limits. Only once in 100 times would a coin of greater bias give, by chance, equal numbers of heads and tails. If it is really necessary to bracket the penny's bias with greater confidence, it would have to be tossed more times. In statistics there is always this trade-off between the information necessary and the reliability of the knowledge it yields, with complete certainty forever unattainable. The art of practical statistics lies in knowing the probability that suffices for the task in hand and knowing what is the sufficient amount of data to collect in order to derive it.

Making good and bad guesses

Insurance companies depend on statistics. Will a client aged 20 die in 40 years time? Nobody knows. But an insurance company, with its records of thousands of men and women, estimates how many clients are likely to die and be the subject of claims and therefore how much it must charge in premiums to keep in business. From its widely amassed survival statistics it can deduce how

dangerous overweight, smoking and so on, are to health. This is achieved by seeking "bias" in the death records of various groups, just as one might seek it in the tossing records of various pennies.

Medical science gains from this too. It was statistical analysis that correlated the taking of the drug thalidomide during pregnancy with deformed babies and cigarette smoking with lung cancer. But such correlations need careful interpretation. Statistics cannot say why smokers are more likely to contract cancer than non-smokers. Perhaps people predisposed to lung cancer also tend to have a taste for smoking – an odd hypothesis, perhaps, but one that is statistically feasible. Similarly cancer of the cervix in women shows a slight but definite correlation with the number of children they have borne. Does this mean that childbirth causes cancer? Further studies show that the correlation fails for Jewish women. This clue leads to the conclusion that the correlation is with sexual activity rather than with its natural outcome. In fact the correlation arises because of the irritant substances that can form under the

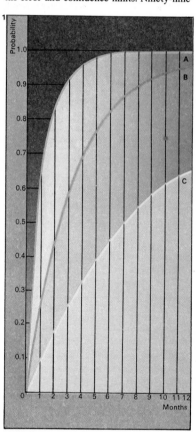

1 Conception depends on many small chances, even when intercourse occurs during ovulation. A fertile couple's chance of conceiving might be as curve A, reaching 0.9 (90%) in 3 months. An average couple [B] might have a 60% chance of conceiving in this time and one of low fertility [C] of only 25%, with only 60% chance of conceiving in a year.

2 Computer calculations show the range of family size 1,000 couples of each type might expect after 25 years. A will probably have 21–23 children; B 15–21 and C probably 10–17.

3 Even in a primitive community very large families are rare. Limiting factors include the death of the mother or her becoming infertile. If, for such reasons, the chances of a family being complete after the birth of the first child is assessed as 4%, at 8% after the birth of the second child and so on, then families of high, average and low fertility each have an average of five or six children and produce the same curve, shown here.

4 A rain of balls through this Galton board is distributed in the bell-shaped "normal error" curve. This and similar curves are commonplace in statistics. It shows the outcome of events under many individual chances – most stay near the average; a few stray farther away.

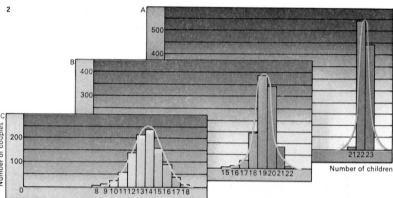

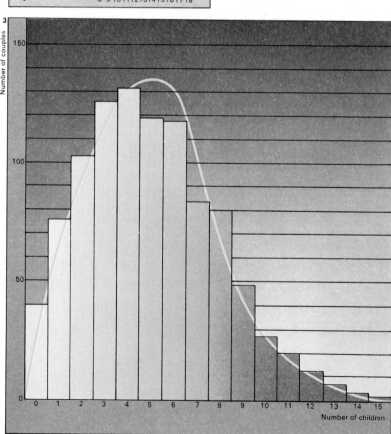

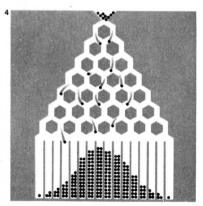

foreskin of an uncircumcised man if he is careless about personal hygiene. Jewish men, being circumcised, do not expose their wives to this slight hazard. So mathematicians must not jump to hasty conclusions. Correlations are not causes (merely clues), and statistical data are dangerously easy to misuse.

Molecules and magnetic tape

In a sense the whole world is ruled by statistics for its individual atoms and molecules are, by the uncertainty principle, not completely predictable. Only when considered in countless millions is their behaviour reliable. It is most unlikely, for example, although theoretically possible, that all the air molecules around someone would chance to rush away spontaneously and leave him to suffocate. On a smaller scale chance molecular fluctuations are inevitable and modern technology, in its quest for sensitivity, occasionally encounters them. A good audio amplifier with the volume turned up, for example, produces a slight hissing which is the amplified random motion of the electrons in the input circuit. It is as if the

amplifier handles information by "tossing electrons" and residual uncertainties cannot be avoided.

In a similar way magnetic recording maps an audio signal onto millions of metal-oxide particles on the tape [Key]. Each can have one of just two magnetic states, equivalent to heads and tails. The faster the tape runs, and the wider the track processed by the recording head, the more particles are used to record a given sound by the changes in their distribution and magnetic states. For this reason the best quality machines use high speeds (38cm/sec [15in/sec]) and wide tracks (up to 1.26cm [0.5in]) to reduce tape-hiss to the minimum. Domestic recorders use lower speeds down to only 3.75cm/sec (1.5in/sec) and track widths down to 0.05cm (0.02in). They suffer accordingly from the smaller sample of magnetic particles from which they must reconstruct the signal. The same statistical principles underlie extraction of information from the tossing of pennies, the fate of smokers and the reading of magnetic tape – and make it highly likely that you will be able to draw your next breath.

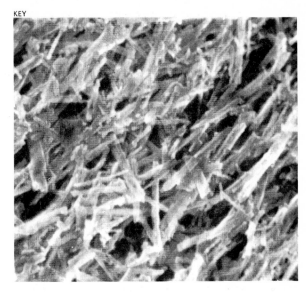

Metallic particles on recording tape, here highly magnified, have their magnetic state changed by the recording process. The quality of the recording depends on how many are affected.

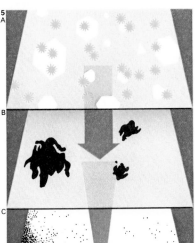

5 In photographic film light-sensitive grains are distributed in gelatine. Two photons (light particles) must hit a grain [A] to render it developable [B]. In a random hail of photons this is pure chance for any one grain. But there are so many [C] that statistically the number of developed grains follows the illumination closely [D]. There is a remote chance that the picture might look like something completely different.

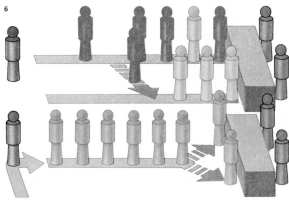

6 People arrive at a counter quite unpredictably. How many clerks are needed for an efficient service? This is a question for queuing theory, which predicts that one queue served by two clerks is more efficient than two queues served by one each. It also decides how much switchgear a telephone exchange needs to install in order to handle randomly arriving calls, how many machinists a machine-shop needs to employ in order to cope with irregular repairs, and so on. Queuing theory can be used to prove that if a queue is not to grow infinitely long, the person or machine serving it must be idle some of the time – a fact that some managers hate to face!

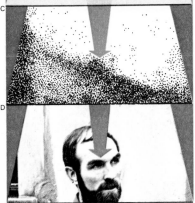

7 A person treading on a step removes a certain amount of stone from his path. Over the years the stone wears away according to the average distribution of paths down the steps. Since most people aim to go down the middle, but deviate randomly to either side, the steps tend to wear into the bell-shaped "normal error" curve. This is a statistical curve that, in time, draws itself.

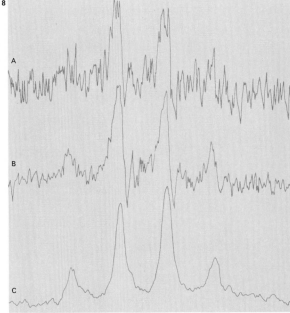

8 Many scientific instruments must register a weak signal against a background of random interference. One strategy is to keep repeating the measurement. The signal is always there, the interference is positive or negative and statistically tends to cancel out. The top trace [A], from a nuclear magnetic resonance spectrometer, shows a spectrum heavily degraded by random interference. In B 16 scans have been added and in C 256 scans.

9 A liquid of one colour is decanted into another and left. Soon the boundary becomes fuzzy and in due course the mixture is uniform. Any one molecule wanders at random, but the statistical effect of all their travels is a perfect mix, the most disordered arrangement possible. The gradual but inevitable increase of disorder is a basic law of physics.

Odds and probability

A businessman worried by the prevalence of aircraft sabotage consulted a mathematician. "Don't worry," he was told, "there is only one chance in a thousand of a plane having a bomb on board." "But I do such a lot of flying," said the businessman. "Then always carry a bomb yourself," came the reply, "because there's only one chance in a million of a plane having two bombs on it!"

How to find the probabilities

This is an elementary but popular fallacy about probability theory. If two independent events each have a known probability such as one-thousandth, the chance of their both occurring together is indeed obtained by multiplying the two probabilities giving in this example one-millionth. But they must be independent: the chance of one cannot be altered by tampering with that of the other – such as ensuring its certainty.

This multiplication rule is one of the two great pillars of probability theory. The other, the addition rule, says that given two mutually exclusive events (such as rolling a one or a two with a die – both cannot be rolled), then the chance of either occurring is the sum of their probabilities. In this case each has a 1/6 probability; so if either one or two win, the chance of success is 1/6 + 1/6 = 1/3.

These two rules, carefully used, can solve most problems of probability. They rest on a subtle sort of probablistic "atomic theory" that takes any chance event as being compounded from a set of basic "equiprobable events". By calculating what combination of these will result in the desired chance coming up, its probability is obtained. But the notion requires subtle handling. Many misleading arguments depend on a deceptive choice of basic equiprobabilities. What is the chance of there being monkeys on Mars, for example? Either there are or there are not – and it could be argued that, since nobody has yet been to Mars, these mutually exclusive situations are equally probable. Then each has half a chance of truth and there is a 50 per cent chance that there are monkeys on Mars.

More subtly, what is the chance of getting one head and one tail on two tosses of a coin? It might be reasoned that there are only three basic possibilities: two heads, head and tail, and two tails. Only one of these is favourable, so the chance is 1/3. But this is not so. There are actually four "atomic" equiprobabilities: HH, HT, TH and TT (where H stands for heads and T stands for tails), of which two are favourable. The chance is 2/4, or one half.

Calculating the chances of success

In mathematical notation, chances vary from 0 (impossible) to 1 (certain). If there are 7 equiprobable possibilities, and 2 of them will result in success, the chance of success is 2 in 7, or 2/7, or 0.2857. This can also be expressed as 28.57 per cent, or in betting parlance 2 to 5 on, or 5 to 2 against. Such figures make most intuitive sense when applied to situations that can occur many times. In a run of 7,000 trials each with a 2/7 chance of success, about 2,000 successes would be expected. A gambler would break even in the long run by accepting odds of 7 to 2 (that is £7 return for a £2 stake). Where the basic equiprobable events are clear and knowable (as in the fall of coins, dice or cards), probability theory can give unambiguous chances of success for any outcome. All casinos and

1 The bookmaker aims to offer odds that give him the same predictable profits whichever horse wins. Thus if he received £3 on one horse and £5 on another, he might offer odds of 7:3 on the first (4 to 3 on) and 7:5 (2 to 5 on) on the second. Whichever wins, he pays out £7 and makes £1 profit. So his odds reflect the money bet. "Outsiders" attract little money, so he offers long odds on them. The chances of six horses are shown in A; 1, 2, 3 are outsiders with very long odds against them. But novice betters find them unreasonably seductive, so the money placed distributes itself as in B. The bookmaker changes the total odds upwards in his own favour, as in C. He is sure of a profit in the ratio of C to B. But even so, some winning odds – on the favourite [6] – are undervalued in C compared to the "reality" of A: 40% (ie offering a return of 100 to 40) compared to its actual chance of winning, 45%. Hence 6 favours the punter and a series of such bets should clear an average of 10% profit to him. But the gullible backers of outsiders, in the long run, also lose. The same mathematical calculation of odds – probabilities – occurs throughout science. In atomic theory, for example, the location of an electron within an atom is defined in terms of probabilities.

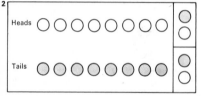

2 A tossed coin can land either "heads" or "tails". On each toss the probability of a head (or tail) is 1/2 (0.5) – the chances are evens. If a coin lands heads (or tails) eight times in succession, a gambler might be tempted to expect that a tail (or head) is more likely to occur on the ninth toss. But the mathematical probability of either outcome is still exactly 1/2 – an even chance.

3 Crown and anchor uses three dice inscribed with the six symbols of the matrix below, which shows all outcomes for the first die "diamond" (five other matrices are similar). Players bet on their symbols against a banker, who returns twice the stake for one symbol displayed, three times for double and four times for triple. Assume each symbol is backed, giving six stakes "input" per throw. 20 out of 36 times (by the matrix), three different symbols come up and the banker makes no gain, returning three 2-fold stakes to the winners. On doubles (15 in 36) he pays out two on the singlet and three on the doublet and keeps one. On the only triple, he pays four and keeps two. So in 36 rounds he has gained (with one unit staked on each symbol) 15+2 = 17 of the 216 stakes: 7.9% return.

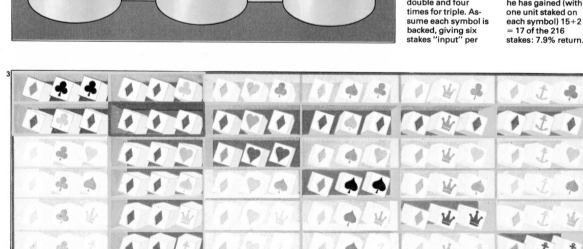

gambling houses use this principle to set fixed odds that give them a small advantage.

In sports and business assessments, odds are subjective and different people guess them differently. By betting on the favourite in a horse-race with a number of unproven "outsiders", however, the gambler's chances of winning are demonstrably better [1]. If one of the horses is known to be doped, or a rival's business strategy is known, it is possible to place investments with better-than-average insight. This is the province of "game theory" – the theory of competing for gains against opponents who possess assumed aims and knowledge.

In the child's game of button-button a button is hidden in one hand and the opponent has to guess which. He wins a penny if he is correct and loses one if he is wrong. What is the best strategy for the holder? If the same hand is always played, or hands are switched regularly, the opponent will soon outguess the holder. Game theory proves that the best strategy is to decide the switch at random, for example by tossing a coin before each round. This is entirely foolproof; even if the oppo-

nent discovers the strategy he cannot win more than he loses in the long run. But if two pennies are lost for a right-hand disclosure and only one penny for a left-hand one, the opponent could then win steadily by always choosing the right hand, and making on average bigger gains than losses. For this modification, game theory prescribes for the holder "weighted random switch" of 2:1 towards the left – say by tossing a die and playing to the right on 1 and 2, but to the left on 3, 4, 5 and 6.

Uses in real-life conflicts

In real-life conflicts such as war and business, game theory is often used for clarifying options, but seldom slavishly followed. If two people make an agreement, for example, game theory recommends to each that he double-crosses the other, for he will gain more if the other is honest. And in a world of unique events that either happen or do not, the whole concept of probability needs careful handling. Be warned by Peter Sellers's parody of a politician, who "does not consider present conditions likely"!

KEY

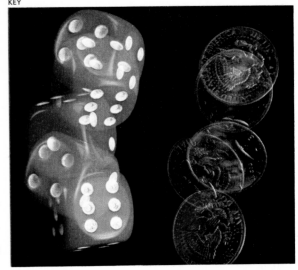

Probability theory cannot predict the outcome of a chance event such as the rolling of a die or the tossing of a coin. But in the long term (thousands of rolls) any one number on a die will occur with a probability of 1/6 (0.16666).

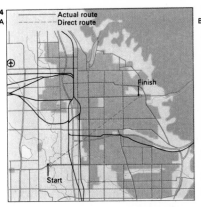

4
A
— Actual route
- - - Direct route
Finish
Start

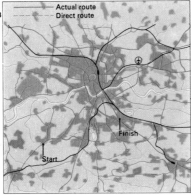

B
— Actual route
- - - Direct route
Finish
Start

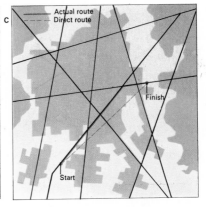

C
— Actual route
- - - Direct route
Finish
Start

4 Is the rational grid layout of Salt Lake City [A] more efficient than the rambling European city of Cracow [B]? A diagonal journey on a grid forces you to traverse the equivalent of two sides of a triangle, even if you zigzag. Probability theory shows that to facilitate many unpredictable point-to-point journeys, a random distribution of straight lines is best [C], a style close to Cracow's.

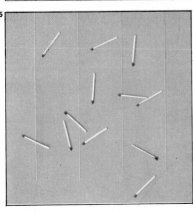

5

5 In the "buffon needle problem", a match is thrown at random on a striped cloth. If the stripes are *n* match-lengths wide, the chance of it coming to rest across a line is $2/n\pi$. It is surprising to find π in this answer: it enters because the match can lie at any angle; like a spoke in a wheel thrown onto the stripes. Mathematicians have evaluated π experimentally by repeated throwing.

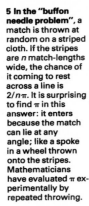

7
A
B
C
D
2 1
3

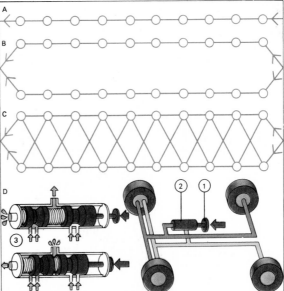

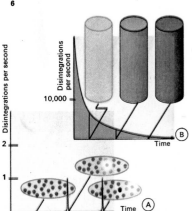

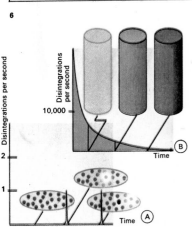

6
Disintegrations per second
Disintegrations per second
10,000
Time B
2
1
Time A

6 Radioactive atoms have a certain chance of decaying which is not affected by the presence or absence of other atoms. The rate of disintegration of a radioactive material is proportional to the amount of radioactive substance present multiplied by the chance that an atom will decay. Whilst we cannot say when a single radioactive atom will decay [A], if ever, we can forecast the average behaviour of a number of radioactive atoms [B]. Electrons, gamma rays or helium nuclei can be emitted.

7 A chain of components, all of which must work if the system is to function, is less reliable than its members. With 10 elements each of 99% reliability [A], the whole thing has about 90% reliability. One improvement is dupli-

cation [B]; with two such chains in parallel, the chance of at least one of them working is 95%. But it is better to parallel each element separately, so that a paralleled pair will still function if either of its members is not working [C]. Then

each pair has a reliability of 99.9% and the whole chain of them has 99.9%. The principle is built into a car's dual braking system [D]. Pressing the pedal[1] moves pistons in the master cylinder [2]. Three brakes work even with a leak [3].

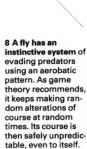

8 A fly has an instinctive system of evading predators using an aerobatic pattern. As game theory recommends, it keeps making random alterations of course at random times. Its course is then safely unpredictable, even to itself.

41

The scale of the universe

Every object around us – indeed, all matter – is made up of countless tiny fragments called atoms. And the Earth is but a tiny speck in the vastness of the universe [Key]. But how large are these fragments? How big is an atom? And how large is the universe?

According to current thinking, the observable universe is about a billion billion billion (10^{36}) times as large as a single atom. But this statement gives no clue to the absolute size of either of them. To define the sizes of atoms, galaxies and the universe – as for a table or a garden – scientists use a series of units. An understanding of these is essential to a proper understanding of modern science – and to helping the imagination to grasp the range [1] between the immensity of the universe and the smallness of an atom.

Units of scale

Small objects can be measured in millimetres (about 0.04 inch) and longer distances are quoted in kilometres (about 0.621 mile). It is difficult to imagine the number of millimetres in a kilometre. But 10mm=1cm; 100cm=1m; 1,000m=1km. Or, writing the numbers as powers of ten, 10^1mm=1cm; 10^2cm=1m; and 10^3m=1km. Therefore one million, or 10^6mm=1km. To denote something smaller a negative index is used: 10^{-1}cm (a tenth of a centimetre)=1mm.

Today an atom is visualized as being almost all empty space with a few tiny sub-atomic particles near the centre which are surrounded by electrons. Very roughly, a sub-atomic particle [2] may be thought of as having a diameter of 10^{-13}cm. Ten billion (10^{13}) of them stretched out in a row might extend through a centimetre. The nucleus of an atom is made up of such particles – protons and neutrons – and may be 10^{-12}cm in diameter. An atom is the next jump in size; measured by pioneers of X-ray crystallography in ångström units, Å = 10^{-8}cm, an atom is about 100 thousand times as large as a proton. Atoms can be bound together to form molecules that can be grouped to make a volume of any size: molecules of gas; a crystal; a droplet of liquid; or all the water in the oceans. The paper of this page is about a few million atoms thick.

The wavelength of visible light is 4×10^{-5}cm to 7.2×10^{-5}cm. As a result, particles with a larger diameter than this can be seen using an ordinary microscope. To make smaller objects visible scientists use electron microscopes, because fast electrons have much shorter wavelengths. The smallest living organisms, such as bacteria, are microscopic. Smaller bodies such as viruses [3], which are submicroscopic, cannot live and develop alone but are parasitic on the cells of living organisms. All visible living things are made up of many millions of atoms.

Distances – from men to the stars

The tallest men are about 2m (6.5ft) in height and the Earth is more than 12,000km in diameter. The diameter of the Sun is more than a million kilometres. The nearest heavenly body to Earth is the Moon, about 384,000km away. Since man landed on the Moon and looked back to the Earth [7] this distance has acquired a more tangible reality.

The Sun is about 1.5×10^8 (150 million) km away from the Earth and the planet Pluto nearly 6×10^9km. These numbers are already becoming difficult to visualize and the whole

1 Within the known universe the dimensions of tiny, subatomic particles and the distance attainable by astronomers' telescopes stand in a ratio of about $1:10^{40}$. The objects shown spanning this staggering range are a proton [1]; an atomic nucleus [2]; an atom [3]; a giant molecule [4]; a virus [5]; a small cell, an amoeba [6]; a large cell, a diatom [7]; a flea [8]; a hen's egg [9]; a man [10] 2m (6.5ft) high and one of his buildings [11]; the Earth [12]; a giant star [13]; an interstellar gas cloud or nebula [14]; our Galaxy [15] and the limits of the theoretically observable universe [16]. The 10m symbol is 10m (32.5ft) tall as a man - and the skyscraper [11] is more than 10^2=100m (325ft) tall, enough to dwarf the men and the bus.

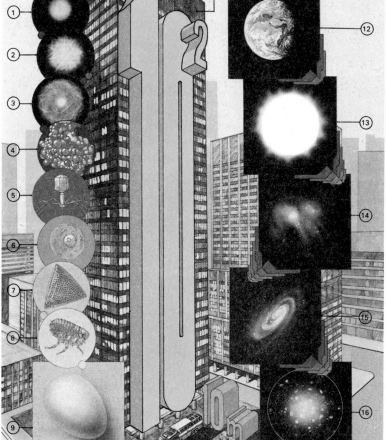

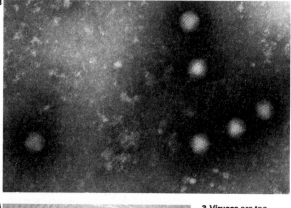

2 Particles are so remote from our experience that indirect methods must be used to make them visible, such as the cloud chamber invented by Charles Wilson in the 1920s and developed by Patrick Blackett. It uses water vapour condensing on ions to reveal particle tracks and therefore identify them. Particles can also be tracked in bubble or spark chambers, or by using stacks of special photographic plates.

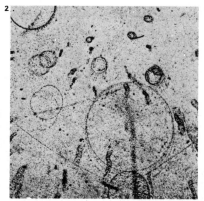

3 Viruses are too small to be seen under an ordinary microscope but can be seen by using an electron microscope. They are non-living matter but affect the properties of living cells.

4 The unique pattern of a fingerprint exemplifies the enormous number of individual cells that make up even the smallest piece of living matter visible to the naked eye. There are about 10 million cells in each cm² of skin.

Solar System, the Sun with its planets and smaller bodies [8], is the merest speck in space. Therefore to describe the geometry of the stars a different unit of distance is used: the light-year, or the distance light travels in a year. In just one second light travels 3×10^5 (300,000) km. In a year light travels about 10^{13}km and the nearest star is more than four light-years from the Sun. Another common unit is the parsec, equal to 3·26 light-years.

The atomic nucleus is formed of densely packed particles, but the atom is almost all empty space. Similarly, in the universe the atoms on the planets and stars are closely packed to form solids, liquids or gases. But the stars are separated by huge distances compared with their diameters and so the universe around us, like the atoms of which we are made, is nearly all empty space.

Towards infinity

The stars themselves, at their immense distances are grouped into great systems called galaxies or extragalactic nebulae. So huge are the numbers of stars that through telescopes the galaxies look like great white clouds. In our Galaxy alone, the Milky Way, there are more than 10^{11} stars. The Galaxy is about 10^4 light-years thick in the middle and 10^5 light-years across.

Galaxies have greatly differing appearances according to the wavelengths of the light used to observe them. One of the most rapidly developing branches of astronomy is radio astronomy in which observation is made by radio waves. The largest known object in the universe is a galaxy designated 3C236, observed by radio telescope. A curious object in which the principal radio sources are two bulges at each end, it measures about 2×10^7 (20 million) light-years from end to end. The nearest large galaxy to our own is 2×10^6 light-years away. The farthest objects probably lie at a distance of about 10^{10} light-years.

The scale of the known universe from the atomic nucleus to the farthest star is about 10^{40}. But what is beyond the limits of present-day astronomy? Does the universe stretch to infinity? Or could it be curved in a curious way so that the nebulae that seem farthest away are in reality near to our own?

The spiral galaxy in Andromeda has a measurable size, but it is difficult to grasp: 120,000 light-years or 10^{18}km across.

5 "Man is the measure of all things" said Protagoras in the 5th century BC – a humanist view that established man at the centre of the universe and related objects to a human scale. The personification of nature was a theme of such Renaissance painters as Botticelli (1444–1510), who painted "The Birth of Venus". Modern science uses other units and man is no longer the standard of length.

6 Man's most visible artefact, the Great Wall of China, runs for more than 2,400 km (1,500 miles), about five per cent of the circumference of the Earth. It can be seen from well out in space.

7 The Earth, as a body floating in space, has acquired a new reality since man left his own planet and looked back at his terrestrial home. For the first time, it has been seen as merely one, minute, heavenly body in immeasurable space. The idea of other planets having other life forms is no longer regarded as improbable and current estimates put the number of possibly inhabited planets at many millions.

8 The Solar System has been brought within man's reach by interplanetary rockets. But beyond it the galaxies stretch endlessly – the nearest to Earth is 2 million million million km away.

What is an atom?

The first recorded suggestion that matter might consist of separate particles was made in the fifth century BC probably by Leucippus of Miletus [1] and the idea was developed by his pupil Democritus, who adopted the word *atomos* (from the Greek word meaning indivisible). John Dalton (1766–1844) revived the word at the beginning of the nineteenth century when he provided a scientific basis for the simple Greek idea. To Dalton an atom was a tiny indivisible particle, the basic unit of matter that takes part in chemical reactions.

The atom and electricity
The simple Daltonian view of the atom was overturned in 1897 when J. J. Thomson (1856–1940) discovered that atoms could emit even smaller particles of negative electricity (later called electrons) [5]. Clearly the atom itself must have some form of internal structure. Thomson's discovery also implied that an atom must also contain positive electricity. He suggested that electrons were like currants dispersed throughout a positively charged bun. This model failed to explain a

number of the properties of atoms, but a better one had made use of the discovery of radioactivity by Antoine Becquerel (1852–1908). He found that certain heavy atoms spontaneously emit radiation. Three forms of this are now known: beta rays (negatively charged electrons), alpha particles (positively charged helium nuclei consisting of two protons and two neutrons) and gamma rays (short-wave X-rays).

The Rutherford model
In 1911 Ernest Rutherford (1871–1937) produced an entirely new model of the atom based on the results of his own experiments and those of Hans Geiger (1882–1945) and his co-workers (who measured the scatter of alpha particles when shot at gold foil). Rutherford's suggestion was that the positive charge and most of the mass of the atom were concentrated in a central nucleus and that the electrons revolve around it. We now know that the atom is mostly empty space with a minute central nucleus some tens of thousands of times smaller than the atom. The atoms themselves are extremely small –

ten million of them side by side would form a line measuring only about 1mm (0.039in).

Rutherford later discovered that the positive charge of the nucleus is carried by particles 1,846 times heavier than electrons; he christened them protons. The charge of the proton is equal, but opposite, to that of the electron. A hydrogen atom consists of a single positively charged proton (the nucleus) with one electron travelling in an orbit around it [Key].

Heavier atoms have increasing numbers of protons in their nuclei, but the number of protons in the nucleus (called the atomic number) is always balanced by an equal number of orbiting electrons. It was later discovered that all atoms except hydrogen have another type of particle in their nuclei. These are uncharged particles (and are therefore called neutrons) and they have almost the same mass as the proton.

Quantum theory and spectroscopy
Two other fields of investigation helped the Danish physicist Niels Bohr (1885–1962) to construct the next important atomic model

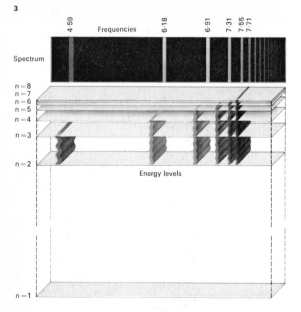

1 The city of Miletus was the first known home of natural philosophy. Thales (*c.* 630 BC) was born there. He was a member of the Ionian School, the earliest known in Greek philosophy. He discovered the electrical properties of amber. Anaximander also dwelt there, as did Leucippus (*c.* 400 BC), credited by Aristotle with atomic theory that formed a central part in the evolution of Western scientific thought.

2 Modern science pictures matter as having a dual existence as waves and particles. Waves are seen on the sea and when a pebble drops into a pond, and sound and electromagnetic radiation such as light and X-rays are known to travel as waves. The wave theory of atomic particles such as electrons, protons and neutrons has led to an improved understanding of atoms and nuclei.

3 Lines in the spectrum can be observed in light given out by incandescent elements. These are emission lines, which result from the emission of light by atoms. One of the successes of the Bohr theory was its ability to explain the wavelengths of the lines in the spectrum of hydrogen in terms of electron energy level changes.

4 Possible orbits of an electron around an atomic nucleus can be pictured [A] as circles that exactly accommodate a whole number of wavelengths, denoted by the principal quantum number n. A two-dimensional analogy (a vibrating drum skin) is described by two quantum numbers n and l [B], and the shape of a real atom [C] in terms of three (n, l and m).

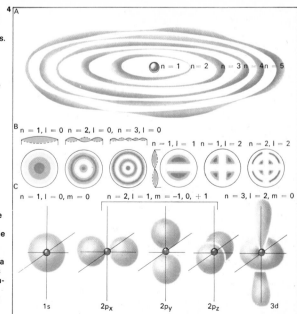

[Key]. The first was the quantum theory, the other was the science of spectroscopy. Quantum theory was proposed by Max Planck (1858–1947) [7] in 1900 as a way of explaining the emission of heat (and light) by a hot body. He realized that energy can be emitted and absorbed only in discontinuous amounts, discrete "packets" of energy that he called quanta.

Spectroscopy began when Isaac Newton (1642–1727) passed a ray of sunlight through a glass prism, breaking the ray into all the colours of the visible spectrum. In 1814 Joseph von Fraunhofer (1787–1826) had discovered that the spectrum of sunlight contains a number of black lines, which were later found to coincide with the position of coloured lines in the spectrum formed by electric discharge in hydrogen gas [3]. Bohr postulated that the circulating electron in an atom of hydrogen can exist only in fixed orbits [4A] and that the spectral lines correspond to the absorption (black lines) or emission (coloured lines) of a quantum of energy when this electron jumps from one fixed orbit to another. This theory, later modified by Arnold Sommerfeld

(1868–1951), has been extremely successful in explaining the hydrogen spectrum.

Modern developments of the quantum theory suggest that the fixed orbits of Bohr should be visualized less precisely and that the position of an atomic electron should be treated as a probability that it will be in a certain place at a certain time. This treatment, known as quantum mechanics [2], was largely the work of Werner Heisenberg (1901–76) and Erwin Schrödinger (1887–1961). The substitution of a probability for a fixed orbit is a reflection of Heisenberg's uncertainty principle: if the momentum of a particle is known precisely there must be an uncertainty as to its position. In wave mechanics, invented by Louis de Broglie (1892–), matter in the form of atomic particles is treated like light in that some of its properties are best explained in terms of particles, others in terms of waves. A stream of electrons behave like particles in cathode rays and like waves in an electron microscope. But for the purpose of chemistry the concept of the atom as the smallest unit of matter that can take part in reactions remains supreme.

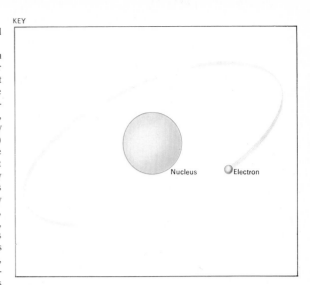

Nucleus   Electron

The pictorial representation of the model of the atom proposed by Niels Bohr is an established part of the iconography of modern physics, even though Bohr's ideas have largely been superseded by various forms of quantum mechanics. This example is a hydrogen atom.

5

5 Geissler tubes, Victorian toys for adults, depended on electronic rays in a near-vacuum long before the principles of cathode rays were understood. The study of the rays, principally by J. J. Thomson, a British physicist, was the crucial one in the elucidation of the structure of the atom, by establishing the mass and charge of the electron, in conjunction with other experiments.

6

6 The new ideas about atomic physics were brought together at a series of conferences, such as this Solvay meeting at Brussels in 1911, attended by Bohr, Rutherford, Planck, Curie and others.

7

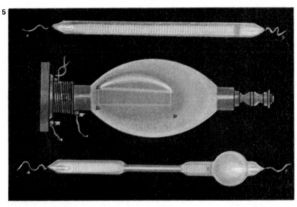

7 Max Planck suggested in 1900 that light was absorbed and emitted in packets or "quanta", with energies proportional to the frequency of light. This is known as the quantum theory.

8 A   B

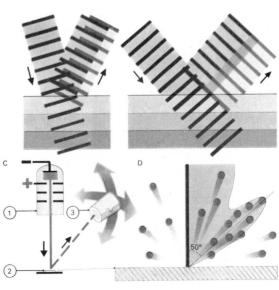

8 When waves are reflected from parallel surfaces they are out of step [A] or in step [B]. An electron beam [C] from a gun [1] can be reflected from nickel [2] into a detector [3] and the angles plotted [D].

9 Erwin Schrödinger played a principal part in the mathematical development of the modern model of the atom. He developed wave mechanics from de Broglie's picture of wave-particle duality.

9

Nuclear physics

Nuclear energy plays a decisive part in shaping the modern world: nuclear weapons not only haunt the statesman but cast a threatening shadow on every living person [Key]. And while the mirage of limitless nuclear power attracts a civilization hungry for energy, the disposal of radioactive waste threatens lasting pollution of the world. In fact, life has always depended on nuclear energy: nuclear fusion heats the sun [1], and radioactivity in the earth [2] heats the liquid core and contributes to the mobility of the continental plates. Nuclear energy is derived from splitting the atomic nucleus by radioactivity or fission, and secondly from fusion, which is the joining of a pair of light nuclei.

Radioactivity: its discovery and source
Radioactivity was discovered by Antoine Becquerel (1852–1908). With the isolation of radium it became clear that enormous amounts of energy were involved. Radium decays over many decades and in fact contains 2×10^5 times as much energy as an equal mass of coal. A nucleus, a few times 10^{-12}cm in diameter, is made of protons (positively charged particles) and neutrons (neutral particles of nearly equal mass to the proton). Hydrogen is unique in having a single proton (and no neutrons) in its nucleus. Most elements consist of a mixture of isotopes, whose nuclei differ in their numbers of neutrons. The total number of constituents (protons and neutrons) in a particular isotope is indicated by a superscript, for example He^4. It is on the properties of individual isotopes that nuclear power depends.

Deliberate transformation of one nucleus into another was achieved by Ernest Rutherford (1871–1937) [4] in 1919: $He^4 + N^{14} \rightarrow O^{17} + H^1$. In words, an alpha-particle (the nucleus of helium) and a nitrogen nucleus momentarily combine and then split into the oxygen isotope O^{17} and a proton.

As mass spectrometers [7] – instruments that measure the individual masses of ions and thus of the nuclei – became more accurate, it was found that the masses of the nuclei of the various isotopes were not equal to the sum of the masses of the constituent protons and neutrons. This discrepancy, according to Einstein's relativity formula, $E = mc^2$, is the source of nuclear energy. Modern theory views the nucleus to be rather like a "liquid" droplet of neutrons and protons. Any such system tends to decay – that is to say transfers itself – into a state of lower energy. If it does so by breaking into two nearly equal parts, that is called fission; if a nuclei gives off one or more particles, that is radioactivity; if two nuclei join together, that is fusion. Two nuclei are both positively charged so one of them must be accelerated to high speed to achieve fusion, or both must be moving fast due to high temperature.

Generating nuclear energy
The generation of nuclear energy in large quantities by fission requires a chain reaction, first achieved with uranium [6]. When a neutron is absorbed by the isotope uranium-235 it induces fission into two major fragments and two or three neutrons. If, on average, more than one neutron from each fission causes a second fission, the process may accelerate exponentially into a run away chain reaction.

In order to generate electricity the pro-

1 **The sun** is powered by nuclear fusion which needs temperatures of the order of hundreds of millions of degrees centigrade. On earth the necessary conditions and temperatures for fusion reactions have so far been achieved only in bombs. Nuclear energy by controlled fusion remains a dream.

2 **Volcanic energy** is provided in part by radioactivity that is naturally present. This is such a powerful source of energy that radioactive atoms, slowly decaying inside the earth, contribute significantly to maintaining the temperature of the molten core. Thus natural radioactivity indirectly helps power volcanic eruptions.

3 **Marie Curie** (1867–1934) and her husband Pierre Curie (1859–1906) formed one of the most famous husband and wife teams in the history of science. During investigations of the radiations given off by uranium, they found an inexplicably high level of radiation. Through painstaking chemical detective work they tracked down and isolated its source in the radioactive elements radium and polonium.

4 **Ernest Rutherford** [A], a New Zealand-born physicist who first worked at Cambridge University in 1903, established the nuclear theory of the atom in 1911 and later achieved the first splitting of the atom when he produced protons from the nuclei of nitrogen atoms. He and his team used remarkably simple (including "home-made") apparatus at the Cavendish Laboratory [B] and were able to change our picture of the structure of atoms.

cess must be slowed down and controlled, and means must be provided for removing the heat. An atomic pile to produce electric power is merely a special kind of furnace. There is a higher probability of fission occurring in U-235 if the neutron absorbed is moving relatively slowly, about 2km (1.2 miles) per second. For this reason special materials, called moderators, are incorporated in the atomic pile to slow the neutrons.

Atomic piles may be classified according to the material used as moderator, typically graphite, water or heavy water. Heavy water is water in which the hydrogen is a heavy isotope, deuterium, and it absorbs far fewer neutrons than ordinary water.

The amount of fissile material brought together is crucial for a sustained chain reaction. If more neutrons are lost by absorption or escape than are produced, the reaction will not be self-sustaining. If more neutrons are produced than are lost on average, a self-sustaining and expanding reaction occurs. The smallest amount in which fission is self-sustaining is called the critical mass. In an atomic pile it is necessary to keep the flux of neutrons nearly in balance and constant. To control a pile, rods of neutron-absorbing material can be moved in and out [8].

Fast reactors and their make-up

Structural supports in atomic piles are made of materials that absorb as few neutrons as possible. Fast reactors have a small core of fissile material and no moderator to slow the neutrons. There is little absorbent material and few neutrons are wasted. Natural uranium is 99.3 per cent U-238 and 0.7 per cent U-235. While U-235 is spontaneously fissionable, U-238 is not, but after absorbing a neutron can decay radioactively to plutonium Pu-239, which is. Atomic bombs and fast reactors require fairly pure fissionable material so U-235 must be separated out – for example in a giant diffusion plant – or U-238 turned into Pu-239 in a reactor and separated chemically. In a fast reactor, the fissile core is surrounded by a blanket of natural uranium so that neutrons escaping from the core can turn U-238 into Pu-239. If more fissionable material is made than consumed, the reactor, is a breeder reactor.

The mushroom cloud of an atomic explosion haunts our civilization. Although the spread of nuclear weapons has been banned by treaties, and some nations have accepted technical limitations on testing, the number of nations with access to nuclear weaponry continues to grow.

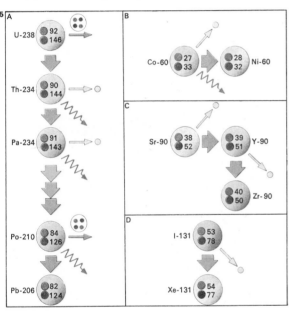

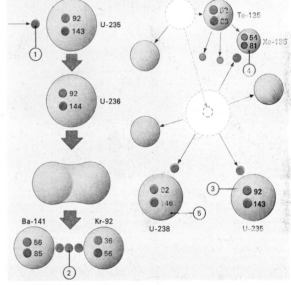

5 The nucleus of an atom, with protons (red) and neutrons (brown), may change, giving radioactivity: gamma rays (electromagnetic radiation, violet), electrons or beta rays (grey), positrons, or alpha particles (helium ions, orange). Naturally radioactive uranium-238 [A] decays as shown to form lead. [B] shows the decay of cobalt-60, [C] strontium-90 and [D] iodine-131.

6 When uranium-235 is hit by a slow neutron [1] it may split by stages and release energy and more neutrons [2]. One of these may strike more uranium-235 [3] and lead to a chain reaction, or be absorbed by other atoms [4] or U-238 [5].

7 The mass spectrograph of Francis Aston (1877–1945) showed that elements are formed of separate isotopes, each nearly an integral multiple of the mass of a proton. Later spectrographs gave exact measurements of nuclear masses and are used to distinguish isotopes.

8 Nuclear reactors are the powerhouses of the future and to some extent of the present. But the formidable problems they create in disposal of radioactive wastes have not yet been satisfactorily solved. Here engineers are carefully stacking the rods that go to make up the central core of an atomic pile. Control rods are also inserted to regulate the reaction rate.

Beyond the atom

One of the characteristic features of science is the way in which it attempts to explain a collection of different phenomena in terms of a few basic concepts. A striking example is the atomic theory of John Dalton (1766–1844) in which many different substances are considered to be made up of a few different types of atom. According to this view atoms are the fundamental "building blocks" of all matter.

In the late nineteenth and early twentieth centuries evidence accumulated to show that atoms themselves have an internal structure. By 1932 it had been realized that atoms are combinations of sub-atomic particles: protons and neutrons (together forming a small positively charged nucleus) with orbiting negatively charged electrons.

Interactions between particles

To give a full description of matter it is necessary to describe not only the particles but also the way in which they are held together – that is, the way in which they interact with one another. Four types of interaction are recognized; two of these are fairly well known

because they are observed in matter in bulk as well as on the atomic scale. The gravitational interaction [1] produces an attraction between objects that depends on their masses. It is an extremely weak effect and plays no part in the binding within atoms, but it is responsible for the forces between heavenly bodies. The electromagnetic interaction [2] occurs between particles that have an electric charge. This force is many millions of times stronger than the gravitational effect and is responsible for the force of attraction between the nuclei of atoms and the orbiting electrons.

Within the nucleus itself a quite different effect must occur. Here neutrons and protons are held together strongly in spite of the electromagnetic repulsion between them. This strong interaction is independent of charge, for it acts between neutrons as well as protons, and is about 7,000 times stronger than the electromagnetic interaction. Moreover, it falls off sharply with distance – its influence extends only over distances comparable with the dimensions of the atomic nucleus, generally less than 10^{-12} cm.

The fourth type, known as the weak interaction, is about one-thousandth of the strength of the electromagnetic interaction. It is observed in certain processes in which transformations of particles occur, as in beta decay, where a neutron changes into a proton, an electron, and an antineutrino.

Fields of force

The four types of interaction take place through free space. One way of explaining this action-at-a-distance uses the idea of a field of force. A charged particle, for instance, is thought of as affecting the surrounding space in such a way that another charged particle placed in this region experiences a force. The region of influence is called an electromagnetic field. Similarly a mass has an associated gravitational field in the space surrounding it.

A different model, based on quantum mechanics, uses the idea of an exchange of virtual particles. Two charged particles interact by emitting and absorbing photons (particles of light). Gravitational interaction is similarly explained by exchange of

1 **The force of gravity is encountered** in all its power and immediacy by a weightlifter. The gravitational force was the first to be studied quantitatively and the first to receive, in Isaac Newton's *Principia* (1687), detailed discussion of its theoretical principles.

2 **Electromagnetism** (used in an electric bell) was the second interaction of which man became aware. Magnetism and static electricity were known earlier but the combination of electricity and magnetism in a single theory was achieved only in the nineteenth century by the work of Oersted, Faraday and Maxwell.

3 **Hideki Yukawa** (1907–) predicted a particle, later identified as the pi meson, as the quantum of the strong nuclear force. It was found in cosmic ray photographs by C. Powell (1903–69) at Bristol University.

4 **Enrico Fermi** (1901–54) developed the theory of beta decay, which depends on weak interaction. He was largely responsible for the development of the first atomic pile (nuclear reactor).

5 **The existence of a particle** equal in mass to an electron [A] but having negative energy was predicted by Paul Dirac (1902–). The discovery of the positron [B] confirmed this. If the two meet, they annihilate each other, releasing their combined mass-energy [C]. Positronium – an electron and positron in orbit – is known to exist briefly and as other anti-particles are known it is possible to imagine anti-atoms such as anti-hydrogen in some other world.

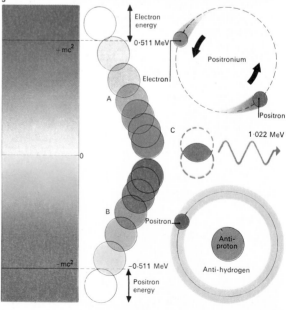

hypothetical particles called gravitons. In 1935 Hideki Yukawa [3] suggested that the strong interaction holding the nucleus together was due to the exchange of a particle with a mass between that of the electron and the proton. This particle is now known as the pi meson (or pion). Another particle, the intermediate vector boson, has been suggested as being responsible for weak interactions, but so far scientists have been unable to prove its existence.

Other fundamental particles
In 1932 only three particles were necessary to explain atomic structure. Since then the situation has been complicated by the discovery of many more particles through work on cosmic rays and experiments using particle accelerators [6, 8]. It is found that high-energy collisions between particles lead to the production of new ones. Now more than 200 are known, most of them very unstable [7]. They are characterized by their mass and charge. They also have other characteristic properties, such as average lifetime, that describe the ways in which they interact.

The numerous sub-atomic particles are classified into groups: particles that partake in strong interactions are called hadrons (including nucleons, hyperons, and mesons). Particles that do not take part in strong interactions are called leptons (including electrons and neutrinos).

The problem of high-energy physics is to produce a single theory explaining the existence and behaviour of this multitude of particles. One suggestion is that the particles themselves are made up of even more basic particles. It is possible, for instance, to describe all nucleons as combinations of three particles called quarks. These have charges that are one-third or two-thirds the size of the electron charge. According to this theory protons and neutrons, for example, are not completely indivisible.

Another goal is the creation of a single theory to account for all the types of interaction. So far some success has been achieved in unifying the electromagnetic and weak interactions, but a single mathematical theory encompassing all four types of interactions is still far off.

The essence of matter summed up in the Chinese symbol of yin and yang was a symmetry of complementary principles – aptly representing the modern theory of particle-wave duality.

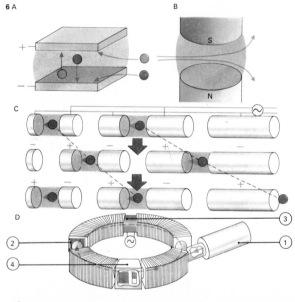

6 Particle accelerators use the principle that an electric field [A] accelerates or deflects positive [red] or negative [blue] particles parallel with the direction of the field, whereas a magnetic field [B] makes them curve at right-angles to the field. In a "drift-tube" accelerator [C, E] oscillating electric fields speed up at the same rate as the particles. A synchrotron [D] is used for particles brought close to the speed of light by a linear accelerator [1]. A magnetic field [2], increasing to balance the growth of centrifugal force, causes particles to circulate through an accelerating field [3], seen through a viewer [4].

7 Type of particle	Symbol	Mass in units of electron mass	Electric charge
Photon	γ	0	0
Leptons			
Neutrino (electronic)	υ	0	0
Antineutrino (electronic)	$\bar{\upsilon}$	0	0
Neutrino (mesonic)	υ_μ	0	0
Antineutrino (mesonic)	$\bar{\upsilon}_\mu$	0	0
Electron	e^-	1	−1
Positron	e^+	1	+1
Mu (muon) plus	μ^+	207	+1
Mu (muon)	μ^-	207	−1
Mesons			
Pi plus	π^+	273	+1
Pi minus	π^-	273	−1
Pi zero	π^0	264	0
K plus	κ^+	967	+1
K minus	κ^-	967	−1
K zero	κ^0	974	0
Anti-K zero	$\bar{\kappa}^0$	974	0
Nucleons			
Proton	p^+	1,836	+1
Antiproton	p^-	1,836	−1
Neutron	n	1,839	0
Antineutron	$\bar{n}$	1,839	0
Hyperons			
Lambda zero	Λ^0	2,183	0
Antilambda zero	$\bar{\Lambda}^0$	2,183	0
Sigma zero	Σ^0	2,332	0
Antisigma zero	$\bar{\Sigma}^0$	2,332	0
Sigma minus	Σ^-	2,328	−1
Antisigma minus	$\bar{\Sigma}^-$	2,341	+1
Sigma plus	Σ^+	2,328	+1
Antisigma plus	$\bar{\Sigma}^+$	2,328	−1
Xi plus	Ξ^+	2,566	0
Antixi zero	$\bar{\Xi}^0$	2,580	0
Xi minus	Ξ^-	2,580	−1
Antixi minus	$\bar{\Xi}^-$	2,582	+1

7 Fundamental particles are now so numerous that the term fundamental seems inappropriate, but there is insufficient information for a unified theory and some vital clues may be missing. Perhaps one day order will be brought to the apparent chaos of information, just as Niels Bohr clarified atomic theory.

8 The ring cyclotron was invented by Professor Ernest Lawrence (1901–58) at the University of California in 1930. Its vacuum chamber, in which charged particles were accelerated by being circulated past two D-shaped electrodes with a high-frequency voltage, measured only 9.8 cm (4in) across. The giant machine now at CERN in Geneva has a diameter of 4.8km (3 miles). Accelerated to high speeds in cyclotrons, particles can be used to bombard nuclei – with the creation of other particles.

The nature of energy

Energy is required for work to be done – work being the operation of a force over a distance. Thus energy is expended when a golf ball is struck, when a dumbbell is lifted, when a spring is compressed or stretched, when a bomb explodes and when electrons flow in a wire as an electric current.

Additionally, energy is needed to raise the temperature of any substance and living organisms need energy for movement and growth. Green plants get their energy as light from the sun [Key], which they utilize by photosynthesis. Animals use the chemical energy of food – the energy of plants or other animals that they eat. From these examples it can be seen that energy exists in many forms. To a scientist, it exists in only two distinct ways: as potential (or stored) energy, and as kinetic energy (which a body possesses by virtue of its motion).

The essence of potential energy

Potential energy can be considered as stored energy. The potential energy of food and fuels such as coal and oil, for example, is the chemical energy stored in these materials.

The potential energy in the water of a dam is equivalent to stored gravitational energy; the earth tries to "pull down" the raised mass of water with a force proportional to its mass [1] – the force of gravity.

In a coiled spring, the potential energy is proportional to the square of the compression or extension. A copper sphere insulated from electrical leakage can be charged with static electricity (unmoving electrons) and the electrical potential energy of the sphere is determined by the amount of static electric charge and the associated voltage.

What is internal energy?

The total energy of any system is called its internal energy. This quantity is not usually measurable and not all of it can be used to do work. A hot object does work in cooling, for example, but even if it is cooled to near absolute zero, namely $-273°C$ ($-460°F$), its molecules still possess most of their internal energy. The potential energy of a sytem is measured not as the total internal energy but as the part of it available to do work.

When matter is in motion it is said to pos-

sess kinetic energy. For this reason, molecules of a gas always have kinetic energy because they are always moving. The temperature of a gas is a measure of the average kinetic energy of its moving molecules – the faster they move, the higher the temperature.

The pressure of a gas is also a measure of its kinetic energy, because the pressure is a measure of the number and energy of the collisions made by gas molecules on the walls of its container. Gas pressure is often used, as in pneumatic drills and lifts, to do useful work. Finally, the kinetic energy of the gas molecules, or of any other moving object, can be expressed in absolute mathematical terms as $\frac{1}{2}mv^2$, where m is the mass of the object and v is its velocity.

Conservation of energy

Heat energy can be regarded as energy of movement. To take the example already used, a gas has kinetic energy proportional to its absolute temperature (its temperature above absolute zero). If the same gas heats an object, the molecules of the object gain

1 A dam holds water at a height and when the water is released its potential energy changes to kinetic energy that can be converted into useful electrical energy by water turbine generators. Other hydroelectric processes rely on the kinetic energy of water moving in the form of waves and tides.

2 In batteries the energy of chemical reactions is converted into electrical energy, which is used for many familiar purposes. Batteries run down as their chemical activity declines. Accumulator batteries (secondary cells) can be recharged by electricity, which is converted back to stored chemical energy.

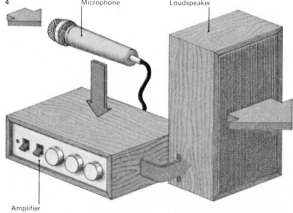

3 A nuclear power station uses the great energy released when the nucleus of an atom disintegrates. Under controlled conditions the nuclear energy of uranium or plutonium is carefully released, mostly as heat, which is used to raise the temperature of water in boilers and produce steam. This heat energy is converted in steam turbines into mechanical energy, then to electrical energy in generators.

4 In a microphone-loudspeaker system a double energy conversion takes place. Sound energy is converted by a microphone into electrical energy. The loudspeaker reverses the conversion process.

Microphone

Loudspeaker

Amplifier

kinetic energy. This transfer of kinetic energy takes the form of a flow of heat from the hot gas to the cooler body.

Useful energy is usually thought of in such terms as the heat of burning coal, the electricity flowing in electric fires and the mechanical energy produced by burning petrol in a car engine. But in each of these familiar examples, energy has had to be converted from one form to another to be of practical use. The chemical potential energy of coal is released by burning the coal and is thereby converted into useful hot gases and radiant energy; in a power station these are further converted into useful electrical energy by a system of water boilers, steam turbines and electricity generators. The chemical potential energy of motor fuel is released by rapid burning as kinetic energy of gas, which is translated into the useful mechanical energy that propels the car.

Energy conversions always involve a loss: no conversion is 100 per cent efficient. A coal fire, for example, releases only about 20 per cent of the chemical energy of the coal as useful heat. An electric motor converts about 80 per cent of the electrical energy supplied to it into mechanical energy [7].

The principle of conservation of energy is usually stated as "energy can neither be created nor destroyed". In energy conversions the amount of energy output to do useful work is always less than the input energy. The total energy of the system, however, always remains the same, the "missing" energy being wasted energy. Not all the electricity flowing through a lamp filament, for instance, is converted into light, most being wastefully converted to heat. The heat and light together are equivalent to the input electricity and so energy is conserved. But after the conversion, less energy is available to do work; as a whole, the energy is at a lower level.

What happens in this particular instance is true for the sum of all energy reactions in the universe at any one time; the overall result of these reactions being a degradation in energy level. Perhaps at some remote time in the future, all energy will have degraded to a level where no work can be done: the universe will then have "run down".

The sun is the ultimate source of energy for all life on earth. Here it is reappearing from behind the moon after an eclipse.

5 Solar cells, as fitted on this satellite, convert radiant energy from the sun directly into electrical energy. A solar cell contains a wafer of semiconductor material, usually silicon. This is made in such a way that when light falls upon it, electrons move in one direction within it and "holes" (positively charged regions) in the other direction. In a circuit, each solar cell produces about half a volt.

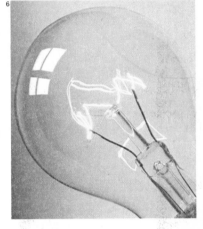

6 In the filament of an electric light bulb some electrical energy is converted to light but most is wasted as heat. A fluorescent lamp contains a vapour and fluorescent coating that together convert electricity to light with less heat and greater efficiency. The element of an electric fire converts electricity mainly to heat.

7 An electric motor converts electrical energy into mechanical or kinetic energy. Most familiar is the rotary type in which a rotor revolves within a fixed stator.

8 The hydraulic ram raises water by converting its kinetic energy into gravitational potential energy. A lake or reservoir [A] supplies water [1] through a pipe [2] to the ram chamber, which is at a lower level, ensuring that the water has adequate kinetic energy on reaching the chamber [3]. This fills with water [B] which briefly escapes through a spring valve [4] before closing it. The water passes on round a one-way valve [5] into a second chamber [6] where air is first compressed by the water [C] then re-expands to force water up the delivery pipe [7]. A back-surge allows the spring valve to reopen and the process to be repeated.

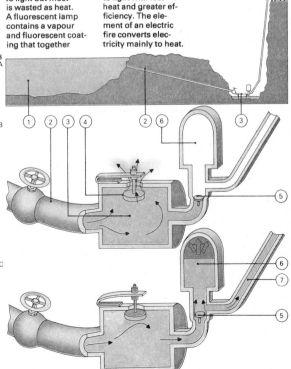

Statics and forces

The sudden movement of an object with seemingly no cause – for example, the unexpected movement of a table in the middle of a room – would obviously cause consternation to the observer. Most people would probably think a trick was responsible for such a happening because they expect a cause for this effect of motion. The scientific name for the cause is "force" – it is anything that causes an object to start to move when it has been at rest, or vice versa. A force is also required to change a condition of motion that already exists – to change the direction of an already existing motion or to alter the velocity of the motion. Once made to move, an object continues to move without stopping or changing direction until it is acted on by another force. This idea has now become almost self-evident following its original expression and generalization by Isaac Newton in the late 1600s, and is generally known in physics as Newton's first law of motion.

In many cases the cause that stops, or modifies, already existing motion is provided by the force of friction. This acts in the direction opposite to the movement of an object. It is produced by the rubbing together of the surface of the moving object and the surface it is moving on or, in a gas or a liquid, the medium it is moving through.

States of equilibrium

When several forces act at the same time on the same object, each tries to move the object along a line pointing in its own direction at a rate that depends on the size of the applied force. If it happens that the object does not move as a result of all these forces, then it is said to be in equilibrium [5].

The magnitude and direction of any one of the forces is balanced by the total effect of the other forces and there is no resultant movement. The study of forces applied to objects in a state of equilibrium is called statics (as opposed to dynamics, the study of forces acting on moving objects).

Someone sitting still on a chair is an everyday example of an object in equilibrium – the upward force of the chair on the person balances the downward force of the earth's gravitational attraction that is trying to pull the person through the chair to the floor. A

tree standing upright in the ground is a similar example – its downward gravitational force, commonly known as its weight, is balanced by the upward force of the ground in which it is rooted. As a consequence of this equilibrium, neither the person nor the tree is in motion up or down. This state of affairs can be modified only if another external force is brought into the arrangement – for example, by the person moving about on the chair and possibly making it topple or, in a most extreme case, by chopping down the tree [7]. Thousands of everyday objects stay where they are and do not move unaided because of the existence of this equilibrium of forces both in magnitude and direction.

Moments and levers

So far, only those forces that try to move objects along straight-line paths have been considered. There are many other forces, however, that can act on objects and try to rotate them around a central point. These forces have an effectiveness that depends on how far from the central point they are acting. Everyone knows that a much greater

1 The balance point of the lever (itself assumed weightless) [A] can be found by dividing each load into equal small weights and distributing them along the lever [B], keeping the centre of gravity of each load where it was. The lever balances at the centre of gravity of the whole line. This point is halfway along the line [C] of equal weights at the distance from the weights that is inverse to the ratio of the weights themselves [D]. The product of the weight and its distance from the fulcrum (pivot) is the same on each side – the moments are equal and opposite.

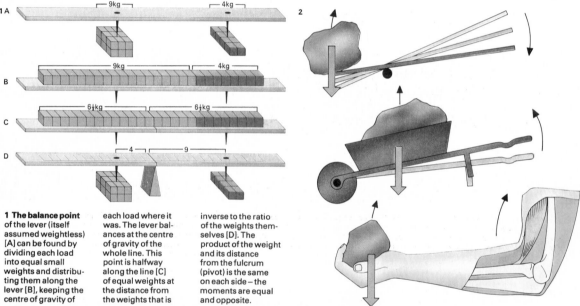

2 The see-saw principle is used in the first order of levers and has the fulcrum, or balance-point, between the load and the applied effort. The wheelbarrow is a familiar example of the second order of levers, with the load between the fulcrum and the effort. Finally, the third order of levers, with the effort between the fulcrum and the load, is used when lifting a weight with the forearm – the elbow is the fulcrum. If both lever and load remain the same in all three cases, the principle of moments shows the required force is the greatest for the third order and least for the second order, which is the best form of leverage.

3 The force needed to turn this threshing machine is lessened if the animal pulls on the outer harness chain, because the leverage (that is force × perpendicular distance to the axis) is greater. But in doing so the animal must walk further.

4 A steelyard is a balance often used by butchers for weighing carcasses that are too heavy for ordinary scales. The small sliding jockey weight is moved along the long arm of the steelyard until the whole beam is horizontal. The

Object being weighed, suspended from point close to the pivot

Small counterweight distant from the pivot

sliding weight, at a greater distance from the fulcrum than the heavy load, can be much lighter. The principle involved here is the same as the first order of levers – like the see-saw. Its first recorded use was in 315 BC.

turning effect is achieved by pulling on a wrench or spanner that has a long, rather than a short, handle. The combined effect of the magnitude of the force multiplied by the perpendicular distance from the turning point (called the axis of rotation) is called the moment of the force. The greater the applied force or the distance of action, the greater is the resulting moment or turning effect. Simple machines that employ the phenomenon of moment of a force belong to one of the various classes of levers [2].

Of course several forces may simultaneously act on an object through more than one point within its boundary. In this case, each has its own moment about a particular axis, through which the object can still be in equilibrium if these moments produce no collective rotational effect. That is, if the total magnitude of the clockwise moments about the axis exactly balances that of the anticlockwise moments, there is no movement. This result is called the principle of moments and it may apply to an object at the same time as the equilibrium, mentioned previously, that arises from forces acting through a par-

ticular point trying to move the object in a straight line.

For the example of a person sitting still on a chair and being in equilibrium for vertical motion, it is clear that if someone tries to tilt the chair backwards, the seated person will topple over unless someone or something pulls the chair in the opposite direction with an equivalent force. The vertical equilibrium through the point of contact of the chair with the floor acts at the same time as the equilibrium for the moments of the forces trying to twist the chair around at the same point.

How couples operate

One further type of force that a study of statics includes is called a couple [6]. Actually this is the application of two equal forces arranged so that they both tend to rotate the object in the same direction. The couple produces only rotation with an *equal* moment about any point between the forces, and does not produce any straight-line motion. Consequently it can be balanced only by another equal or opposite couple if an equilibrium state is to be achieved.

The principle of moments is used in most of the activities in a children's playground. The see-saw obviously demonstrates the lever, as shown here; in addition, the umbrella, roundabout and swings all use the moment of a force about their axis or fulcrum to achieve movement.

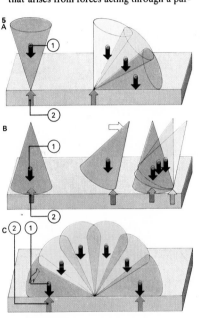

5 If a cone standing on its point [A] is slightly displaced, its weight produces a moment that continues to topple the cone about the point of contact. This is an unstable equilibrium position. With the cone on its base [B], displacement produces a moment that restores the original position – a stable equilibrium. If the cone lies on its side [C], displacement produces no moment since the weight and its reaction [1, 2] still act along the same line – the cone remains in its new position and is in neutral equilibrium. The very low centre of gravity of the bus [D] keeps it in stable equilibrium even for large displacements.

6 The moment of a couple is equal to the product of one of the forces and the distance between the two. This hand is applying an equal force to each end of the top of a tap, producing a rotating effect about the central axis to turn it on and off. Both these forces are trying to turn the tap in the same direction, and together form a couple; the larger the tap-top, the larger the couple.

7 A tree stands in equilibrium (its centre of gravity acts downwards in a straight line through its base) until a wedge is cut into its trunk. This starts to destroy the equilibrium by allowing the tree's weight to develop a toppling moment that is not balanced by an equal and opposite reaction.

8 Two forces act simultaneously on an object in different directions. The resultant force, and the direction of any subsequent movement, is defined by the diagonal of a parallelogram whose sides are drawn parallel to the applied forces with lengths proportional to their magnitudes. This is an application of vector diagrams.

Attraction and repulsion

To many people, the most mysterious natural forces are those that produce an effect on objects at great distances, reaching across even empty space without any material contact between the body producing the force and that being affected by it. This phenomenon is often called "action at a distance", and there are several fundamental forces of nature that act in this way. They are gravitational, magnetic and electric. Other fundamental forces act within the limits of the atomic nucleus, over short ranges only.

The inverse-square law
The three forces acting at a distance obey a common law that describes how the magnitude of the force depends on the object producing it, the object affected by it and the distance separating the two. It is called the inverse-square law [Key]. If the distance between two bodies is doubled, then the force between them falls by one-quarter (the inverse square), and so on.

Isaac Newton (1642–1727) was first to realize this type of law applied to the gravitational force of attraction when performing calculations on the speed of the moon in orbit round the earth. His law of gravity [1] states that "the attractive force between two bodies is proportional to the product of their masses divided by the square of the distance between them" and it should be noted that this force is a mutual one – there are equal and opposite forces on the two objects.

About 100 years later, in 1789, Henry Cavendish (1731–1810) used this theory of gravitation to produce the first estimate of the mass of the earth [2]. He was also responsible for one of the best experimental verifications (in 1785) of the use of the inverse-square law to describe the force between electrostatic charges (that is, electric charges at rest). Its use was further verified in 1870 by James Clerk Maxwell (1831–79) who showed that the inverse-square law was true to one part in 20,000. More modern methods have taken this limit to one in 1,000 million.

The volume of space within which the force exerted by a body produces a detectable effect (usually by causing movement of a second body) is normally called the field of force. The directions along which movement can occur are known as the lines of force. These are merely imaginary "lines" in space that are used to help describe the possible directions of any motion within the field – they spread out from the force-producing object, filling the complete field.

Gravitational and magnetic force
Any object with mass, however small, can produce a gravitational force field. The force is always positive because no object can have a negative mass. This indicates that the force of gravity can only be one of attraction. (A negative value for a force indicates repulsion, not attraction.)

It is gravitational attraction that gives all objects their weight, trying to pull them towards the centre of the earth [3], and which keeps the planets in orbit around the sun. In some circumstances, gravitational attraction can be balanced by an equal and opposite force to achieve a weightless condition. This is most commonly accomplished by the centrifugal force caused by the revolution of an orbiting satellite. As a consequence, objects

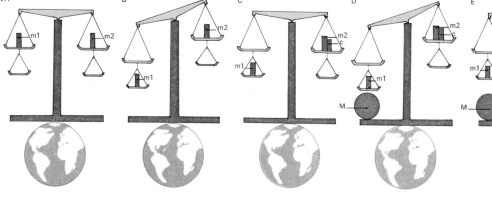

1 The earth's mass W can be measured by means of a tall balance with two pans on each side. Initially, m1 balances m2 [A] but when m1 is moved to the lower pan it weighs more, being closer to the earth [B]. Mass c is used to restore the balance [C]. Next, the large mass M is used to make m1 weigh more, by gravitational attraction [D]. Balance is restored [E] with weight n. If R is the earth's radius, d is the distance between m1 and M, then Newton's law states:
$$\frac{m1 \times M}{d^2} = \frac{n \times W}{R^2}$$
The distance between the pans on each side must be great enough to prevent M from having significant gravitational pull on the other masses.

2 In 1798, Henry Cavendish determined the earth's mass using a quartz fibre torsion balance. Two small lead spheres were attracted by two larger lead spheres and from the size of the deflection, the force of attraction between the spheres was calculated. To work out the mass of the earth, Cavendish compared this force with the gravitational pull of the earth on the spheres (that is, their weight).

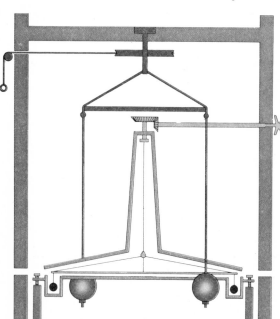

3 On a roller-coaster, power is needed to pull the car to the top of the highest incline against the gravitational force exerted by the earth. The resulting potential energy of the car is then transformed into kinetic energy of motion as it is allowed to free-wheel down the track. According to the principle of energy conservation, the total kinetic energy at the bottom of an incline should equal the potential energy at the top; the car would be able to travel to the top of another equally high incline with no further application of external power. Some of the potential energy, however, is lost as a result of its conversion to heat energy by friction between the speeding car and the track. Therefore the remaining kinetic energy will allow the car to climb only a smaller vertical height each time it travels downwards. To raise the height of the car again, it would be necessary to apply additional power against the force of gravity.

within the satellite are able to float freely within its confines.

Magnetic force [4] is familiar in connection with the working of a normal compass. This force also acts over large distances, although in this case both attractive and repulsive forces may occur, a fact that is easily tested with two simple bar magnets. The ends, or "poles", of the magnets are distinguished by being called north and south and it is always found that two north or two south poles will not remain in contact, whereas a north and south combination will. This fundamental effect is summarized by the rule: "like magnetic poles repel each other, unlike poles attract".

The different poles are given the descriptive labels north and south for historical reasons – the north pole of a magnet is the one that is always attracted to the North Pole of the earth, though in fact a magnetic south pole must be sited there to achieve this magnetic effect [5]. The inverse-square law determines the magnitude of the magnetic force, although this is now proportional to the product of two magnetic pole strengths

that can be positive or negative (instead of two masses that can only be positive, as in the case of the gravitational force).

Electric force [6] can also be either attractive or repulsive since its source, an electric charge, can be either positive or negative. According to the type of charge either a positive (attractive) or a negative (repulsive) force is obtained by the inverse-square law.

What is an electric charge?

Every electric charge is in fact a multiple of a unit charge that is equal in magnitude to the irreducible charge associated with a single electron, a fact first noted and evaluated in 1909 by the American physicist Robert Millikan (1868–1953). However the dual nature of the electric charge had been known from Greek times and is best demonstrated, as then, by electrostatic effects. If a glass rod is rubbed with silk the two objects attract each other, while two glass rods rubbed in the same way repel each other. Each rod acquires a net positive electric charge, whereas the silk collects excess electrons by the action of friction and becomes negatively charged.

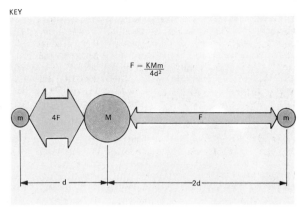

KEY

$$F = \frac{KMm}{4d^2}$$

The inverse-square law governs gravitational, electric and magnetic forces. M and m represent the masses of two bodies for the gravitational force, their charge values for the electric force and their pole strengths for the magnetic force.

In all cases, d represents the distance between the bodies. K is a constant quantity that has a different value for each of the three forces. Gravitational force is much the weakest, the gravitational attraction for two electrons

being about 10^{42} times less than the electric force of repulsion. (Consequently one is aware of gravity only when great masses such as the earth are involved.) The inverse-square law equation thus varies for the three forces according to the value of K.

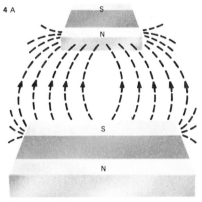

4A

B

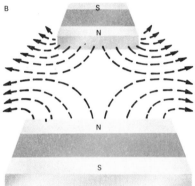

4 A field of force exists all round a magnetic material and the associated lines of force indicate paths along which a unit magnetic north pole would move. Iron filings sprinkled on paper laid over a pair of magnets will display negative [A] or positive [B] lines of force. In a similar way, a small compass needle will line up along lines of force with its north pole pointing out the field direction [C].

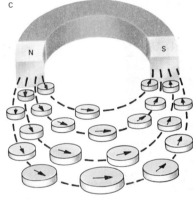

C

5 The earth's magnetic field is created by phenomena below the crust as if it had been formed by an immense bar magnet with its south pole approximately aligned with the north geographic pole sited at one end of the earth's rotational axis [A]. The needle of a ship's magnetic compass [B] swings to a position where its ends point to north and south, along a line of force of the earth's magnetic field.

5A

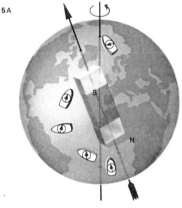

6

B

○ Molecule in bulk liquid

● Molecule at surface

6 Electric forces that exist on a molecular and atomic scale within a substance are responsible for the cohesive forces that hold it together and give it shape and strength. Both attractive and repulsive forces exist in a state of

equilibrium, the attractive holding the substance together and the repulsive effectively preventing the atoms collapsing in on each other. A striking result of these cohesive forces between atoms is seen in liquids. Within the

body of the liquid, any one atom has equal and opposite forces on either side of it in any direction; there is therefore no resultant force. But at the surface there is a net force pulling atoms into the body of the liquid and as

a result the surface appears to behave like an invisible elastic "skin" pulled across the liquid. This surface tension effect is used by insects such as water boatmen and mosquito larvae to keep themselves floating on a pond's surface.

Speed and acceleration

Cars, rockets, falling weights and footballs all move under the action of forces. The branch of physics that studies movement, and the forces that produce and influence it, is called dynamics. It was given a firm scientific basis as a result of the work of Isaac Newton (1642–1727), who formulated the fundamental three laws of motion.

Principles of motion

The first law [1] summarizes the principle of inertia – the basic tendency for anything moving to continue moving and for an object at rest to remain at rest. It states that "an object will remain at rest or in motion at constant velocity unless acted on by a force". Once a car is in motion, both it and its passengers carry on moving unless acted on by a force – such as a braking force. A head-on collision may stop the car, but the inertia of the passengers will cause them to fly forwards from their seats. They may be thrown against the windscreen unless held in place by safety belts which exert a restraining force.

As a result of this law, it is apparent that the greater the applied force on an object the greater its change of velocity. Velocity is merely speed in a certain direction and change of velocity in a given time is called acceleration. So the greater the applied force, the greater the acceleration. The second law of motion states that, in addition, acceleration is inversely proportional to the mass of the object being moved.

The third law considers the way forces act against each other. If an object rests on a table, the table exerts an upward force equal and opposite to the downward force of the object's weight. The third law generalizes this by saying that "for every applied force there is an equal and opposite reaction". Two spring balances hooked together and pulled in opposite directions register the same force. Another much more spectacular application of this law is the rocket. The force of the expanding gases in a rocket's combustion chamber acts equally in all directions. The forward thrust is produced by the reaction to the displacement of mass that occurs when the burning gases escape through the nozzle of the rocket.

Newton's laws of motion also connect with several other concepts. Thus the second law describes how acceleration (a) is dependent on mass (m) and applied force (F) in the equation $F=ma$. This can be used to calculate the weight of an object, because weight is the force with which a body is attracted towards the centre of the earth. This force equals the product of the mass and the acceleration with which a falling object drops to the ground (called the acceleration due to gravity). Consequently mass and weight are completely different quantities, having different units to describe their magnitudes. Mass is a property of an object due to the quantity of matter it contains; weight, a force which acts on it due to gravity. Unfortunately in the past the same units (pounds, kilogrammes and so on) have been used for both mass and weight; the modern scientific units are the kilogramme (or pound) for mass and the newton (or poundal) for weight.

Definition of momentum

The equation of the second law also shows that, because acceleration is the rate of change of velocity, force can be expressed as

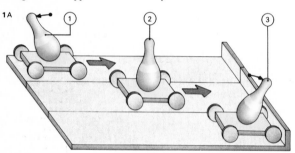

1 Newton's first law describes inertial effects. [A] An object resists being moved from rest by toppling backwards [1], although moving steadily it is undisturbed, as if at rest [2]. When stopped it resists slowing and tends to continue moving [3]. The second law explains that acceleration or deceleration is proportional to the force producing it. [B] A ball falling on to a soft material [4] sinks deeper than into a harder one [5] because the deceleration force is smaller. The third law states there is an equal and opposite reaction to every force. [C] A rifle recoils when fired [6], although the bullet's velocity is much greater. Successive firings cause successive recoils [7]. A rocket ejects gas and moves forwards [8] because of reaction.

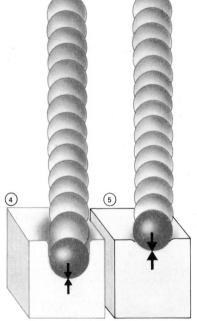

2 A heavy gun recoils when firing and an equal and opposite reaction propels the shell forwards. The principle of conservation of momentum, states that the total momentum before and after is zero but the shell is given its forward velocity because it is lighter than the gun. The chemical energy stored in the propellant explosive charge is transformed into the kinetic energies of gun and shell.

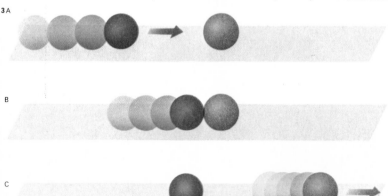

3 A stationary ball is hit by another of similar mass moving towards it. Before the collision (A) the moving ball has a certain momentum (equal to the product of its mass and its velocity). At the moment of impact (B), this momentum is transferred to the stationary ball, which had no momentum. As a result, the stationary ball moves while the ball that was moving formerly becomes stationary (C). In all such collisions momentum is conserved – after impact the momentum of the second ball equals that of the first.

the rate of change of the product of mass and velocity. This product is called momentum and can be thought of as a quantity of motion that, for a definite velocity, increases with the object's mass. In effect the momentum indicates the effort needed to move an object or to stop or change the direction of its motion. For instance, a brick carefully placed on someone's foot does not hurt. But the pain caused when the brick is dropped from a height of a metre or so testifies to the effect of momentum.

Probably the most important reason for calculating momentum is that it is conserved throughout events involving changes of motion – for example, sudden collisions or explosions. This means that the total momentum before and after such an event stays absolutely constant [3]. Following the event, momentum may be lost through the action of friction reducing the velocities, but during its occurrence this law of conservation of momentum holds exactly.

Another phenomenon occurring during this kind of event is the transfer of energy. It can exist in many forms such as heat, light,

sound, chemical and electrical energy. All of these can be transformed into one another – petrol's stored chemical energy is transformed in the combustion engine to mechanical energy for moving a car. If the energy transfers occurring in any process are considered collectively, very careful measurements have shown that energy is never created or destroyed. This is the law of conservation of energy and it implies that no machine can produce a net gain of energy.

Two forms of energy
For the study of dynamics two forms of energy are fundamental – kinetic energy, possessed by objects that are in motion, and potential energy, possessed by objects that are at rest and able to do work by virtue of their position [5]. The pile driver has work done on it to lift it against the earth's gravitational force and then can expend the stored energy when again allowed to fall. In fact, the potential energy is transformed to kinetic energy as the hammer falls and it is the kinetic energy that finally does the work of driving the pile into the ground.

Galileo's legendary experiment, dropping a cannon ball and a pebble from the tower at Pisa, showed that objects of different masses fall to the ground together, proving that the acceleration due to gravity is the same for all objects. With objects of different cross-sectional area, air resistance to downward motion may also be different and prevent the objects hitting the ground together. If resistance equals the gravitational attraction a limiting velocity is reached. Also there will not be a total transformation of potential to kinetic energy as the objects fall because some heat energy is lost by the action of friction with the air.

4 A motorway pile-up can occur after one or two cars stop. Other cars that are unable to stop in time collide with the stationary vehicles and transfer their forward momentum to them, causing a "knock-on" effect which ripples along an ever-extending chain. Conservation of energy controls the transformation of a car's mechanical kinetic energy to wasted heat and the energy imparted to the stationary cars.

5 The change from potential energy (due to an object's position) to kinetic energy (due to its movement) and back again occurs with a bouncing ball (A), a ball rolling in a hemispherical cup (B) and a swinging pendulum (C). Before a ball is dropped it possesses only potential energy. This is converted to kinetic energy as the ball falls and reaches a maximum at the moment of impact – when potential energy is zero. Potential energy is regained as the ball rises to become stationary again at the top of the bounce. The same sequence of transitions occur in the bob at the end of the pendulum and with the ball rolling in its cup.

6 A steam catapult, driven by the pressure of gas built up in the rams, is effectively storing a great quantity of potential energy that, when released, can be transformed to the kinetic energy of movement. As a result, even the large mass of an aircraft can be accelerated to a speed that will allow it to take off from rest in the very short distance available on an aircraft carrier's deck.

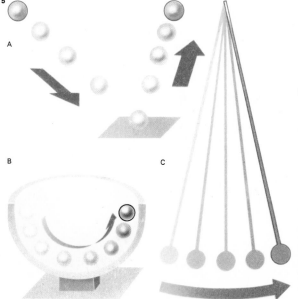

7 In 1798 Count Rumford (1753–1814) noticed that, in the boring of cannon barrels, the barrels, borer and metal chips all became hot despite there being no apparent heat source, except for friction. He realized that the mechanical energy needed to turn the barrel against this friction was being converted to heat energy. Subsequently other experimenters, notably James Joule (1818–89), demonstrated the transformations between other forms of energy.

Circular and vibrating motion

If a driver presses the accelerator pedal of his car, the car speeds up – in scientific terms its velocity changes. But even when he goes round a bend at constant speed, the car's velocity also changes. This is because velocity is speed in a certain direction; if either its magnitude or direction alter, velocity changes.

Motion in a circle

The rate of change in velocity is called acceleration. Thus an object which changes direction while travelling at constant speed experiences an acceleration. When a stone is tied to the end of a string and whirled round in a circle at constant speed, the velocity's magnitude is unchanged but the direction alters continuously. If the string were cut at any instant, the stone would fly off along a tangent to the circle (as seen in the sparks flying off a rotating catherine-wheel).

A force must be acting on the rotating stone to produce its acceleration. Here the force is due to the tension in the string and one can feel this force on the hand as the stone is whirled round. It is called the "centripetal force" because it acts towards the centre of the circle. The acceleration it produces is therefore similarly directed towards the centre. For a car moving round a circular track, frictional forces at the ground acting on the wheels provide the centripetal force.

Newton's laws are applicable only to non-accelerating frameworks. For these laws to hold true in the accelerating framework of a rotating system, we must introduce centrifugal force as a fictitious force acting outwards from the orbit centre. The effect of this force is used in the domestic spin-drier to squeeze the water out of wet laundry and, on a larger scale, in the centrifuge machines that subject astronauts and pilots to the high acceleration forces encountered in flight.

Periodic motion

Both centripetal and centrifugal forces depend on the mass (m) of the object and its velocity (v) in the circular motion (circle of radius r). A heavy object needs a greater centripetal force to hold it in orbit and a greater force is also required for high speeds of rotation. Experiment shows that, in addition, the required force (F) is inversely proportional to the radius of motion, and $F = mv^2/r$ where v^2/r gives the magnitude of the centripetal acceleration.

Uniform circular motion is periodic – that is, the events recur over and over again. The time taken for a complete revolution of the object remains constant. This periodic character is further demonstrated by considering how the object's distance from any fixed diameter of the circle varies with time. If a graph of these distances is plotted, the resulting curve is one of a uniformly oscillating displacement [1], resembling a sine wave.

For a swinging pendulum, the force which pulls the bob back through the central vertical position is its weight. It undergoes oscillatory motion with an acceleration that is proportional to its distance from the point of suspension and it is also directed towards that point. Movement of this type is called "simple harmonic motion" and for the pendulum the time taken for a complete cycle of forwards and backwards swing (the oscillation "period" t) is proportional to the square root of its length (l). The number of cycles completed per second is called the "fre-

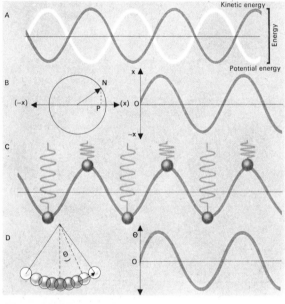

1 All periodic motion involves the continuous interchange of kinetic and potential energy, as shown in the graph [A]. Simple harmonic motion (SHM) is one form of periodic motion that is characterized by the shape of a sine wave [B]. The point [P] on the diameter of the circle around which N is moving is an example of SHM. The mass on a spring [C] performs linear SHM and a pendulum [D] performs angular SHM.

2 Circular motion of the "aeroplanes" produces an apparent centrifugal force that lifts the planes off the ground. The equal and opposite centripetal force is provided by tension in the arms.

3 The constant periodic time of oscillation of a pendulum is used to control clocks, especially case clocks [A]. The periodic time needed to drive the escapement correctly can be exactly matched by choosing a pendulum [B] of correct length. It can be calculated from the equation $t = 2\pi\sqrt{l/g}$ where t is the oscillation period, l is the length and g is the acceleration due to the earth's attraction – gravity.

4 The moons of Jupiter, as well as all other natural and artificial satellites, move in orbits around their mother planet at great speeds. The force of gravity between them provides the centripetal force towards the centre of motion that keeps a moon in orbit and produces its centripetal acceleration. As the speed of rotation remains almost constant, it is the continuously changing direction of the moon which implies acceleration. If the inward gravitational force were removed the moon would continue in a straight line, hurtling out into space. The orbits are not exactly circular, so that the speed of rotation does not remain completely constant; the associated forces are analogous to those of a system performing circular motion.

quency" of oscillation (measured in hertz).

The displacement in all types of simple harmonic motion rises and falls like a sine wave. Many other wave motions behave in this way. If a long rope is clamped at one end and its free end is whipped, a wave-like disturbance travels along the rope and the amplitude of the rope's displacement at any point from the fixed end is described by the waveform shown in illustration 6.

Moving and standing waves

The characteristics of this wave picture describe amplitude changes for the plane waves that move through the sea, the circular waves (ripples) that spread from the point at which a stone is dropped in a pond, the air pressure waves of sound and the electromagnetic waves of radio and light (which are distinguished by their wavelengths). For all these waveforms, energy is transmitted in the direction of the wave motion. Actual vibrations of the medium in which they travel may occur in the same direction, producing "longitudinal waves" such as those of sound, or in a direction at right-angles to the motion,

producing the transverse waves of all the other examples. In water, a floating object merely bobs up and down as the waves pass, and it does not move in the direction of the wave motion.

If a string is clamped at both ends and then plucked, it still vibrates but in this case the wave appears to stay in the same place – a stationary, or "standing", wave has been produced as the ends are fixed and allow no forward motion. The string vibrates at its natural frequency, which is inversely proportional to its length and directly proportional to $\sqrt{T/m}$ where T is its tension and m is its mass per unit length.

This state of vibration is called "resonance" because it occurs with the natural frequency of the string. Blowing into the end of an organ pipe makes the air in it resonate at a natural frequency that depends on the pipe's length. Similarly, when struck, a tuning fork vibrates with one particular frequency. There are many useful applications of resonance, as in tuning circuits on radio receivers [8], and in musical instruments – perhaps the most satisfying application of this effect.

Many fairground rides depend on circular motion and the resulting centrifugal forces for the excitement they can provide. They all use different variations of this type of motion, ranging from the slow revolutions of the merry-go-round to the much faster and more complex movements of the aeroplane "spinners". The magnitude of the centrifugal force depends on the mass of the circling object. On this "chairoplane" the heavier children experience greater centrifugal force than the lighter ones, but do not fly higher because the force is balanced by their greater weight. In ultra high-speed centrifuges small molecules can be separated according to their different mass.

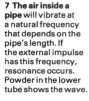

5 Sea waves move with a transverse wave motion that transmits energy in their direction of motion, while floating objects move only vertically up and down as the waves pass them.

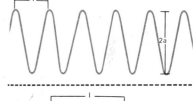

6 The forward velocity (v) of a wave of frequency (f) and wavelength (l) is given by v = fl. Such waves can be drawn as sine waves. Two waves can have the same amplitude (a) even though the wavelengths differ.

7 The air inside a pipe will vibrate at a natural frequency that depends on the pipe's length. If the external impulse has this frequency, resonance occurs. Powder in the lower tube shows the wave.

8 A circuit [1], with the AC source from an aerial [2], is "tuned" so that its natural frequency matches one of the incoming radio signals [3]. Resonance excites it to oscillate and work the radio [4], [5].

Quarter wavelength

Powder

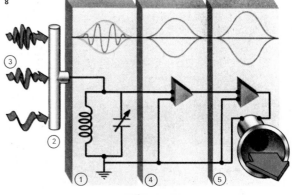

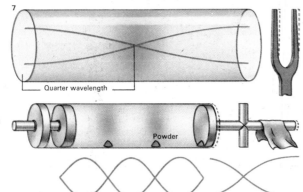

9 Freak winds can begin to produce oscillations in very large and heavy structures. If they continue, the oscillations may gradually increase in amplitude and if their frequency equals the natural vibration frequency of the structure resonance may occur, leading to catastrophic break-up of the structure. This has happened with bridges (the most renowned probably being the Tacoma Narrows Suspension Bridge, USA, shown here) and tall structures such as skyscrapers.

Pressure and flow

The branch of physics that deals with the forces and pressures that act within liquids and gases is called hydrostatics. It also examines how these forces affect any surface they touch and what uses they can be put to. It includes, for example, problems ranging from deep-sea diving to aeroplane altimeters and from floating and sinking to the design of hydraulic lifts and other machinery.

Archimedes' principle
Hydrostatics explains what happens to an object immersed in a fluid. Both liquids and gases are fluids and each is able to exert or transmit a force. If a cork is pushed below a liquid surface and then released, it immediately bobs to the surface. The cork has experienced an upward force, called the "upthrust", due to the liquid, and it is this that keeps the cork floating on the surface. In exactly the same way, an upthrust must act on a floating balloon, although here it is produced by a gas rather than a liquid.

It was the Greek scientist Archimedes (287–212 BC) who first quantified this fact by stating that "when an object is totally or

partially immersed in a fluid the upthrust on it is equal to the weight of fluid displaced". Using Archimedes' principle [1] the magnitude of the upthrust can always be found and it makes itself apparent as a loss of weight of the object.

For this reason, a floating object has its weight exactly balanced by the upthrust. But if the object is too dense, the upthrust may not be sufficient to counterbalance its weight and the object sinks. This principle of flotation is used directly by a hydrometer, an instrument for measuring liquid densities. A hydrometer floats at a level that depends on the weight of a liquid it displaces and, since the submerged volume is known, the density of the liquid can be calculated.

Internal forces in fluids
As well as being able to exert a force such as an upthrust, a fluid can produce an internal force at any depth due to the weight of the fluid above it. It is normal to measure this effect as the force per unit area, or pressure, developed by the fluid's weight; this increases with depth (in both liquids and

gases). Thus the greater water pressure at the bottom of a dam requires a form of construction in which strength also increases with depth – a triangular cross-section getting thicker with depth is generally used. For a similar reason, the suit of a deep-sea diver must contain a jacket of compressed air whose pressure counteracts the external water pressure, so that he can breathe without his muscles having to expand his chest against this pressure.

Another example of a fluid is the earth's atmosphere. The weight of air produces a pressure at the surface, commonly called atmospheric pressure, which is about 14.7 pounds per square inch at sea-level. In other unit systems it is equal to 760mm of mercury, 101,325 newtons/m^2 or 1,013 millibars. Variations in this pressure affect the weather and are caused by atmospheric disturbances. They are measured by the common barometer. The simplest form of barometer measures the height of a column of liquid, often mercury, supported by the atmospheric pressure. An aneroid barometer transforms the effect of pressure on a thin-walled metal

1A

1 Archimedes' principle states that for an object immersed in a fluid the upthrust on it equals the weight of fluid that its volume displaces [A]. The round object suspended on the balance has weight p in air and lesser weight q when immersed in a liquid. The difference in its weight is equal to the upthrust on it in the liquid; that is, to the weight of displaced water in the beaker, which equals r minus s and which in turn equals p minus q. An application of Archimedes' principle is the hydrometer [B], which is used to test the condition of a car battery by checking the acid density. The tube is immersed in the battery acid and the bulb is squeezed to expel air; it is then released to suck acid into the main stem. The hydrometer then floats in the acid, at a depth that depends on the liquid's density.

2A

2 The manometer is a U-shaped liquid column gauge used to measure differences in fluid pressure. The "well-type" has one column [1] of relatively small diameter whereas the second that is wider acts as a reservoir [2]. The difference in columns ensures that the level in the reservoir does not change much with pressure, but that in the small diameter column does, so making for accuracy in reading these variations. Small positional adjustments of the scale with the help of the level indicator [3] compensate for the small reservoir changes. At first [A] both columns are at equal levels. With the reservoir pressurized [B] the new level shows pressure.

3 In the lift-pump, the piston [1] is moved upwards by the downwards stroke of the lever, producing a partial vacuum in the cylinder [2]. The piston valve [4] is kept closed by the water already in the pump chamber. Water is then forced into the cylinder by atmospheric pressure acting on the surface of the water outside the pump. This water passes through the open valve [3] filling the upper chamber. On the upward lever stroke the piston moves down, valve 3 closes and valve 4 opens to allow the piston to move through the trapped water. On the next downward stroke this water is lifted out of the pump and the cycle begins again. In theory, atmospheric pressure "lifts" up to 10m (34ft).

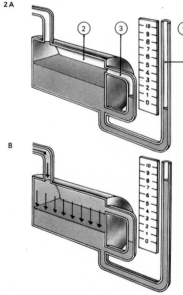

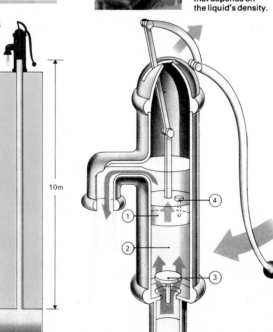

4 A water cannon has water pumped into it under great pressure and forced through an exit nozzle of relatively small diameter. As a result a great force propels the water forwards (pressure is the force per unit area) and accelerates it to a high velocity. This means that the water acquires considerable momentum and kinetic energy which can be used to cut relatively soft china clay from a quarry wall. The great power of the water cannon is also often used to clean the outside walls of buildings. In this case, an abrasive in the form of a powder can be put into the water to increase the corrosive effect of the water jet as it strikes the surface to be cleaned, removing accumulated dirt.

cylinder into the mechanical movement of a needle moving across a calibrated dial. This form is used as an altimeter in many aircraft.

The possibility of supporting a column of liquid by gas pressure is also used in a manometer [2]. This generally consists of a U-shaped glass tube containing a liquid that moves round the U-bend by an amount depending on the difference between two pressures applied at each end. The same principle is employed in the common pump that lifts water from a well. It "taps" a column of water supported by atmospheric pressure acting on the surface of the water source. The height of this column can theoretically be 10.36m (34ft), although in practice the so-called lift-pump [3] can raise water from a depth of only about 8.5m (28ft).

External pressure can be used to move a fluid, but its own internal pressure can also be most effectively employed. A liquid is virtually incompressible, so that pressure developed at one point is transmitted equally in all directions. This fact can be utilized in a hydraulic press or jack to exert very large forces. A force acting on a very small area

produces an enormous pressure (force per unit area) which can be transformed into a much greater force acting over the large area of the hydraulic jack ram [5], since the pressure is constant throughout a liquid.

The study of hydrodynamics

All these effects use the static properties of fluids. But by definition a fluid is something that flows and the properties resulting from motion are described by hydrodynamics.

Motion changes the pressure within a fluid, and this can be difficult to predict accurately. The flow can be either smooth (streamlined) or turbulent, when the fluid is broken up into eddies; it is then harder to calculate the pressure at different points within the fluid. The Swiss scientist Daniel Bernoulli (1700–82) first noticed that pressure decreases as fluid velocity increases (although this holds accurately only for streamlined flow) and this principle creates the necessary lift on an aircraft's wing [Key]. The wing shape is arranged to produce a greater flow velocity above than below and so there is a net upward pressure or lift.

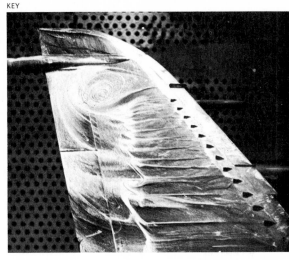

The way air flows around objects can be studied using a wind tunnel. Thus the aerodynamic properties of aircraft wing shapes, or of complete planes and cars, for example, can be investigated. Tiny plastic spheres are injected into the airstream so that the flow patterns can be photographed and perfectly streamlined designs created.

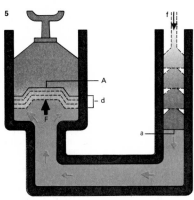

5 An hydraulic lift works on the principle that an incompressible liquid transmits pressure equally in all directions. The small force f acting on area a produces pressure f/a which is converted at the much larger area A to the correspondingly larger force F so that F/A = f/a. The larger force can be used to move great weights. But the weight moves through only the small distance d.

6 The principle of hydraulic lift has many applications, the most familiar of which is probably the car lift used by motor mechanics in garages. Other types of hydraulic machinery have many other applications in agriculture and industry, as in this hydraulic hoist used by an engineer to rig or maintain overhead telephone and electric power lines. If such machines worked exactly as described in illustration 5, the pressurizing force would have to move several metres to produce a small movement of the actuating piston. The hydraulic fluid is therefore pressurized by a pump, which transfers the necessary pressure.

7 A shock absorber is used to reduce or dampen oscillating motions. Several damping systems can be employed – oil damping is shown in A, air damping in B and friction damping in C. The most common type is the oil damper D, which is used especially in road vehicles. It consists of a plunger that on its downward stroke allows oil to pass through a small valve in the piston. The viscosity of the oil and the size of the valve determine the damping characteristics; that is, the manner and speed with which the oscillation is reduced. For rapid loading conditions, where speed of application makes damping solid, a second valve channels oil into a reserve.

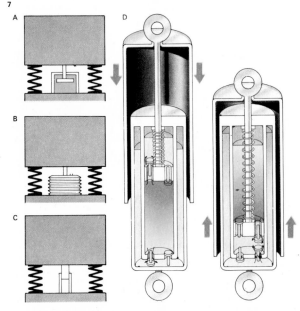

8 A stream of gas tends to adhere to any adjacent solid surface, a phenomenon called the Coanda wall-attachment effect. A gas stream that is free to enter two identical channels [A] chooses one of them by adhering only to its walls. A small side-stream [B] can then deflect it to other output channels [C] where it remains even when the disturbance ceases. This is the fluidics analogue of an electric switch.

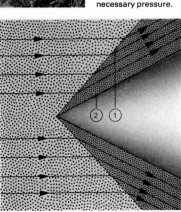

9 When the velocity of a gas is low compared to that of sound its flow can be described without considering the compressibility. Above 0.3 of the speed of sound (Mach 1) a gas is compressed when it meets a solid and there is a consequent temperature change. Above Mach 1 compression occurs abruptly and a shock wave forms. The diagram shows a Mach 4 shock wave [1] at an aircraft nose-cone [2]. At the shock-front the direction of flow changes and the gas becomes more dense.

What is sound?

Sound is energy and, like other forms of energy, can be useful to man. The vast range of expression that characterizes both speech and music makes sound a highly efficient medium of communication and ultrasound – sound above the hearing range of man – is used like radar by bats, dolphins and whales. Even loud sounds do not represent a great deal of energy. A symphony orchestra playing as loudly as possible involves sound energy equivalent to the light and heat energy from only a low-powered electric lamp. Our hearing sense is more easily saturated (in energy terms) than our visual sense.

How sound is produced

Sound is a particular form of kinetic energy (energy of motion) produced when any object vibrates. Vibration is the cause of all sounds, although generally it is not visible. The sound of a car crash booms out as the surfaces of the two colliding vehicles vibrate with the force of the collision; music comes from a radio as the cone of a loudspeaker vibrates; and talking and singing result from vibrations of the vocal cords in the larynx.

As an object vibrates it sets the air molecules around it vibrating. The vibrations move out through the air, forming a sound wave, but the air does not move along with the wave. Where the air molecules gather together a region of higher pressure (compression) forms. Where they move apart a region of lower pressure (rarefaction) occurs. A succession of compressions and rarefactions move through the air as the sound wave passes. At the ear, they set the eardrum vibrating and we hear sound.

If a surface vibrates more strongly the pressure difference between the compressions and rarefactions is greater and the sound is loud [1]. The frequency of vibrations affects the pitch, or note, of the sound. If it is fast, the compressions and rarefactions are close together and the pitch is high. A slower speed of vibration causes the compressions and rarefactions to be farther apart and the sound is lower in pitch.

A sound wave moves out from its source in all directions, travelling at a speed of 331m (1,087ft) per second or 1,194km/h (741mph) in air at sea-level. The speed is slower at high altitudes as air is less dense there and faster in water and metal because these substances are more elastic than air and transmit vibrations more rapidly. Sound **cannot move through a vacuum** because there are no gas molecules to vibrate and transmit the sound.

Like other waves of energy, sound normally travels in straight lines, but sound can turn corners. It is reflected whenever it strikes a surface such as a wall [2] or floor and is diffracted or spreads out as it passes through an opening such as a window [3].

Dynamics, pitch and frequency

The loudness of a sound can be measured with a decibel meter and the result given as a number of decibels (dB). Strictly, the meter measures the intensity of the sound, which is related to the pressure differences in the sound wave. The scale is logarithmic – an increase of 10dB is produced by 10 times the intensity. Loudness varies with the cube root of intensity, so that a sound 10dB greater sounds about twice as loud. The human ear does not hear all frequencies of sound in the

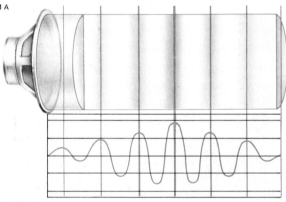

1 A sound wave consists of pressure differences, shown as dark and light bands [A]. The curve shows how pressure changes with time. This wave has a constant frequency (a single note) but decreases and increases in intensity. It would have a "wah" sound. A falling note [B] would be heard as this sound wave passes. The frequency decreases as the note becomes lower, but the intensity remains the same.

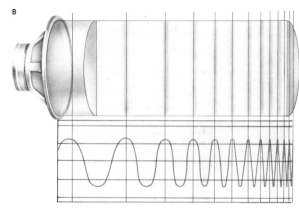

Source of sound

Window

2 The Whispering Gallery in the dome of St Paul's Cathedral in London is renowned for its acoustics. A sound whispered against the wall on one side of the gallery can be heard clearly on the other side. Being circular in shape and made of stone, the walls reflect the sound of the whisper all round the gallery and concentrate the sound at the opposite side, 32.6m (107ft) away. Normally, a whisper would be inaudible at such a distance.

3 Both reflection and diffraction enable a sound to be heard even though the person or object producing the sound is hidden from view. Sound is reflected from surfaces such as walls, floors and ceilings and, moreover, undergoes diffraction at an opening such as a door or window. As they pass the edges of the opening the sound waves spread out and hence the opening appears to be the source of the sound.

same way and a low sound is perceived as being less loud than a high sound of the same intensity.

The number of compressions that pass in every second is called the frequency of the sound wave and is measured in hertz (Hz), equal to cycles per second. This scale is not logarithmic and a note of 440Hz (the A above middle C in music) sounds twice as high as, or an octave above, one of 220Hz (the A below middle C). In other words, the higher the frequency, the higher the pitch.

Noise and acoustics

Noise does not have any particular pitch and covers a wide frequency range [4]. Very loud noise is dangerous as well as a nuisance, because continuous exposure to sound of more than 100dB – the levels produced by jet aircraft [5] and machines in many factories – soon results in a permanent reduction in hearing ability. Low-frequency noises are particularly hazardous because they do not seem to be as loud as higher sounds and tests have shown that very high levels of low-frequency sound and infrasound (sound

below the hearing range of the ear) quickly result in vertigo, nausea and other physical effects; military scientists have even conducted experiments with infrasound as a potential weapon.

Acoustic engineers work to reduce noise and improve sound in many ways. A consideration of acoustics in the design of a machine such as a jet engine can reduce the amount of noise it makes. Buildings can also be designed to prevent the transmission of sound through them. A steel framework tends to distribute sound throughout a building, but the use of soft sound-absorbing materials in and on floors, walls and ceilings prevents sound from getting into and out of rooms. In concert halls the reflection of sound inside the hall is rigorously controlled to provide an exact amount of echo and give the best quality sound [6]. This may be assisted by electronic amplification, although very loud music loses clarity in a concert hall. Some recording studios have completely absorbent walls to remove all echo and ensure total clarity whatever the type of music being played.

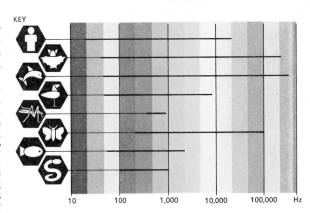

KEY

The range of hearing varies widely in man and other animals. Birds and man have fairly similar hearing ranges and both use sound to communicate. Bats and dolphins are sensitive to ultrasound (beyond human hearing), which they use to avoid obstacles and to find their prey by echo-location. There is good evidence that dolphins and other whales communicate by means of ultrasound. Night moths make use of ultrasound to avoid predators. Mosquitoes hear a narrow range of sound, corresponding to their own buzzing. The range heard by fish is also extremely small.

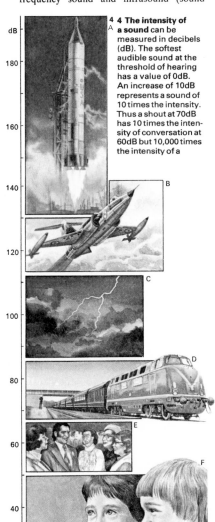

4 **The intensity of a sound** can be measured in decibels (dB). The softest audible sound at the threshold of hearing has a value of 0dB. An increase of 10dB represents a sound of 10 times the intensity. Thus a shout at 70dB has 10 times the intensity of conversation at 60dB but 10,000 times the intensity of a whisper at 30dB. The chart shows the intensity of some sounds near their sources. At 140dB sound causes pain. These fairly common sounds illustrate the range that can be heard by human beings: [A] space rocket at lift-off, 140–190dB; [B] a jet aircraft on take-off, 110–140dB; [C] thunder, 90–110dB; [D] a train, 65–90dB; [E] loud conversation, 50–65dB; [F] quiet conversation, 20–50 dB; and.[G] a rustling of dry autumn leaves, 0–10dB.

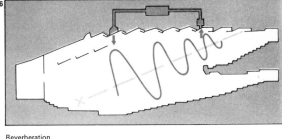

5 **Noise is a hazard,** particularly near an aircraft, and airport personnel who work on the tarmac may wear earmuffs for protection. Farther away, noise is a severe nuisance but not physically dangerous. Near an airport noise levels are about 90dB – sufficient to drown all conversation – and for miles around noise levels may be 80dB – roughly that of heavy traffic. The problem is worse when aircraft are landing than at take-off. A landing aircraft flies nearer the ground for a longer time and its noise consists of disturbing high-pitched whines. After take-off an aircraft climbs rapidly and leaves a smaller area affected; also its sound is more of a rumble. The new generation of jet aircraft – supersonic airliners excepted – have quieter engines and may affect an area only a tenth the size of that disturbed by older jet aircraft.

6 **The acoustics** of a London concert hall were altered when it was discovered that the reverberation time – the time taken for the sounds made on the stage to die away in the hall – was too short for the lower frequencies. Electronically amplified resonators were placed in the ceiling to add echo to the hall. The graph shows the reverberation time before [1] and after [2]. The result was a more balanced and pleasing sound throughout the hall.

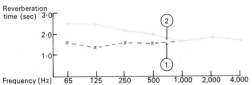

Reverberation time (sec)

Frequency (Hz)

Musical sounds

Why should one musical instrument sound so different from another? Instruments are played in various ways; some are struck, some are blown, while others are bowed or plucked to produce many kinds of sounds. But what is different about the sound itself?

Frequency and pitch

Every instrument produces a sound by making something vibrate and the frequency of the vibration is related to the pitch of the note produced. If the vibration is more rapid, the number of vibrations in the sound wave that reaches the ear (the frequency of the wave) is greater and the pitch is higher or more to the treble. If the frequency is less, the pitch will be lower or more to the bass.

The frequency of a sound wave (number of vibrations per second) is measured in hertz (Hz). The audible range of frequencies for most human beings lies between 20 and 20,000Hz. But some animals, bats and dogs for example, hear over a far wider range.

Every instrument produces a certain set of notes within a particular range of pitch. But each note is in fact a combination of

many more notes. The pitch of the main note heard by the ear is called the fundamental, and above it every instrument also produces a group of higher-pitched notes called harmonics. The harmonics are produced because the vibrating object making the sound vibrates at several frequencies at once and the extra frequencies are simple multiples of the fundamental frequency.

These higher notes can sometimes be produced deliberately on certain instruments – on brass instruments by blowing harder and on string instruments by a particular method of fingering – but normally they are not heard individually. If they were, each note on an instrument would sound like a vast chord. Instead, all the harmonics combine with the fundamental note to produce a complex waveform. Each instrument produces its own particular waveform because the relative intensity of the harmonics is different. The modern music synthesizer works by producing several waveforms of basic shapes – a sine wave, a saw-toothed wave and a square wave – and then combining them to make all kinds of sounds.

Not all instruments produce a note of definite pitch. Several, such as drums and cymbals, produce noise, which consists of a wide range of frequencies without any particular dominant frequency.

The effect of volume

Volume, or the degree of loudness, is another quality of musical sound. Music employs contrasts of volume on a large time scale for dramatic effect, but on a small time scale the change of volume at the beginning of a note is essential to the quality of a sound. The starting characteristics [3], called transients, determine whether a note begins quickly or takes some time to build up; transients are complex and involve changes in the waveform as well as in volume as the instrument begins to sound. Transients are vital to recognition; if the transients are removed from a recording of an oboe, for example, the character of its sound changes until it sounds more like a mouth organ.

Two other qualities often present in a musical sound are echo and vibrato. Echo is often believed to improve music, giving it a

1 Sound waves combine and the waveforms show that the first tuning fork [A] has twice the frequency of the second one [B]. The combination [C] produces a sound equal to the differences in frequencies and the altered shape of the waveform [green curve] shows that it has changed in tone. Two waves that are only slightly different in frequency combine to give a slow beating (pulsing) sound.

2 The waveforms of a flute [A], oboe [B] and clarinet [C] show the differences in tone of the instruments. The flute's rounded waveform indicates a gentle, fluid sound. The clarinet wave has a similar shape with "jinks" reflecting the instrument's more reedy sound. The jagged waveform of the oboe shows that its sound is even more reedy. Every note of an instrument has a fundamental

frequency but also vibrates at frequencies that are simple multiples of this, to give a range of harmonics above the fundamental. For example, G below middle C has a fundamental of 196Hz

with harmonics of 392Hz, 588Hz etc. Harmonics collectively colour the basic note by combining with it to give a complex waveform. The relative intensity of the harmonics shows that the

fundamental is less intense than some of the harmonics. But it is reinforced because the harmonics interact to give notes with frequencies equal to their differences.

1 A

B

C

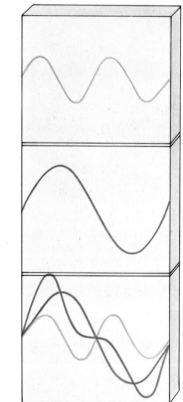

2

A

B

C

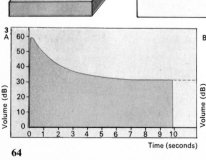

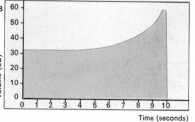

3 A

B

3 The start of a sound must be heard if it is to be recognized. The graph shows that a piano note, for example, reaches its peak volume very soon after it has been struck [A]. It then begins to fall away with great rapidity

at first, before tailing away slowly for several seconds. This is what gives the instrument its "attack". The same note produced on a gong takes a comparatively long time to build up and, although of the same pitch,

sounds completely different. The same piano note played backwards on a tape recording [B] slowly increases in volume and then suddenly stops. Shorn of its start, the sound is totally unlike a piano and rather like an organ.

more rounded sound, and it is produced by the reflections of sound from the walls of a concert hall or added artificially to recordings. Vibrato is a slight wobble in pitch that many musicians like to use; a violinist moves his left wrist to and fro to produce vibrato.

The nature of the vibrating object is the basis of family grouping of instruments. In string instruments – the violin, viola, cello, double bass, guitar, piano, harpsichord and harp – a taut string is vibrated by stroking it with a bow, plucking it with the fingers or a plectrum, or striking it with a soft hammer. A longer string produces a lower note, and the pitch of notes from an instrument is altered either by pressing the string against a fingerboard to change its length, or by playing a string of a different length. The tension and thickness of the string also affect the note, a tauter or thinner string giving a higher note.

Types of musical instruments

Wind instruments work by making a column of air vibrate. In brass instruments – the trumpet [5], trombone and horn – the player's lips vibrate in the mouthpiece. In some woodwind instruments such as the bassoon, oboe [2B] and clarinet [2C], the mouthpiece contains one or two vibrating reeds and in the flute [2A] the player blows across a hole to set the air column in the instrument vibrating. When a player presses down keys or valves, he alters the length of the air column and produces notes of different pitch [6]. Also, he can obtain some harmonics instead of the fundamental.

Some percussion instruments are played by striking either a taut skin, as in a drum, or a solid object of some kind – a disc of metal in a cymbal, for example. Tuned percussion instruments give definite pitches. They include the vibraphone [7] and xylophone, in which metal or wooden bars of different lengths are struck to sound various notes.

Electric instruments pick up the vibration of a string, as in an electric guitar, or a rod in an electric piano, and convert the vibration into an electric signal that passes to an amplifier and loudspeaker to produce the sound. Electronic instruments include the electronic organ and synthesizer, in which oscillator circuits produce electric signals.

KEY

Musical instruments, from the deepest to the highest members of each family, cover almost the entire range of human hearing. The woodwind family has a particularly wide compass, the lowest note of musical instruments, mingling the acoustic sounds of trumpet, saxophone and drums with the electric sounds of synthesizer, electric piano, bass guitar and electric guitar. the contrabassoon and the harmonics [dotted line] of the piccolo nearing the limits of audibility.

4

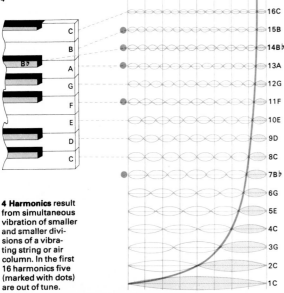

16C
15B
14B♭
13A
12G
11F
10E
9D
8C
7B♭
6G
5E
4C
3G
2C
1C

4 Harmonics result from simultaneous vibration of smaller and smaller divisions of a vibrating string or air column. In the first 16 harmonics five (marked with dots) are out of tune.

6

6 Resonance is an important part of musical sounds. It can be demonstrated with a milk bottle and a tuning fork. The fork is struck and held over the neck of the bottle. The bottle can also sound, but its frequency depends on the length of the air column inside. It is possible to "tune" the bottle by adding a liquid until the remaining air space resonates at the same frequency as the tuning fork. The sound of the fork is then much louder. Many musical instruments make use of resonance. The low-volume sound produced by the vibrating string of a violin or guitar, for example, is made much louder by the air resonating inside the accurately shaped body of the instrument.

5 A modern jazz-rock band contains all families of

5

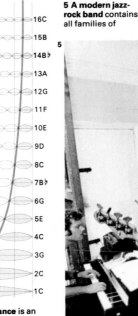

7

7 Sound production in musical instruments often involves resonance. Amplification of sound is achieved in the vibraphone in the same way as in the tuning fork and milk bottle. Beneath each bar is a tube of sufficient length to resonate at the frequency produced by the bar when it is struck. Small motor-driven fans over the top of each tube blow air into it and at slow speeds produce a "wavy" vibrato quality in the notes produced.

States of matter: gases

Everything in the world – all matter – exists in just one of three basic states. It is a gas, a liquid or a solid. Some substances can exist in all three states, depending on the temperature. Water, for example, is a liquid at ordinary temperatures. But above 100°C (212°F) it changes to a gas (steam) and below 0°C (32°F) it becomes a solid (ice).

All matter is composed of atoms or molecules and these are held together in liquids and solids by what are called intermolecular forces. The molecules are in continuous motion whose vigour depends on temperature. This "thermal motion" is restrained by the intermolecular forces of attraction, which hold the molecules together. Scientists call this view of matter the kinetic theory ("kinetic" means relating to movement or motion).

Kinetic theory of gases

In gases, thermal motion predominates and the molecules move rapidly in space, constantly colliding with each other and with the walls of their containing vessel. Collisions account for the pressure exerted by a gas [1].

Scientists have made measurements that confirm the kinetic theory of gases. At 0°C (32°F) and a pressure of 760mm (29.9in) of mercury, known as standard temperature and pressure (STP), a litre (1.75 pints) of oxygen is known to contain about 3×10^{22} (30,000 million million million) molecules. They move with a speed of about 430m/sec (1,411ft/sec). Molecules are extremely small and measured in ångström units ($1\text{Å} = 10^{-10}$m). Each oxygen molecule is 3.5Å across. The molecules are, on average, 70Å apart, and they travel about 905Å between collisions; this distance is called the mean free path.

Boyle's law and Avogadro's principle

As temperature rises the kinetic energy of the molecules (their energy of motion) increases by an amount that is proportional to the change in absolute temperature. In a mixture of gases the average kinetic energy becomes the same for each kind of molecule.

When a gas is compressed – that is, if its volume is made to change at a constant temperature – the volume is inversely proportional to the pressure. This relationship is known as Boyle's law [3] after its discoverer, the British scientist Robert Boyle (1627–91). It exists because, when the volume is reduced, collisions with the container walls become more frequent and the pressure rises. If the temperature of a gas rises but it is not allowed to expand (its volume is held constant), the pressure again increases because molecular collisions with the walls become more forceful as well as more frequent.

Another basic gas law is called Avogadro's principle after the Italian physicist Amadeo Avogadro (1776–1856). It states that, at the same temperature and pressure, equal volumes of all gases contain the same number of molecules. A litre of a dense gas such as carbon dioxide contains the same number of molecules as a litre of a light gas such as hydrogen.

Gases slowly diffuse through the walls of a porous vessel because their molecules are smaller than the minute holes in the walls of the container. The rate at which they do so is inversely proportional to the square root of

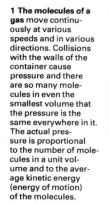

1 The molecules of a gas move continuously at various speeds and in various directions. Collisions with the walls of the container cause pressure and there are so many molecules in even the smallest volume that the pressure is the same everywhere in it. The actual pressure is proportional to the number of molecules in a unit volume and to the average kinetic energy (energy of motion) of the molecules.

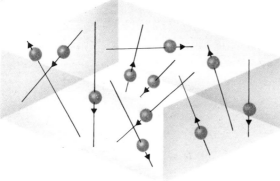

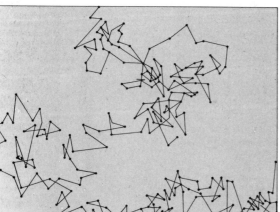

2 A compressed gas is a store of potential energy and it can be made to do useful work when it expands to atmospheric pressure, as in pneumatic drills, hammers and "guns" for spraying paint.

3 When the pressure exerted by the piston is doubled, the gas volume is halved (provided temperature does not change). This is an example of Boyle's law: pressure is inversely proportional to volume.

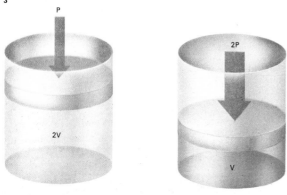

4 In this diagram of Brownian movement [A] – which is evidence for kinetic theory – the dots represent the position of a particle recorded after equal small intervals of time and the lines joining them indicate the paths taken by the random motion of the particle. A beam of sunlight passing through smoke [B] is made visible by reflection from the smoke particles. The same principle is used to view Brownian movement with a microscope.

their density. Discovered by the British physicist Thomas Graham (1805–69), this relationship is called Graham's law [7]. It is explained by the kinetic theory: if different gas molecules have the same average kinetic energy, the lighter ones must move more quickly. Thus light gases diffuse through pores more quickly than dense ones.

Brownian movement

More direct evidence for the kinetic theory is provided by the phenomenon known as Brownian movement [4]. Smoke can be seen in a sunbeam crossing a room. This effect can be produced in the laboratory by looking through a microscope at smoke particles in a box. Specks of light can be seen moving in a haphazard manner, first a short distance in one direction, then in another, and so on. The cause is unequal bombardment of the smoke particles, from different sides, by air molecules. The movement is less with larger smoke particles because they and the air molecules have the same kinetic energy, so the larger particles move more slowly.

When a gas expands it has to do work against the external pressure. As a result it becomes cooler because the necessary energy must come from the kinetic energy of the gas. This phenomenon accounts for the coldness of the air escaping from a car tyre, for example. When such a change in pressure or volume occurs without heat entering or leaving the gas it is called an adiabatic change. The pressure changes in air as a sound wave passes are adiabatic.

The amount of heat needed to raise the temperature of unit mass of a substance through 1°C is called its specific heat capacity. A gas has two principal ones: that measured at constant pressure (c_p), and one at constant volume (c_v).

Subjected to sufficient pressure most gases turn into a liquid. But above a certain "critical temperature" it is impossible to liquefy a gas using pressure alone [5]. This is because, above this temperature, the kinetic energy of the molecules is sufficient to overcome the intermolecular attractions of their neighbours. Scientists therefore apply the cooling effects of adiabatic expansion in order to liquefy gases [6].

KEY

Gasometers store coal gas or natural gas and do not, as their name suggests, merely measure quantity. They enable the pressure of the supply to consumers to be kept almost constant, even with fluctuating demand. A gasometer consists basically of a large movable cylinder with a water seal at the base.

5 A

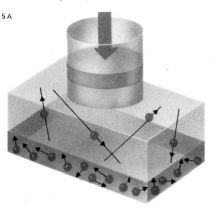

B

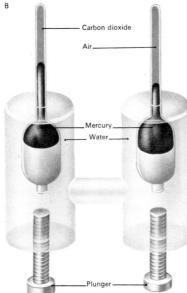

Carbon dioxide
Air
Mercury
Water
Plunger

C

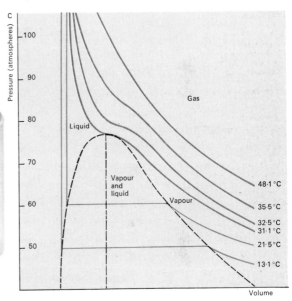

Pressure (atmospheres)

Gas
Liquid
Vapour and liquid
Vapour

48·1°C
35·5°C
32·5°C
31·1°C
21·5°C
13·1°C

Volume

5 In early attempts to liquefy gases [A] they were subjected to high pressure. Some gases liquefied under these conditions and a dynamic equilibrium was established between the liquid and vapour states – molecules left and entered the surface at the same rate. The experiments of Thomas Andrews (1813–85) [B] resulted in techniques that allowed other gases to be liquefied. Pressure is increased by screwing in the plungers and transmitted through the water to the gas and air in the upper tubes. The air is assumed to obey Boyle's law so that its change in volume is a measure of the pressure. Graphs of volume against pressure, called isothermals [C], reflect the various states of the gas. The horizontal blue line shows liquefaction and does not appear until temperature falls below 31.1°C (86°F), the critical temperature of carbon dioxide.

6 In an air liquefier, air free from water vapour and carbon dioxide is compressed and cooled by a refrigerator to −25°C (−13°F). It moves the piston part of an adiabatic engine and is further cooled to −160°C (−256°F). This air cools the other part of the high-pressure air flowing down the central pipes. Final cooling occurs by the Joule-Thomson effect as the air expands through the valve.

7

6

Refrigerator
Heat exchanger

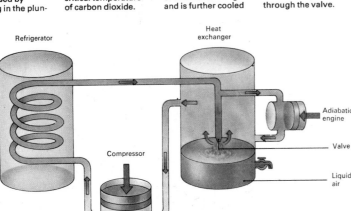

Compressor
Adiabatic engine
Valve
Liquid air

7 The rate of diffusion of a gas is inversely proportional to its density. This principle (called Graham's law) was used to separate the isotopes of uranium during World War II to make the first atomic bombs and nuclear reactors in this plant at Oak Ridge in the USA. The uranium had to be converted into its fluoride, which is a volatile solid.

States of matter: liquids

A liquid occupies a definite volume and yet it can flow. The first property is evidence that a liquid's molecules are attracted to each other, whereas the second shows that they have greater freedom than those locked in the lattice of a solid. In a liquid, the molecules vibrate continually (at a rate of a million million times a second) and they change places with each other at nearly the same rate.

A stationary liquid cannot support any stress trying to shear it (as can a solid), because the pressure at any point is the same in all directions. The actual value of the pressure is the product of the depth, the density of the liquid and the acceleration due to gravity. For this reason, solid objects can float in a liquid and even a submerged one is acted on by an upthrust equal to the weight of the liquid displaced. This fact is known as Archimedes' principle.

Structure of liquids

Scientific methods used to study the structure of solids (such as X-ray diffraction) reveal that there are sometimes small volumes in a liquid with molecules in an ordered array.

But there is no overall order as in a solid. In a hexagonal close-packed solid, for example, each molecule has 12 nearest neighbours. In a liquid the number varies between four and 11 and is continually changing.

The average distance between a liquid's molecules is greater than between those of a solid, which explains why most solids take up more room (expand) when they melt. But in a liquid the molecules cannot be squeezed close together (a liquid is almost incompressible). As a result, a liquid can transmit pressure along a pipe [5].

Evaporation and boiling

When a liquid is heated, its molecules move more and more until, at the boiling-point, the liquid turns into a gas or vapour. The heat energy needed to vaporize it is called the latent heat of vaporization. Similarly, when a liquid is cooled, its molecules move less quickly until they take up fixed positions and the liquid freezes into a solid. The heat needed to melt a frozen solid back to a liquid at the same temperature is called the latent heat of fusion.

Even at ordinary temperatures (below boiling-point) some molecules "jump" out of the surface of a liquid to form vapour – they evaporate. In a closed vessel there is an equilibrium between a liquid and its saturated vapour; the rate at which molecules leave the liquid is the same as that at which they re-enter it.

When a liquid boils, some work has to be done by the escaping vapour to overcome atmospheric pressure. If the pressure on a liquid is reduced it boils at a lower temperature. If the pressure is increased the boiling-point rises. But if there are no tiny particles in the liquid on which vapour can form bubbles, boiling is suppressed. This effect causes the "bumping" that takes place when pure water is boiled and is the principle of the liquid hydrogen bubble chamber [6]. Water does not follow many of the general rules that apply to liquids [3]. Most substances expand by between five and 15 per cent on melting, for instance, but water contracts by about ten per cent and expands on freezing. These properties arise from the highly directional nature of intermolecular forces in water (due to hyd-

1 At the surface [A], the force between a liquid's molecules causes the surface to behave like a stretched membrane. The surface in a glass container [B] curves depending on whether the glass attracts liquid weakly (eg mercury [1]) or strongly (eg water [2]). An oily liquid [C] adhering to cloth [3] is weakly attracted by water [4]; a detergent forms a new surface layer [5] attracted to both (detergent [6] is partly oil-like and partly salt-like). Some detergents [D] prevent gas bubbles [7] collapsing, making it possible [E] to separate ore [8] clinging to them from earth and sand [9] by flotation.

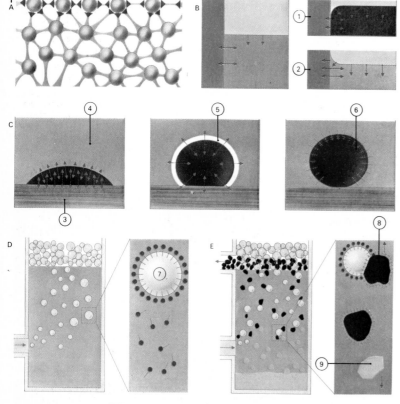

2 Oil is a prime source of energy and chemicals, and huge quantities of crude oil are carried in tankers from the producing countries to highly industrialized ones, such as the USA, Japan and Western Europe. By Archimedes' principle a tanker displaces its own weight of seawater in order to float and the cargo (oil) is less dense than water. The tanker sinks slightly deeper in warmer water and on the return journey water ballast is carried in the tanks to keep the vessel stable. If a mishap occurs, escaping oil floats on the water: oil slicks are a form of pollution.

3 In all materials the atoms or molecules are in continuous motion. The energy of this motion depends on the temperature. In a liquid, the motion prevents any permanent intermolecular structure from forming, but forces of attraction govern the overall volume. In water there are many temporary linkages (shown blue) between the molecules; very small cavities [1] form and vanish, giving water an ever-changing structure.

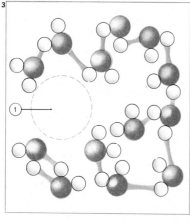

4 All the molecules in a liquid exert attractive forces on their immediate neighbours. Within the main body of the liquid the effects of these attractions cancel each other out. But on the surface the attraction can take place only inwards (there are no molecules outside the surface to counteract it). As a result the surface is in tension. This surface tension behaves like a "skin" which pulls a droplet of water into a spherical shape.

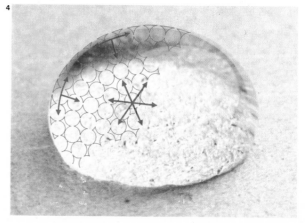

rogen bonding). In the solid state (ice) it produces a very open structure, which disappears on melting. Water has its maximum density at about 4°C (39°F), probably due to a crystal-like ordering of small groups of molecules which disappears on warming.

Surface tension and viscosity
In the centre of a liquid each molecule is attracted by all those surrounding it and their net effect is zero. But at the surface there can be no upward forces to balance the attractive downward forces. As a result a surface molecule tends to be pulled into the body of the liquid [4]. The number of molecules at the surface becomes the smallest possible, and the surface behaves as if it were in tension and had a "skin" on it. The membranous effect of surface tension allows small, dense objects, such as needles or insects, to "float" on the surface of water. If the cohesive forces of attraction between a liquid's molecules are large, it has a high surface tension and a large viscosity (stickiness).

Water wets glass because the cohesive force between a water molecule and a glass molecule is greater than that between two water molecules [1]. The opposite is true of glass and a liquid such as mercury. A liquid such as water rises in a fine capillary tube dipped into it and the meniscus (shape of the surface) curves inwards, or is concave. Mercury, on the other hand, is depressed in a capillary tube and possesses a convex (outward curving) meniscus.

Water pours more easily from a jar than does treacle and treacle is said to be more viscous than water. A simple model of what happens shows one layer of liquid molecules under a shearing stress sliding over another layer. For this to happen any molecule in the faster-moving layer must overcome the attraction of the nearest one in the adjoining layer. And having moved one place along the line it must repeat the process. To do this it must use some energy and this slows it down. The relative velocity between the layers is reduced and the result is viscosity. Heating a liquid provides it with more energy and, as expected, viscosity falls with increasing temperature. For this reason, warm treacle pours more easily than cold treacle.

Various liquids differ in their physical properties such as boiling-point and viscosity (stickiness). Water and wine have roughly the same boiling point and low viscosity. Oil is more viscous and boils at a higher temperature whereas exceptionally viscous liquids such as honey and tomato ketchup have extremely high boiling temperatures.

5 Liquids are almost incompressible and as a result can transmit pressure. This important principle finds many applications in the branch of engineering called hydraulics. Many trucks have an hydraulic jack in which pressure transmitted by means of oil is used to tilt the load. A pump is used to provide the pressure and provision has to be made for the oil to run back when the pressure is released.

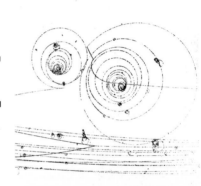

6 In a bubble chamber, a dust-free liquid in a perfectly clean vessel is heated to a temperature above its boiling-point and extra pressure is applied to stabilize it. If charged particles are then directed into the chamber, bubbles form on the charged "nuclei" left by the particle along its track, making it visible. Liquid hydrogen is generally used as it is a good source of protons on which bubbles can form.

7 A water drop at the end of a glass tube takes its shape because of surface tension. The attraction between its molecules leads to a spherical shape as the "skin" effect caused by inward-acting forces in the surface holds the bulk of the liquid back. But a water droplet becomes a distorted sphere because gravitational as well as surface tension forces are acting on it.

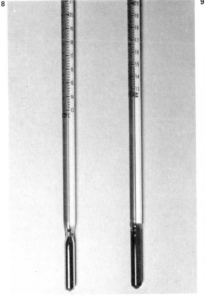

8 The most common method of measuring temperature makes use of the expansion of a liquid on heating. A mercury thermometer (left) has a wide range (−39°C to 360°C), but needs a large bulb (reservoir) and a narrow stem if small temperature changes are to be detected. Alcohol can be used in thermometers for measuring lower temperatures; it expands more, but boils at 78°C. The great advantage of liquid-in-glass thermometers is that they can be read directly and carried easily.

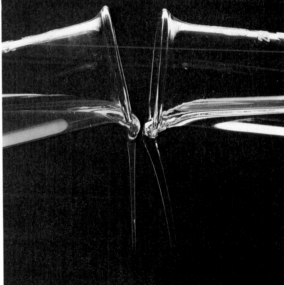

9 Motor oil is more viscous than water, as can be seen when each is poured; the water flows much more easily than oil because layers of water molecules slide over each other more easily than do layers of oil molecules. Normally, the viscosity of a liquid decreases with rise in temperature. Oil for a particular application must have the right lubricating properties and much research has been done to produce the correct oils for car engines and gear-boxes, including oils whose viscosities change only a little when they get hot. When a liquid flows in a pipe in stream-lined motion, the region in contact with the pipe is still and that near the axis has the greatest velocity.

States of matter: solids

The crystalline shapes of many solids indicate that the atoms in them take up some kind of regular arrangement. In the amorphous or non-crystalline substance, there is no regular order. There are seven main crystalline structures, of which the cubic system is the simplest. Sodium chloride (common salt) is composed of sodium ions and chloride ions. In the solid salt these ions take up what is called a face-centred cubic structure. This and other arrangements can be confirmed by making the crystals diffract an X-ray beam, then experts can use such X-ray photographs to work out the structures of complex crystals.

Sodium chloride is an example of an ionic crystalline substance. Other crystalline substances, such as diamond, consist of a regular array of atoms linked to each other by covalent chemical bonds, in which one or more electrons are shared between neighbouring atoms. In waxes and similar substances, molecules are held together only weakly by what are called Van der Waals' forces. And a metal has a lattice of positive ions in which free electrons occupy the spaces. Applying a voltage across the metal makes electrons drift between the ions, which is the reason why metals and their alloys are good conductors of heat and electricity.

Vibrating and slipping atoms
All intermolecular forces can be thought of as electrical in origin, causing attraction between molecules at relatively large distances and causing repulsion at close quarters. The elastic properties of solids can be explained in terms of such forces. When a material is stretched, the distances between its atoms increase slightly and the resulting strain is found to be proportional to the stress producing it (the relationship known as Hooke's law). Compression moves the atoms closer together, while shearing makes layers of atoms slide over each other.

The atoms in a solid – even a crystalline one – vibrate about their average position in the lattice. Heating a pure solid makes its atoms vibrate more vigorously. Sufficient heat energy overcomes the forces holding the atoms together, the crystalline structure "falls apart" and the solid melts.

A single crystal of a pure metal is much weaker than might be expected. This may be due to imperfections in the lattice which cause dislocations [7]. Under stress, the layers of atoms move in such a way that the dislocation shifts towards the edge. An ordinary metal is polycrystalline, consisting of an irregular arrangement of many small crystals. Stress makes layers of atoms in individual crystals slip over each other. But atoms of an impurity within a crystal can "anchor" dislocations and prevent slipping. Consequently an alloy is usually harder than the two or more metals of which it is composed.

Metal fatigue: cause and cure
Strain deforms some solids over a period of time in the phenomenon called creep. This can be due to the movement of dislocations in crystalline grains, slip between grain boundaries, or slip along well-defined glide planes. "Fatigue" is the name given to a change in metallic properties that may result in sudden breakage. It resembles work-hardening (caused by hammering) in that dislocations in crystallites interlock, causing brittleness.

Scientists can make thin fibres of sub-

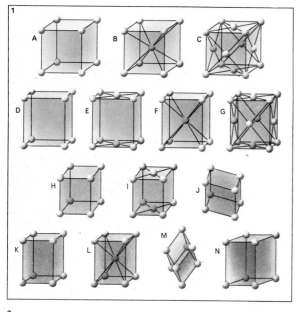

1 **Crystals** are formed by the regular stacking of identical building blocks. The elementary block is called a unit cell and may contain a single atom, such as in copper, or it may contain hundreds or thousands of many different types, as in some protein crystals. The regularities and symmetries in crystals are a great help in identifying and solving their structure. The unit cells of all crystals can be classified into one of 14 basic types called space lattices. They are conveniently grouped into seven systems: cubic [A, B and C] orthorhombic [D, E, F and G], monoclinic [H and I], triclinic [J], tetragonal [K and L], trigonal [M] and hexagonal [N].

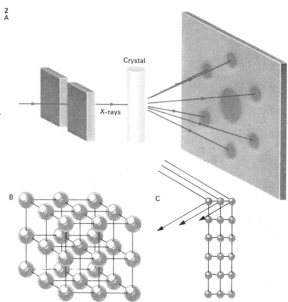

2 **X-rays** diffract from the periodic regular array of unit cells in a crystal to produce a pattern of diffraction spots [A]. X-ray waves reflecting from successive planes need to be a whole number of wavelengths out of step in order to produce a diffraction spot [C]. Symmetries and regularities in the pattern help the crystallographer to decide which type of unit cell is present. For instance the diffraction pattern in [A] shows hexagonal symmetry, so a unit cell such as those in [B] cannot be present. From the relative intensities of the spots and their phases one can calculate the crystal structure.

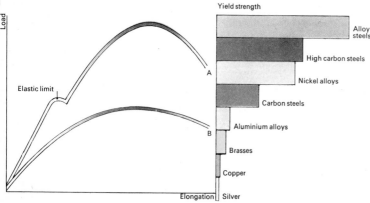

3 **Tensile strength** is tested by stretching. A metal extends overall at first, but later expansion concentrates around the point of fracture. Curves A and B show typical extensions. Curve A, for mild steel, remains linear to its elastic limit. If the load is released early, the metal returns to its original length. Curve B is typical of softer metals. A range of relative strengths of metals is also shown (right).

4 **Engineers** use high-grade steel girders in their work because good steel is usually highly resistant to cracking. If a crack does appear, the metal is generally ductile enough for the edges of the crack to flow together, which will diminish the danger of the crack extending far. In poor steels cracks may develop rapidly. This is a particular danger in bridges where the steel has to resist changes in temperature.

stances free from any dislocations. Called whiskers, they are very strong and when incorporated into a matrix of another substance produce a strong composite material.

Structural effects in solids

Molecules in natural and man-made polymers have a complex arrangement. X-ray photographs reveal that, when rubber is stretched, its coiled long-chain molecules line up. When tension is released, the molecules snap back into their former shapes, and as a result giving rubber its elasticity. Similarly a stretching process during the manufacture of nylon lines up long chains of molecules.

Semiconductors – the key to modern solid-state devices such as transistors – make use of subtle variations in an otherwise normal crystal lattice. The basic element, such as silicon or germanium, has incorporated in it minute traces of a deliberately introduced impurity element. The impurity has either one more or one fewer electron in its atoms than the basic semiconductor element. As a result, there is a slight excess of electrons or a slight deficiency (an absence of an electron is in this context called a "hole"), and it is the movement of these electrons or holes that gives the materials their special electrical properties. When extra electrons are present the semiconductor has negatively charged current carriers and so is called an *n*-type semiconductor. The holes in the second type are considered to be positive carriers and it is called *p*-type.

X-ray diffraction enables scientists to study the microstructure of solids. Other methods reveal the overall or macrostructure. The grain structure of a metal, for example, can be revealed by etching the surface and viewing it by reflected light through an optical microscope.

Higher magnifications are possible using an electron microscope. Scientists make a copy of the etched surface by depositing on it a layer of carbon or plastic and stripping it off as a thin film to be viewed with the microscope. They may use a very thin foil of the metal to be studied. The fine structure of the surface is revealed in three-dimensional detail by a scanning electron microscope.

KEY

Seen through a microscope, salt crystals are revealed as regular cubes. Perfect – that is, unbroken – crystals have precise shapes (although here tumbling of the crystals has knocked the corners off some of them). There are six other basic shapes.

5 Metalworkers hammer sheet metals to harden them without making them brittle. The hammering moves dislocations along intersecting slip planes until they meet and stop. These meeting places act as barriers to the movement of any other dislocations, making the metal stronger.

6 Foundryworkers separate metals from ores by smelting them. Metals are heated to break down the lattice of atoms so that the metal flows. They are poured into moulds or cooled and rolled into sheets. Melting-points of metals range from mercury which melts at −38.8°C (−38°F) to tungsten which melts at 3,410°C (6,170°F).

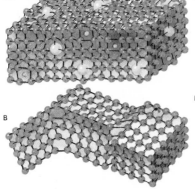

7 Strong metals restrict the free movement of dislocations. A metallurgist may achieve a strong metal by making an alloy, or he may make the metal's crystals as small as possible. In A, large atoms are at the crystal corners and small ones in the lattice centre, distorting the whole crystal and preventing any free dislocation movement. In B the crystal boundaries are mismatched and they too have the effect of creating barriers against dislocation movement.

Where dislocation of the atomic lattice occurs, or where there is slipping between grain boundaries and along glide planes, the metal will fail. Frequently repeated strains and fluctuating loads may eventually cause metal fatigue [C]. The edges of the fractures may show signs of metallurgical recrystallization. Strain over a long period produces a similar effect, called creep failure [D]. The example of failures C and D occurred in a nickel alloy turbine blade.

8 Increased pressure lowers the melting-point in substances such as water, which expand when they solidify. Ice melting under the pressure of a skate acts as a lubricant that makes the skater's motion both smooth and easy.

Heat and temperature

A bicycle pump becomes warm when pumping up a tyre, an effect that can be explained by the kinetic theory of heat, first suspected by Isaac Newton (1642–1727) and developed by eighteenth and nineteenth century scientists. The theory describes heat as the kinetic energy (energy of motion) of the vibrating atoms or molecules that make up every substance. In the bicycle pump, air molecules are speeded up by collisions with the pump's piston. The increase in their kinetic energy takes the form of heat.

Thermal agitation and molecular motion

According to the third law of thermodynamics, absolute zero – the temperature (−273·16°C) at which molecules cease all motion – is unobtainable. As a result, molecules perform a continuous motion known as "thermal agitation", which increases in vigour as heat is transferred to an object. Indirect evidence of this incessant motion was first obtained by the botanist Robert Brown (1773–1858) in 1827. He discovered that tiny pollen grains suspended in water were continually making jerky movements. It is the continual unequal bombardment of each tiny speck by the molecules of the liquid that produces this "Brownian motion". The smaller the particle, the more violent is the motion.

The kinetic theory also explains why, when a hot gas is mixed with a cooler one, a common temperature is eventually reached. Molecular kinetic energy of the hot gas molecules is transferred by thousands of collisions to the cold gas molecules, until the average kinetic energies of both gases are the same. The molecules all travel with different velocities, changing after each collision. For this reason the temperature of the gas (or other substance) is a measure of the average molecular kinetic energy.

The changes of state that may occur when a substance is heated can be described by the kinetic theory [1]. In a solid, the atoms or molecules are tightly bound together and vibrate only about an average position. As the solid is heated its internal kinetic energy increases and the particles vibrate more vigorously. They move farther and farther apart until eventually the attraction between them is insufficient to keep them in a fixed position. They can then slide about and exchange partners – the solid melts and a liquid is formed. The heat needed to achieve this change of state from tightly bound solid to loosely bound liquid at the same temperature is called the latent heat of fusion. If yet more heat is applied, the atoms or molecules gain more kinetic energy, move with greater velocity within the liquid and the proportion of these escaping from the surface increases (vapour pressure increases). Eventually, at the boiling-point, so many atoms have enough energy to escape from the liquid that the vapour pressure equals atmospheric pressure. In the gaseous state the atoms or molecules move almost independently; the conversion of a liquid at its boiling-point into a gas requires latent heat of vaporization.

Changes of temperature

Instead of changing the state of a substance (for which latent heat is needed), applied heat energy may merely raise its temperature. The temperature change depends directly on the quantity of heat transferred

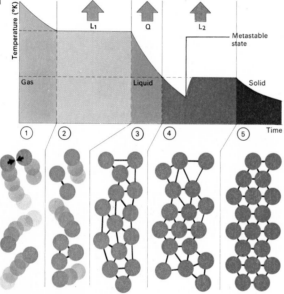

1 Vibration of atoms and molecules in a substance governs its temperature. In a gas [1] atoms move independently and their average velocity and mass determine the internal energy and temperature. After cooling, loss of latent heat of condensation [L₁] converts the gas at boiling-point to a liquid state [2] when its atoms become locked in a weakly bonded arrangement. Further cooling [3] to freezing-point loses a quantity of heat [Q] and a solid then forms through [4] release of latent heat of fusion [L₂]; the atoms then become rigidly bonded together [5]. A colder "metastable" phase can precede actual freezing.

2 The three ways in which heat moves all take place when a pan is heated [A] – conduction through the metal walls of the pan [1], convection by fluid motion [2] and radiation from the heat source to the pan [3]. In theory an insulated good conductor with ice at one end and boiling water at the other varies in temperature linearly with distance along the bar [B], as in the straight-line graph. With poor insulation a curve like the dotted line results. A vacuum flask [C] has a vacuum [4] to prevent conduction and convection and silvered walls [5], to minimize heat loss by radiation.

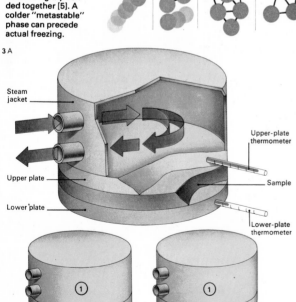

3 Conductivity is the amount of heat passing in unit time across unit cross-section per unit of temperature gradient. It can be measured [A] by noting the time taken for a known quantity of heat to pass through a sample. Two plates of equal area [2] are put against the material [3]. Thermometers on each side measure the temperatures as the upper plate is heated by a steam jacket [1]. Materials of high conductivity [B] are tested in a cylinder [8] heated at one end by steam [4] to 100°C [5]. Other thermometers [6] measure the temperature of the sample and the rise in temperature of water circulating through a jacket attached to the other end [7], and give a way of calculating conductivity.

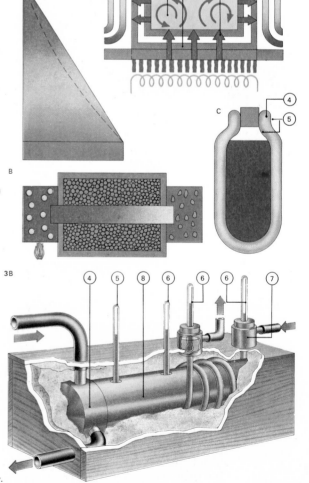

3 A

Steam jacket

Upper plate

Lower plate

Upper-plate thermometer

Sample

Lower-plate thermometer

and this is measured in units called calories or joules (4.2 joules=1 calorie). The calorie is defined as the quantity of heat that raises the temperature of 1 gramme of water by 1°C. So the quantity of heat needed to raise the temperature of 1 gramme of any substance by 1°C can be measured in these units – and this is called the specific heat of the substance. The quantity of heat that raises the whole bulk of substance by 1°C is called the thermal capacity of the given mass.

It is possible for heat to be transferred from place to place and there are three ways in which this can occur: by conduction, convection and radiation [2]. The first two methods rely on the fact that atoms that have received kinetic energy from a heat source can, in collision, transmit this to their neighbours. In a tightly bound solid only nearest-neighbour collisions occur and any heat transfer through the solid is called conduction. In a fluid (liquid or gas), the medium itself can move and transport atoms of high kinetic energy to the cooler parts of the fluid where they then transfer their heat – this is convection. Even when no physical contact

exists between atoms, heat can still be transferred. For instance, heat from the Sun reaches the Earth through the near vacuum of space. This method is radiation. Different substances conduct heat at different rates. Their ability to transmit heat is known as their thermal conductivity [3].

Measuring temperature

All methods of measuring temperature changes are based on the ways in which materials change physically when heated. The most commonly used characteristic is the expansion of solids or liquids when heated. Usually the physical change caused by a temperature change is made visible against a calibrated scale on the measuring instrument or thermometer. In making any type of thermometer [5, 6, 7], two constant temperatures or "fixed points" must first be marked. The range between them can then be subdivided as finely as desired. The numbers assigned to the fixed points and the numbers of degrees between them define the temperature scale, such as Celsius (or centigrade), Fahrenheit and Kelvin (or absolute) [4].

A furnace converts the chemical energy in coal to heat energy used to produce the steam that drives an engine. The heat of the furnace brings the water to its boiling-point and provides latent heat of vaporization to turn it into steam.

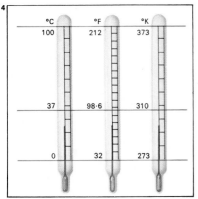

4 Temperature scales are arbitrary both in their range and in their division into degrees. The freezing-point of water is set at 32° Fahrenheit (°F), 0° Celsius or centigrade (°C) and 273° Kelvin (°K). Between this point and the boiling-point of water there are 180°F, 100°C and 100°K. The Kelvin scale is unique in setting its lowest fixed point at absolute zero, which in practice is unobtainable.

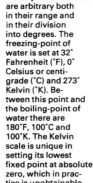

5 A / B / C

5 The indicators in a maximum and minimum thermometer [A] are pushed along by mercury in a U-tube and stay put at the farthest point of travel. Liquid in a cylindrical reservoir senses the temperature and its contraction [B] or expansion [C] displaces the mercury along scales at each side of the U. The steel indicators can be reset simply by moving a small magnet along the outside of the tube.

6 A bimetallic strip thermometer uses a helical metal strip that unwinds when heated and rotates a pointer over a calibrated scale. When warmed, the inner metal (usually copper) expands more than the outer one, so causing the bimetallic strip to unwind. The material used for the outer strip is usually Invar, an alloy of iron and nickel, which has a low coefficient of thermal expansion.

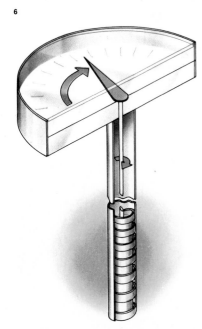

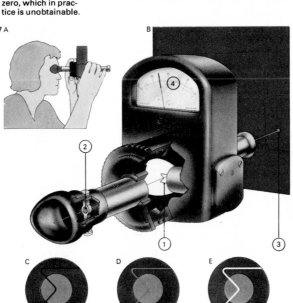

7 A / B

C / D / E

7 An optical pyrometer allows very high temperatures to be measured at a distance from the temperature source [A]. It exploits the fact that two solids at the same high temperature radiate light with the same spectrum and show the same colour. To measure the heat of a furnace [B], an electrically heated filament [1] fixed in the tube of a telescope with a special lens [2] is heated until it glows with the same colour as that emitted by the furnace [3]. Comparison with the background image shows if the furnace is hotter [C], as hot [D] or colder [E] than the wire. A meter [4] indicates the current passing through the wire and this can be calibrated directly in temperature degrees.

8 Liquid air can be produced by cooling air, which is normally gaseous at room temperature. During the change to a liquid state, latent heat of condensation is released. To cut down heat input the liquid is kept in a Dewar vacuum flask. But if it is poured out of this flask, heat from the surroundings makes the liquid boil rapidly. Large amounts of gas are generated during this process and cause a fog of condensed water vapour to form above the liquid.

Order and disorder: thermodynamics

Thermodynamics (meaning "the movement of heat") deals with the ways in which heat energy travels from one place to another and how heat is converted into other forms of energy. In a heat-transfer process temperature, pressure and volume may each or all undergo various changes. Much of thermodynamics consists of ways of mathematically manipulating these and other parameters to be able to make predictions about the ways in which they will and do change.

The four laws of thermodynamics

Historically scientists first derived three laws called the first, second and third laws of thermodynamics. Then an even more fundamental law was recognized. It has been labelled the "zeroth" law of thermodynamics.

If a hot and a cold object are brought into contact, they finally reach the same temperature [1]. The hot object emits more heat energy than it receives and the cold object has a net absorption of heat. Both objects absorb and emit energy continually, although in unequal quantities, and the exchange process continues until the temperatures

equalize. Each object is then absorbing and emitting equal amounts of heat and the objects are said to be in "thermal equilibrium". The zeroth law states that, if two objects are each in thermal equilibrium with a third object, then they are in thermal equilibrium with each other.

The first law really has two parts – the first is the law of conservation of energy and the second effectively defines "heat energy" and how types of energy can be converted into one another [2]. If heat energy is supplied to a system, then the first law states that this equals the change of internal energy of the system together with the mechanical energy that allows the system to do external work. Thus in a petrol engine an air/petrol vapour mixture is ignited after being compressed. The burning of the mixture releases heat energy from the chemical reaction, thereby causing the gases to expand and do work against the piston by moving it. The burned gases are finally hotter than the system was before the explosion, so there is a change in the internal energy of the petrol engine system. The sum of this energy change and

the external work done equals the released heat energy.

Following the zeroth law, which defines temperature, and the first law, which describes energy conversion, the second law of thermodynamics governs the direction of flow of heat energy between objects at different temperatures. It says that, of its own accord, heat can flow only from a hot to a cold object. The heat transfer increases the motion of the molecules of which the colder object is composed and so effectively increases its internal "disorder".

Cooling substances

The third law of thermodynamics states that it is impossible to cool any substance to absolute zero. This zero of temperature would occur for example in a gas whose pressure was zero. All its molecules would have stopped moving and possess zero energy, so that extracting further energy and achieving corresponding cooling would be impossible. A substance becomes progressively more difficult to cool as its temperature approaches absolute zero ($-273 \cdot 16°C$).

1 The thermic lance produces enormously high temperatures. If it is directed on to a substance the intense heat rapidly melts the substance in the region of the lance so that the substance becomes fluid and can be carved at will as the lance advances. Here a lance is being used to cut through a huge concrete block.

2 Friction occurs whenever two surfaces rub together, and this in turn generates heat. The sudden surge of power at the beginning of a dragster race spins a car's rear wheels and the heat generated burns the rubber of the tyres. Similar heating occurs in a car's brakes when they are used.

3 Carbon dioxide, released as a solid from a fire extinguisher, turns into a gaseous form and prevents oxygen reaching the fire.

4 Heat can be converted to mechanical work by allowing a heated gas to expand. Maximum efficiency comes from the Carnot cycle of alternate adiabatic [BC, DA] and isothermal [AB,CD] processes. The former take place without gaining or losing heat, the latter without changing temperature. From A to C the gas raises the piston and performs work equal to the area below the curve, that is, $V_A ABCV_C$. From C to A it uses work equal to area $V_A ADCV_C$. The net work obtained equals area ABCD.

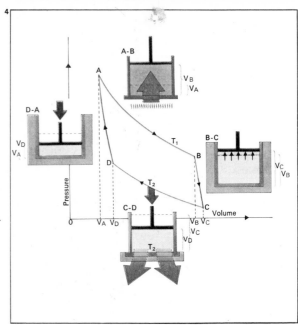

From the statement of the second law, a heat transfer process naturally proceeds "downhill" – from a hotter to a cooler object. There must be some property or parameter of the system that is a measure of its internal state (its order or disorder), and which has different values at the start and the end of a possible process (one allowed by the first law). This parameter is termed "entropy", and the second law maintains that the entropy of an isolated system can only remain constant or increase.

Careful observation of machines shows that they consume more energy than they convert to useful work. Even if no energy is wasted in friction or lost by necessity, as in a radiator, the available mechanical energy is less than that supplied by the heat source. The entropy of the system is a reflection of its inaccessible energy, and the second law says that it cannot decrease. Heat is a random motion of atoms and when the energy is degraded towards the inaccessible energy pool, these atoms assume a more disorderly state – and entropy is a measure of this disorder.

Under the constraints imposed by the laws of thermodynamics it is possible for a system to undergo a series of changes of its state (in terms of its pressure, volume and temperature). In some cases the series ends with a return to the initial state, useful work having been done during the series.

Heat cycles and efficiency

The sequence of changes of the system is called a heat cycle and the theoretical maximum efficiency for such a "heat engine" would be obtained from following the so-called Carnot cycle [4] which is named after the Frenchman Nicholas Carnot (1796–1832). If it were possible to construct a machine operating in cycles which, in any number of complete cycles, would generate more energy in the form of work than was supplied to it in the form of heat then the dream of the perpetual motion machine would be possible [5]. The first law states the impossibility of achieving this result and the second law denies the possibility of even merely converting all the heat to an exactly equivalent amount of mechanical work.

KEY
A flame applied to one end of a metal bar transfers heat energy to the atoms of the metal. This **raises their kinetic** energy so that the **atoms begin to vibrate** much more vigorously about their
fixed mean positions within the lattice network of the metal. As the extent of vibration increases, collisions with neighbouring atoms occur so that energy is transferred to these atoms causing them to vibrate. Heat energy is eventually transmitted to the other end of the bar and if the flame is kept in position for some time the temperature at each end of the bar will tend to equalize.

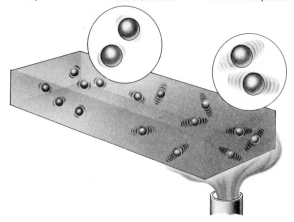

5

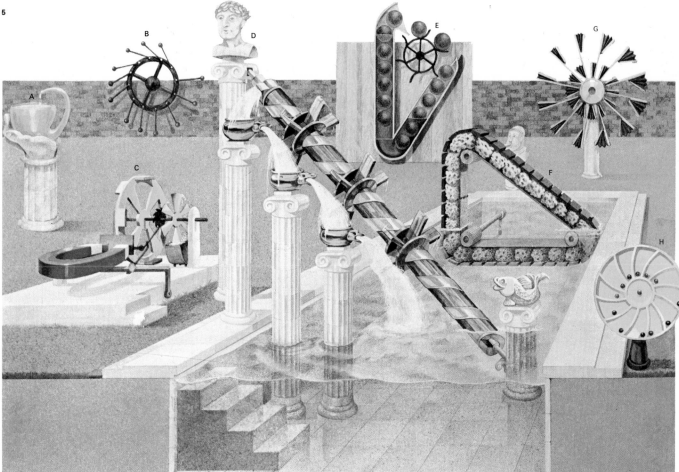

5 Perpetual motion machines can be classified according to which of the laws of thermodynamics they attempt to violate. The continual operation of a machine that creates its own energy and thus violates the first law would be called a perpetual motion machine of the first kind. There is nothing in the first law to preclude turning the heat of the ocean completely into work and hence drive a cargo ship across the ocean. The second law insists that some of the heat utilised be given up to a heat reservoir at a lower temperature. Thus the temperature difference between the top and bottom of the ocean could be used to do work providing some heat is given up to the colder sea water. If not then the second law is violated, and this machine would be an example of perpetual motion of the second kind. The machines illustrated here are nearly all stopped by friction and not by the laws of thermodynamics. Some may apparently work in defiance of the laws but on closer inspection an unexpected source of energy can be found. Device A uses capillary action to overcome gravity but would exchange heat with the atmosphere in the process. The validity of the laws of thermodynamics has been demonstrated by countless indirect scientific experiments, and no perpetual motion machines have been produced that contravene them. A device could conceivably exist that might be kept in motion without violating these two laws, with only dissipative forces such as friction to slow it down. If the device could be made frictionless then its continual motion would be termed perpetual motion of the third kind. Machines B to H all attempt to gain something for nothing using an apparently greater leverage on one side of a device to turn it. The reasoning behind these attempts to break the first law is faulty and they would remain stationary even without friction. Machines C, D, E, and F had the added dissipative forces of water viscosity or magnetic eddy currents to overcome. Historically thermodynamics was devised for machines containing millions of molecules. Yet single protein molecular machines obey the same laws.

Towards absolute zero

Every substance contains a certain amount of heat, even a relatively cold substance such as ice. The heat is the result of the continual motion of the substance's molecules which, by that motion, possess kinetic energy. Temperature is a measurement of the average kinetic energy of the molecules. The cooler a substance becomes the less its molecules move. Thus it should be possible to continue cooling to the point at which molecular movement ceases completely. This point, "absolute zero", is of great interest to scientists but in practice is unattainable. At temperatures close to absolute zero some materials exhibit remarkable properties, such as superconductivity [6] and superfluidity [Key].

Calculation of absolute zero
On the centigrade temperature scale, absolute zero is 273.16 degrees below the freezing-point of water. Its value can be predicted as a result of the behaviour of gases when they are heated or cooled. When heated, a "perfect" gas expands in volume (V) proportionally to its absolute temperature (T) if its pressure (P) is kept constant. Its pressure increases in the same proportion if its volume is kept constant. The reverse occurs on cooling, according to the equation $PV = RT$ where R is known as the universal gas constant. The pressure actually falls by a factor of 1/273.16 for every 1°C temperature decrease. Thus at −273.16°C zero pressure would be reached and this must be the absolute zero of temperature.

Absolute zero is usually denoted as 0° on the Kelvin scale of temperature, named after the British scientist William Thomson, Baron Kelvin of Largs (1824–1907). Its temperature increments equal those on the centigrade or Celsius scale [1]. Thus 0°K is the same as −273°C (absolute zero temperature is usually rounded to −273°C, or −460° on the Fahrenheit scale) and 273°K equals 0°C – the freezing-point of pure water.

Aiming at absolute zero
Gas temperatures can be lowered by first compressing the gas in a fixed-volume enclosure and then removing the resultant heat with, for example, a surrounding water jacket. If the gas is then allowed to escape into a larger volume it becomes even cooler because its molecules lose kinetic energy during the expansion. This cycle is used in a refrigerator and can liquefy and even freeze many gases.

The gas most useful in experiments at very low temperatures has been helium, the gas with the lowest boiling-point, 4.2°K (−269°C). The temperature of liquid helium can be further reduced to 1°K by vacuum pumping the gas above the level of the liquid to reduce its pressure and thereby force down the boiling-point. Liquid helium is generally produced in an air liquefaction plant as one of the rare gases left after oxygen and nitrogen have been liquefied [2].

Below 1°K it is difficult to achieve further cooling and a low-temperature effect that occurs in some solids is used [3]. Some salts act as magnets when immersed in a strong magnetic field but stop being magnetic when the field is removed, a phenomenon known as paramagnetism. When the salt is magnetized its molecules line up in the field but are disarranged when the

1 The temperatures on this diagram are stated in both the Kelvin (absolute) and Celsius (centigrade) scales, below a temperature equivalent to the melting-point of ice in equilibrium with water.

°C	°K	
0	273	Water freezes
−7	266	Bromine freezes
−33	240	Ammonia boils
−39	234	Mercury freezes
−107	166	Xenon boils
−112	161	Xenon freezes
−152	121	Krypton boils
−183	90	Oxygen boils
−186	87	Argon boils
−196	77	Nitrogen boils
−210	63	Nitrogen freezes
−218	55	Oxygen freezes
−240	33	Critical point of hydrogen
−246	27	Neon boils
−253	20	Hydrogen boils
−269	4	Helium boils
−272	1	
−273	0	Helium freezes under pressure

Absolute zero

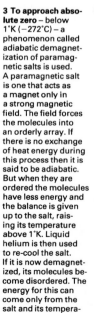

2 In a helium liquefier, which can be carried by road [A], a mixture of helium gas and air is first compressed and the heat generated removed. Air contains, in addition to oxygen and nitrogen, other "inert" gases such as argon, neon, krypton and xenon. At about 20°K all the gases of air except helium can be liquefied in the separator [B]. The helium can be expanded through a nozzle and liquefied.

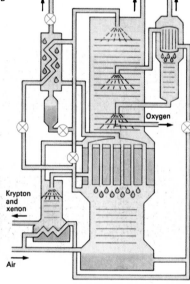

B

Helium and neon
Nitrogen   Argon
Oxygen
Krypton and xenon
Air

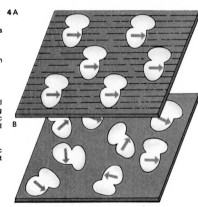

3 To approach absolute zero – below 1°K (−272°C) – a phenomenon called adiabatic demagnetization of paramagnetic salts is used. A paramagnetic salt is one that acts as a magnet only in a strong magnetic field. The field forces the molecules into an orderly array. If there is no exchange of heat energy during this process then it is said to be adiabatic. But when they are ordered the molecules have less energy and the balance is given up to the salt, raising its temperature above 1°K. Liquid helium is then used to re-cool the salt. If it is now demagnetized, its molecules become disordered. The energy for this can come only from the salt and its temperature falls below 1°K.

To pumps
Liquid helium
Coil producing magnetic field
Paramagnetic salt
Liquid hydrogen coolant

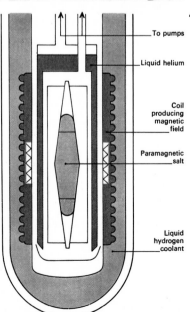

4 A

B

4 The molecules of a paramagnetic salt are normally in continual disordered motion, even if the temperature is as low as 1°K (−272°C). As long as the molecules behave in this way there is no part of the salt that appears to be like either pole of a magnet. As soon as the salt is placed in a magnetic field [A], however, the molecular magnets line up along the field and endow the bulk substance with north and south magnetic poles. Molecular disorder returns when the field is removed [B].

field is removed [4]. If a paramagnetic solid is cooled to 1°K by liquid helium that is allowed to evaporate, heat energy is removed from the solid. When a strong magnetic field is switched on, the molecules align themselves and create heat by their motion. This is removed by the surrounding helium gas, which is pumped away. When the field is switched off, the molecules become disordered and cause a further lowering of the solid's internal energy. The cold salt can then absorb heat from a second helium container. A cycle of magnetization and demagnetization can produce temperatures of a few thousandths of a degree Kelvin.

Superfluidity and superconductivity

Liquid helium at very low temperatures is not only difficult to produce but behaves in a most unusual way. Fast boiling occurs as the vapour pressure falls but at 2.18°K the internal bubbling of helium gas suddenly ceases, although boiling continues. Below this so-called "lambda point" liquid helium exhibits "superfluidic" properties [Key].

Near absolute zero, certain substances show remarkable properties; for example, a kind of perpetual motion in electric current becomes possible – that is, some metals and alloys exhibit superconductivity [6]. As their temperature is lowered (for example, to 7.2°K for lead) the electrical resistance of the material disappears completely. If an electric current can be made to flow in a ring of such metal it continues to flow. Current has been kept flowing unattenuated in this way for up to several years.

Superconductivity was discovered by the Dutch physicist Heike Kamerlingh Onnes (1853–1926). It can theoretically be used as the basis for some computer memories, for once stored in a superconductor, information remains unaltered. A magnetic field of sufficient strength can destroy the superconducting state and this effect can be used to achieve a high-speed current-switching facility. As a superconducting material has zero electrical resistance, very high currents can pass through it. As a result, superconducting windings for electromagnets can be used to generate extremely powerful magnetic fields.

KEY

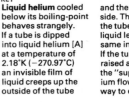

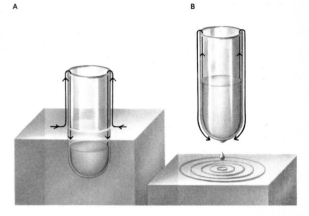

Liquid helium cooled below its boiling-point behaves strangely. If a tube is dipped into liquid helium [A] at a temperature of 2.18°K (−270.97°C) an invisible film of liquid creeps up the outside of the tube and then down the inside. The helium fills the tube until the liquid levels are the same inside and out. If the tube is raised a little [B] the "superfluid" helium flows the other way to equalize the levels. Drops of the liquid drip off the bottom of the tube. The thickness of the liquid film can be measured (by light polarization) as about 3 millionths of a centimetre at a height of 1cm above the liquid.

A

B

5 Liquid air has a temperature of only 83°K (−190°C) and thus a flower dipped in it will solidify completely as all the fluid in its cells freezes [A]. When this happens the flower becomes so brittle that it can be broken into small pieces with a blow from a hammer [B]. Liquid air is used industrially for freezing other substances and for the commercial production of oxygen and nitrogen.

6 The superconducting magnets [A] of a particle accelerator, such as those used in the giant proton synchrotron at CERN in Geneva, Switzerland [B], are products of low-temperature physics. Normally superconductivity is destroyed by a high magnetic field. But materials such as niobium-zirconium alloy, with distorted crystal structures, remain superconductive in fields of up to 100 thousand gauss.

6 A

5 A

B

6B

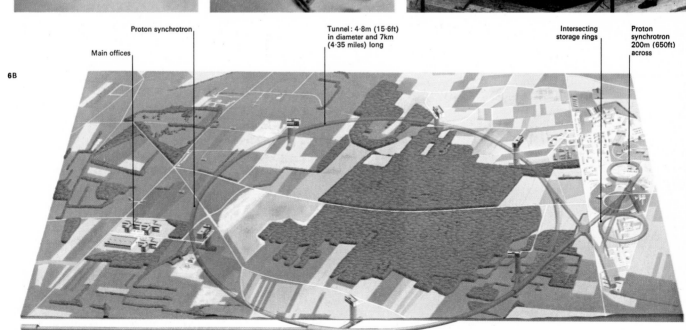

Main offices

Proton synchrotron

Tunnel: 4·8m (15·6ft) in diameter and 7km (4·35 miles) long

Intersecting storage rings

Proton synchrotron 200m (650ft) across

Extremes of pressure

The extremes of pressure – ultra-high vacuum (low pressure) and very high pressure – have varied and sometimes remarkable effects on different materials.

Matter exists as either solid, liquid or gas, and all are compressible to various degrees. Perfect gases are compressible to almost any extent, following at low pressures Boyle's law (which states that the volume of a gas varies inversely with its pressure). But liquids are much less compressible and the changes in their volume brought about by pressure follow no simple law.

Solids are the least compressible. Their rigid structure, in which atoms have their mean separation distance fixed by very strong forces, is the most resistant to externally applied pressure. Their structure can be distorted or destroyed by sufficiently high pressures, but the way in which they actually behave is governed by their internal atomic or molecular arrangement.

The compressibility of a gas can be calculated by its equation of state, but that of a liquid or a solid has to be determined experimentally. For the liquid metal mercury at 0°C (32°F), for example, it has been shown that the volume changes by less than one-millionth part over a pressure range of 0–7,340 kg/cm² (0–7,000 atmospheres).

Effects of pressure

Pressure applied to any substance can, under certain conditions, cause a change of state. Thus below a certain critical temperature pressure can turn a gas to liquid.

Extremely high pressures find many industrial applications. Hydraulically generated and transmitted pressures are employed for lifting extremely heavy loads. In the motor industry they are used to press completely shaped car body panels [3] from flat metal sheet. The behaviour of metals under compression is also the basis for processes involving rolling and forging. Again, if sufficiently high pressures are brought to bear, metal enters what is called its "plastic" range. That means that the metal continues to yield (ie, to extend its dimensions), even though the load applied remains constant. In the normal elastic range, the dimensions change in direct proportion to the applied load and return to normal when the load is removed. The plastic property is used in processes such as extrusion [2], but enormous pressures must be applied to achieve it.

At the other end of the pressure range is the vaccum, which can be of varying degree. To obtain a vacuum, gas atoms or molecules are removed from an enclosed vessel. The number of intermolecular collisions is correspondingly reduced and thus there is a reduction in the internal energy and pressure of the gas.

The creation of vacuums is not, however, limited to vessels that previously contained nothing but gas. A partial vaccum can also be achieved above the surface of a liquid – but the space is filled by the vapour of the liquid. As the gas pressure above the liquid is reduced by pumping, the liquid boils at a lower temperature than it does at atmospheric (that is, normal) pressure.

Vacuums in industry

As with high pressures, high vacuum states also have many industrial uses. The process of vacuum deposition by evaporation allows

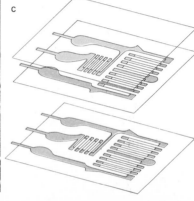

1 The pressures operating on large structures, such as the bridge spanning the Severn [A], are measured by an electrical strain gauge [B]. This device uses the phenomenom (first noted by Lord Kelvin in 1856) that if a wire is strained, its electrical resistance is changed. The principle was first employed practically in the United States in 1938 and now the strain gauge is the most common instrument used for analysis of stress. Gauges can consist of a grid of fine metal wire that is then bonded to a thin backing but, more commonly, a grid of wire filaments is obtained by printing onto a metal foil [C]. In either case, the gauge is cemented onto the structural surface and changes in its resistance are measured; the readings are then recorded automatically.

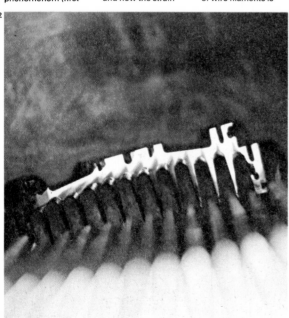

2 Metal forms of complicated shapes can be made by the process of extrusion. Cold metal is forced through a hole of the required shape and size and the great pressures exerted on the metal cause it to assume a "plastic" condition, so that it is able to "flow" smoothly through the extrusion die, as in this machine.

3 Hydraulic presses can make shaped body panels, in one stage, from single flat sheets of metal. A piston carries a former of the shape required and then a hydraulic ram presses this against the metal sheet with tremendous force. The high pressures generally needed call for costly presses, but their speed justifies the expense.

solid objects to be thinly coated with metal [4]. Here, the object to be coated is placed in an enclosed vessel that can maintain a high vacuum. When the coating metal is vaporized within that vessel, it forms a thin mirror-like film over the object.

There are other manufacturing processes in which the controlled deposition of impurities on substances or objects is performed by means of high vacuums. Sophisticated electronic circuitry is based upon this use of an ultra-high vacuum [5].

But technological processes are not the only applications of extremes of pressure. Given that all substances are compressible to some degree, consideration of the effects of increasing pressure on materials to be used in construction work is obviously important. Compression and tension tests of various building materials provide the necessary information and increase our knowledge of the extremes of stresses and strains sustainable by different substances.

The behaviour of materials under the two extremes of pressure is well demonstrated in the varying conditions of space. Extremely high vacuum conditions exist in interstellar space, with probably only a few atoms per cubic centimetre. Separate chemical radicals have been found in interplanetary space.

Pressure and gravitation
During the early evolution of stars, clouds of gas and dust (nebulae) condense under the influence of gravitation. Heat is generated, leading to a build up of high internal pressures that tend to resist further gravitational contraction. Compression ceases when these opposing forces of pressure and gravitation are in balance.

Within the stars, the radiation temperatures and pressures are extremely high. At the centre of the Sun the temperature is probably about 10 million °C (18 million °F) and the density fifty times that of water; the pressure amounts to about 400,000 million kg/cm^2 (6 million million lb per sq in).

In other stars, the pressures can be so great that the normal arrangement of an atom is completely broken. Protons and electrons are squashed together, creating immense densities of several tonnes per cm^3.

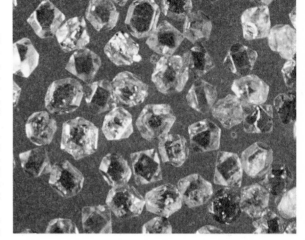

Artificial diamonds are produced when graphite is subjected to very high pressures and temperatures. Most of the stones are inferior to those that have been produced by nature.

4 Vacuum deposition is widely used to form metal coatings on plastic objects. The object to be so treated is enclosed in a chamber [A], along with a wire filament carrying beads of the metal that is to be deposited. Then the chamber is pumped down to a very low pressure and an electric current is passed through the wire. The beads melt, vaporize and deposit a metal film on the objects [B].

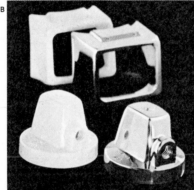

5 Silicon "chips" can be modified by the use of high-vacuum methods so that whole electronic circuits can be integrated into a single piece. To achieve this, certain "impurities" are diffused into or layered onto the base material; these impurities affect the conductivity of the base and perform equivalent functions to electronic components such as transistors, diodes, capacitors and resistors. The pure silicon base is held in a vacuum during the implantation or layering process. Connections to the circuit are made by fine wires welded to it from gold-plated contacts.

6 Testing materials to destruction is often necessary to discover their real strengths and their weaknesses. These tests are carried out in a machine that is capable of exerting both compressive and tensile (pulling) forces and it records automatically the applied pressure on the material at the very instant of its failure. Such tests are not confined to ductile metals (those that can be drawn out as wire), but also applied to brittle materials such as this fibreglass.

7 Young stars and a large nebula are seen in the region of Messier 8. In the cluster on the left, star formation appears to be almost complete and very high pressures, accompanied by intense internal heat, prevent the stars from collapsing further.

Light and colour

We are surrounded by various forms of energy, namely light, heat, chemical and mechanical energy. Of these, light is as necessary as heat energy and chemical energy – and all are essential to life; few sightless people can survive without the aid of people who can see. By virtue of its basic nature light enables people to sense the world around them in great detail. This is because light consists of a wave motion of extremely high frequency. If human beings were sensitive instead to radio waves, which have a much lower frequency than light, they would detect no more detail in their surroundings than the blurred outlines seen on a radar screen.

How light travels
Light travels in waves, as sound does. In light the vibrations of the wave consist of vibrating electric and magnetic fields, whereas in sound they are vibrations of a medium such as air or water. Both kinds of waves may vary in intensity, producing stronger vibrations. In sound an increase in intensity causes an increase in loudness and in light it produces an increase in brightness.

Light waves also possess a range of frequencies – the number of vibrations passing every second. In sound, people hear different frequencies as sounds of different pitch; in light they see different colours. Blue light, for example, has a higher frequency than red light. Light may also be considered in terms of wavelength – the distance between successive vibrations in a wave; blue light has a shorter wavelength than red light. Light frequencies are very high and the wavelengths are very short (about 55 millionths of a centimetre).

Paint manufacturers include white and black among their ranges of colours, but these are not strictly colours at all. Black is simply an absence of light and therefore of colour and white light is made up of a mixture of several basic colours. This can be shown by passing sunlight through a prism. The white light of the sun is split up into a band of colours called a spectrum. The spectrum looks exactly like a rainbow [5], which is no coincidence because raindrops act as prisms and split up sunlight to produce a rainbow. The beam of colours from a prism can be made to

recombine and produce white light once more. This is a proof that white light is a mixture of all the colours.

The science of spectroscopy
Splitting up light to form a spectrum is important in science [Key]. Different elements glow with different colours when they are heated sufficiently or subjected to an electric discharge – examples are gases in sodium street lights or neon advertising signs. By passing the light from a glowing substance through a prism and examining the resulting spectrum, which has a different pattern for different elements, the glowing substance can be identified. This is useful in all kinds of analysis, but particularly in finding out which elements are present in the Sun and the stars. This branch of science is called spectroscopy.

Most of the colour that reaches our eyes comes from objects that are naturally coloured, painted or dyed. When white light strikes the surface of a red object, red light is reflected from it, but all the other colours in the white light are absorbed by the surface. Colour is also produced in other ways. A sub-

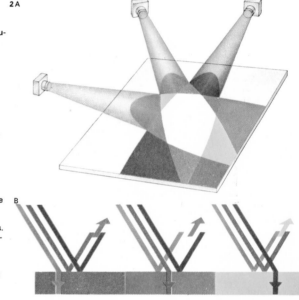

1 Colour is used as a means of imparting simple information quickly and unambiguously. On the road, for example, red tail-lights on cars indicate "stop" or "danger".

2 Mixing colours depends on whether coloured lights or pigments are being used. Lights combine by additive mixing [A] in which three basic or primary colours, red, green and blue, combine to give white. Yellow, cyan and magenta are secondary colours formed by mixing equally two primaries. Pigment colours combine by subtractive mixing [B] in which some colour is absorbed before mixing of the remaining colours occurs.

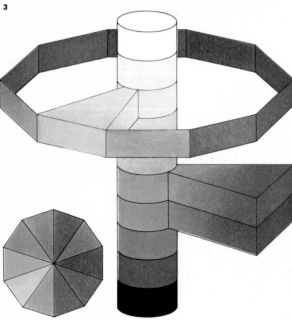

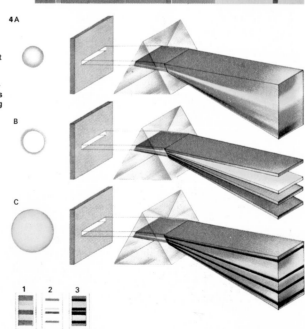

3 The Munsell colour tree is a system of grading any colour. The hue (basic colour), chroma (amount of colour) and value (degree of lightness or darkness) are measured and the colour's position found among all those in the tree. Hue is denoted by its place on the circumference of the tree; chroma by its distance from the trunk; value by its place up the trunk.

4 A solid or plasma under pressure heated to incandescence emits a continuous spectrum [A]. At low pressure a gas produces an emission spectrum [B]. In the Sun [C], light from the inside [1] is partly absorbed as it passes through the outer regions [2] to form an absorption spectrum [3].

stance can be heated so much that it glows with colour and luminous compounds such as the phosphors in a colour television screen light up with colour when they are struck by invisible cathode rays (beams of electrons) or ultra-violet rays.

Humans (and many other animals) can perceive colour because the retina in the eye contains three kinds of light sensors. These detect different ranges of light frequencies, roughly corresponding to red, green and blue. All other colours can be produced by combining light of these three basic colours in various amounts. Red and green combine to produce yellow; green and blue to give cyan; and blue and red to make magenta. All three basic colours combine to give white light.

Additive and subtractive mixing

It may seem strange, to anyone used to mixing red and green on a paint brush and obtaining brown, to read that red and green make yellow. This is because coloured lights and coloured paints combine in different ways. A colour television set produces coloured light and close examination of a lit screen reveals that it contains patterns of red, green and blue dots or stripes. At a distance the dots or stripes merge into a colour picture. But close up, the yellow light can be seen to be made up of red light and green light. This kind of colour mixing, in which light combines directly, is called additive mixing [2]. Any three coloured lights, such as red, green and blue, that combine to form any other desired colour or in the right proportions to form white light are known as the primary colours.

In producing colours by mixing paints, dyes and inks, subtractive mixing occurs [2]. The colours form not by mixing the three basic colours directly, but by absorbing some of them from the light that illuminates the surface of a painted object. Thus yellow paint absorbs blue from the illuminating white light but reflects red and green, which combine to reach the eye as yellow. Cyan paint absorbs red light, leaving blue and green to mix and make cyan. Mixing yellow and cyan subtracts red and blue from the white light, but leaves green to be reflected: so cyan and yellow paints mix to give green.

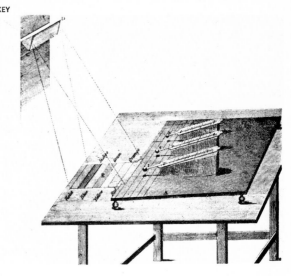

Dispersion of light by a prism produces a spectrum of colours. In 1800 the British astronomer William Herschel placed thermometers just beyond the red end of the spectrum and observed a rise in temperature. He deduced that the prism was dispersing invisible heat rays (now called infra-red rays).

5A

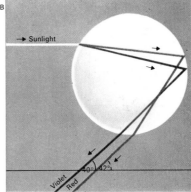

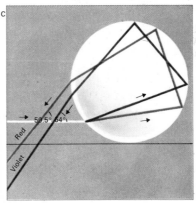

5 A rainbow is a natural demonstration of the mixture of colours, or wavelengths that make up white light. Drops of moisture in the atmosphere act as prisms, dispersing the light into its component colours. The observer sees the various colours of the spectrum emerging from many droplets. The completeness of the rainbow he sees depends on his position between the Sun and the drops of moisture and on his horizon; from aircraft at high altitudes a circle can be seen. Sometimes two rainbows are visible (A): an inner – called a primary bow – and a larger outer one, or secondary bow. The colours are in opposite sequence in the two rainbows. In the primary (B), light is dispersed on entering a rain-drop, and the colours reflected from the back of the drop towards the observer. Some rays may be reflected twice within the drop (C) to produce a reversal of the colours in the secondary.

6

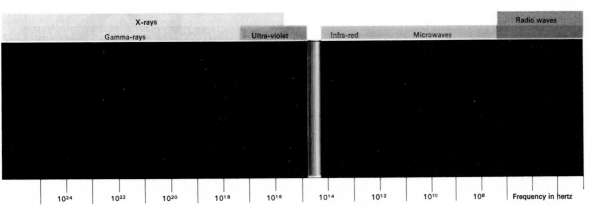

6 The spectrum of visible light is only a small part of the much greater spectrum of all electromagnetic radiation. Beyond the blue end lie the invisible ultra-violet rays, X-rays and gamma-rays, while infra-red rays (heat rays), microwaves and radio waves lie beyond the red end. All electromagnetic radiation has the power to penetrate matter to a certain extent. High frequency radiation – that is, X-rays and gamma-rays – penetrates most.

Mirrors and lenses

Nearly everyone looks in a mirror at least once a day and people with less than perfect vision spend most of their lives looking through spectacle or contact lenses. Telescopes, binoculars, microscopes, cameras and projectors help us to examine the world about us in far more detail than can be perceived by the unaided human eye. All these visual aids and optical instruments use mirrors or lenses. They work using the simple laws of optics, but before these laws and their application can be understood it is necessary to appreciate how an image is formed.

Light rays and images
Any illuminated or luminous object sends out light rays that spread in all directions in straight lines. An image forms if any of the light rays coming from the same point on the object happen to meet. Normally images do not form because there is nothing to bend the light rays to make them meet, but a lens will do this. The image produced can be seen on a card or a screen placed at the point where the rays meet. If the rays meet exactly a sharp image is formed and the image is said to be in

focus. It is known as a real image and is the kind produced in a camera or by a projector. If the incoming light rays are parallel, the image is produced at a distance called the focal length of the lens.

Plane (flat) mirrors, on the other hand, produce images that cannot be shown on a screen. In this case the light rays are bent but they continue to become farther apart (diverge) rather than closer together (converge). But the human brain always assumes that light rays reach the eyes in a straight line, and we therefore see an image at the point that the object would be occupying if the rays were not bent [6]. This kind of image is called a virtual image and it is always sharp.

Except when illuminating the deepest black objects, light is reflected from every surface it strikes. A dull or matt surface scatters the rays at all angles. But a very smooth surface acts as a mirror and reflects all rays so that the angle of incidence equals the angle of reflection. A plane mirror, being flat, bends all the rays that strike it by the same angle and so a virtual image, unchanged in size and shape, is seen in it. Left and right are inter-

changed because a light ray leaving one side of the object is reflected by the mirror to the opposite side of the eye from the one it would otherwise strike [1].

Curved mirrors [2] produce images changed in size and shape. A convex mirror, one that bends outwards towards the observer, gives a smaller virtual image. It makes the rays diverge more than if they came from a plane mirror, producing a smaller virtual image behind the mirror. A concave (inward-bending) mirror may make the rays from the object converge, giving a real image in front of the mirror. If the object is very close, the rays diverge less than with a plane mirror, giving a magnified virtual image behind the mirror.

Bending of light
If light rays meet a transparent object most of the rays enter the object and emerge from the other side. The rays are bent as they pass through the surfaces, being deflected away from the surface if they are entering a denser medium and towards the surface if they are leaving a denser medium. This effect is called

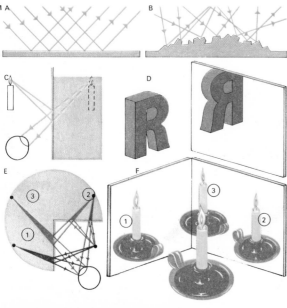

1 A plane mirror reflects all light rays at the same angle [A] whereas a matt surface [B] scatters light. The brain imagines that light rays reaching the eye from a mirror come to it in straight lines and it therefore sees an image at that point where the rays would originate if their paths were not bent by the mirror [C]. The image is seen laterally inverted [D], because the reflected rays reach opposite sides of the eye. An image can be seen right way round in two plane mirrors at right-angles [E]. Although an image reflected once appears laterally inverted [1, 2], one reflected twice [3] is seen correctly [F].

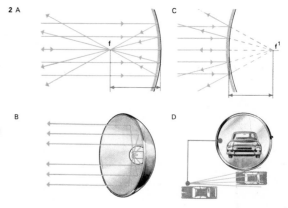

2 Curved mirrors form real and virtual images. A concave mirror [A] reflects the rays of a parallel beam of light so that they converge and meet at the focus of the mirror [f]. A real image of a distant object will be formed on a screen placed at the focus. Also, if a light source is placed at the focus, a parallel beam of light is given. The reflector of a car headlamp works in this way [B]. A convex mirror [C] makes the rays of a parallel beam diverge as if they were coming from the focus [f¹], which produces a diminished virtual image, as in a driving mirror [D].

3 Lenses form images because light rays are bent by refraction as they pass through a lens. The rays are made to converge on passing through a convex lens [1] or diverge through a concave lens [2], regardless of the direction in which the rays are moving. Thus convex lenses can make light rays meet and produce real images, whereas concave lenses give only virtual images.

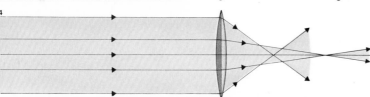

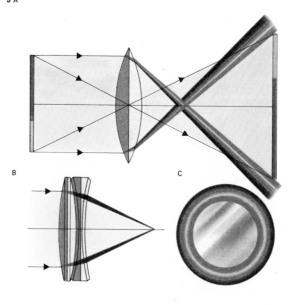

4 Spherical aberration produces a blurred image. Rays passing through the centre of the lens are brought to a focus at a different point from rays passing through the edge of the lens and there is no place at which all the rays come to a single focus and give a sharp image. Spherical aberration may be reduced by narrowing the lens so that rays do not pass through the edges and by combining lenses to cancel out the defects in each kind of lens.

5 Chromatic aberration produces coloured fringes around the lens edges, and parts of the image may not be sharp [C]. This aberration occurs with single lenses because they behave like prisms and bend blue light more than red light [A]. Combining the lens with a weaker concave lens [B] made of a different glass cancels out this dispersion effect, and both red and blue rays are brought to the same focus to produce a sharper, more distinct image.

refraction. Some of the light is reflected instead of being refracted. If, on leaving the denser medium, the light rays strike a surface at or below a certain angle, called the critical angle, they are all reflected back (none is refracted) and the light stays inside the denser medium. The amount of bending depends on the refractive index of the medium; the greater the refractive index the greater the amount of bending.

Refraction and lenses

Refraction explains why objects seen in water appear to be less deep than they really are. Light rays from the submerged object bend as they leave the water but the eye, as always, imagines that the rays have come in straight lines from the object.

Lenses work by refraction [3] and are shaped to bend the light rays passing through them by different amounts. In a convex lens – one in which the surfaces curve outwards – light rays passing through converge and meet to form a real image. The lenses in a camera, a projector and in the eye work in this way. But if the object is very close to the lens,

the light rays diverge after passing through the lens. When viewed from the other side, a large virtual image of the object will be seen behind the lens. This is how a magnifying glass works. Concave lenses – which curve inwards – make light rays diverge and produce small virtual images. These lenses are used in spectacles to correct short sight, converging lenses being necessary for long sight.

Single lenses produce several kinds of aberrations [4, 5], or distortions, of the image. Coloured fringes may be seen around the edges, and parts of the image may not be sharp. When several lenses are combined the aberration is reduced by cancelling out defects in each kind of lens, and high-quality lenses consist of several different elements grouped together to give a perfect image. Each element has to be carefully shaped and positioned with great accuracy.

Most optical instruments use lenses to produce images [8, 9, 10]. But the largest telescopes used in observatories all have a concave mirror to produce a real image of a distant planet, and this image is then viewed with a magnifying lens to enlarge it.

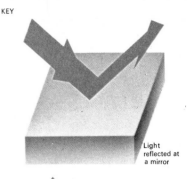

Mirrors and lenses alter the paths of light rays in accordance with simple laws. A mirror reflects light rays so they leave the mirror at the same angle as they strike the mirror. The brain assumes that the light rays reaching the eye have travelled from an object in straight lines, and it therefore sees an image behind the mirror. A transparent material refracts light passing through it so that the path of the rays is bent at the surface by a certain angle, which depends on the refractive index of the material. The brain assumes that light moves only in straight lines and the image it sees of an object is displaced.

Light reflected at a mirror

Light refracted through a glass block

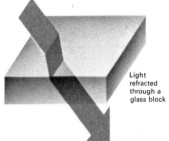

6

(A) (B) (C)

6 Images form when the eye receives light rays coming from the same point on an object and bends them to meet at the retina. The tree reflects light rays in all directions. The eye may see it directly [A], see a virtual image of the tree "behind" a mirror [B] or view a real image of it formed on a screen by a lens [C]. The images are located at the points from which the light rays appear to originate.

7 A periscope, in its most simple form, consists of two mirrors angled at 45° one above the other so that an image is reflected from the top of the instrument down to the observer at its base. A submarine periscope works on the same principle, but has prisms instead of mirrors and a system of lenses to produce a magnified image or a wide field of view. Optical adjustments can be made with the handles.

7
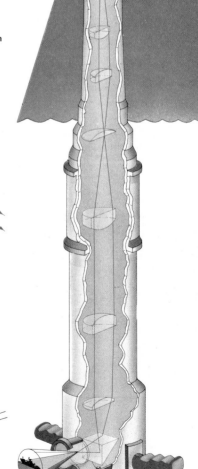

8 In a microscope an image of the specimen is formed by the objective lens and this image is then viewed by the eyepiece lens so that it is magnified and an extremely close view obtained.

1 The field lens forming part of the objective
2 The eye lens of the eyepiece
3 Specimen placed on the glass slide
4 The objective of the eyepiece
5 The microscope effectively increases the angle at which

light, from the specimen, enters the eye, and the final virtual image appears to lie in this plane
6 Mirror reflects light on to specimen

9
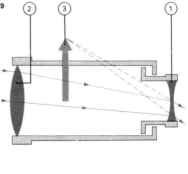

8
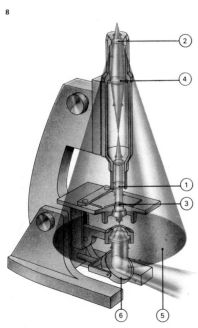

9 Opera glasses have a pair of telescopes known as Galilean telescopes. The concave eyepiece lens [1] is placed inside the focus of the convex objective lens [2] to obtain a magnified upright image [3] of the object. The lenses have low-power magnification. Galileo discovered the moons of Jupiter using a similar instrument.

10 An astronomical telescope has a similar optical system to a microscope. It consists of an objective lens [1] (of focal length f_o) and an eyepiece lens [2] (of focal length f_e). Parallel light from a distant object converges to form an inverted image [3]. Light rays then appear to come from the large upside-down image [4].

10

f_o f_e

Light waves

In the seventeenth century scientists were divided in their opinions about the nature of light. Some believed it to be made up of streams of particles of some kind, while others argued that it consisted of waves. Reflection was easy to explain by the particle theory; it could be pictured as a bouncing of particles off surfaces rather as balls bounce from the sides of a billiard table. (The modern form of this theory envisages light travelling as "packets" of energy called photons.) Refraction was more difficult to explain – why should some particles bounce off and others pass through a surface? Other effects were impossible to account for by the particle theory and the wave nature of light became accepted as more convincing.

The wave motion of light
In those early days no one knew exactly what vibrated in light to make it behave as a wave motion, nor how the waves could be produced. These problems began to be solved in the 1870s. It was discovered that a light wave consists of vibrating electric and magnetic fields travelling through space; the two fields vibrate at right-angles to each other and to the direction of motion. In fact light waves are part of a whole group of electromagnetic waves that include X-rays, ultra-violet rays, infra-red rays and radio waves. Light waves can be produced by changing the orbits of electrons inside atoms. If an atom receives energy in some way – perhaps as heat, light or electrical energy for example – the electrons move away from the nucleus to orbits of higher energy. They then jump to a lower energy orbit and give out energy in the form of electromagnetic waves as they do so. In this way objects produce light [1].

Light spreads out from any point producing it or reflecting it in ever-expanding spheres, rather as ripples spread out in circles over a pond. Each ray of light can be thought of as moving in a straight line, producing a continuous series of ever-expanding vibrational movements through space. In all the rays leaving a point the vibrations add up to give a set of spherical wavefronts consisting of alternate peaks and troughs of energy. Each peak and trough are maxima of vibration but in opposite directions.

The shadow of an object is rarely seen to have sharp edges, but this is because a source of light always has a certain size [Key]. If the source were infinitely small we would expect it to give shadows that are totally sharp because light rays are considered as straight lines, but this is not so. All waves spread round the edge of an object – an effect called diffraction [2]. In the case of light the edge is illuminated and points close to it can act as sources of light waves that spread out in all directions so that the rays are effectively bent by the edge. The wavelength of light is so short that this effect is hard to detect at edges, but it becomes clearly apparent when light passes through very small openings about the same size as the wavelength. This happens in a diffraction grating [3] in which light passes through or is reflected from extremely narrow slits.

The effects of interference
The wavefronts that spread out from the two edges of the opening cross each other. Where two peaks of the waves meet, an increase in brightness occurs, but where a peak meets a

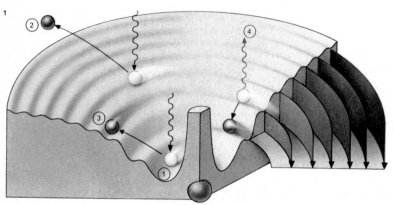

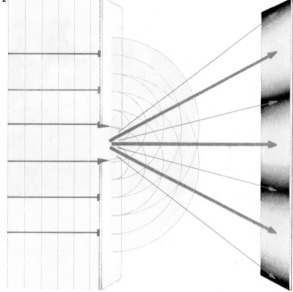

1 Light production can occur when electrons accelerate or when atoms lose energy. In an atom an electron can be pictured as circling the nucleus in a certain orbit (1). If the atom absorbs energy the electron may escape (2) or move to a higher orbit (3). It may then fall to a lower one, giving out visible (4) or invisible radiation depending on the energy gap between the two orbits.

2 Diffraction occurs when a wave passes an edge, causing it to spread around that edge. Often this effect is too slight to be noticed, but it is marked when waves pass through an opening of the same size as the wavelength (with light, about 55 millionths of a centimetre). The light waves spread out from the edges of the opening and patterns of light and dark are formed where they cross.

3 A diffraction grating has a fine mesh. When white light passes through it is bent in many directions and split up into a spectrum of colours: each wavelength is bent a different amount.

4 Interference occurs when two waves of the same wavelength [1, 2] travel over the same path. The waves interact to give a new light wave [3]. If the waves are in phase [A] the new wave is brighter than either of the original waves. If they are slightly out of phase [B] the new wave has about the same brightness as the original waves. If they are totally out of phase [C] the peaks and troughs cancel each other out and so no new wave is produced.

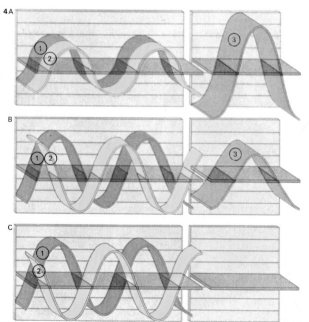

trough they cancel each other out so that no vibration occurs and there is no light. As a result a series of light and dark fringes is produced instead of a single image of the opening [2]. This effect, in which waves reinforce each other or cancel each other out, is called interference [4].

If a ray of light is divided into two rays that later recombine then interference effects are seen if one of the divided rays travels a longer path than the other before the recombination. The peaks and troughs may be out of phase (not exactly 'together) and the light is affected. This happens between two surfaces that are very close together, as in a thin film or two pieces of glass pressed together, and it produces colourful fringed patterns [5]. The iridescent colours seen in the plumage of some birds and some butterflies' wings are produced by the phenomenon of interference; the fine structure of the feather or wing resembles either a diffraction grating or a thin film.

Because interference can be produced by a path difference of only a wavelength or so, interference effects can be used to detect very small changes in length. Interferometers are used for this purpose. They produce interference by dividing a ray of light into two or more beams and then recombining them.

Polarization of light waves

Another effect to be seen with light waves is polarization [7]. In an ordinary light wave the electric and magnetic fields vibrate in many randomly orientated planes about the direction of wave motion; in polarized light they vibrate in only one plane. Light is polarized by passing it through a filter that cuts out all vibrations except those in one particular plane. The polarized beam will then pass through a second filter only if it is set at the correct angle to allow the vibrations through. Otherwise the beam is stopped. Light reflected from surfaces at certain angles is polarized, and polarizing sunglasses [8] cut out glare by stopping reflected beams in this way. Solutions of some chemical substances, such as various sugars, rotate the plane of polarization of light passing through them. The effect is used in chemistry for analysing such solutions.

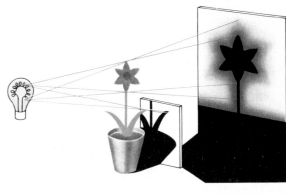

Shadows form with sharp edges when they are cast on a nearby object, but the outlines become less distinct the farther away they are cast. This can easily be explained because light travels in straight rays and every light source has a certain size. The ray paths show that a region exists at the edge of the shadow that is partially illuminated; this region, the penumbra, makes the outlines of the shadow fuzzy. The dark part of the shadow, the umbra, is completely shielded from the light source. The penumbra is less broad the closer the shadow is to the object casting it, and so nearby shadows look sharper.

5

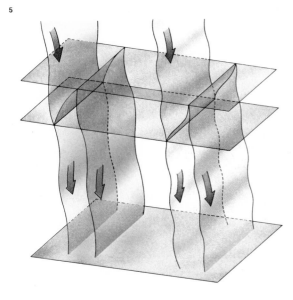

5 A thin film, such as a soap bubble or oil film, glistens with colour. Part of the light passing through the film is reflected between the inner surfaces of the film and emerges to interfere with the rest of the light that passed straight through. Travelling paths of different lengths, some of the waves are in phase and reinforce each other [red] while others [blue] cancel each other out and are not seen.

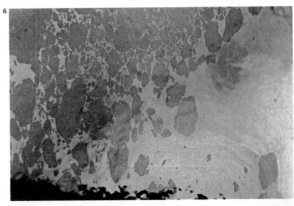

6

6 Interference is responsible for the coloured reflections from bubbles and oil films on water. The light reflected from the top of the film interferes with light reflected from the lower surface.

7 A

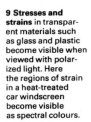

C

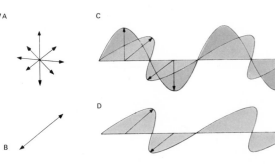

D

B

7 Unpolarized light consists of vibrations in all planes at right-angles to the direction of the light wave; the arrows show the wave approaching head on [A]. Polarized light consists of vibrations in one plane only [B]. Light rays consist of vibrating electric and magnetic fields at right-angles [C]; only the electric vibration denotes the plane of polarization [D].

8 A

B

8 Light reflected from glass or water is partly polarized. Here [B] a reflection makes it difficult to see through a shop window. A similar photograph taken with a polarizing filter over the camera lens gives a reflection-free view [A]. Polarizing sunglasses reduce glare this way.

9 Stresses and strains in transparent materials such as glass and plastic become visible when viewed with polarized light. Here the regions of strain in a heat-treated car windscreen become visible as spectral colours.

9

The speed of light

Every time we press a light switch, light floods the room instantaneously – or almost instantaneously. It does take a fraction of a second for the light to pass from the light bulb to our eyes but the time taken is far too brief for us to be aware of it. To early scientists light seemed to take no time to propagate; many claimed its velocity to be infinite.

Determining the velocity of light

Others, notably the Italian astronomer Galileo (1564–1642), challenged this view. He attempted to measure the velocity of light by trying to find out how long light took to travel between two hills a known distance apart. His experiment was inconclusive but it did show that if light has a particular velocity then it is very great. Confirmation of this view came with observations of the moons of Jupiter by the Danish astronomer Olaus Roemer (1644–1710) in 1675 [1]. The moons, which had been discovered by Galileo in 1610, are often eclipsed by Jupiter but Roemer found that predictions of the eclipse times were as much as 22 minutes out. Roemer reasoned that the variations occurred because the dis-

tance between Earth and Jupiter varies depending on their positions in their orbits around the Sun, and light therefore takes different times to reach the Earth from Jupiter. Knowing the distances involved Roemer made a good estimate of the velocity of light, obtaining a value of 227,000km (141,000 miles) a second. The true velocity is almost 300,000km or 186,000 miles a second.

Another astronomical determination of the velocity was made by the English astronomer James Bradley (1693–1762) in 1728. He observed that the stars are seen in slightly different directions depending on the position of the Earth in its orbit. This phenomenon, called stellar aberration, is caused by the Earth's motion and the differences in direction are simply related to the difference between this motion and the velocity of light. Bradley was therefore able to obtain a value for the velocity of light, and it was of the same order as Roemer's figure.

Later determinations of the velocity were completely terrestrial and sensitive instruments were used to measure very precisely the time light took to travel a known distance.

The instruments contain mirrors to reflect a ray of light along a particular path and time its passage by a variety of shutter mechanisms. Modern methods use an electronic shutter capable of very rapid action.

The accepted value for the velocity of light is now 299,792.58km (186,181 miles) a second. This is the velocity in a vacuum, for light slows when it enters a medium such as air, water or glass. The change in velocity causes the light to bend on entering a different medium and refraction occurs. The refractive index of a medium is the ratio of the velocity of light in a vacuum to its velocity in the medium. For example, the refractive index of water is 1.333 or $^4/_3$, and thus the velocity of light in water is only three-quarters of its velocity in a vacuum.

The mystery of the ether

Having determined that light has a certain velocity scientists began to wonder how light waves could travel through space. Other wave motions need a medium in which to travel – sound, for example, moves through air – and light had to have a medium too.

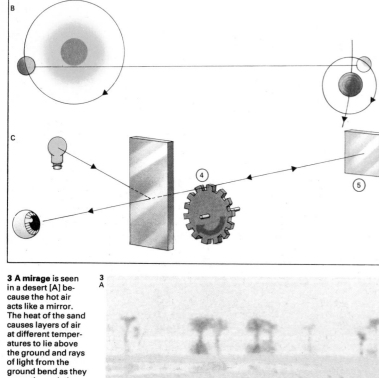

1 The velocity of light was first determined by Olaus Roemer in 1675 [A]. He saw the eclipses of Jupiter's moons [1] by Jupiter [2]. Light from the moons takes less time to reach the Earth [3] when its orbit nears Jupiter than when it is far away towards the other side of the Sun [B]. Knowing the distances and times involved he could calculate the velocity of light. Another determination was made by Armand Fizeau (1819–96) in 1849 [C]. Light was reflected through the teeth of a rotating wheel [4] to a mirror [5] and back through the teeth to the observer. The light was seen only when the wheel spun so fast that no teeth blocked its return journey. From the spacing of the teeth, the speed of rotation of the wheel and the distance of the mirror (8km [5 miles]), the velocity of light could be accurately calculated.

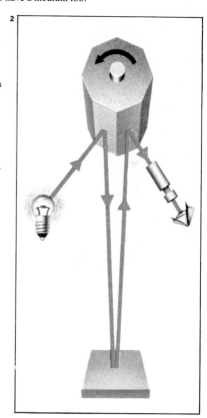

3 A mirage is seen in a desert [A] because the hot air acts like a mirror. The heat of the sand causes layers of air at different temperatures to lie above the ground and rays of light from the ground bend as they move through the layers [B]. Each layer has a different refractive index. In extreme conditions the light rays bend so much that they are deflected back towards the ground and an image of an object over the horizon is seen.

2 A rotating mirror was used by Michelson to measure the velocity of light in 1927. Light travelled from one face of the mirror to a plane mirror 35km (22 miles) away and then back to another face and an eyepiece. An image of the light source was obtained with the mirror first stationary and then rotated at sufficient speed for the image to be seen in the same position. At such a speed the mirror turned so that the next face moved into position as the light made its 70km (44 mile) journey to and from the plane mirror. Velocity of light was calculated from the speed of rotation.

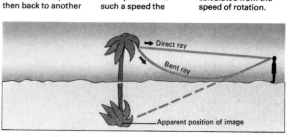

Direct ray
Bent ray
Apparent position of image

As the medium through which light moved could not be seen to exist, one was invented; it was called the ether and it was supposed to pervade the whole universe. Thorny problems surrounded the ether. Known wave motions move more rapidly in denser, more elastic substances and a wave motion as fast as light should theoretically need a medium denser than steel. Yet the planets continue to sail through space, unimpeded by the ether. There were many other contradictions and so an experiment was made to detect the motion of the Earth through the ether.

In the 1880s two American physicists, Albert Michelson (1852–1931) and Edward Morley (1838–1923) [5], made a simple instrument to detect the ether. In it a beam of light was split into two beams at right-angles and the two beams reflected from mirrors before recombining. Combined beams show interference effects if one travels a slightly longer path than the other. Michelson and Morley observed the combined beams in one direction and then turned the instrument at right-angles and observed the beams again. If the light were travelling in an ether it would have to move over a different path in the direction of the Earth's motion from at right-angles to it. Turning the instrument at right-angles should show a difference in the interference effects if the ether existed. None was observed and none has been observed in many repeats of this classic experiment.

The basis of relativity
The conclusion of the Michelson–Morley experiment was that ether does not exist and light does not need a medium for its propagation, or that the ether can never be detected. Without a stationary ether there is no basis in the universe against which the absolute motion of everything can be measured, except for light. The Michelson–Morley experiment showed that the velocity of light is the same in the direction of the Earth's motion as at right-angles to it and is always the same whatever the observer's motion. These conclusions had profound implications but to realize them it took a genius – Albert Einstein (1879–1955) – who used them as a basis for the theory of relativity.

Light that reaches us from heavenly bodies does not travel instantaneously. It takes 1.25 seconds to get to Earth from the Moon, 8 minutes from the Sun, over an hour from Saturn and the outer planets, and over four years from the nearest star. We see the galaxies as they were millions of years ago.

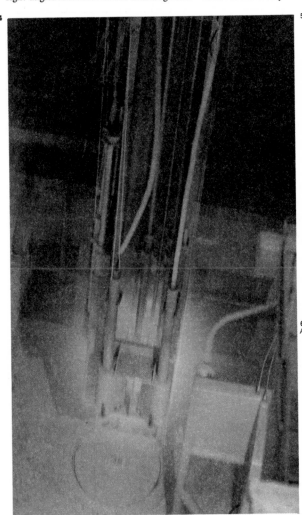

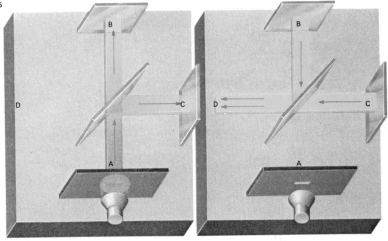

5 The Michelson-Morley experiment, first made in 1881, used an interferometer to produce a pattern of interference fringes from two beams at right-angles. The Earth's motion was expected to make the light move faster along one path [ABD] than along the other [ACD] so that on turning the interferometer a change in pattern would be seen. In the experiment no change was detected.

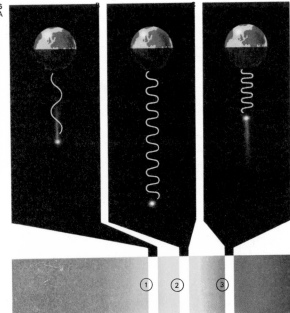

4 The blue glow coming from the water surrounding this nuclear reactor is known as Cerenkov radiation. It is produced because nuclear particles emitted by the reactor are moving faster than light does itself in water, which slows light by about a quarter. The particles cause a shock wave to be produced in the water, just as a supersonic plane produces a shock wave in the air. We hear the sound shock wave as a supersonic boom and see the light shock wave as blue light. The production of Cerenkov radiation is used as a method of detecting fast-moving particles in nuclear physics. The radiation was first observed by the Russian physicist Paul Cerenkov (sometimes known as Cherenkov) in 1934.

6 The motion of an observer does not affect the velocity of light but it does change the colour or wavelength of light to give the Doppler effect. However, only stars move fast enough to show the effect. If the star and the observer are moving apart [A] the wavelength increases because the individual waves are encountered less frequently. The light is more red than if the star were stationary [B] and this red shift shows as a shift in the lines of the spectrum of the star from [2] to [1]. If a star and observer are approaching [C], wavelength decreases and the light appears bluer [3]. A similar shift of frequency is used in radar to detect the movement of aircraft or cars.

The idea of relativity

Relativity sought to eliminate from physics the idea of absolute values for space and time. Such values were held to be fixed and quite independent of the person measuring them or of the instruments used. To Isaac Newton (1642–1727) they existed as a backdrop against which he could formulate general "laws" about such quantities as acceleration and force. It was the genius of Albert Einstein (1879–1955) that, through the special and general theories of relativity, showed that such absolutes did not exist and that Newton's laws were not universally true.

The special theory of relativity

Einstein's special theory of relativity (1905) was based on the idea that all uniform motion is relative – that is, an object can be seen to move uniformly only in relation to some stationary frame of reference. The classic experiment made by Albert Michelson (1852–1931) and Edward Morley (1838–1923) determined that the speed of light is always the same in a given vacuum regardless of the speed of the source of light, of anyone observing it or of its wavelength [1, 2]. From these results Einstein deduced an astonishing set of conclusions. They showed that the mass, length and time interval of an object will appear to change when the object begins to move relative to an observer.

If, say, an astronomer were to observe an extremely fast-moving spaceship, then his instruments would indicate that the mass of the spaceship had increased, that all lengths in the direction of the spaceship's motion had decreased, and time aboard was slower. Yet in the spaceship itself nothing would appear to have changed, although if the pilot looked back at the astronomer – who would be in the same motion relative to him – he would observe that mass, length and time there had changed in exactly the same way.

The light clock [4A] shows why time varies with motion and by how much. Normally the effects of special relativity are undetectable in an object until it is travelling at nearly the speed of light (300,000km [186,000 miles] a second) [3], although very sensitive atomic clocks have been used to detect clocks "going slow" on aircraft in flight. The effects do become large for sub-atomic particles moving at close to the speed of light. Thus, because of their high speed, very fast unstable particles in cosmic rays live longer in the Earth's atmosphere than would otherwise be expected [4B]. Sub-atomic particles can be so speeded artificially that their masses are increased many thousand-fold; particle accelerators have to be specially designed to allow for this effect.

It is Einstein's famous equation "$E = mc^2$", relating the energy E and mass m of a moving particle with c the velocity of light that shows why in special relativity a particle given ever greater energy will increase its mass. Because c^2 is so large, only a small amount of mass is equivalent to a vast amount of energy. The conversion of mass into energy takes place in nuclear reactors, in atomic power stations, in nuclear weapons and in the Sun and other stars.

As the speed of a particle approaches that of light its energy increases indefinitely. But there is a limit to the amount of energy available to any particle and so it can never travel faster than light. The light barrier cannot be crossed, but there may exist parti-

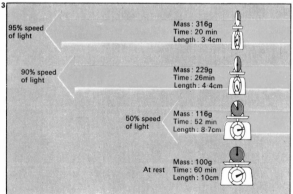

1 **Relativity** hinges on the simple idea that all motion is relative. A sailor in a yacht hauls a pennant up the mast [A]. To him, it appears to move vertically up [1]. To a man on the shore, the pennant appears to move forwards and up [2], because it is being carried past him as it is raised. A passenger in a passing aircraft sees the pennant disappearing rapidly behind him as it is raised [3]. Each observer records the same motion differently [B]; none is any more "correct" than the rest, for the planet on which all this happens is also moving. Their views confirm the relativity of all motion.

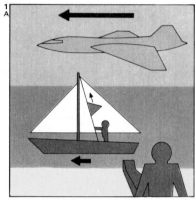
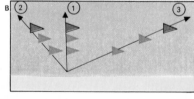

95% speed of light — Mass : 316g / Time : 20 min / Length : 3·4cm

90% speed of light — Mass : 229g / Time : 26min / Length : 4·4cm

50% speed of light — Mass : 116g / Time : 52 min / Length : 8·7cm

At rest — Mass : 100g / Time : 60 min / Length : 10cm

3 **Einstein's first theory** states that the measurement of mass, length and time depends totally on the relative motion of the measuring instrument and the object being measured. Compared with measurements made at rest, the mass will be increased, length decreased in the direction of motion, and time will be slowed. The effects are apparent only at extremely high speeds. At 90% of the velocity of light, mass more than doubles, length reduces by over a half and a clock takes an hour to record 26 min. At the velocity of light, mass would become infinite, length zero and time would slow to a complete stop – an impossible situation – which means that nothing can overtake the speed of light.

2 **The special theory** of relativity states that all uniform motion is relative and that the velocity of light is always constant. When two spacecraft pass each other in orbit, each travelling at 8km (5 miles) a second as measured by radar at the tracking station below, the pilots detect that they are travelling relative to each other at 16km (10 miles) a second. If the spacecraft and the tracking station then measure the velocity of light from the Sun, they all get the same result. The spacecraft moving towards the Sun does not give a value that reflects its motion relative to any other body.

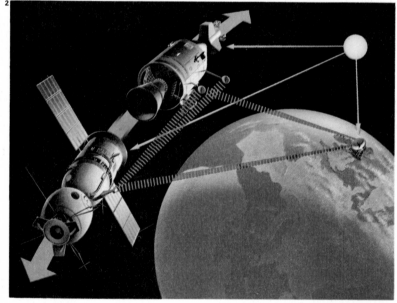

4 **A light clock** [A], in which light is reflected to and fro between mirrors, shows the principle of time slowed by motion. As the clock and its mirrors move, the light travels farther between reflections than when the clock is stationary, and therefore takes longer to reach the mirrors – observed time is slowed. Time slowing was proved [B] when particles created by cosmic rays (purple tracks) and predicted from observations at high altitudes to have lives shown by the red tracks, reached the ground in unexpectedly great numbers, shown by the yellow tracks.

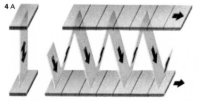
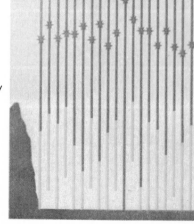

cles that are always travelling faster than light. These particles, called tachyons, have been looked for but not yet found.

The general theory of relativity

To take account of acceleration [8] and of the force of gravity, Einstein's general theory of relativity (1915) incorporated the fact that all bodies fall equally fast at the surface of the Earth. In other words, the effect of the Earth's gravitational field is an intrinsic feature of the space around the Earth. Einstein described this feature in terms of the curvature of space: the greater the distortion the greater the gravitational force. If time is included with space in this distortion it is possible to incorporate the idea that all motion is relative. The amount of space-time distortion caused by massive bodies can be quantified and it was Einstein's genius that showed how the amount of this curvature depends on nearby massive bodies.

Experimental observations, for example of small deviations in the motions of planets from those predicted by Newton [7], make the general theory of relativity the most satisfactory of a whole range of similar theories. Confirmation also comes from the bending of the path of a ray of light near a massive body. Light has energy – and hence mass – and therefore moves in a curved path in the distorted space around the body [9]. Such bending of light by the Sun was confirmed at an eclipse [10].

Holes in the heavens

All these effects involve weak gravitational fields and cannot put general relativity through the most searching test. When stars have used up their nuclear fuel they may evolve into extremely condensed objects in which strong gravitational fields occur and so they are good testing grounds for general relativity. It is postulated that very heavy stars collapse in on themselves so completely that the escape velocity on their surface is greater than the speed of light. As a result, nothing can ever escape from them again – not even light – and so they are known as "black holes". Good candidates for black holes in our own Galaxy are the variable X-ray stars such as Cygnus X-1.

ALBERT EINSTEIN 1879-1955

R HUGUENIN

Albert Einstein, working without the aid of a laboratory or university post, thought out the revolutionary concepts of the first theory of relativity from simple and seemingly unconnected ideas. Einstein was 26 and working as a patent officer when he published his special theory of relativity in 1905. Ten years later he announced his general theory of relativity. Einstein's fame was worldwide, but this did not stop the Nazi rulers of his native Germany from persecuting him for his Jewish blood. From 1933 he lived in the USA.

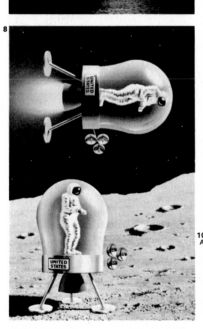

5 Nuclear weapons are one consequence of Einstein's discovery that mass can be converted into energy. But so too are atomic power stations and our understanding of the Sun's energy.

6 Low velocities accumulate by simple arithmetic. If a tank moving at velocity V fires a shell that leaves the gun at velocity v, then the shell will be travelling at $V + v$ [A]. Addition of velocities near that of light (c) is different. If a hypothetical body moving relative to Earth at 0.5c had a supergun that fired a shell at 0.5c, the shell would appear from Earth to move at only 0.8c [B].

7 The orbit of Mercury puzzled astronomers because its perihelion (point of nearest approach to the Sun) continually shifted more than could be accounted for by the influence of the other planets. Einstein's general theory of relativity accounted for this movement. He explained that gravity distorts space so the orbits of the planets do not follow the simple orbits described by Newton.

8 The principle of equivalence on which Einstein based his general theory of relativity states that gravity cannot be distinguished from acceleration. An astronaut is pulled to the floor of his stationary craft by gravity [bottom], in the same way as the floor is pushed towards him when the craft accelerates [top]. The effects are identical; if he let go of an object it would "fall" in either situation.

9 A ray of light passing a rotating wheel bearing a line of people would appear to be straight to an outside non-rotating observer [A]. As it passes, the people are carried away from it by the movement of the wheel. To them the ray appears to bend [B]. This analogy shows that light bends in an accelerating system and therefore, by equivalence, in a gravitational field.

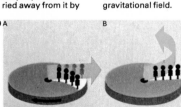

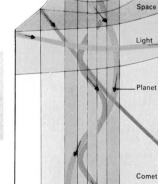

10 The bending of light by gravity was detected by photographing two stars normally [A] and in a solar eclipse [B]. As the light rays pass the Sun, they are bent by its field of gravity. As a result, the two stars appear to be farther apart [D] than usual [C].

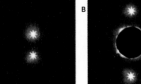

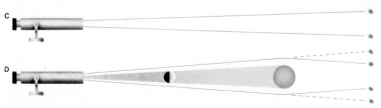

11 The dimension of time is as necessary to describe the location of any body as are the three dimensions of space. Einstein realized that if light always travels at the same speed, then space and time must therefore be equivalent. This diagram shows the Sun, planets and a comet moving in time as well as space. The varying velocity and widely changing path of the comet demonstrates the effects of the various gravitational fields on its motion, as Einstein correctly predicted in his general theory of relativity.

Light energy

Light is energy and, in systems of constant mass, energy cannot be created but only changed from one form to another. Light can therefore be produced only from the conversion of some other form of energy. Electrical energy is changed into light in an electric lamp or discharge tube; heat is converted into light in a fire or a red-hot poker; chemical energy is changed into light in luminous animals such as glow-worms. The conversion may also go the other way – light produces electrical energy in a photoelectric cell.

Radiation and quantum theory

The conversion of energy involving light puzzled scientists at the end of the 1800s. A perfectly black object absorbs all light falling on it and all the invisible radiations such as ultra-violet rays and infra-red rays. However, when it is heated, the object gives out radiation, but only at certain definite colours or frequencies. Like the poker in the fire, it first gives out infra-red rays (which can be felt as heat rays), then it glows red, yellow and finally white as it gets hotter. If it could be heated hot enough, it would glow blue-white

and emit ultra-violet rays, as do the hottest stars. The wave theory of light [1] could not explain why a black object should differ in the radiation it produces when heated. According to the wave theory, all frequencies should be produced when the object is heated, not different ranges of frequencies at different temperatures.

In 1900, the German physicist Max Planck (1858–1947) put forward a convincing, although revolutionary, theory. He suggested that all energy, including light, consists of whole units of energy: an object can have one unit or a million, but not 0.8, 2.5 or 354.67 units, for example. Each energy unit is called a quantum of energy, from the Latin for "how much". The amount of energy in a quantum is minute and we are unable to make out the individual quanta in light rays as they strike the eye. A quantum of light energy is called a photon.

The quantum theory therefore explains why a poker glows in the way it does. As more heat is applied to the poker, the light produced has more energy, and this is shown by a change in colour – a "blue" photon has more

energy than a "red" photon. Planck explained that the energy content of each photon of light depends on its frequency; the higher the frequency (more towards the blue or ultra-violet), the greater its energy.

Particles and waves

The idea of light existing in indivisible units was a return to the particle theory of light. A light quantum is included in the fundamental particles that make up matter. If light consists of streams of particles, then it will cross empty spaces with no need for the medium of "ether" that scientists had sought in vain. But such effects as diffraction and interference could be explained only if light behaved as waves. Scientists solved this by assuming that light can behave both as particles and as waves, depending on the situation. This was not just an easy way out of a difficult problem, because the duality can be shown to exist – both experimentally and mathematically. Also, fast-moving particles were found to have wave-like properties. A beam of electrons acts as a wave in an electron microscope, for example.

1 The wave nature of light can be demonstrated by passing a narrow beam through two slits [A]. On reaching the screen the resulting two beams overlap to produce a pattern of light and dark stripes – interference fringes. Where two wave peaks, or two troughs, reach the screen in step the combined intensities produce a bright line [B]. A dark line [C] results from a peak and trough arriving together and cancelling out one another.

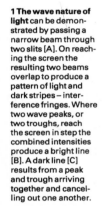

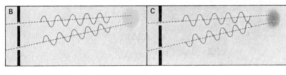

3 The photoelectric effect was explained by Einstein in 1905 as the absorption of a quantum of energy [A] by an atom and the resulting emission of an electron [B], which can form an electric current.

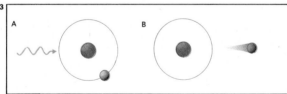

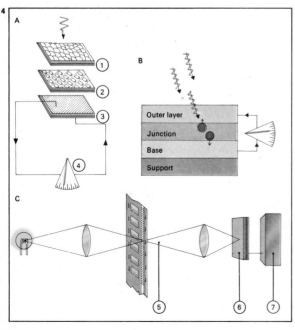

4 A light meter [A] contains a glass honeycomb [1] and a grid [2] through which light travels to a light-sensitive metal element [3]. There it causes electrons to be excited and these pass round the circuit to the meter [4]. The solar cell [B] is another application of photoelectricity. It consists of layers of semiconductor, usually silicon. Light crosses the outer layer and produces electrons at the junction. These are emitted and travel towards the base, producing a current. The optical sound track [C] on a cine film transmits a varying light signal [5] to a photoelectric cell [6] which produces an electric signal that goes to an amplifier and loudspeaker [7].

2 Light exerts pressure on any object it encounters. A vane [1] struck by light [2] moves under this pressure, and the movement is counterbalanced by a horizontal mirror [3] onto which light is directed by a vertical mirror [4]. The torsion heads [5] first level the balance arm. The mirror [6] reflects light from a lamp [7] onto a scale [8]. A timer [9] detects motion of the light across the scale and adjusts a power source [10] to change the intensity of the lamp [11] illuminating the mirror [4] and thus keeps the arm in balance. Deflection of the mirror is detected by the torsion head [12].

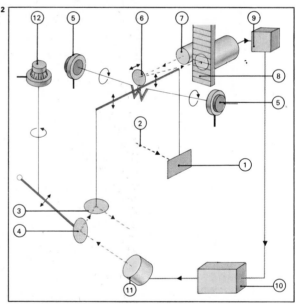

5 A photographic exposure meter measures the light coming from a scene. The light strikes a photoelectric cell which produces an electric current that varies in strength according to the intensity of the light. The current is low but sufficient to move a needle across a dial and give a value for the light. Many single-lens reflex cameras have built-in exposure meters that measure the light entering the lens of the camera.

The quantum theory – especially its application to light – finally resolved the problem that had divided scientific thought for centuries. Isaac Newton (1642–1727) had championed the particle theory and Christiaan Huygens (1629–95) had maintained that light travels as waves. With Max Planck's proposal the dilemma ceased to exist – light can be regarded as behaving as particles *or* waves, depending on the phenomenon being investigated.

Certain metals emit electrons when light falls on them – a phenomenon known as the photoelectric effect [3]. It had been observed that brighter light produces more electrons than dim light but not electrons of greater energy; whereas blue light always gives electrons of greater energy than red light, regardless of the intensity of the light. In 1905, Albert Einstein (1879–1955) explained that each electron is released by one photon of light; a bright light has more photons of the same energy than a dim light, but a blue light has photons of greater energy than red light.

Changing the frequency of light, or converting an invisible frequency into a visible one, has several uses. Fluorescent substances take up light of several frequencies and immediately radiate them at a different frequency, making the resulting colour very bright because extra light has been transformed into it [9]. The fluorescent paints and inks used in some advertisements work in this way. Some washing powders contain optical brighteners that convert invisible ultra-violet rays into blue light and thus making the washing look brighter.

Effects of phosphorescence

Phosphorescence is similar to fluorescence, but the production of light continues for some time after the initial radiation has ceased. Television screens contain phosphors that glow for a short time after being struck with the electron beams inside the cathode ray tube and give a picture on the screen. Many instruments make use of the light produced by phosphors to detect invisible rays such as X-rays and fast-moving particles such as cosmic rays. Some phosphorescent paints store light for a long time after being exposed to it and glow in the dark.

The radiometer, invented by William Crookes (1832–1919), measures radiant energy. When sunlight falls on it, the vanes move round, seemingly pushed by the light. In fact, heat is absorbed by the black side and the few gas molecules left in the bulb's vacuum rebound faster, exerting pressure on that side.

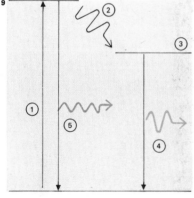

6 A discharge tube contains a gas at low pressure through which electricity is passed [A]. Electrons (negative particles) and ions (positive particles) move towards the electrodes [B]. Ions strike electrodes to produce more electrons [C]. Light is produced as electrons collide with gas atoms [D].

7 Advertising signs contain a gas such as neon or are coated with phosphors to give various colours.

8 An infra-red view of the Colorado River and Lake Powell taken by a satellite shows vegetation in various shades of red and water as black. Diseased plants can be detected by colour.

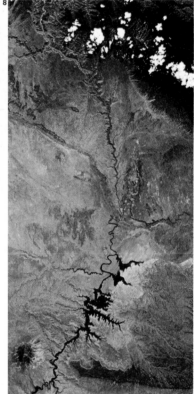

10 Automatic letter checking utilizes ultra-violet light. Invisible phosphor codes printed on the stamp glow as the letter passes an ultra-violet scanner, classifying it as first or second class.

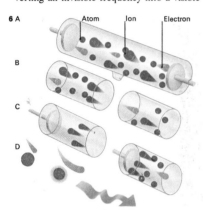

9 Fluorescence occurs when an atom receives light energy [1] and divides emission of the energy into two stages: a small energy change producing infra-red [2] to an intermediate energy state [3] and a large change giving light at a lower frequency than that received [4]. Normal light production occupies one change [5]. Phosphorescence is similar but stage two takes some time.

11 An image intensifier gives a bright picture of a dimly lit scene. Light from the scene is focused onto the photocathode, which emits electrons. These pass to the electron multipliers that contain tubes lined with electron-emitting substances and produce more electrons from each electron entering the tubes. The resulting intensified electron beam is focused on a fluorescent screen which is viewed through an eyepiece.

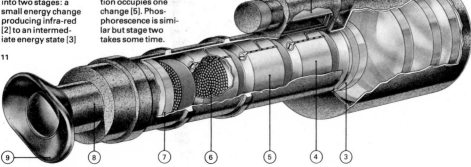

1 Night lens system
2 6·75 volt mercury battery
3 Photocathode
4 15kV channel plate
5 30 kV channel plate
6 45kV channel plate
7 Fluorescent screen
8 Ocular lens system
9 Eyepiece

Energy from lasers

From boring holes through diamonds to performing delicate eye operations, from spanning space between the Earth and the Moon to detecting the smallest movement, the laser has found an amazing range of uses during its short life. Its future looks no less extraordinary with the promise of three-dimensional television and cheap nuclear power. Clearly the laser is no ordinary source of light.

What is a laser?

A pulse laser is basically a device for storing energy and then releasing it all at once to give a very intense beam of light. The heart of the laser is a crystal or tube of gas or liquid into which energy is pumped [1]. This is usually done by surrounding it with a device to produce a powerful flash of light or an intense beam of radio waves or electrons. As pumping occurs, more and more of the atoms inside take up energy and are excited to high energy states. Suddenly an atom spontaneously returns to its first energy state and gives out a particle of light (a photon). This photon strikes another excited atom and causes it to produce another photon. Very rapidly, a cascade of photons develops. The crystal or tube is closed at both ends by mirrors and the photons bounce to and fro between them, building up the cascade. A proportion of this light is able to escape through one of the mirrors, which is half-silvered, and an intense flash of light emerges from the laser.

The first pulse laser, invented by Theodore H. Maiman in 1960, contained a ruby crystal and produced a short flash of red light. Continuous wave lasers now produce continuous beams of many colours and some give out infra-red rays or ultra-violet rays.

The activities of photons

The atoms that discharge photons are stimulated to emit them by the arrival of other photons, which make up light radiation. The light that is pumped into the laser consists of many frequencies but what emerges is a far more intense light at a single frequency.

The result - *light amplification by the stimulated emission of radiation* – gives the laser its name.

Each photon triggers the production of another one and so they all travel together and produce light waves that are exactly in step. This light is said to be in phase, or coherent. (In ordinary light, the waves are all out of phase.) Because the waves are all in step, they reinforce each other and laser light is very bright. The construction of the laser produces a narrow beam that hardly spreads at all – even at the distance of the Moon, a laser beam directed from the Earth is only 3km (2 miles) wide [3]. A narrow beam of intense, coherent light is extremely concentrated in energy and, if a laser beam is focused to a point by a lens, it will heat the air to a state of incandescence (bright and glowing with heat) or burn a hole in a steel plate. A straight, narrow beam of laser light can be used for precise alignment in the construction of tunnels and pipelines, for example. The beam is directed along the proposed route and can be seen by the construction engineers only when they are directly in line with it.

Other uses of lasers

Laser beams can also be used to measure distances and speeds. These have included firing a laser beam at the moon to reflect it from a

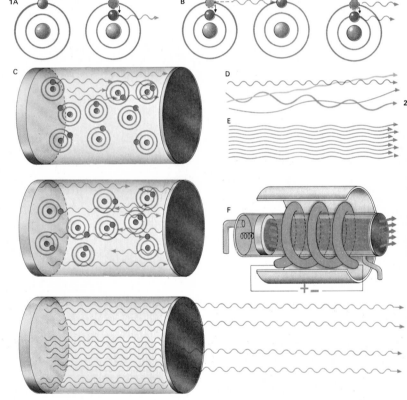

1 Normal emission of light occurs when an electron in a high-energy orbit falls to low orbit [A]. Stimulated emission [B] is triggered by light emitted from another atom. In a laser [C], most atoms are brought to a high-energy state by pumping in energy. Some begin to produce light by normal emission and mirrors at each end reflect the light to and fro, producing stimulated emission until all the atoms are in a low-energy state. The light leaves the laser through one of the mirrors. Ordinary light [D] is a mixture of different frequencies moving in various directions, whereas laser light [E] has a single frequency and moves in the same direction with all waves in phase. The first laser [F] contained a synthetic ruby crystal surrounded by a flash tube (to pump in light energy) and a pair of reflecting mirrors.

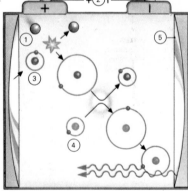

2 The helium-neon gas laser contains two gases and operates continuously. Ions [1] accelerate in an electric field produced by a high voltage [2] to excite helium atoms [3]. Through collisions they transfer their energy to equal energy levels in the neon atoms [4]. Light amplification occurs when a passing photon stimulates excited neon atoms to radiate. After several reflections from partly silvered mirrors [5] the laser beam emerges.

4 A detached retina is quickly and painlessly welded into place by a laser beam, instantly curing partial blindness. The surgeon lines up the laser by directing a beam of ordinary white light into the unaffected eye. When the white beam is in place, the laser is fired briefly and the green laser light enters the other eye and is focused on the affected retina to seal it in place.

3 Laser communication would be ideal for interplanetary missions because the narrow, powerful beam [B] can reach a small, distant target. A laser carries a television or other signal by modulating the beam at the transmitting end, focusing the beam on a detector at the receiving end and demodulating the signal produced [A]. Ordinary light is unsuitable for communication because it has many frequencies that interfere with each other; only the laser can be used.

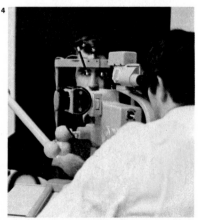

special mirror placed there by the Apollo astronauts and thus give a very accurate measure of the moon's distance.

In meteorology, laser beams are used to detect invisible air layers and movements as well as clouds, and they are useful in studies of air pollution.

The intense heat of lasers gives them all kinds of uses in medicine and industry. A laser beam directed into the eye at insufficient power to damage the lens is focused by the lens onto the retina, where it can painlessly weld a detached portion back in place and restore failing sight [4]. Laser beams can burn away skin growths without surgery, by firing the beams along fibre-optic tubes inserted into the body, and painlessly drill decayed teeth. In industry, lasers cut out patterns, drill holes in diamonds to make dies for wire manufacture and shape and weld parts for microelectronic circuits [Key].

Communication by laser beams instead of radio waves is desirable because light beams can carry many more channels of information than can radio. Data, sound and pictures can be transmitted by a laser beam, which routes it along an enclosed path of some kind to avoid loss of signal strength from having to pass through fog or mist in the air.

One of the most amazing consequences of producing coherent light in lasers is the development of holography, with which three-dimensional images can be made [5, 6, 7]. Although three-dimensional colour television and motion pictures may one day result from it, holography has several uses now. Double-exposure holograms record any movement of the object between the exposures and so readily picture the vibrations in a surface. Vibration analysis is essential to the design of components such as aircraft and engine parts which must perform faultlessly for long periods at high speeds and stresses.

Another field that may be revolutionized by the laser is nuclear energy. Research is being carried out to see if thermonuclear fusion (the reaction that takes place in a hydrogen bomb and in the stars) can be initiated by a laser beam instead of producing a high-temperature plasma by means of a powerful electric discharge.

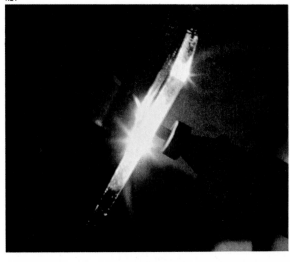

A laser beam contains sufficient energy to "burn" a hole in hard materials such as steel and diamond. Here a laser beam is drilling a hole in a sheet of toughened glass. Laser-drilled diamonds are used as dies for drawing metal into extremely fine wires.

5 Holography reconstructs light waves. An illuminated point produces spherical wavefronts [A]; an object surface makes a complex wavefront [B]. When two plane waves from a common source fall on a photographic plate a uniform pattern of black and white interference fringes results [C]: a hologram. The pattern is altered when a plane and a complex wave interfere [D].

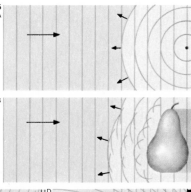

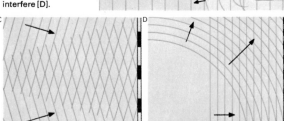

6 When a laser beam passes through a hologram of circular fringes [A] two wavefronts emerge [B]: one converges [1] to form a real image, the other diverges [2] as if from a virtual image. A hologram is made [C] by illuminating an object by a laser light, which then falls on a photographic plate. Part of the laser beam is reflected directly on to the plate as a reference beam [3]. The image is recreated [D] by illuminating the hologram with laser light. An observer sees a three-dimensional virtual image of the object [4], the appearance of which changes with viewing angle. A real image can be recorded photographically [5].

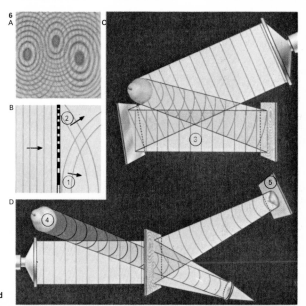

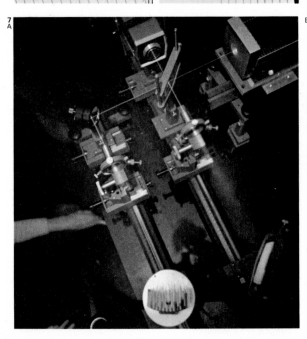

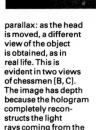

7 Images in 3-D can be obtained by holography. A hologram of an object is made by the technique described in illustration 5, using apparatus such as that shown in A. It is arranged so that laser light reflected from the object travels about the same distance as the reference laser beam reflected onto the photographic plate by a mirror. When the hologram is illuminated from behind with laser light, an image of the object is seen which is not only 3-dimensional but also demonstrates parallax: as the head is moved, a different view of the object is obtained, as in real life. This is evident in two views of chessmen [B, C]. The image has depth because the hologram completely reconstructs the light rays coming from the object and striking the plate. The colour of the object can also be produced by using several lasers of different colours. It is possible that holography may one day give us a totally realistic cinema or television picture.

93

What is electricity?

To the man in the street, electricity is the cause of a lightning flash [1–3] or the form of energy that powers his television set and washing machine. He knows that electric trains use electrical power and he is reminded of his dependence on it by the network of power lines criss-crossing the countryside, or by a power cut, when he has to read by candlelight. But there are other less well-known everyday processes that involve the use of electricity. A beating heart, a running athlete, a dreaming baby and a swimming fish all generate a form of electricity just as surely as a power station does.

Electrons and protons

To a scientist, electricity results from the movement of electrons and other charged particles in various materials. A scientific understanding of electricity therefore depends on a knowledge of atoms and the sub-atomic particles of which they are composed. The key to this understanding is the tiny electron – tiny even when compared with the minute atom in which it may be found.

Atoms of all materials have one or more electrons circling in orbits of various sizes – much as the planets move round the sun. Normally the number of electrons equals the number of protons in the nucleus. The protons, however, being much heavier than the electrons, are virtually stationary in the atom's centre. This extremely simplified model of the atom is sufficient to explain the basis of electricity.

The electrons and protons each have an electric charge (but of opposite polarity) and attract each other. Charges of the same polarity repel each other. To distinguish the proton's charge from that of the electron the former is called positive and the latter negative. An atom that has more, or fewer, electrons than normal is called an ion. If it is deficient in electrons, it is called a positive ion; if it has an excess of electrons, it is called a negative ion.

When an electron moves away from an atom the atom is left with a net positive charge. The electron, deprived of its positive counterpart in the atom's centre, eventually moves about another atom or possibly returns to the ion it has left.

Why do electrons move at all? There are a number of possible causes. A common one is simply that, if an incoming electron or light pulse hits an atomic electron, the latter can be knocked out of its orbit. Heat makes atoms dance faster, causing the electrons to move so energetically that they may shoot away from the parent atoms. Chemical activity will also cause electrons to move out of atoms.

A good example of the relationship between chemical and electrical activity is found in the muscles. Muscle fibres contract when they are electrically stimulated [4]. Normally, this is caused by the release of a chemical from an associated nerve, following the receipt of an electrical signal from the nervous system. When part of this system is damaged and muscles become weak or fibres are destroyed, it is possible to apply external electrical signals to stimulate muscle activity and strengthen their fibres.

Conductivity

The electrons of some materials move more freely than others. This characteristic is known as conductivity. Most metals, hot

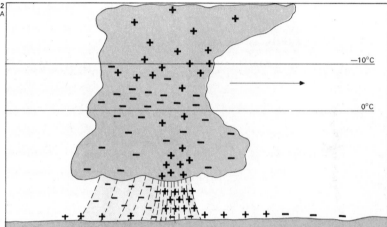

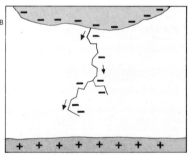

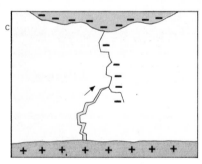

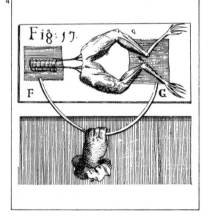

1 Lightning strokes were not properly explained until about 200 years ago. They are caused by an electrical imbalance between clouds or between clouds and the earth. The base of the cloud can have an excess of electrons and then draws positive ions to the ground underneath it. The potential difference grows until there is a sudden flow of electrons (the flash), neutralizing charges on both the ground and the cloud.

3 Benjamin Franklin (1706–90) was the first man to recognize the true nature of lightning. During a thunderstorm he induced a flash of lightning to flow along the string of a kite to the earth.

4 Galvanism was the term used to describe the twitching effect produced by an electric current on a pair of frog's legs. Luigi Galvani (1737–98) used this to show the connection between muscle activity and electricity.

2 Formation of lightning starts with a big storm cloud [A], within which there is a significant temperature difference. Electrons move downwards and positive ions move upwards within the cloud, causing positive ions to gather on the earth below. When there are sufficient electrons, a sudden breakdown of the air occurs and a stream of electrons shoots earthwards [B] to be met by an upward stream of ions [C].

gases and some liquids are good conductors. Air, rubber, oil, polythene and glass are bad conductors so that they can be used to cover good conductors without themselves taking part in electron flow [6].

These bad conductors are called insulators. No insulator is "perfect". Under certain circumstances the electrons of any atom can be forced out of it. But the conditions required are generally so unusual and difficult to arrange with these materials that, for practical purposes, they can be considered inactive.

There is also a group of materials – the semiconductors – that behave partly as insulators and partly as conductors. Among these are germanium, silicon and copper oxide. Their properties can be exploited for many purposes. For example, using one of the semiconductors it is possible to make an electric "valve" that, like the valve on a bicycle tyre, allows easy electron movement in one direction only. This device is called a rectifier; it is used in both tiny radio sets and large power stations to change an alternating current to a direct current.

Heat is simply a chaotic form of molecular activity or electronic motion and temperature is a measure of its vigour. When the temperature of most metals is reduced, it is easier for electrons to move freely; that is, the electrical resistance (to free electron movement) falls as the temperature drops and the conductivity of the metal increases.

Superconductivity
If in certain materials the temperature drops low enough, the resistance to electron flow ceases completely and electrons, once started on their journey, continue to move indefinitely provided the temperature is kept sufficiently low. The condition of zero resistance is called superconductivity. It occurs in metals such as tin, lead, aluminium and niobium [7] at a few degrees above absolute zero ($-273°C$ or $-460°F$).

Electricity, therefore, is simply the movement of electrons or other charged particles. These particles are among the smallest components of matter, and yet the way in which they move and interact has a great influence on every aspect of life.

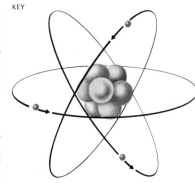

The electron is the basic unit of electricity; it is also a fundamental particle found in all kinds of atoms. In this simple model of an atom of the metallic element lithium, three electrons [red] can be seen circling the central nucleus. Larger particles called protons [blue] and neutrons [grey] make up the nucleus. Each electron carries a negative electric charge and each proton carries a positive one, so that the three electron charges are exactly balanced by the three proton charges, making the whole atom

electrically neutral. In a conductor – ie most metals – an external electromotive force (voltage) causes electrons to "drift" from atom to atom and it is this flow of electrons that constitutes an electric current. Electron movement occurs because in a conductor the outermost electron is not tightly bound to its nucleus. In a non-conductor or insulator the electrons are too tightly bound to leave the nucleus easily and so such substances do not conduct electricity. In some situations atoms can completely lose or gain one or more electrons to become permanently charged. Such charged atoms, called ions, can also act as current carriers.

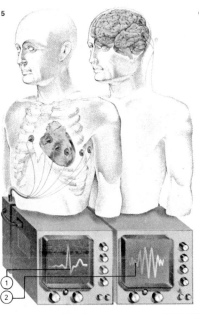

5 The beating heart generates tiny electrical currents which, after being suitably amplified, can be displayed on a cathode-ray tube. These current shapes can be recorded permanently on paper, in which form they are called electrocardiograms for the heart [1] and electroencephalograms [2] for the brain. Existing or potential malfunctions of both these vital organs can be diagnosed with their aid.

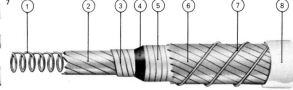

6 Domestic wiring uses copper wires encapsulated in rubber or plastic [A, C]. In fire-proof wiring [B], the wires are embedded in a noninflammable powder surrounded by a copper tube.

1 Helical conductor support
2 Strips of inner conductor
3 Inner conductor screen
4 Lapped tape dielectric
5 Outer conductor screen
6 Strips of outer conductor
7 Helical skid wires
8 Helium pipe

7 Perfect conductors can be made out of alloys of metals (eg tin, lead and niobium) at temperatures close to absolute zero ($-273°C$). Once electrons become detached from their parent atoms they

move through the supercooled conductor, without slowing down or coming to rest, for indefinitely long periods. At such low temperatures the atoms in the metal vibrate only very slightly.

9 Extremely high voltages can be produced with the Van de Graaff generator [B]. If a body having an excess of positive ions is placed inside a container, the inside acquires electrons [A] and the outside an equal number of positive ions. If the charged body touches the inside, all the free electrons flow into it, thus making it neutral. The outside of the container still retains its positive ions. In the Van de Graaff generator, positive ions are sprayed from a suitable source [1] onto an endless conveyor belt which carries them inside a metal sphere. The belt connects to the inside wall through a conductor in the form of a comb [2], thus permitting an electron flow to the belt. This causes positive ions to form on the sphere's outside wall [3]. The effect may be enhanced by using two generators connected as shown [C].

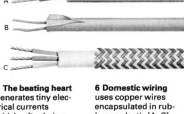

8 A high velocity particle passing through a gas knocks electrons off the otherwise neutral atoms [A]. As it sweeps through the gas, it leaves behind a stream of free electrons [B], shown here in blue. If these break free

with sufficient energy, they can knock other electrons out in a Geiger counter [C, D], subatomic particles enter the chamber where they are accelerated to produce more free electrons. These are attracted to the positive

plate and are led from there to drive a meter or earphones. The current flow depends on the voltage v between the plates [E]. The meter reading or frequency of clicks indicates the amount of radioactivity of the source.

Current per particle

Voltage V

What is an electric current?

Electricity flowing along a wire is known as an electric current. The wire is the conductor. When an electric lamp is connected across a battery and switched on, current flows along a wire from one terminal of the battery to the lamp, through its filament, making it glow white hot, and back along a second wire to the other battery terminal. If the switch is turned off, the circuit is broken, current flow stops and the lamp is extinguished.

Movement of electrons
The current carriers in most circuits are electrons from the metal making up the conductors. In all conductors, and a few other materials as well, there is always a random movement of electrons (minute charged particles), even when no current flows. The electrons may be relatively free to move or more tightly bound. Good conductors have freer electrons and hence more electron movement than do bad conductors, or insulators, in which most of the electrons are too tightly bound to their parent atoms to move easily. Sometimes, through natural or contrived processes, there can be a net movement of electrons in a

specific direction. This concerted flow is the electric current and it is measured in amperes, generally given by the abbreviation A. Other current carriers include ions (charged atoms or molecular fragments) in gases and solutions, and "holes" (a deficiency in electrons in some types of semiconductors – the holes behave as positively-charged carriers of electric current).

A force has to be applied to cause a net flow of electrons in one direction. In nature this force can be derived from a number of sources such as sunlight, magnetic action or chemical activity. Some of these have been exploited to generate electric current. Two common devices designed for this purpose are the generator [9], which utilizes magnetic effects, and the cell (sometimes called a battery) [6], which depends on chemical action. Both devices force electrons to move in one direction round a circuit by virtue of the electromotive force (emf) they generate. The electromotive force is measured in volts, using a voltmeter.

The voltage of an emf and current flow are related in a similar way to water pressure

and water flow. In a household, all the pipes are full of water at a certain pressure. But there is no movement until a tap is opened, allowing water to run.

An electrical circuit may be connected to a source of emf without causing any specific electron flow (current) until a path is provided through which the electrons can move. This may be a light bulb [Key] or a vacuum cleaner; an electric switch is like a tap that turns on the current.

Relationship between voltage and current
As the voltage in a circuit increases, so does the current. An electrical circuit is, however, made up of a number of different parts. There is normally a switch, conductors and the appliance that is being supplied with electricity. All these taken together have a resistance to current flow, which is constant (provided the temperature remains the same) for that particular group of components. Therefore although the same voltage may be applied to a light bulb and an electric iron, the actual current flow is different in each, because each has a different resistance. So it

1 Metal is a good conductor of electricity because its atoms [1] easily give up their outer electrons [2], which move freely within the crystal lattice of the metal [A]. An electric current flows only if the "free" electrons have a net motion in one direction [B]. A voltage [3] from a battery, say, can cause such a flow. In a thermocouple [C], a temperature difference between the two junctions of a circuit, made of two dissimilar metals, will produce a current, indicated by a meter [4], which is proportional to the temperature difference. In a thermopile [D], several thermocouples are connected in series to increase the voltage of the circuit.

2 Circuit-breakers can be used either in conjunction with, or in place of a fuse to interrupt dangerously high currents. When too large a current flows through the coil [1], a magnetic field is produced which activates the catch [2], causing the spring-loaded contact [3] to rise. The current is interrupted, thereby protecting the circuit of which the breaker is a part. No further current can flow until the circuit-breaker is closed again, which is achieved by pressing the reset button [5]. To test the circuit-breaker, or to operate it manually, a push button [4] is pressed to move the contact.

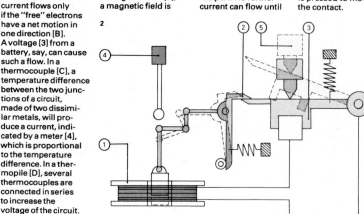

3 A gas discharge lamp gets its light from the energy changes in gas atoms. A positive and negative electrode (anode and cathode) at opposite ends of a gas-filled glass tube [A] attract electrons and positive ions.

Reducing the pressure [B] speeds this up. As ions hit the cathode [C] they dislodge electrons which speed towards the anode, colliding with gas atoms on the way. The atoms absorb the energy for a moment, then release it in the form of light [D].

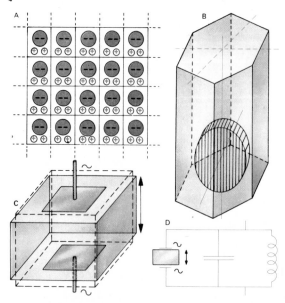

4 Certain crystals, including quartz and sapphire, exist in the form of "cells' in a delicate state of electrical equilibrium [A]. Applying a varying voltage across the crystal disturbs the delicate balance and causes the crystal to vibrate and emit sound or ultrasonic waves, generally at a specific angle to the direction of the applied voltage [B]. Conversely, when such a crystal is vibrated, it generates a voltage. This effect – which is known as piezoelectricity – is made use of in a gramophone pick-up [C] and in crystal microphones. In the pick-up, the movement of the stylus in the record groove rapidly vibrates a piezoelectric crystal and generates a small electric current. In a

crystal microphone, sound waves vibrate a diaphragm coupled to a crystal and generates a current that can be amplified and fed into a tape recorder or sound system. Most crystals respond strongly to only one frequency, depending on their dimensions. Radio transmitters make use of this property to "hold" a particular fixed frequency [D]. Vibrating quartz crystals are able to keep almost perfect time. They are used in quartz clocks and watches, which are accurate to within a few seconds over a period of several years. Piezoelectric crystals are also used to generate the electricity for the spark that ignites the gas in certain kinds of "electronic" cigarette lighters, which do not need any batteries.

is not only the magnitude of the voltage that determines how much current flows through a particular piece of equipment, it is also the resistance of that equipment and the conductors. This property of electrical resistance is measured in ohms (Ω). For any conductor, or system of conductors and equipment, the relationship between voltage, current and resistance is given by the formula: voltage = current × resistance. This is the mathematical expression of Ohm's law, named after Georg Ohm (1787–1854) who was the first person to specify the interdependence of these three factors in a precise way.

The resistance of electrical conductors depends on their dimensions and on the materials they are made of. As the cross-sectional area increases, the resistance falls; but as the length increases, the resistance rises. A long thin conductor therefore has more resistance than a short thick one with the same volume of material. Silver has a lower resistance than copper, whereas aluminium and iron have higher resistances.

Current flows at the same rate at all points around a circuit at any one time. According to a convention adopted before the nature of electricity was properly understood, a direct current (that is, current from a battery or dynamo) is assumed to flow from a positive point to a negative one. As it happens, electrons move from negative to positive, so that electron movement is opposite to the assumed current flow.

Effects of current flow

Three phenomena that typically occur when a current flows (and by which it can be detected) are heating, chemical and magnetic effects. Its heating effect is used to provide warmth in electric fires, cookers and industrial furnaces. Such heating can also be unwanted; large cables carrying thousands of amperes have to be cooled to prevent the current-generated heat melting the insulation or even the wires themselves.

The chemical effect of current is used in electroplating and in energy storage, particularly in cells, the most familiar of which is the lead-acid accumulator or battery [7]. The magnetic effect is used in motors, electromagnets and many other devices.

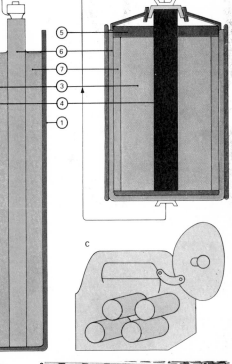

Heat generated by the passage of electric current is the source of light in a so-called "filament" or "incandescent" lamp. Because it is enclosed in a vacuum, or inert gas [1], the filament [2] cannot oxidize when the current passes through, causing it to become hot. It is made of a tungsten alloy, combining mechanical and thermal strength. Though it is extremely thin, it glows white hot when enough current passes through it. It is supported on two glass columns [3] through which the connecting wires pass. The whole assembly is enclosed in a thin glass envelope [4]. Only about two per cent of the electrical energy is converted into light.

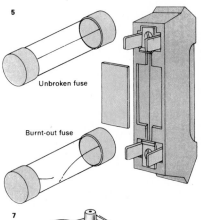

Unbroken fuse

Burnt-out fuse

5 The heating effect of an electric current is used in a fuse, which consists of a thin wire that melts when excessive current passes through it, thereby cutting off the electricity supply.

6 The Léclanché cell [A] consists of a leakproof jacket [1] containing a porous pot [2] in which there is a paste of manganese dioxide and carbon granules [3] surrounding a carbon rod [4]. The top can be sealed with pitch [5]. A zinc rod [6] stands in a solution of ammonium chloride [7], and is connected to the carbon rod via a circuit and a light bulb [8]. The zinc dissolves in the solution, setting up an electromotive force. The ammonium ions migrate to the carbon anode and form ammonia (which dissolves in the water), and hydrogen ions. Torch dry batteries [B and C] use wet paste cells of the Léclanché type.

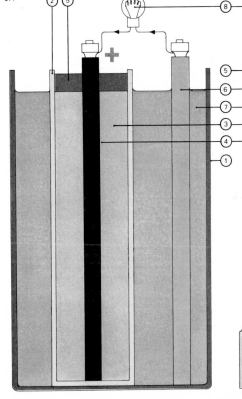

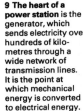

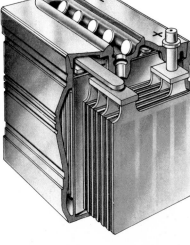

7 A 12-volt car battery has six two-volt cells connected in series. The cells have anodes of brown lead oxide and cathodes of porous grey lead immersed in sulphuric acid. An electric current flows if the electrodes are connected through a conductor. When the battery supplies current the sulphuric acid converts the anode to lead sulphate, thus reducing the strength of the acid. This process is reversed during recharging. Each cell of the battery is made of several anodes and cathodes separated by porous insulators. The cells are housed in a hard rubber case and the various cells are interconnected with lead bars.

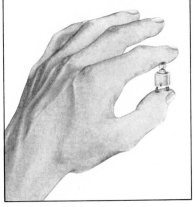

8 Tiny electric motors, such as this one, which is used for driving a miniature tape recorder, emphasize the enormous range of size and applications of electrical equipment.

9 The heart of a power station is the generator, which sends electricity over hundreds of kilometres through a wide network of transmission lines. It is the point at which mechanical energy is converted to electrical energy.

Magnets and magnetism

Magnetism and electricity are not two separate phenomena. The error of thinking they were arose from the fact that their interrelation was not appreciated until 1820. In that year the Danish scientist Hans Christian Oersted (1777–1851) showed that an electric current flowing in a wire deflects a compass needle close by. Whenever an electric current flows, whether from cloud to ground in the form of lightning or through a muscle in the body, a magnetic field is created.

Thousands of years before electricity was recognized and used, magnetism was observed and applied – mainly for navigation. Eventually, when science became aware of the atomic nature of matter, it was finally realized that the properties of magnetism and electricity are both bound up in the nature of the physical structure and arrangement of atoms and their electrons.

Whenever magnetism can be detected there must be a current of electricity. Those materials that appear to be magnetic without any external source of electricity depend on electron movements within their atomic structure to provide the electric current; this is the class of magnetism dealt with here.

The property of attracting iron and iron-based materials occurs naturally in a mineral called lodestone [3], itself a chemical compound of iron. It is likely that some form of lodestone was used in the first magnetic compasses that the Chinese are thought to have made [1]. It is relatively easy to transfer deliberately magnetic properties between various materials, of which iron and steel are the best known common examples.

Permanent magnets

Iron-attracting materials form a class of so-called permanent magnets, although they may retain their magnetic properties for only a limited time. In the form of a bar, a permanent magnet experiences a force due to the earth's magnetism such that, if it were free to move, one end would point roughly in the direction of the earth's North Pole and the other to the South. The two ends are named the north-seeking (or north) pole and south-seeking (or south) pole.

Unlike magnetic poles attract each other. A magnet that attracts other material does so by first turning the material into a weak magnet. Like poles repel each other (although this is not so obvious as attraction) because whenever an iron or steel object comes within the influence of a magnet, and itself becomes a magnet, it acquires the opposite polarity. As a result it is automatically attracted. But when two identical magnets of equal strength are positioned with their *like* poles close to each other, each experiences a repulsive force equal to the attractive force that results when the two unlike poles are placed close to each other.

It is not only ferrous (iron-containing) materials that are affected by magnetism. But its effects are easiest to observe in pure metals such as iron, nickel and cobalt.

Domain strengths

In general the metals affected by magnetism consist naturally of tiny magnets within the structure of the material, all of them aligned in a random manner. These magnets occupy areas known as domains [6], which can be seen with an electron microscope. In the unmagnetized material, the result of these

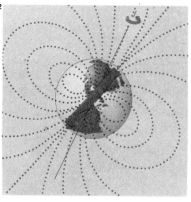

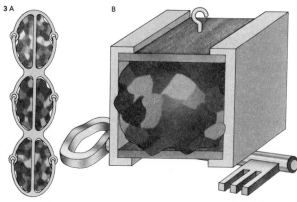

1 The Chinese were probably the first to realize the directional properties of magnetic materials and built compasses to help them navigate at sea as well as overland. By the 12th century magnetic compasses were in use in the West. This 13th-century one consists of a disc of lodestone (meaning "way stone") marked with the compass points, mounted on a block of wood and floating in water.

2 A simplified model of the earth's magnetic field may be made by picturing a long bar magnet lying in the centre of the earth. Magnetic materials on the globe's surface tend to align themselves so that their north-seeking poles point to what is called north (actually the south pole of the imaginary magnet) and their south-seeking poles point to the south (north pole of our magnet).

3 In an early "magnet" the magnetic properties of lodestone were intensified by placing lumps of the material within a soft iron structure [A]. This provided a path of low resistance to the magnetic flux of the lodestone, and had the effect of concentrating the flux. The attractive force depends on the square of the flux density, so that by directing the flux through a small section the lifting power of the lodestones was increased. Further improvements to lodestones' attractive qualities were gained using iron pole-pieces [B]. The flux lines follow the iron path to produce the two poles.

4 A simple way to magnetize materials such as iron and its alloys is to stroke it with a bar magnet [A], the nearness of which, coupled with its movement, tends to align the magnetic domains within the material. They then reinforce each other rather than keeping their normally random arrangements. The south-seeking ends of the domain try to follow the movement of the original magnet's north pole so that the right-hand side of the new magnet becomes a south pole. The domains lie with their south poles to the right, and so their north poles are to the left. Another way to magnetize a bar of suitable material is simply to hit it [B]. The domains receive a mechanical shock and the earth's field tends to align them with itself. Adapting the technique shown in [A] it is possible to make a bar magnet of suitable material using two magnets [C]. In this case, the right-hand side acquires a south pole and the left-hand side a north pole.

5 William Gilbert (1544–1603), an English physician and philosopher, demonstrated magnetic phenomena to Elizabeth I. His *De Magnete* was the first major work in Europe to describe the characteristics of magnets and magnetism in an organized way. Some of the theory is now known to be incorrect but it was still the most important contribution to the subject for many years. He suggested that the earth itself is a large magnet. The compass was already at that time used as a navigational aid – an important tool for the long commercial and military ventures of the 16th century – but the process by which the compass worked had never been explained. This painting is by A. Ackland Hunt.

millions of tiny magnets, acting in different directions, is to produce a neutral field – one with no magnetic properties whatsoever. It is as if hundreds of children were all tugging equally at a maypole from different positions; the result of their combined efforts is that the pole does not move.

The process of magnetizing consists of causing all the domains to assist each other by lining them up in the same direction. As they all come into line the total effect is additive and the whole of the material begins to display the properties of a magnet. If all the domains become perfectly aligned then the material has reached the limit of its magnetic capability. As a result, the magnetic strength of a material depends ultimately on its domain strength, and this is determined, in turn, by the way its individual atoms are structured within the domains.

Earth's magnetic field

The magnetic field of the earth has been accurately measured and charted but it still cannot be adequately explained [2]. In very simple terms, it is as if a single bar magnet lies between the geographic North and South Poles to produce some of the observable effects. But this does not explain the very unusual variations of strength, and even change of direction, of the magnetic forces over the earth's surface. Nor does it explain why millions of years ago the magnetic poles were oppositely aligned to their present direction, nor why they are slowly but constantly moving.

Both terrestrial magnetism and that exhibited by small pieces of iron can be better understood by considering that lines of magnetic force (often called flux lines) leave the north pole and enter the south. But this is an entirely arbitrary concept, in the same way as lines of latitude and longitude on a map are drawn merely for the sake of convenience.

In a simple bar magnet, lines of flux [Key] are pictured as forming an approximate cylinder stretching in air from one pole to another and enclosing the magnet itself. The flux lines are of the same polarity so they repel each other. They all start from and end at the same poles, but they each follow unique paths that can never cross.

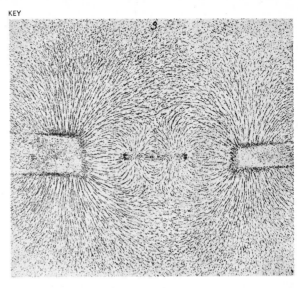

The pattern of iron filings in a magnetic field demonstrates how the lines of magnetic flux are distributed. The lines never cross and their mutual repulsive effects push each other away.

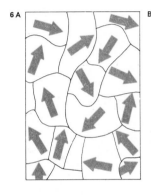

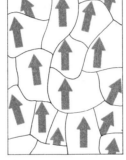
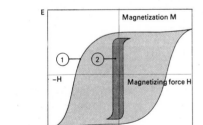

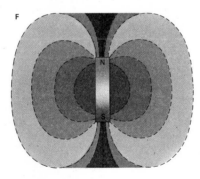

6 6 A B C D E F

6 The random arrangement of domains in unmagnetized materials [A] becomes highly ordered in a strong external magnetic field [B]. On removing the field the domains do not revert completely but retain some degree of alignment [C]. Domains on each side of any breaks ensure that large bar magnets always split up into smaller replicas of themselves [D]. Increasing the magnetizing force beyond a certain limit [E] cannot increase perfect alignment, and the material "saturates". Reversing H causes demagnetization. Different materials have similar shaped curves [1 and 2]. Removing H leaves the material partly magnetized [F].

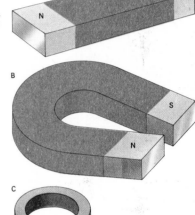
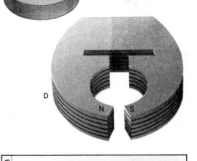

7 Magnets can be made in almost any form, from the bar [A] to a horseshoe [B], a ring [C] or a shape like that of D, used in an electrical measuring instrument. The poles are marked as N and S.

8 Magnets of complicated shapes can be made using powdered iron, mixed with a suitable bonding agent and cast into the required form. In granular form the structure is similar to bricks and mortar, the bricks being the particles, the mortar the bonding agent. Each magnet is separated from the next by non-magnetic material. For this reason the whole structure makes a weaker magnet than it would be if made from solid material.

9 Powdered iron can also be bonded as needle-like particles magnetized in such a way that their poles correspond to their points. The flux lines tend to run along the axes so that the bonding agent has a limited weakening effect.

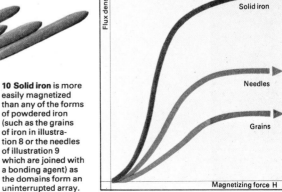

10 Solid iron is more easily magnetized than any of the forms of powdered iron (such as the grains of iron in illustration 8 or the needles of illustration 9 which are joined with a bonding agent) as the domains form an uninterrupted array.

Iron particle ___ Bonding agent ___

Electromagnetism

Electromagnetism is the effect by which electrical currents produce magnetic fields. Occasionally the process is unwanted, such as when a current flowing through a piece of equipment or cable on a ship produces magnetism that deflects the ship's magnetic compass. Often the effect passes unnoticed because it is very weak. But sometimes electricity is deliberately used to produce magnetic fields of great strength, as in the electromagnets that lift scrap iron [5].

Current flow and magnetic flux

The strength of a magnetic field is measured in flux lines or webers (Wb). These lines are produced whenever a current flows; and in air there is a simple proportional relationship between electric current flow and magnetic flux. A straight wire carrying a current can be looped to form a single turn. Provided the radius is reasonably small, the effect of forming a loop is to increase the concentration of magnetic flux without having to increase the current.

This concentrating effect can be further intensified by using more turns of wire to form a coil [4C]. At the point of maximum flux density – that is, maximum flux lines per unit area – the relationship between electric current A, turns of wire T and magnetic flux B is such that AT is proportional to B. Additional turns are simply a way of making the same current pass the same way more than once, and 12 amps flowing through three turns has precisely the same magnetic effect as three amps flowing through 12 turns.

Solenoid is the name given to a coil of wire wound to produce a magnetic field. Solenoids may be wound on iron (iron-cored) or on a non-magnetic support (air-cored). As far as flux is concerned, any non-magnetic core has the same properties as air, which means that the relationship connecting current, turns and flux holds good.

The presence of iron influences the magnetic field in two ways. It enhances the magnetic effect of the current, often by a factor of a thousand or more, but it also destroys the simple relationship applying to air-cored coils. Both these effects are a result of the structure of iron.

Microscopic regions called domains in the iron tend to align themselves with the magnetic field produced by the current. The iron provides an easy path for the magnetic flux passing through it. As a result, a given current produces more flux per unit cross-sectional area – that is, there is a high flux density. When all the domains have been aligned, further increase in current (or in the number of turns of wire in the coil) increases the flux density only negligibly.

Limiting characteristics

An iron-cored solenoid has a vastly stronger magnetic field compared with that of an air-cored one but is limited by the characteristics of iron. Theoretically there is no maximum to the magnetic field produced by an air-cored solenoid. But generally the enormous currents required to make them comparable to iron-cored ones are too expensive and technically difficult to produce.

A changing magnetic field can produce a current just as a current can produce a magnetic field. As a magnet moves towards a conductor the flux lines sweeping past cause an electromotive force (voltage) to be

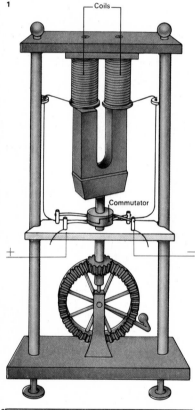

1 An electricity generator devised in 1883 by a Frenchman, Hippolyte Pixii, consisted of a horseshoe magnet set on end between two coils. The magnet was rotated through a gear system driven by a hand crank. As the magnet rotated, an alternating voltage was induced in the coils. A commutator, added later, enabled positive voltage to be picked off one side, and negative off the other, to produce direct current.

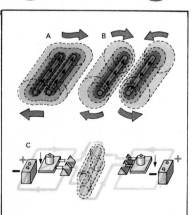

3 An electric current carried by a wire sets up a magnetic field around itself. As a result when parallel wires carry currents in the same direction [A] they attract each other, but when the currents flow in opposite directions [B] they repel. The ampere balance [C] measures the force of attraction or repulsion between two electric current-bearing conductors. Such forces can be very destructive when the currents are high and the conductors close.

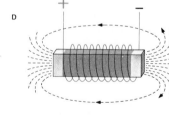

2 A moving electric charge generates its own magnetic field. This will interact with the field of a magnet to deflect the charge [A]. If the charge is moving in a wire, the wire will be deflected, as in an electric motor. Conversely, if a magnetic field is moved near a conductor, electrons will move so that their own magnetic field opposes the changing field [B]. This is the basis of the electricity generator.

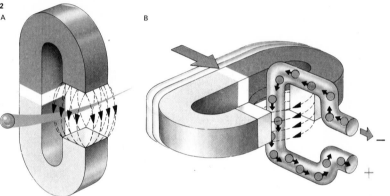

4 Electrons generate a magnetic field when they move. To determine the shape of the field the direction in which the "free" north pole of a small compass moves, at various points within the field, is noted. When a current flows at uniform velocity along a wire the magnetic field produced is a set of concentric rings in any plane drawn at right-angles to the wire. The number of lines of force drawn – dotted lines in B, C and D – by convention, represents the strength of the magnetic field. The direction of the field can be found by applying the "right hand grip rule" [B], that is, when the wire is held in the right hand with the thumb pointing in the direction of the current flow – conventionally opposite to that of the electron flow – the curled fingers indicate the field direction. If the wire is bent the field follows the change in shape. When the wire is wound, in a coil or solenoid, the force lines of the field all point in the same direction through the centre of the coil; overall, the field resembles that produced by a bar magnet with the north pole, in this example, on the right. If an iron bar is inserted into the core of the solenoid, the lines of force prefer to remain within it and this results in a high concentration of lines at the end of the bar. This device, called an electromagnet, can produce a very strong magnetic field which varies with the current in the wire, the number of turns in the solenoid and its cross-sectional area.

induced. The polarity of the induced voltage depends on the polarity and the direction of flux movement. The effect is greater in a coil than in a single wire, and is in proportion to the number of turns of wire in the coil. Similarly if the coil is iron-cored the induced voltage is more than in an air-cored coil because the flux changes are larger.

In inducing a voltage in this way there must be relative movement between the flux and the conductor (or coil). If not, flux lines will not move relative to the conductor and no voltage will be induced.

How power is produced

Electric generators produce current using precisely these principles [1]. In their basic form a magnet is rotated between coils. A voltage is induced depending on the factors outlined previously – that is the strength of the magnet and its speed of rotation (since this determines the rate of flux change). The voltage in a conductor is directly proportional to the rate at which flux sweeps past it.

In many generators the magnet is replaced by a solenoid that must be energized

or "excited" with current to produce the magnetic field necessary for the generator to function. It is the combination of voltage and current that constitutes the electrical power output from a generator.

Another aspect of the interrelationship between current in a conductor and magnetic flux makes use of the flow of an electric current in a magnetic field to produce physical movement. This is the principle on which motors and some electrical measuring instruments operate [6] but electrical power must be supplied to cause movement against a mechanical force.

Magnetic fields far stronger than ever before are now created by means of superconductivity, the zero-resistance effect in some metals at temperatures approaching absolute zero. As a result, current can flow without losses or heating, and it is possible to use vast currents in air-cored coils, avoiding the limitations of saturation imposed by iron. These enormously strong magnetic fields open up prospects for electromagnetic levitation and new forms of motors and generators capable of high outputs at reduced costs.

The "lift" obtainable using magnetism has been applied to make a working model of a magnetic levitation train, which is seen here end-on. The train has no wheels, but instead "floats" over a long magnetic strip that takes the place of a conventional track, below which a series of electromagnets generate the necessary magnetic field. The electric current can be supplied to these electromagnets in such a way that they behave as a linear motor, so driving the train along the track. Such trains are frictionless, pollution-free and virtually silent; a full-scale experimental prototype train has been built and tested in West Germany.

5 **Electromagnets** are often used in scrap metal yards to lift ferrous metals. This method not only reduces manhandling but also provides a means of separating the iron from other scrap materials.

6 **In electrical indicating instruments** a coil [1] turns when energized in a magnet's field [2]. The pointer [3] shows the strength of current on the scale [4]. The hairspring [5] returns the pointer to rest.

7 **Relays** are used to allow a low-power source to switch a high voltage circuit. When the coil [1] is energized by a small current, magnetic flux appears between the poles of the core [2] attracting the armature [3]. The moving contact [4] then engages the fixed contact [5], closing the high-voltage circuit. When the coil is de-energized, the balance weight [6] overcomes the weakened magnetic field and opens the circuit.

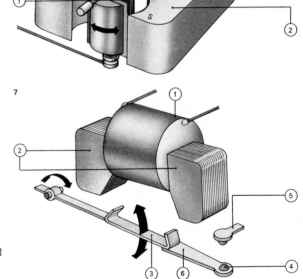

8 **In an electric bell**, the magnetic field of an electromagnet is effectively turned on and off rapidly to make a hammer strike the bell. Pressing the switch [A] allows current from a battery to energize the magnet, pulling over a spring-loaded armature and with it the hammer [B]. This action also breaks the circuit at a point contact and "turns off" the electromagnet. The armature springs back, re-makes the circuit [C] and the whole sequence is repeated.

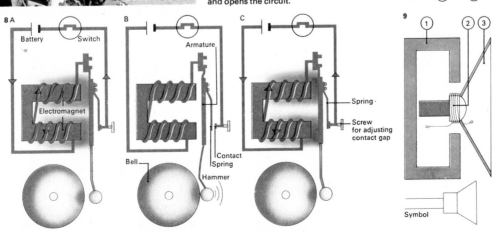

8 A Battery Switch

B Armature

C Spring

Screw for adjusting contact gap

Electromagnet

Contact Spring

Bell

Hammer

9 **A loudspeaker** commonly has a permanent magnet [1] to provide a magnetic field in which a coil [2] attached to a fibre cone [3] is held balanced, but is free to move backwards and forwards. A varying electrical current is fed to the coil from the amplifier output, resulting in a varying magnetic flux in the coil. This reacts with the permanent magnet's field, causing the coil and hence the cone to move back and forth, producing sound.

Symbol

Using magnets

The two main types of magnets used in apparatus such as electric bells, motors, dynamos, speedometers and the like are permanent magnets and electromagnets. Permanent magnets, chiefly made from iron-based alloys, retain their magnetism all the time. An electromagnet consists of a coil of wire, sometimes wound round a soft iron core, and behaves as a magnet only when an electric current flows in the coil.

The magnetic field

Those processes that generate motion by creating a strong and then a weak magnetic field (as in an electric bell) expend more electrical energy in the electromagnet than is gained from the resulting mechanical motion. But weakening a magnetic field (or alternatively "turning it off") is in fact the basis of many important devices that have characteristics that would be difficult or expensive to obtain in other ways. In permanent magnets the field cannot be turned off without destroying it. But it can be diverted.

The best example of diversion of the magnetic field is the magnetic chuck [Key].

This is a device for holding ferrous metals tightly onto a work table. The chuck is used almost exclusively in grinding machines because a vice could distort the metal, or not hold it level relative to the grinder.

The chuck comprises a number of small bar magnets embedded on a movable metal plate so that north and south poles are pointing vertically. The metal plate is of a material with low magnetic properties and the poles of the magnets are positioned alternately north–south and slightly separated. A second metal plate is placed above the magnet assembly. This incorporates soft iron pieces that correspond to the position of the magnets fixed in the base plate.

When a workpiece is placed on the upper plate it provides a flux circuit for the embedded magnets through the soft iron pieces of metal and is attracted to them, holding the workpiece in position. However, the operation of a simple lever allows the lower plate to be moved horizontally in such a way as to bring the magnet poles out of alignment with the pieces of soft iron in the upper plate. This causes the magnetic flux to

be diverted from the workpiece and it goes instead through the metal of the upper plate to link the embedded magnets north to south. The workpiece is then free to move.

Magnets in railway service

A system in which permanent and electromagnets complement each other for reasons of safety is commonly used in railways. A strong permanent magnet is attached close to the track at a set distance from the signals. As a train passes over the magnet it causes a pivoted permanent bar magnet in the cab to swing (like a see-saw) through a small angle and rest in this new position. The bar magnet's movement closes a switch to bring into action an alarm bell or hooter signal. A few seconds later the cab passes over an electromagnet connected to the signals. If they are set at "clear" the electromagnet is energized and the pivoted magnet in the cab is repelled so that it returns to its first position, turning off the alarm.

But if the signals are set at "stop" or "caution", the electromagnet is not energized and, after a short pre-set delay, the brakes

2 A system of permanent magnets attached to movable metal plates can be suspended above a fixed set of magnets. Provided there is a guide-rail to stop sideways motion, it can be used to move heavy loads around a factory or within an area where it is convenient to build a magnetic "track". The advantage over comparable methods such as rail systems is the absence of friction and moving parts.

1 Magnetic mines took a great toll of merchant ships during World War II. Placed in busy shipping lanes, the strong magnets built into the devices were attracted to metal-hulled ships which caused the mine to explode. Countermeasures such as electrical cables to reduce the ships' magnetic fields were devised, and are sometimes used in places where mines may still be located.

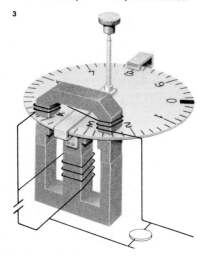

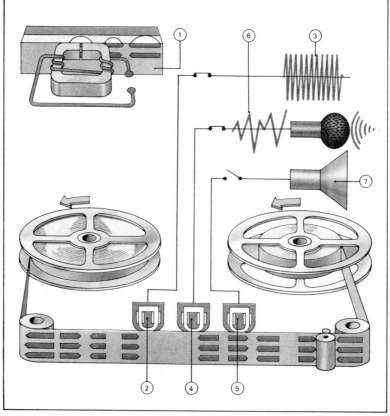

3 A domestic electric meter – a watt-hour meter for recording the amount of electricity consumed – makes use of electromagnets. When current is being used, it flows in coils that energize magnets and make a disc rotate. The disc is coupled to a counter reading in kilowatt-hours.

4 Magnetic metal oxide development has led to a revolution in the sound-recording industry. Metal oxides in powder form are bonded to flexible plastic tape [1], usually PVC, forming a moving surface on which magnetic patterns can be imposed corresponding to sound, visual or other signals. These tapes are used in machines that consist of an erase head [2] using high-frequency input [3] to demagnetize the tape as it is driven past, and a record [4] and replay head [5]. These either magnetize the tape according to the signal input [6] or reconvert the previously imposed magnetic patterns into the signals that formed them (ie plays back) [7]. Stereo or twin-track recording combines two record/replay heads in one. The erase head is taken out of circuit when playing back and, to prevent accidental erasure, most tape recorders have a built-in fail-safe arrangement.

are automatically applied if the driver fails to apply them. The brake-time circuit (like the audible alarm) is energized from the moment the pivoted magnet moves. If this magnet is returned to its original position (within the pre-set time) the brakes are not applied.

Meters and medicine

A phenomenon associated with magnetic fields is the eddy current. When there is relative motion between an electrical conductor (not necessarily one with magnetic properties) and a magnetic field, currents called eddy currents are induced. These, in turn, produce another magnetic field of opposite polarity. There is a tendency, because of the attraction between the opposite fields, for the conductor and original magnetic field to move together while the motion exists.

This principle is the basis of the car speedometer. A permanent magnet within the instrument housing rotates at a speed related to the crankshaft speed. It turns within a specially shaped aluminium disc which itself can rotate, but only through about 270° because of the restraint of a spring. As the magnet rotates, eddy currents are induced in the disc, which tries to follow the magnet. The strength of these currents is proportional to the speed of rotation and therefore the disc moves according to the speed of the car. A pointer attached to the disc moves over a scale calibrated in kilometres or miles per hour.

An electricity meter [3] works on similar principles. Current used by the consumer passes through an electromagnet, which induces eddy currents in an aluminium disc. In this case the disc can rotate freely through 360° and its movement is coupled to a gear train that drives the indicating dials.

Medical science also benefits from the use of powerful magnets. Experiments are taking place in the application of magnetically guided "pills" within the body. The "pill", which may be swallowed or inserted in a vein, is a minute radio, capable of transmitting information about such factors as temperature and salinity. It incorporates a "nose" of suitable metal and may be guided to particular organs by a magnet operating outside the body, thus aiding doctors in diagnosis.

KEY

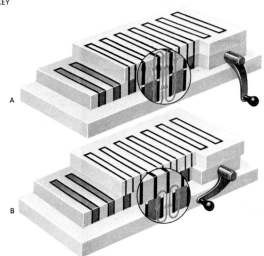

A permanent magnet cannot be switched off as electric currents can. Instead, its magnetic flux can be diverted. A magnetic chuck holds a workpiece in position on a grinding machine. Flux enters the workpiece and holds it in place [A]. When the flux is cut, the work is released [B].

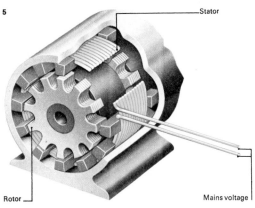

5

Stator

Rotor

Mains voltage

5 Magnetically polarized rotators are essential elements of modern timing devices and similar equipment. Because the mains frequency is fixed precisely at the power station, motors whose rotation is tied to this frequency have a highly accurate speed. Using magnets in the rotor (often permanent for ease of manufacture and reliability) ensures that once it is "locked" to the stator frequency, the rotor follows the speed exactly. The rotor is made from thin sheets of silicon steel cemented together to form a cylinder. The ridges are then magnetized to form poles.

6

6 Electricity meters are often difficult to read. The cyclometer type shown here suffers from the disadvantage that the digits representing the high numbers (on the left) rotate slowly, to give ambiguous readings. A version developed by Ferranti has a small magnet attached to every wheel behind the figure 7. A bar magnet is fixed over the wheels as shown. When the wheels move from 9 to 0 magnetic attraction ensures a quick changeover of figures. Only the highest number wheel is excluded from this arrangement because when it changes to 0 all the other figures will change to 0.

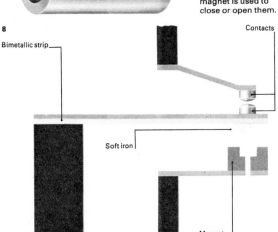

7

7 The reed switch, used as a safety switch and in electronic counters, has its contacts enclosed in a glass envelope to protect them from corrosion. A magnet is used to close or open them.

8

Bimetallic strip

Contacts

Soft iron

Magnet

8 A thermostat often incorporates a bimetallic strip, which moves to open or close a circuit according to the temperature. One way of ensuring a quick "on" or "off" is to use a fixed magnet and a soft iron pellet (armature) attached to the moving contact arm. As the bimetal starts to curve it is either attracted swiftly to the magnet or else is released suddenly, providing a fast "snap" action.

9

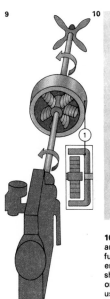

9 The electromagnetic clutch, often used on ships, has a soft iron cup [1] attached to the propeller shaft and has electromagnets on the engine shaft. Energizing the coils produces a strong field and transmits the drive motion.

10

10 Magnetic catches are used on doors of furniture and refrigerators to hold them shut. A common type on a refrigerator uses "magnetic rubber" (rubber with ferrous particles magnetized to form a convenient pole pattern) on the edge of the door. The type shown here, on a cupboard, uses metallic magnets in a plastic housing fixed to the frame. It "catches" on an iron plate on the door.

103

Transformers, motors and dynamos

The transformer, one of the most essential and efficient of electrical machines, has wide uses in the supply of electricity. It is used in power stations and at sub-stations – in the former to boost voltages for transmission over power lines and in the latter to reduce voltages to levels suitable for industrial or domestic use. Transformers are also used in many electrical appliances – such as radios, television sets and battery chargers – wherever alternating voltages different from the mains supply are required.

Motors and generators

A transformer, with its two main elements, magnetic and electrical, linked by a laminated soft iron core [Key, 1], has no moving parts and is up to 99 per cent efficient. Electric motors and dynamos, however, have rotating elements and therefore cannot be made quite as efficient.

Motors and dynamos (or generators, as they are now more usually called) are basically the same in construction, although their functions are different. Motors are supplied with electrical power to provide mechanical power; generators are supplied with mechanical power to give electrical power. But it is important to remember that they are so similar that some machines can act as motors or as generators, depending only upon whether they are supplied with electricity or mechanical power.

The two essential elements of each of these machines are the field and the armature. The field is a magnetic field, which may be derived from permanent magnets or electromagnets. The former are cheaper but the latter are more convenient because with an electrically energized field it is easy to increase or decrease their strength. It is, however, a convenience gained only at the expense of having to provide the coils for the electromagnets that form the field (field "windings") and to do all the work that goes into insulating and installing them.

How the armature works

The armature is also a winding but is arranged differently from the field. It is essentially a conductor (or conductors) arranged to cut the field's magnetic lines of flux at right-angles. The armature conductors may be wound onto a cylinder that rotates in a field. Or they may be fixed to the inner walls of a cylinder, within which the field windings rotate. The static part of the machine is called the stator and the revolving part the rotor. Both the field and the armature may be on either the stator or the rotor.

By a basic principle of electromagnetism, a voltage is induced in a conductor that moves in a magnetic field and a conductor in a magnetic field experiences a force and tends to move when a current flows in it.

To make the best use of this basic effect, the magnetic and electrical elements in electrical machines (the field and the armature) have to interact in the most efficient manner possible. The armature is generally wound on an iron core which concentrates the maximum number of magnetic flux lines. The field coils are also wound on iron cores, to produce the maximum flux for a given current. The iron for both the field and the armature is sometimes laminated – that is, made up of slices [1]. This prevents the currents from circulating and "eddying" in the iron

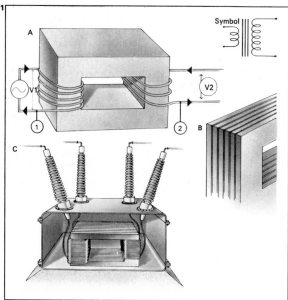
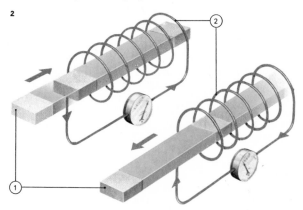

1 In the transformer [A], the input or primary current [1] causes lines of magnetic flux to form in the iron core, linking it to the output or secondary [2]. As the supply alternates the flux lines collapse and reform in the same pattern, but with different polarities. They induce a voltage in the output coil. The ratio of input to output voltage (V1 to V2) is the ratio of turns on the input and output coils. The iron core is laminated [B] to reduce eddy currents. The high-voltage transformer [C] has its terminals insulated to prevent "flashover".

2 Electricity can be generated by a magnet, an electrical conductor and relative movement. Moving the magnet [1] causes the flux lines surrounding it to cut the conductor of the coil [2] and induce a voltage in it – coinciding with the movement; the faster the movement the higher the voltage induced. Opposite movements produce opposite voltages – any current in a circuit between the coil ends flows first one way then the other as the magnet is moved in and out. These are alternating currents and the generators are called alternators.

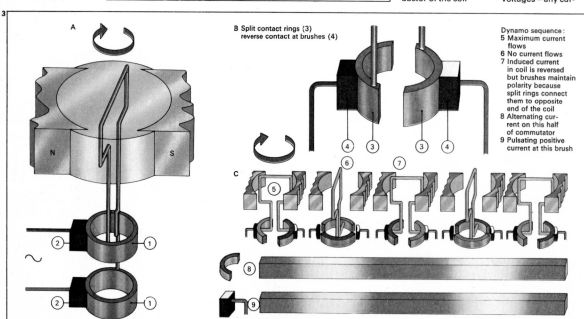

B Split contact rings (3) reverse contact at brushes (4)

Dynamo sequence:
5 Maximum current flows
6 No current flows
7 Induced current in coil is reversed but brushes maintain polarity because split rings connect them to opposite end of the coil
8 Alternating current on this half of commutator
9 Pulsating positive current at this brush

3 Electricity is generated mechanically when a coil is rotated in a magnetic field [A]. An AC voltage is induced in the coil and is connected to the external circuit by contact rings [1] and carbon brushes [2]. A current flows when a circuit is made between the brushes. To produce direct current – as in a cycle dynamo – the generator is modified [B]; the contact rings are split [3] and the halves insulated from each other. A fixed pair of brushes [4] contacts the ring segments in turn. The arrangement of split segments is called a commutator; the sequence [5–9] describes how it works in a cycle dynamo.

itself and generating wasted heat, as a result of changing magnetic flux in the machine.

The armature must be supplied with current (through rotating contacts) if it is the rotor in a motor and there must be a way of taking current from it if it is in a generator. The same applies to the field if it is electrically energized. The rotating contact arrangement can be either a set of slip-rings or a commutator [3]. These rotate under fixed contacts, called brushes, made of carbon and held in place by springs. From time to time the brushes have to be replaced when the carbon wears away

Varying the field
The armature and field windings of a motor are supplied with current and, by using a resistor in the field circuit, it is possible to vary the field strength. Weakening it causes the motor to revolve faster – provided the armature current is constant – but with less torque (turning force), and vice versa [4]. In a generator driven at constant speed, strengthening the field increases the voltage output; weakening the field decreases it.

The motors and generators already described are generally suitable either for AC (alternating current) or for DC (direct current) supplies. However, induction motors can be used only with alternating current supplies. The armature is the rotor and can be wound or made in the form of a "squirrel cage" [5]. The flux from the stator field is changing and induces a voltage in the cage. This causes a current to flow which interacts with the stator field to produce torque. No slip-rings are necessary.

The simplest field consists of two coils. As one becomes a north magnetic pole, the other becomes south, unlike DC machines whose field polarities are constant. The rotor experiences a pulsating and reversing field, but not one that appears to rotate; without a starting force the armature will not rotate either. Given a push in either direction, it begins to follow the field as it alternates.

Some induction motors have a wound rotor and slip-rings may be used. The purpose of the rings is not to supply current to the armature but to alter its characteristics with the use of external resistances.

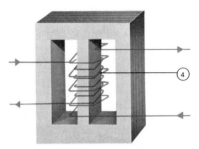
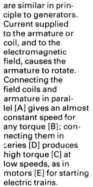

The transformer, a simple and efficient means of raising or lowering AC voltage, consists of three basic elements: an iron core [1], which provides a magnetic link between the primary or input [2] coil and the secondary, output coil [3]. The turns ratio between the input and the output determines the ratio between AC voltages "transformed"; fewer turns on the output side give a proportional decrease in voltage and vice versa, transforming the flow of current. The core may take a number of shapes; sometimes more than two coils are used and sometimes the two coils are wound on each other [4].

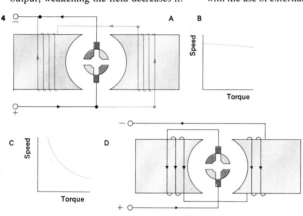

4 Electric motors are similar in principle to generators. Current supplied to the armature or coil, and to the electromagnetic field, causes the armature to rotate. Connecting the field coils and armature in parallel [A] gives an almost constant speed for any torque [B]; connecting them in series [D] produces high torque [C] at low speeds, as in motors [E] for starting electric trains.

5 The induction motor is the one in most widespread use; the coil forming the armature of a simple DC machine is replaced by a "squirrel cage". This consists of aluminium or copper bars connecting each end to a ring, the whole embedded in a laminated iron rotor. The field, at least two coils inside the motor body, is shaped to allow the rotor to revolve inside with a small clearance. Flux lines caused by an alternating current passing through the field cut the cage bars, inducing a current in them – hence the "induction" motor.

6 A
B
C

6 The "rotor" of a linear motor moves length-wise rather than revolving. It is a flat plate, either sandwiched between two long field windings or resting solely on one. Energizing the fields with alternating current causes the plate to move in a linear direction, making use of exactly the same principles as an induction motor [A], from which it can be pictured as being "made" by cutting [B] and opening out [C].

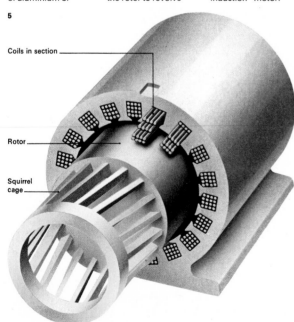

Coils in section
Rotor
Squirrel cage

7 A large linear motor, with field windings similar to those shown here, could be used to drive a silent, non-wheeled train or other vehicle. Smaller motors are already used – for example for opening and closing sliding doors. The armature or metal plate, usually aluminium, is fixed to the upper part of the door and the windings attached to the door frame. When the field is energized, the plate passes horizontally along the field, thus moving the door.

Basic DC circuits

An electrical circuit is the system by which an electric current is directed, controlled, modified, switched on or switched off. Circuits can contain from two or three to many hundred different components, according to the way in which the current is to be controlled, but all share certain characteristics.

The formation of a circuit
The primary requirement of a circuit is that it must form a complete path; electrons must be able to flow round the whole system so that as many electrons pass back into the source of the current as leave it. Certain occurrences, such as lightning strikes or electric shocks, seem to deny this first requirement, but are nevertheless examples of electrical circuits. This apparent contradiction can be resolved by considering the earth and all the structures on it as a vast electron bank. If clouds develop an electron imbalance, the earth makes it up with a flash of lightning and the net result is that on average the numbers of electrons leaving the earth and arriving at it are equal.

Electric currents can also be "carried" by charged atoms, or ions. Ions of dissolved salts

and other chemicals conduct current through the electrolyte in an electroplating bath and gas ions conduct electricity in a fluorescent strip-light. But whatever the current carriers, all circuits share three characteristics: a current (I), a voltage (V) and a resistance (R).

An illustration of electron movement (and the use of high-voltage direct current) is the arrangement of the transmission line from the Cabora Bassa dam in Mozambique to the South African town of Apollo some 500km (310 miles) away. There are two lines to carry the current, one taking electrons to Apollo, the other returning the same number to Cabora Bassa. If one of the lines breaks, the earth itself "replaces" it and carries the electrons in the appropriate direction.

In a similar way, the chassis of vehicles are used as the so-called earth or return circuit, although this is a loose and generally inaccurate term. One terminal of the battery is connected to the bodywork and a single wire is brought from the other terminal through a switch to each piece of electrical equipment. These in turn are also connected firmly to the chassis. The circuit so estab-

lished allows the number of electrons leaving the battery to be matched exactly by the number of those arriving. Using the chassis to complete the circuit in this way makes a second wire to each component unnecessary.

Direct and alternating current
One major practical difference in circuit components (although there are no differences in principle) is determined by whether they are used for direct current or alternating current. Direct current is unidirectional; the electron flow is always in the same direction and although it may stop and start, grow or diminish in quantity, it never reverses.

Current flow (as opposed to electron flow, which is always against the conventional direction of current flow) is assumed by convention to be from a positive to a negative terminal. In direct current (DC) generators, batteries and some other sources, the terminals are determined by the nature of the machine or equipment and are irreversible. The most common example of direct current source is a chemical cell or battery, in which the nature of the chemicals themselves

1 A cell or battery sends electrons round an electrical circuit as a result of chemical action. This unidirectional character of the electron flow is called direct current (DC), even if it varies greatly or stops altogether from time to time. In a primary cell current flow stops as soon as one of the chemicals or electrodes is consumed. A secondary cell or accumulator can be recharged, often forming these gas bubbles.

2 Electrical generators can be AC or DC machines. The output of a DC machine does not depend on an exhaustible chemical process, so it usually gives a steadier direct current than chemical sources. Large generators like these supply alternating current (AC), characterized by a rapid periodic reversal of electron flow. In an AC system the current falls to zero every time the direction of its flow is reversed.

3 A method of examining direct current is to measure how it varies over a fixed period. Graph A shows a current, such as that taken by a lamp supplied by a generator, which does not alter over the time it is measured (the vertical axis represents current and the horizontal one time). Graph B shows a direct current typical of a welding circuit. It varies with time, although its value is always positive.

4 The drawings used by engineers and other workers in the electrical industry have to be clear to the reader irrespective of his language. These symbols are just a few of the hundreds used.

5 It is often economical to use direct current at high voltage when transmitting large amounts of electrical power. Only in the last few years has reliable equipment been available to switch large DC voltages on and off. This large thyristor "switch" operates on similar principles to transistors used in radios. Because power stations are being sited farther away from population centres, high voltage DC is increasingly used instead of AC.

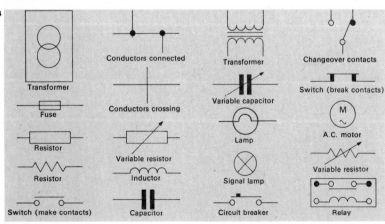
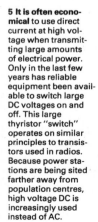

Transformer

Fuse

Resistor

Resistor

Switch (make contacts)

Conductors connected

Conductors crossing

Variable resistor

Inductor

Capacitor

Transformer

Variable capacitor

Lamp

Signal lamp

Circuit breaker

Changeover contacts

Switch (break contacts)

A.C. motor

Variable resistor

Relay

fixes the polarity of the system. Although the output of the cell may vary, the current flow is always in the same direction. The same applies to a DC generator (dynamo), because the structure of the machine determines the polarity. Another device, known as a rectifier, also has fixed polarity. A rectifier is used to convert alternating current to direct current – irrespective of how the input varies, the current direction at the output terminals is always the same.

Alternating current (AC) is the more common mode, although in certain instances direct current is particularly appropriate and alternating current cannot be used. In electroplating, for example, direct current is used because it is vital that the current always flows in the same direction. If it did not, material would pass back and forth from the coating metal to the coated surface and no plating would take place. The recharging of a battery [1], which is a specialized form of "electroplating", can also be carried out only by direct current and mains-powered battery chargers must contain a rectifier.

In systems for transmitting power over long distances, direct current may be chosen because it requires less insulation and uses fewer and narrower conductors for the amount of power transmitted than does alternating current. Direct current, provided it is steady, uses its conductors fully throughout the whole of the transmission period whereas the conductors of an alternating current are not always fully utilized. As a result, a smaller conductor can be used for the same effective power transmission and if the current is to be transmitted over very long distances the savings may be considerable.

Interrupting the flow
Despite some advantages, the use of direct current is beset by one major problem: switching it off quickly. Interrupting a current that is flowing tends to produce a spark between the contacts providing the interruption. Sometimes this can take the form of a spark so large that it melts not only the contacts but the switching device itself. Alternating current, by its very nature, falls to zero many times a second, so that the spark also falls to zero, limiting the damage it can do.

Electroplating of metals was one of the earliest uses of direct current. The inherent electrical properties of certain chemicals in solution make it possible to coat metallic surfaces with a thin durable coating of another metal. In this automatic plating plant car components are given a protective coating of chromium.

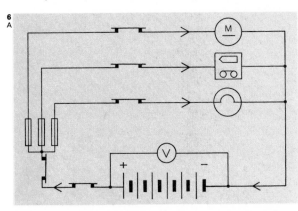

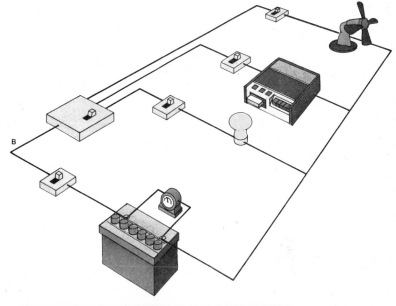

6 This diagram of a circuit [A] shows a typical but simplified electrical system [B] of the kind that is used for equipment powered by a battery. Switches control the current flow into three leads to a lamp and two appliances containing electric motors. The voltmeter records the electromotive force (that is, the voltage) of the battery, which remains virtually constant. The current flowing through the lamp will also remain virtually constant, but those through the appliances may vary, depending on the demands made by the motors in them. Fuses can protect the circuit from current surges.

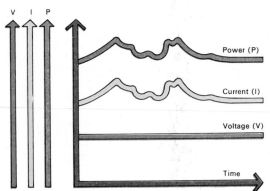

7 The circuit shown in illustration 6 has many interdependent electrical variables. Representing them in the form of a graph indicates how they are related. (There are different scales on the vertical axes but the horizontal axis, time, is the same for all the other variables.) Three of the most important variables – voltage, current and power – are shown. The current (I) is fixed by the battery. If the battery is in good condition the voltage will not vary significantly. The voltage (V) depends on the voltage and the resistance of the appliance it is feeding. This may vary (as it does in the motors) or may be fixed (as it is in the lamp). The power (P) is the product of voltage and current and is measured in watts.

8 Welding is a process of joining metals together with a bond so strong that it is often superior to the parent materials. A large electric current – perhaps 2,000 amps – at low voltage can be used to provide the necessary heat, so that the metal in a particular area is melted. The current passes in the form of an arc from an insulated electrode in the welder's hand and enters the workpiece across a short air gap. The object that is to be welded is connected to one terminal of the current source and the welding electrode to the other. Electric welding generally uses direct current, generated by special equipment because of the very large currents needed.

Basic AC circuits

The physical processes that take place in electrical circuits carrying alternating current (AC) differ from those in direct current (DC) circuits, reflecting the differences between the two types of electricity. Alternating current regularly reverses its direction, becoming zero before each reversal (100 times a second in European countries and 120 times a second in North America, corresponding to 50Hz and 60Hz supply frequencies). With reference to zero, the current is negative and positive alternately. Direct current always flows in the same direction.

Current wave and circuit components

The shape of the "current wave" (the curve representing its change of value with respect to time) can take an infinite variety of forms. For most purposes it is sinusoidal (like a sine wave [Key]).

The number of times the curve repeats the whole alternating cycle in a second is called the frequency and is measured in hertz (Hz) – one cycle per second equals 1Hz. A sinusoidal voltage (V) applied to a circuit produces a sinusoidal current whose value at any instant in the cycle is equal to V/Z, where Z is called the impedance (which depends on the resistance, capacitance and inductance of the circuit and the supply frequency); Z is measured in ohms (Ω). The equation is analogous to that used to express Ohm's law: the direct current flowing through a conductor is directly proportional to the electromotive force (voltage) that produces it and inversely proportional to the resistance.

The three main types of circuit components are inductors, capacitors and resistors. A resistor behaves in the same way in either an AC or a DC circuit; inductors and capacitors, however, do not. In these devices, currents are out of phase with the applied voltage in parallel circuits (in which there is more than one path for the current) and voltages are out of phase with the current in series circuits (in which the source and output devices are connected by only one path).

Phase lead and lag

A simple analogy to the phase differences in alternating current and voltage is the action of a yo-yo, where the hand from which the spinning mass derives its energy can move in the opposite direction to that of the mass. The current taken by a capacitor is out of phase with the applied voltage; it is zero when the voltage is maximum and vice versa. Sine waves may be represented by rotating vectors (a vector is a quantity that has both magnitude and direction) and on a vector diagram the capacitor current is 90° out of phase with the voltage and is said to be leading.

For a pure inductance the reverse applies – that is, the current lags the voltage by 90°. This can be explained in another way by saying that for a capacitor the voltage lags the current by 90° and for an inductor the voltage leads. With a resistance, the current and voltage are in phase [3].

In a circuit that has both capacitance and inductance but no resistance, one current leads by 90° and is equal in magnitude to another lagging by 90°. The overall effect is subtractive – they cancel each other out. When this happens the circuit is said to experience current resonance. In effect, the capacitor's current feeds the inductor and

1 An inductor [A] is a circuit component consisting of a coil of wire. When current flows through a coil a magnetic field is set up whose lines of magnetic flux thread through the coil. Their number and distribution depend on the design of the coil. As the field changes in strength with the changing current, flux lines increase or decrease, cutting the windings of the coil. This is the principle of a generator and an emf (electromotive force) is generated in such a way as to oppose current changes. The effectiveness of an inductor can be changed by screwing a threaded iron core into or out of the coil [B].

Symbol
Iron core
Symbol

2 A capacitor or condenser [A] is a component used primarily in alternating current circuits (particularly in electronic applications). The two parallel plates alternately store electrons as the current varies. The capacitor holds the electrons in balance and releases them at the same rate as the supply current, but out of phase with it. Shown here are (top) a variable condenser consisting of parallel metal plates separated by air gaps, commonly used as the tuning control in a radio set, and an electrolytic condenser (bottom) consisting of a roll of aluminium foil. In [B] a large industrial condenser is shown.

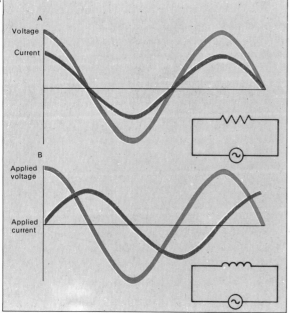

A
Voltage
Current

B
Applied voltage
Applied current

3 In an AC circuit that has only resistance in it [A], the voltage applied and the current flow are exactly in phase, that is, their maxima, minima and zero points always occur at the same instant; this is true no matter how quickly the voltage fluctuates. With only inductance in the circuit, the voltage and current are out of phase. In an inductive circuit [B], current is said to lag the voltage, or the voltage lead the current. In a capacitive circuit, the reverse applies – the current leads the voltage. The inductor and capacitor (unlike the resistor) store energy and release it out of phase with the input – something like flywheels on steam engines.

A
Volts
Current
Average Power

B
Current
Volts
Average Power

C
Volts
Current
Average Power

A Pure resistance, voltage and current in phase
B Pure capacitance, 90° lag or lead
C Capacitance or inductance and resistance, less than 90° lag or lead

4 Power in an AC circuit is the instantaneous product of voltage and current averaged over a fixed period. In a resistive circuit (one that has resistance only) the voltage and current are in phase [A] and the power dissipated is given by the formula VI (voltage × current). In a purely capacitive circuit (one that has capacitance only) the current and voltage are 90° out of phase and the circuit returns as much power as it absorbs [B]. This also applies to a purely inductive circuit (one that has inductance only). There is, however, always some resistance present; the phase angle Φ is no longer 90°, and some power is absorbed according to VIcosΦ [C].

vice versa, because each needs the current at different times in the cycle. It is a repeated borrowing and lending action.

In a normal circuit some resistance R is always present. The phase angle Φ between the voltage and current depends on the inductance, capacitance, resistance and frequency. Resonance can still occur when the phase lags and leads cancel out.

The actual value of the current taken by a capacitor or inductor depends on three factors: the voltage, the frequency and the value (size) of the capacitor or inductor. The higher the capacitance the higher the current, but for an inductor the current is smaller as the inductance rises. Current or voltage vectors may be added or subtracted using special mathematics to give a resultant vector. The process is similar to that applied to mechanical vectors. Pulling a barge with ropes at an angle from each side of a canal, for instance, gives a resultant forward motion.

Root mean square values

In an AC circuit the magnitude of the alternating voltage or current is defined as the rms (root mean square, or "effective") value. It is used because the average value is zero, since during any short interval of time the number of half cycles in one direction equals those in the other. The rms value can be derived using simple mathematics and is that quoted in all descriptions of electrical equipment. On an electric iron, a plate reading "230V, 2A" refers to rms values. The voltage and current in this case vary constantly in the form of a sine wave, reaching ±325V and +2.828A – both 50 times every second.

All electrical appliances that are essentially resistive in structure – such as incandescent lamps, heaters and irons – operate perfectly well in either alternating or direct current circuits (provided they are of the same voltage). But equipment that depends on inductive or capacitive properties, such as some motors, transformers and fluorescent lamps, can operate only with alternating current. Alternating current is preferred for the domestic electricity supply because it can be transmitted efficiently and easily from the power station to the domestic consumer and, is safer when it is switched on and off.

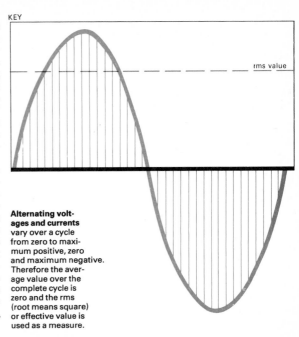

Alternating voltages and currents vary over a cycle from zero to maximum positive, zero and maximum negative. Therefore the average value over the complete cycle is zero and the rms (root means square) or effective value is used as a measure.

5 A vector diagram shows the relationship between the three branches of current in a capacitance, resistance and inductance. Three currents and their phase relationships with the applied voltage are depicted, by convention, by lines whose lengths represent the various values of current (they are vectors): A is said to lead, B to be in phase and C to lag behind the voltage.

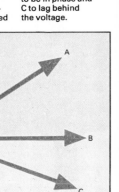

6 Electric clocks connected to the AC network depend on the system frequency for keeping accurate time. This is why the kitchen clock [A] always shows the same time as a master clock in the power station [B]. A reduction in frequency makes the clock read slow and vice versa. Because many essential timing devices depend on the mains frequency, it is maintained at a constant value (normally 50Hz in Europe). Any fall in frequency (when demands are heavy) can be gradually made up by adjusting the frequency. The frequency rarely varies by more than 4 per cent.

**7 A circuit with inductance [H], resistance and capacitance [C] may contain some voltages out of phase with the common current. It is possible for those of leading components to cancel out those of lagging components, when the circuit is said to be resonant. Resonant circuits are used in radio sets.

8 The power given by an AC generator depends on its voltage, current output and frequency. The power to weight ratio becomes more favourable as the frequency increases, which is why aircraft generators operate at 400Hz. Here an auxiliary generator is being used to power electrical circuits in an aircraft while its engines are idle.

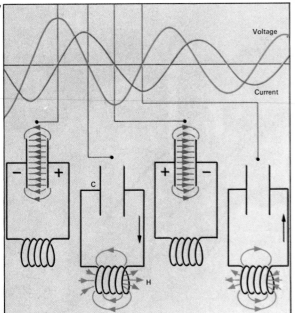

Semiconductors

Metals such as copper and aluminium are good conductors of electricity. Glass, rubber and most plastics are non-conductors, or insulators. But there are some materials, such as germanium and silicon, which are neither good nor bad conductors, and they are called semiconductors. They are used for making transistors and other solid-state devices.

Current carriers

The atoms in a semiconductor easily lose one of their electrons, allowing another from a nearby atom to replace it. Although this electron exchange process goes on, the overall charge of the material is nil; in other words, it is electrically neutral. But by adding some different atoms in the form of a slight impurity, for example with one more electron per atom than the atoms of the material itself, an entirely new material is created. Just one of these new atoms (such as phosphorus, arsenic or antimony) for every one hundred thousand million germanium or silicon atoms can make a semiconductor called an *n*-type material, in which a few extra electrons are available for carrying current.

The opposite situation can be produced, making a material deficient in electrons, by adding atoms with one fewer electron per atom than those of the original material. In this case, aluminium, gallium or indium in the same remarkably small proportion is added to the germanium or silicon to produce *p*-type material [Key]. In both *n*-type and *p*-type materials, the electrons involved in the creation of the particular type of semiconductor are known as the valence electrons – the ones in the outer shell of the atom.

In *n*-type materials, the surplus electrons provide the means for current flow, whereas in *p*-type surplus "holes" are created for the electrons to settle into. And as a hole exerts forces of attraction on the surrounding electrons, it can be thought of as if it were a positively charged particle. The most numerous – electrons or holes – are called majority carriers, or current carriers, in contrast to the minority carriers which are the few residual electrons or holes [1].

The simplest form of semiconductor device, a *p-n* junction diode [3], is made by joining pieces of opposite types of semicon-

ductor material together, attaching a wire to each and enclosing the combination in a metal or plastic shield, with the leads protruding. By connecting a battery, so that the positive terminal is connected to the *n*-type material, a very small current flows consisting of minority carriers only. But if the battery is reversed [4], there is a large current flow, because it consists of majority carriers.

Forming a transistor

When a layer of one type of semiconductor material is sandwiched between two layers of the opposite type, a conventional two-junction, three-layer semiconductor device is formed, known as the junction transistor [5]. This arrangement can be used to form either a *p-n-p* or an *n-p-n* device. Apart from voltage polarities, both can be connected in a circuit to provide current amplifying devices. The voltages in each instance are low – for example, a voltage of 6 volts DC between the collector and base of an *n-p-n* transistor.

When the base/emitter voltage is increased from, say, 600 to 620 millivolts, the collector current might increase from 0.995

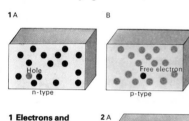

1 Electrons and holes deliberately introduced into the intrinsic (pure basic) material are seen here to be much more numerous than the carriers (holes [A] or electrons [B]) made by thermal activity.

2 In an *n*-type material [A], electrons are attracted by the oppositely charged (positive) terminal of the battery. But for the fact that electrons are also flowing from the negative terminal into the other end of the material, it would be left with a net positive charge. With *p*-type material [B] a similar action ensues, but initial attraction is between positive holes and the negative terminal. The invention of the transistor in 1948 revolutionized the world of electronics. Before this no one had ever considered how vitally important semiconductors would become to the electronics industry.

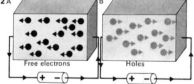

4 Wiring the terminals of a battery across a piece of joined *n*-type and *p*-type semiconductor material, in which a barrier free from carriers has been produced, simply widens the barrier if the positive pole of the battery is connected to the *n*-type [A]. Little current flows. But if the battery is reversed, forward bias is created together with the breakdown of the barrier and a large current flows [B].

6 Most alloy junction semiconductor devices were of the *p-n-p* type with germanium as the *n*-type base material in the form of a wafer. A pellet of "impurity" material, such as indium, was placed on each side and heated. The indium melted, and after recrystallization, *p*-type areas formed. In recent devices, and in integrated circuits, gaseous boron or phosphorous is diffused into wafers of hot silicon to make layers of *p*- or *n*-type material.

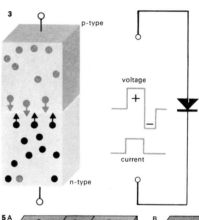

3 Joining together two different semiconductor materials (*n*-type and *p*-type) causes carriers to start drifting across the junction area. As soon as a few holes and electrons have crossed the junction, they make a thin section of each material oppositely charged from the rest. A barrier which is free from carriers is therefore produced. The combination acts as a semiconductor diode.

5 A transistor is a sandwich of *n* and *p* type material, like two diodes back to back, [A] or [B]. In the *n-p-n* device [A, C] electrons readily flow from the *n*-type emitter to the *p*-type base under the influence of a forward bias voltage. The base is doped to give relatively few holes, so the base current is small. Most electrons are attracted across the thin base, by the reverse bias on the second diode, into the second *n*-type area called the collector. The large flow of electrons from emitter to collector is proportional to the small flow of holes from base to emitter. This makes a current amplifier. A voltage amplifier can be made by putting a resistance R in the collector circuit [D].

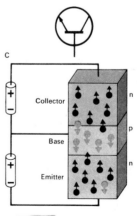

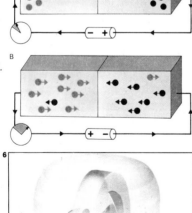

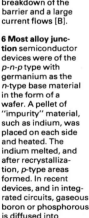

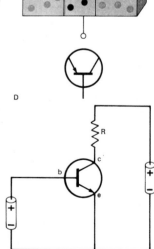

7 Some electrons in a metal are free to flow, provided that losses are made up by a reservoir, such as a battery [1]. An insulator is like an array of ponds – the potential walls around each atom (from the positive nucleii) are too high for electrons to escape – unless the system is "tilted" by a very strong electric field [2]. In semiconductors the potential walls are not so far above the electron "surface". The "tilt" from a small electric field permits electrons to jump from one atom to the next [3].

to 1.990 milliamps (mA), whereas the corresponding base current would probably increase only from 0.005 to 0.010mA. Therefore the gain of 0.005mA in the base current has caused a gain of 0.995mA in the collector current, a current amplification of 200 times.

The earliest transistors were of the point contact type, but this method of manufacture was quickly replaced by the alloy junction [6]. It involves the use of heat to form two regions of p-type material in an n-type germanium wafer. The resulting device is a p-n-p semiconductor, although it can handle only low currents.

Integrated circuits

A more recent method of manufacturing semi-conductors involves the forming of p- and n-type silicon layers on the surface of a silicon wafer, sliced from a single large crystal. Many layers can be added, the atoms of each fresh layer matching up with those on the surface of the original crystal so that they behave, electrically, as if they had always been part of the crystal. The n- or p-type layers may be coated with silicon oxide for protection and insulation, or covered with metal to make contact between devices on the same chip. The shape and size of the surface deposited is controlled by masks, produced photographically or by electron beams, and circuit elements can be made as small as it is possible to make masks – typically 10^{-4}cm for a mask made photographically.

These advances in technology have generated a host of new microelectronic devices. For example, the MOSFET – Metal Oxide-Semiconductor Field Effect Transistor [8] – which can be packed more densely on a silicon chip than the conventional bipolar transistor. This allows the fabrication of quite powerful computers on a single silicon chip [10B]. Some devices have unique properties that cannot be duplicated by discrete components. In the charge couple device [8D], a row of gates act like a "bucket brigade", storing packets of charge under alternate gates to be handed on when required. Charge produced by the absorption of light can be used to drive a solid-state TV camera.

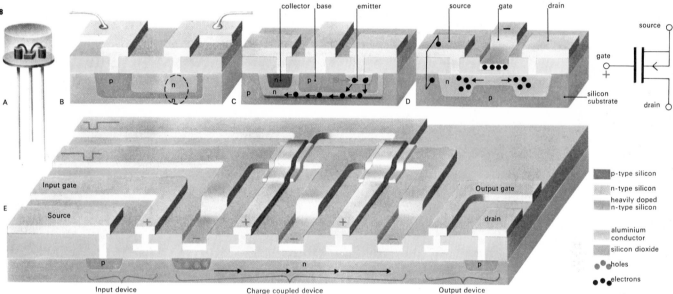

Electron

Impurity atom   Hole

If a "foreign" or impurity atom with three electrons in its outer shell enters an array of atoms that have four electrons in their outer shells, a "hole" is created in the lattice. This hole acts as an attraction to the surrounding electrons; it can be considered as a virtual positive charge.

8

collector   base   emitter   source   gate   drain

source

gate

silicon substrate

drain

A   B   C   D

Input gate

Output gate

E   Source

drain

p-type silicon

n-type silicon

heavily doped n-type silicon

aluminium conductor

silicon dioxide

holes

electrons

8 In a silicon transistor [A], shown in cross-section [B], the important part, the n-p-n junction, is below the surface, protected by silicon oxide [1]. Both n-type emitter and p-type base were formed by diffusion through holes etched into the oxide. These were then filled in with more oxide. The chip itself is used as a collector. The base is thin so that current does not take long to diffuse across it, enabling the transistor to turn on in only 10^{-8} seconds. An integrated circuit [C] may contain many of these bipolar transistors on the surface of a single silicon chip. It is necessary to isolate them electrically or they will interfere with each other. By fabricating the n-p-n device on a p-type substrate, the n-type collector and p-type substrate act as a reverse-biased diode which, with very high resistance, achieves isolation. Field Effect Transistors (FET's), made with Metal, Oxide and Semiconductors (hence MOS device) use only one type of charge carrier, electrons or holes. In this n-MOS transistor [D] two islands of n-type silicon, called the source and the drain, are separated by a narrow channel which normally conducts. A negative potential applied to the gate narrows the channel and reduces the current. A charge-coupled device [E] is like a MOS device with a long string of gates between the source and the drain. A charge packet of holes can be retained by applying a steady negative voltage to a gate. If that negative voltage is reduced and, simultaneously, the next gate in the line is made more negative, the charge moves under the second gate. "Bits" of information, stored as packets of charge, can be passed along the device by applying pulses in sequence to alternate gates.

9 Photographic methods are used in combination with diffusion and etching techniques to produce large numbers of identical circuits on a wafer cut from a single crystal of silicon [A]. An array of fine probes, lined up with the aid of a microscope, is used to test a circuit [B]. The wafer is then sliced up and each chip is individually mounted, connected to terminal pins and protectively sealed against dust and damp.

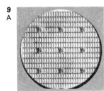

10 Integrated circuits make feasible the miniaturization of all kinds of electronic devices. Such circuits are used in this electronic watch [A] and in this microcomputer [B] which contains a central processor, for performing logical and arithmetical operations, and a memory. Instructions and data are fed in through an input device such as a keyboard; output can be displayed on a TV screen or may be used to control a machine or robot.

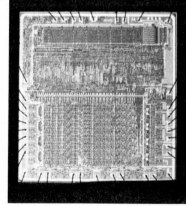

Basic electronic principles

Everything in electronics begins with the electrons that are part of every atom. Scientists have painstakingly built up the modern picture of the atom, but no one has ever seen one because they are so small that even the most powerful electron microscopes have difficulty revealing them. Even smaller are the minute, negatively charged electrons, which can be thought of as orbiting at a distance round the atom's central nucleus where most of its mass is concentrated.

The movement of electrons

Although atoms are normally neutral they can acquire an extra electron and so become negatively charged, or lose an electron and become positively charged. It is this ability of certain atoms easily to "lose" electrons that enables a stream of free electrons – an electric current – to flow in a conductor [1]. By using a battery, or a generator, a surplus of electrons can be provided at one terminal and a deficit at the other, to produce an electromotive force (emf). If a conductor is connected between these terminals the emf causes electrons to flow (or rather "drift" –

the rate is seldom more than 2cm [0.75in] a minute) from the "surplus" terminal (negative) to the "deficit" terminal (positive). This is opposite to the adopted convention that assumes that electric current flows from positive to negative. Unfortunately this convention was firmly established before anyone knew anything about electrons and has been allowed to remain ever since.

In electronic circuits, conductors (in the form of wires or thin copper strips on an insulating material such as paxolin) act as paths for the free flow of electrons from one part of a circuit to another. But elements are needed to control the flow, to allow precise currents of electrons to pass through various circuit components such as valves and transistors. These elements are known as resistors [2], and are available in a wide range of values from a fraction of an ohm (the unit of resistance) up to tens of millions of ohms.

Valves and their components

The diode valve is the simplest form of vacuum tube [3A] and can change an alternating current (such as that at the mains) into

a series of pulses – direct current – by a process known as rectification. A diode with a single anode produces half-wave rectification [3B]. The efficiency of the process is improved by full-wave rectification [3F]. To obtain a direct current that has virtually no pulses in it at all the pulsating current can be fed into additional circuit elements, such as capacitors and chokes, which "smooth" it.

Nowadays valve diodes are usually rejected in favour of their solid-state semiconductor equivalents. Virtually all modern domestic circuitry is made up of solid-state components, apart from a few television sets that still employ one or two valves as well as semiconductors.

Although the solid-state diode [3C] is much smaller than the vacuum tube equivalent it performs exactly the same rectifying function when used in a similar type of circuit [3D]. But it does not have a filament (heater) and so a semiconductor diode does not consume a large amount of power. It thus makes cooling the equipment unneccessary as well as enabling the size and cost of any associated transformer to be reduced.

1 By applying an electromotive force (emf) to the ends of a wire made of a metal such as copper a flow of electrons can be maintained. These electrons, not associated with particular atoms, are free to drift independently of each other throughout the metal. Under the influence of an emf, they flow, on average, in one direction and constitute an electric current.

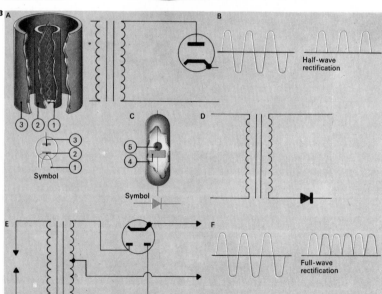

Atom   Electron

2 Carbon resistors usually have their resistance value in ohms (ranging up to millions of ohms) marked on them in an internationally recognized colour code. This resistor has a value of 470

ohms with a tolerance (accuracy) of 10%. The key to this simple code is as follows: end ring [A] has no significance; ring B gives the first figure; ring C gives the second figure; ring D

gives the numbers of noughts to be added to the digits in B and C. If there is a fourth ring E it indicates tolerance: silver 10%, gold 5%. An absence of a fourth ring would indicate a tolerance of 20%.

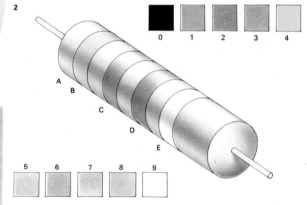

0 1 2 3 4

5 6 7 8 9

4 By adding an electrode called a control grid [3] between the cathode [2] and the anode [4] the current in the valve can be controlled by the voltage on the grid. As with the diode valve, a heater

[1] is essential to start current flow in the resulting triode valve [A]. In practice, it is found that a small change in grid voltage results in a large change in anode current. By using

this effect in the circuit [B] a varying anode current can be converted to a voltage in the resistor R – the result is a signal amplified relative to the input at the control grid [C].

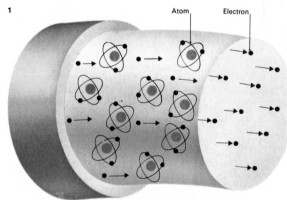

Half-wave rectification

Symbol

Symbol

Full-wave rectification

3 When a voltage is applied [A] to the filament (heater) [1] of a diode valve it causes the cathode [2] to emit electrons that are instantly attracted to the anode [3]. As the anode cannot emit electrons, current flow is possible only

in one direction. Therefore the diode valve is ideal as a rectifier of alternating current, either as a half-wave rectifier [B] or a full-wave rectifier [F] using a different circuit with a pair of anodes to produce a "double diode"

valve [E]. The solid-state component, known as a semiconductor diode, is more efficient for it does not need a heater. This device [C] has a layer of p-type semiconductor material [4] and a bead of n-type [5]. This combination has

a low resistance in one direction and a high resistance in the other, allowing current to flow in only one direction and therefore producing rectification. A half-wave rectification circuit using such a diode is shown in D.

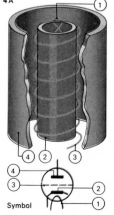

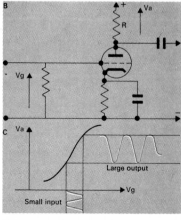

Va

+
R

Vg

Va

Large output

Vg

Small input

Symbol

By adding an extra electrode to the diode valve in 1906 the American inventor Lee De Forest (1873–1961) controlled the flow of electrons between the cathode and the anode [4A]. And by adding other basic circuit elements, in this case resistors and capacitors, the triode valve could be used as a voltage amplifier [4B]. Later, other grids were added to the triode to improve performance, especially in early radio receivers.

The transistor

Following a successful research programme directed by William Bradford Shockley (1910–) at the Bell Telephone Laboratories, Murray Hills, New Jersey, USA, the world of electronics was suddenly presented with the first solid-state three-electrode device, which was destined to end the supremacy of the electronic valve. Shockley, John Bardeen and Walter Houser Brattain were awarded the Nobel prize in physics in 1956 for work on the development of the transistor in 1948.

As a result of this work the world now enjoys the benefits of small, inexpensive portable radios that run on torch batteries [5]. Inspecting a circuit shows that transistors are even smaller than many of the other conventional components, despite the fact that these are now miniaturized. A transistor consists of a layer of one type of semiconductor material between two layers of a different type. These materials are called *p*-type and *n*-type and either of them can form the inner layer. Taking up even less room, an integrated circuit has one or more transistors and other circuit components formed within a single "chip" of semiconductor material.

An interesting feature of practical valve and transistor circuits is the use of "feedback" to improve the quality of the sound produced by an amplifier. This is a refinement to overcome the distortion of the signal that can take place between the input and the output circuits of a valve or transistor or of several such devices. Feedback may be voltage feedback or current feedback.

In small portable transistor radios, there is seldom any output transformer at all because a "single-ended" push-pull output stage is used, reducing cost and weight.

KEY

The mysteries of the atom have fascinated many artists. "Theme on Electronics" by the English sculptor Barbara Hepworth (1903–75) was created in 1957 for the Mullard Electronics Centre in London. It symbolizes the world of the electron. Every atom can be pictured with one or more electrons orbiting a central nucleus (with one or more protons and sometimes one or more neutrons as well). The electron always carries a negative charge and the central nucleus a positive one. Normally these charges balance each other out exactly so that neither the negative nor the positive charge predominates – in other words an atom is normally electrically neutral.

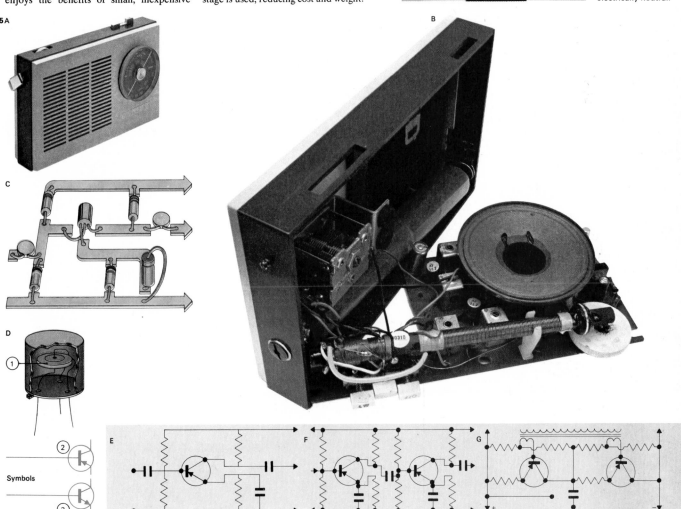

Symbols

5 A modern portable radio [A] owes its existence to the invention of the transistor in 1948. Without transistors such devices as this one were almost out of the question as far as mass production was concerned because valves, and most other parts, were too large. Looking inside the set [B] it is possible to see how many transistors and other components can be packed into such a small space and yet leave room for the batteries and loudspeaker. Within a portable transistor radio there are several types of amplifying circuits. In a typical one-stage transistor amplifier [C], several components are grouped around the transistor, which emphasizes its small size even more. The upper wires of the various capacitors and resistors are cleverly folded back and joined onto the printed circuit board. Basically, the transistor itself [D] comprises a centre layer called the base [1] of one type of semiconductor material sandwiched between two other layers of the opposite type of semiconductor material (the collector and the emitter). The two types are *n*-type and *p*-type and the composition of the sandwich is denoted by the names of the transistor types: *pnp* [2] and *npn* [3]. The essential difference is in the polarities of the three terminals, and the two types of transistors are distinguished by the directions of the emitter arrows in the symbols. The circuit (E) represents the amplifier circuit (C). Increased amplification of small signals can be obtained by using several amplification stages [F]. Where high output is needed a "single-ended", push-pull circuit [G] is used, each amplifying half of the signal.

113

What is chemistry?

Dyestuffs, drugs, synthetic fibres, photographic products, detergents, fertilizers – these are just a few examples of the very many products that have been made through chemistry. But what is chemistry? Every science looks at the world in its own special way; the basic building block with which chemistry is concerned is the atom. Chemistry deals with the properties of different atoms, the ways in which they join together to form molecules, and the interactions of various kinds of molecules with one another.

The stuff of atoms

To the chemist, an atom is made up of three kinds of sub-atomic particles – the proton, neutron and electron. The only difference between a neutron and a proton is that a neutron has no electric charge, whereas a proton has a unit of positive charge. An equal unit of negative charge is carried by the electron, which is much lighter.

In any atom, the protons and neutrons are packed closely together in the central nucleus. Surrounding this, but much less closely packed, are the atom's electrons. The radius of a neutral atom – that is, one in which there are as many electrons as protons – is about 10,000 times larger than the radius of its nucleus. An atom is composed largely of empty space. Because of this, it is much more likely, when two atoms collide, that their electrons will interact with one another than that the two nuclei will ever come into contact. Consequently, chemists are concerned primarily with the electrons in atoms.

Different kinds of atoms result from the combination of different numbers of protons, neutrons and electrons. The number of protons in an atom is its atomic number, and the total mass of all the sub-atomic particles (protons, neutrons and electrons) is its atomic weight. The simplest atom, that of hydrogen, consists of a single proton and a single electron. If a neutron is added to the nucleus of hydrogen, a different kind of atom, called deuterium, is formed. In many ways, the behaviour of hydrogen and deuterium is the same – as one might expect of two atoms each with only one electron. As a result, the hydrogen atom with no neutron (sometimes called protium) and the deuterium atom are classed by the chemist as being different isotopes of the same element. There is also a third isotope of the element hydrogen. This is tritium, with two neutrons and one proton in its nucleus. But if a second proton is added to a tritium nucleus and, to balance the electric charge, another electron is placed round this nucleus, the situation is quite different. The atom shows no resemblance in its chemical behaviour to any of the hydrogen isotopes. It is an atom of an entirely different element – helium.

How elements are built up

The element to which any atom belongs is defined by the number of protons in its nucleus. The number of neutrons can usually vary slightly, to give a range of isotopes. The isotopes of an element have different masses but identical chemical properties. There are many stable isotopes in nature, but among the elements with about 90 or more protons, such as uranium, the isotopes tend to be unstable and the nuclei break down to form atoms of other elements [4]. Nuclear reactors and atomic bombs depend on this instability.

1

2

3

1 This iron rosette, dating from the 7th century BC, once decorated an Etruscan chariot. Techniques of working iron and, earlier, copper and bronze go back thousands of years. They allowed men to make tools and weapons, implements that advanced both agriculture and warfare. Extraction and purification of metals probably developed accidentally, but led to the founding of present-day chemistry.

2 Ancient Greeks, such as Democritus, believed that matter is made from tiny particles, which they called atoms. But "atomism" did not become a useful part of chemistry until John Dalton (1766–1844) proposed that atoms have different weights, and that the weight of any particular atom is constant. By 1808 Dalton had drawn up this list of symbols for the different types of atoms (elements).

3 John Dalton, the son of a weaver, is one of chemistry's most distinguished figures as a result of his work on the atomic theory. He was born in Cumberland, England, in 1766, into a Quaker family. At the age of 12 he became a schoolteacher. He moved to Manchester in 1793 and stayed there until his death in 1844, earning his living by teaching mathematics and natural philosophy (physics). Dalton was colourblind and in addition to the atomic theory, which he developed during the first decade of the 1800s, he also investigated colour-blindness (sometimes called Daltonism) and meteorology.

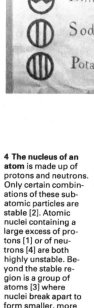

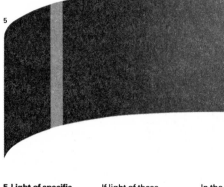

4

5

4 The nucleus of an atom is made up of protons and neutrons. Only certain combinations of these sub-atomic particles are stable [2]. Atomic nuclei containing a large excess of protons [1] or of neutrons [4] are both highly unstable. Beyond the stable region is a group of atoms [3] where nuclei break apart to form smaller, more stable nuclei. Below [5], and above [6], the stable regions are unstable nuclei, which decay into stable elements.

5 Light of specific wavelengths is emitted by an element such as hydrogen when it is "excited" by passing an arc discharge through it.

If light of these wavelengths is passed through the vapour of the same element, it is absorbed to form an absorption spectrum.

In the 1800s men wondered why elements should have such discrete spectra, and why the spectral lines could be divided into four classes – called sharp, principal, diffuse and fundamental. Only when modern atomic theory was developed was an explanation found.

As the elements build up, their nuclei are surrounded by more and more electrons which are arranged according to definite rules. The positive charge of the protons in the nucleus attracts the negatively charged electrons, whose momentum prevents them from "falling" into the nucleus.

Electronic orbitals

The electron in a hydrogen atom spreads out round the nucleus in a spherical shell. It is possible to assign to any point only a probability that the electron is there at an instant in time. The region round a hydrogen nucleus where there is the highest probability of finding the electron is the electron's orbital.

In 1925, the Austrian physicist Wolfgang Pauli formulated rules for electronic orbitals. His major rule was that no two electrons in the same atom can be in exactly the same quantum state. The quantum state of an atom is defined by four different numbers. The first of these, known as the principal quantum number, describes the average distance between the electron and the nucleus. The second quantum number is related to the

shape of the orbital, which is not always spherical, and the third determines its orientation. The final quantum number is the spin of the electron, which can only be $+\frac{1}{2}$ or $-\frac{1}{2}$. The possible values for the second and third quantum numbers depend on the value of the principal quantum number in such a way that, when it is 1, there are only two possible quantum states (and orbitals); when it is 2, there are 8; when it is 3, there are 18; and so on, according to the formula $2n^2$, where n is the principal quantum number.

The energy of any electron depends upon the first two quantum numbers and, because its behaviour depends largely on its energy, chemists have developed a kind of shorthand for describing an electron's energy level. Each electron in an atom can be described by a number followed by a letter. The number is the same as the principal quantum number, but the values 0, 1, 2 and 3 for the second quantum number are represented (for historical reasons) by the letters s, p, d and f [7]. By knowing the numbers of electrons in different orbitals, a chemist can predict the behaviour of any particular atom.

Flasks, beakers and the simple test-tube have long symbolized the chemist's search for new elements and compounds.

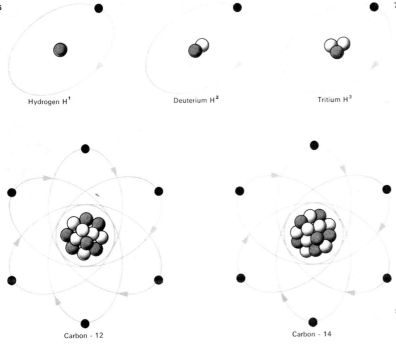

Hydrogen H¹

Deuterium H²

Tritium H³

Carbon - 12

Carbon - 14

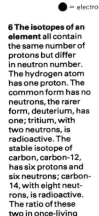
● = electron

= proton

= neutron

6 The isotopes of an element all contain the same number of protons but differ in neutron number. The hydrogen atom has one proton. The common form has no neutrons, the rarer form, deuterium, has one; tritium, with two neutrons, is radioactive. The stable isotope of carbon, carbon-12, has six protons and six neutrons; carbon-14, with eight neutrons, is radioactive. The ratio of these two in once-living material helps determine its age.

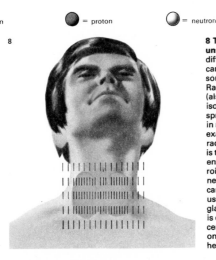

8 The breakdown of unstable isotopes of different elements can be detected and sometimes utilized. Radioactive isotopes (also called radio-isotopes) have widespread applications in medicine. For example, a dose of radioactive iodine is taken up preferentially by the thyroid gland in the neck. Its presence can be detected and used to map the gland, to see if it is diseased, cancerous or (as in the one pictured here) enlarged.

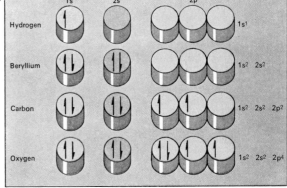

7 The positions of electrons in a neutral atom of any element can be shown in a "pigeon-hole" notation. The orbitals are signified by a number – the principal quantum number that indicates the average distance of the electron from the nucleus – and a letter that indicates the shape of the orbital. The letters used for identification are derived from the initial letters of the four types of spectral lines, s, p, d and f and then proceed alphabetically. Because electrons – shown by half arrows – can spin in opposite directions, each pigeon-hole can hold two electrons.

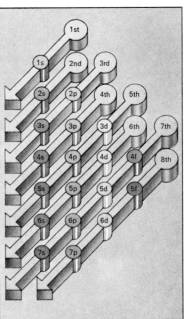

9 Atoms have more and more electrons as they build up to form the heavier elements and the order in which they occupy orbitals depends on the particular binding energy. In general, the closer an electron is to the nucleus, the greater is the energy. As electrons get farther away from the nucleus, the energy relationships become more complex. So that, for example, the 4s orbital is more strongly binding than the 3d orbital, and is filled with electrons before it. The chart shows the general order for the filling of orbitals as atoms get larger. However, even this is an approximation and there are a few exceptions to it.

Classification of elements

Since man first began to purify metals from rocks thousands of years ago, he has been learning how different substances behave and trying to detect a pattern in that behaviour. But the major breakthrough in discovering the pattern of chemistry did not come until just over 100 years ago when the Russian chemist Dmitry Mendeleyev [Key] proposed his periodic system of the elements.

Earlier, the French chemist Antoine Lavoisier (1743–94) had revived Robert Boyle's use of the word "element" for substances that could not be broken down into anything simpler. During the next 75 years, many new elements were discovered [4] and substances previously thought to have been elements were shown to be compounds – two or more elements combined.

Atomic weights

As more elements were discovered, and more of their properties catalogued, it became clear that some elements were similar to others. Sodium and potassium, for example, first isolated in the early 1800s by Humphry Davy (1778–1829), are both soft

metals that react violently with water to produce alkaline solutions. It gradually became obvious that there must be a way of tabulating the elements so that those with similar properties were grouped together.

One property of elements that was being catalogued at that time was atomic weight. An atom is extremely small – a toy balloon might easily hold a quadrillion of them (that is 1 followed by 24 zeros). Nevertheless each atom does have a definite mass. Most of this comes from the neutrons and protons in its nucleus. For example, a deuterium atom – with one proton and one neutron in its nucleus – is almost twice as heavy as a hydrogen atom, with its one proton. An oxygen atom, with eight neutrons and eight protons, is about 16 times as heavy as a hydrogen atom.

Using various analytical skills, nineteenth-century chemists gradually catalogued the comparative atomic weights of the elements with increasing accuracy. The weight of a hydrogen atom was formerly taken as 1 and the weights of other atoms related to it; atomic weights are now based on a value of 12 for carbon-12 (six neutrons

and six protons), making hydrogen 1.008.

By organizing the elements in tabular form in order of increasing atomic weight, Mendeleyev produced a periodic table. Unlike those proposed by other chemists, his had gaps in it. Where the difference in atomic weight between two neighbouring elements seemed exceptionally large, he assumed that there was an element of intermediate weight that had yet to be discovered. Because his scheme also arranged elements in families, he was able to predict the properties of some of these undiscovered elements [6]. Before the end of the nineteenth century, his assumptions were vindicated by the discovery of some of these "missing" elements and by the close agreement between Mendeleyev's predicted and their actual properties.

Atomic numbers

It is known that the physical basis underlying the periodic classification is not the atomic weights of the elements, but their atomic numbers – that is, the numbers of protons in their nuclei. And the regularities observed in different families of elements result from

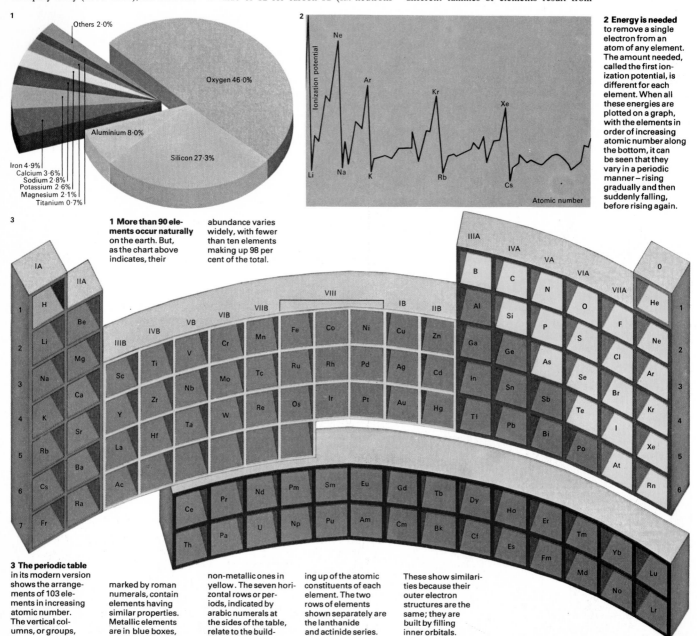

1 More than 90 elements occur naturally on the earth. But, as the chart above indicates, their abundance varies widely, with fewer than ten elements making up 98 per cent of the total.

2 Energy is needed to remove a single electron from an atom of any element. The amount needed, called the first ionization potential, is different for each element. When all these energies are plotted on a graph, with the elements in order of increasing atomic number along the bottom, it can be seen that they vary in a periodic manner – rising gradually and then suddenly falling, before rising again.

3 The periodic table in its modern version shows the arrangements of 103 elements in increasing atomic number. The vertical columns, or groups, are marked by roman numerals, contain elements having similar properties. Metallic elements are in blue boxes, non-metallic ones in yellow. The seven horizontal rows or periods, indicated by arabic numerals at the sides of the table, relate to the building up of the atomic constituents of each element. The two rows of elements shown separately are the lanthanide and actinide series. These show similarities because their outer electron structures are the same; they are built by filling inner orbitals.

similarities in electronic arrangement [5].

Lithium (Li) has three electrons and potassium (K) 19. According to the rules for the occupancy of orbitals (the regions in space where electrons are most likely to be found), lithium has as many electrons as are allowed (two) in the orbital with the principal quantum number 1. It also has one electron left over: this occupies the next lowest energy orbital, called 2*s*. Potassium, on the other hand, has electrons filling all possible orbitals in the first three levels, and one more. This last electron is in the 4*s* orbital. Thus, in both elements, the outermost occupied orbital has a single electron in it.

If two atoms have the same number of electrons in the outermost orbital layer, or "shell" as it is usually called, it is reasonable to expect that their chemical properties should be similar. All the elements beneath lithium in a modern periodic table [3] have only one electron in their outermost shell.

Man-made elements
For many years, it was believed that element 92 (uranium) had the heaviest atoms occur-ring naturally on earth. It was believed that as atomic size increases, the atoms become less stable and any atoms of heavier elements that might once have been present on earth had broken down. Since 1940, chemists in the United States and the Soviet Union have been making "transuranium" elements artificially [7]. Glenn Seaborg (1912–), who has been involved with much of this work, has used the periodic table to predict the likely properties of transuranium ele-ments. His predictions go as far as element 168, although, for physical reasons, few of these elements would be stable for long enough to check whether or not their proper-ties did coincide with Seaborg's predictions.

But another of his theories based on the periodic table has been proved. Because of their chemical similarities, members of the same family of elements often occur in the same minerals. Seaborg predicted that, if there were any traces of transuranic elements left on earth, they would be found in minerals rich in other elements of the same family. In 1971, he discovered naturally occurring plutonium in a sample of uranium ore.

The Russian chemist Dmitry Mendeleyev was responsible for proposing the periodic table of the elements in 1869. This major theoretical breakthrough provided the necessary classification system for making the similarities in the properties of certain elements understandable. Mendeleyev was born in Siberia in 1834 and trained as a teacher in St Petersburg. Subsequently he became professor of chemistry at St Petersburg University, a post which he held until 1890. He died in 1907.

4 The elements, their symbols and atomic numbers

Actinium	Ac	89	Hafnium	Hf	72	Promethium	Pm	61
Aluminium	Al	13	Helium	He	2	Protactinium	Pa	91
Americium	Am	95	Holmium	Ho	67	Radium	Ra	88
Antimony	Sb	51	Hydrogen	H	1	Radon	Rn	86
Argon	Ar	18	Indium	In	49	Rhenium	Re	75
Arsenic	As	33	Iodine	I	53	Rhodium	Rh	45
Astatine	At	85	Iridium	Ir	77	Rubidium	Rb	37
Barium	Ba	56	Iron	Fe	26	Ruthenium	Ru	44
Berkelium	Bk	97	Krypton	Kr	36	Samarium	Sm	62
Beryllium	Be	4	Lanthanum	La	57	Scandium	Sc	21
Bismuth	Bi	83	Lawrencium	Lr	103	Selenium	Se	34
Boron	B	5	Lead	Pb	82	Silicon	Si	14
Bromine	Br	35	Lithium	Li	3	Silver	Ag	47
Cadmium	Cd	48	Lutetium	Lu	71	Sodium	Na	11
Caesium	Cs	55	Magnesium	Mg	12	Strontium	Sr	38
Calcium	Ca	20	Manganese	Mn	25	Sulphur	S	16
Californium	Cf	98	Mendelevium	Md	101	Tantalum	Ta	73
Carbon	C	6	Mercury	Hg	80	Technetium	Tc	43
Cerium	Ce	58	Molybdenum	Mo	42	Tellurium	Te	52
Chlorine	Cl	17	Neodymium	Nd	60	Terbium	Tb	65
Chromium	Cr	24	Neon	Ne	10	Thallium	Tl	81
Cobalt	Co	27	Neptunium	Np	93	Thorium	Th	90
Copper	Cu	29	Nickel	Ni	28	Thulium	Tm	69
Curium	Cm	96	Niobium	Nb	41	Tin	Sn	50
Dysprosium	Dy	66	Nitrogen	N	7	Titanium	Ti	22
Einsteinium	Es	99	Nobelium	No	102	Tungsten	W	74
Erbium	Er	68	Osmium	Os	76	Uranium	U	92
Europium	Eu	63	Oxygen	O	8	Vanadium	V	23
Fermium	Fm	100	Palladium	Pd	46	Xenon	Xe	54
Fluorine	F	9	Phosphorus	P	15	Ytterbium	Yb	70
Francium	Fr	87	Platinum	Pt	78	Yttrium	Y	39
Gadolinium	Gd	64	Plutonium	Pu	94	Zinc	Zn	30
Gallium	Ga	31	Polonium	Po	84	Zirconium	Zr	40
Germanium	Ge	32	Potassium	K	19			
Gold	Au	79	Praseodymium	Pr	59			

5 The periodicity of the elements is now known to be due to their electronic structures. The elec-trons in any atom can be envisaged as occupying "shells", each of which can hold only a certain number of electrons. For the first three shells, the numbers are 2, 8 and 18. If the outermost shell is either completely filled, or holds 8 electrons, the ele-ment is chemically unreactive: the gases helium (He), neon (Ne), argon (Ar) and krypton (Kr) all fulfil this condi-tion. Lithium (Li) and potassium (K) are similar because they both have one outer electron, and both differ chem-ically from magnesium (Mg) and bromine (Br).

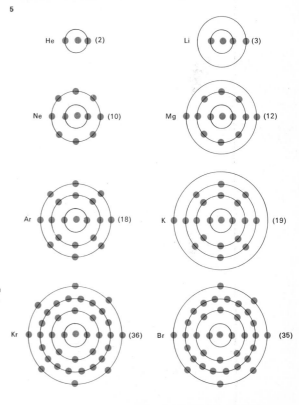

He (2)   Li (3)

Ne (10)   Mg (12)

Ar (18)   K (19)

Kr (36)   Br (35)

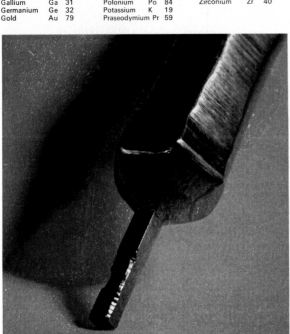

6 Germanium, a metal "grown" in this form for making tran-sistors, was unknown when Mendeleyev proposed his period-ic table. However, in 1871 he predicted the existence of an ele-ment with the proper-ties of germanium and called it eka-sili-cium, from silicium (the old name for silicon) and the Sanskrit word *eka*, meaning "one". Germanium was dis-covered in 1886, 15 years after he had made his prediction.

7 The first samples of element 94, plu-tonium, were pro-duced in 1940 in an American laboratory. One of 11 "transuran-ium" elements that have now definitely been synthesized, it is used as a fuel in some types of nuclear reactors.

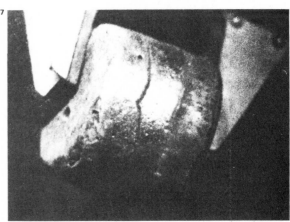

Survey of groups of elements

Atoms of all elements consist of a central nucleus surrounded by a "cloud" containing one or more electrons. The electrons can be thought of as occupying a series of well-defined shells. The behaviour of a particular element depends largely on the number of electrons in its outermost shells. Other factors, such as the total number of electron shells, also play a part in determining behaviour but it is the dominance of the outer electron configuration that underlies the periodic law and justifies the grouping of the elements into groups or families.

The s-elements and their reactions

Each electron shell is made up of various volumes in space called orbitals, known as s-, p-, d- and f-orbitals, and each is at a higher energy than the one below it. Those elements in which the outermost shell can have only one or two electrons can be grouped together as the "s-elements" (because it is only the s-orbital that is occupied in the outer shell). These are (in addition to hydrogen and helium) lithium, beryllium and the elements directly below them in the periodic table [1].

All but helium readily form positive ions by the loss of their outer electrons and they are therefore mostly found as components of ionic compounds, commonly called salts. Many common substances contain these elements – for example, soda (sodium, Na), potash (potassium, K), gypsum (calcium, Ca) and carnallite (magnesium, Mg).

The s-elements with only one electron are more reactive than those with two. Thus if dropped on to water, sodium reacts so violently that it catches fire; if magnesium is dropped into hot water the reaction (release of hydrogen) gives off light, but is less violent.

The energy levels of electrons in the heavier elements are slightly complicated and, for this reason, many elements have a filled s-level but only a partly filled d-level below it. The part of the table ten elements wide beginning with scandium (Sc) includes the "transition" elements in which a d-level is successively filled. The outermost electron shell of these elements has an s-configuration, but it is the underlying layers of d-electrons that determines the element's chemical behaviour. The lanthanide and actinide series form further sub-groups: in their cases an f-group on a lower level begins to fill while the levels beyond contain one d-electron and two s-electrons.

The d-elements: "rare earths" and metals

For the elements scandium, yttrium (Y) and lanthanum (La), as well as the entire 14-element lanthanide series, the chemical behaviour is very strongly influenced by the presence of the single d-electron. All these elements tend to form positive ions by the loss of this electron and the two s-electrons – giving ions with a charge of +3. The elements are all fairly reactive and all are rare, but some of these "rare earths" have found commercial uses, for example in the manufacture of specially tinted spectacles.

The other sub-series, the actinides, is of greater importance as it contains the nuclear reactor fuel elements uranium and plutonium. But the importance of these elements is based on their nuclear instability rather than their chemical properties.

The other transition elements [4] are also important because they are all metals and

Li	Be											B	C	N	O	F	Ne
Na	Mg											Al	Si	P	S	Cl	Ar
K	Ca	Sc	Ti	V	Cr	Mn	Fe	Co	Ni	Cu	Zn	Ga	Ge	As	Se	Br	Kr
Rb	Sr	Y	Zr	Nb	Mo	Tc	Ru	Rh	Pd	Ag	Cd	In	Sn	Sb	Te	I	Xe
Cs	Ba	La	Hf	Ta	W	Re	Os	Ir	Pt	Au	Hg	Tl	Pb	Bi	Po	At	Rn

1 Elements are won from minerals in different ways, according to their position on the periodic table. In the red group are reactive metals usually extracted by electrolysis. In the orange group, the elements frequently occur in ionic compounds, often combined with oxygen. These elements are often prepared by electrolysis. The third group (coloured green) is commonly found as sulphides and the elements are obtained by roasting these and reducing the resultant oxides. Group four (coloured yellow) are relatively unreactive elements, found free or as compounds that give the element when they are heated to a certain temperature. The fifth group (light brown) are non-metals that occur free or as negative ions that can be converted to elements by electrolysis.

2 Magnesium is one of the reactive s-elements. It burns with an intense white flame, which made it useful in early "flash" photography. It is now used in flames that burn under water.

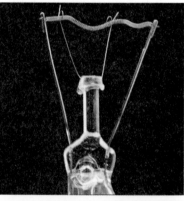

3 Tungsten was discovered in 1783 by the brothers Fausto and Don Juan d'Elhuyar. A fine wire made from tungsten becomes white hot when carrying an electric current, as in an electric lamp.

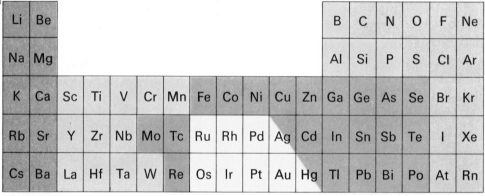

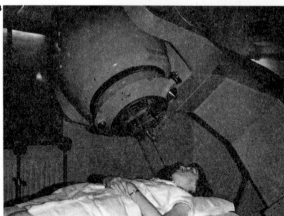

4 Cobalt, one of the transition metals, is the basis of various blue pigments. It is also an important constituent of some biological molecules. However, a most important use in recent years has been in the medical "cobalt bomb". A radioactive isotope of cobalt (cobalt-60), which gives off high-energy gamma-rays, is used to direct this cell-destroying radiation at tumour sites in humans. It is used extensively in hospitals to treat cancers and arrest their growth.

5 A compound exhibits a specific colour when it absorbs white light – a mixture of all colours – by selectively reflecting a few wavelengths. Many salts of transition metals, such as iron and nickel, are coloured. The exact colour depends on which other atoms are associated with the metal. Thus chromium compounds have for centuries been used to provide painters with yellow pigments. Vincent van Gogh's "Sunflowers", shown here, is a good example of their use.

many of them have large-scale industrial uses. All of these elements – except copper, silver and gold [6] – have two electrons in an outer s-orbital and between two and ten electrons in the underlying, but more strongly bonding d-orbital. Silver, copper and gold could be expected to have two s-electrons and nine d-electrons. But, because the complete filling of a d-shell increases stability, they have only one s-electron and a full complement of ten d-electrons.

The transition elements are characterized by the ability to form several different ions, because of the complex behaviour of electrons in the d-orbitals. Thus iron is found in ionic compounds as both Fe^{2+} (ferrous, with two electrons lost) and Fe^{3+} (ferric, with three electrons lost from the atoms).

The p-elements and their grouping

To the right of the transition elements in the periodic table are the p-elements. In the groups headed by boron, carbon, nitrogen, oxygen, fluorine and helium, it is the three p-orbitals (capable of holding a maximum of six electrons) that are the most important in determining chemical behaviour. From left to right through this group the p-orbitals become increasingly filled, until the "completed octet" (two s- and six p-electrons) of the noble gases – the group that includes neon. These elements are unreactive, and only recently have chemists made compounds including them.

The group headed by fluorine – the halogens – all need only one electron to complete the octet and they readily do this to form ions carrying a single negative charge. The oxygen group can form double-negative charged ions, but tend more to link with other atoms through covalent (non-ionic) bonds. The tendency towards covalent bonding is even more marked in the groups headed by nitrogen and carbon. The group headed by boron, where there are two s-electrons and one p-electron, like the group headed by scandium, shows more of a tendency to form ions. Aluminium, for example, readily loses its three outer electrons to form Al^{3+}, but aluminium chloride ($AlCl_3$) is not an ionic compound. The bonds joining the chlorine and aluminium atoms are partly ionic and partly covalent.

Elements such as iron and lead have been known since antiquity. Others were first purified by alchemists such as Hennig Brand (died c. 1692), shown praying after discovering phosphorus.

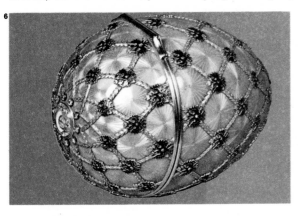

6 Precious metals often occur as the free elements in nature. Not only gold and silver, which for centuries have been used in jewellery and ornamentation, such as this Fabergé egg, but others such as platinum and iridium also come into this category. Silver and mercury are borderline cases. Mercury, for example, occurs as its sulphide but heating releases the metal, which readily alloys with other metals.

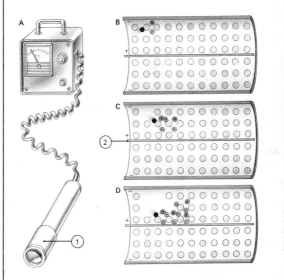

7 A Geiger-Müller counter [A] detects radioactivity in a chamber [1] containing neon atoms at low pressure [B]. The chamber has neon atoms [grey] that are ionized by beta particles [black] to form positive ions [red] and electrons [blue]. [C] An electric field round an anode [2] accelerates electrons, which collide with other neon atoms [D] and split them to release more electrons, to be recorded by the anode.

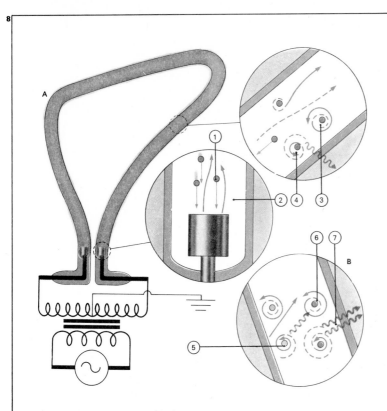

8 Neon is an unreactive element yet it can be used to produce coloured lights [A]. Positively charged ions [1] strike a negative electrode, causing emission of electrons [2] which "energize" electrons in neon atoms [3]. When the energized electrons return to their stable "ground" state [4], red light is emitted. Similarly, a mercury vapour lamp [B] emits ultraviolet light [5]. This may be absorbed by a fluorescent substance [6] which can then release the energy in stages [7].

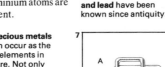

9 Marie Curie (1867–1934) was the first person to win two Nobel prizes; one in physics, the other in chemistry. She discovered polonium and radium and was responsible for much of the early research on radioactive elements.

Joining atoms

Human beings and the world in which they live exist because atoms of elements join together to form compounds or molecules [Key]. Such compounds may have as few as two atoms or they may contain thousands linked together. From the basic building blocks – consisting of fewer than 100 elements – natural processes have produced hundreds of thousands of compounds and chemists have synthesized many more.

Every atom consists of a small central nucleus surrounded by a "cloud" containing one or more electrons. When two atoms approach closely their clouds of electrons interact. Each electron has a negative electric charge and for this reason the electron clouds repel one another. But when two atoms are close together the electrons of each, located in space in "orbitals", are attracted by both the atomic nuclei.

Forming a bond

The net result of these dual forces of repulsion and attraction can be a rearrangement of the electron orbitals to form new orbitals that encompass and hold together both nuclei. When this happens a chemical bond [1] has been formed and a molecule created. The electrons involved in the chemical bond now occupy molecular, not atomic, orbitals.

The rules that apply to electrons occupying atomic orbitals also apply to those in molecular orbitals [4]. Using the normal "pigeon-hole" notation for showing how electrons occupy atomic orbitals it is also possible to show how electrons are distributed in chemical bonds.

In the commonest form of chemical bond, in which a single "pigeon-hole" is involved, the molecular orbital contains two electrons. Such a bond, in which two electrons are shared between two nuclei, is called a single, covalent bond [3]. In some cases an atom may have more than a single electron available for bonding. If it meets up with a similar atom, two (or more) covalent bonds may form between the two nuclei.

The number of electrons in an atom that are available for forming chemical bonds depends on its outer electronic structure. (All the inner electrons are in completely filled atomic orbitals, which generally cannot accept any more.) For this reason elements such as neon and helium that have completely filled outer shells are highly unreactive and form practically no compounds.

Complete electron shells are very stable structures, and there is a tendency for atoms to borrow or share as many electrons from other atoms as they need to complete a shell. If two oxygen atoms meet, for example, to fill their outer shells they each take a share of two electrons from the other. As a result, each nucleus has eight (instead of six) electrons.

Hydrogen needs – and can accept – one electron to complete its shell (it has only one) [4]. This means that if oxygen and hydrogen atoms come together, two hydrogen atoms each form a single bond to oxygen. In the resultant compound, H_2O (water), the oxygen shares two of its own electrons and has a share in two others, so it again completes its outer octet in the molecule.

Exchanging electrons

When two electrons are shared between atoms the bond is said to be covalent [4, 6]. But some atoms have a stronger affinity for

1

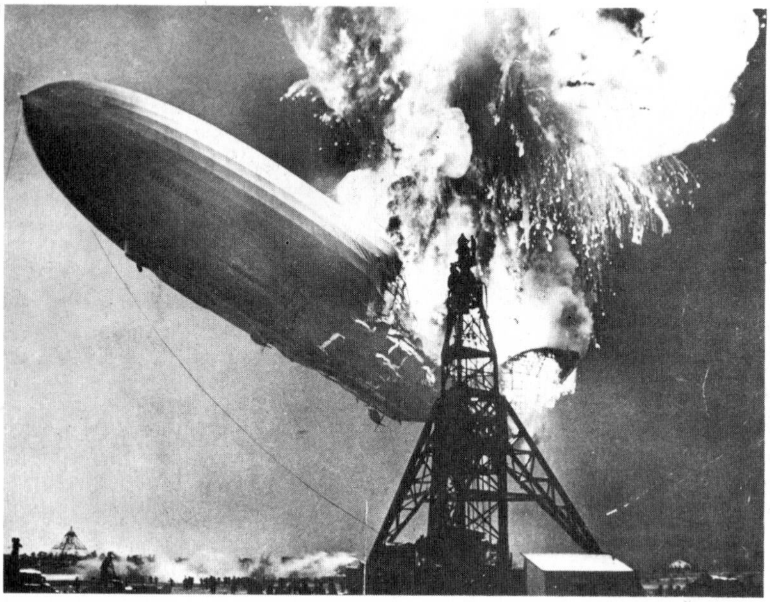

2

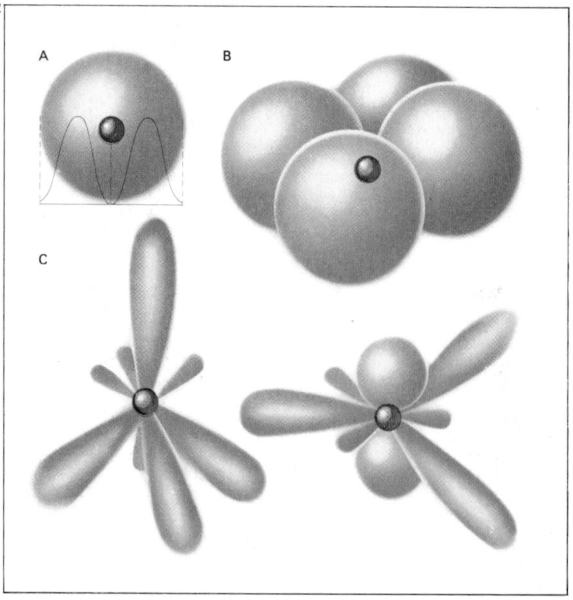
A
B
C

3

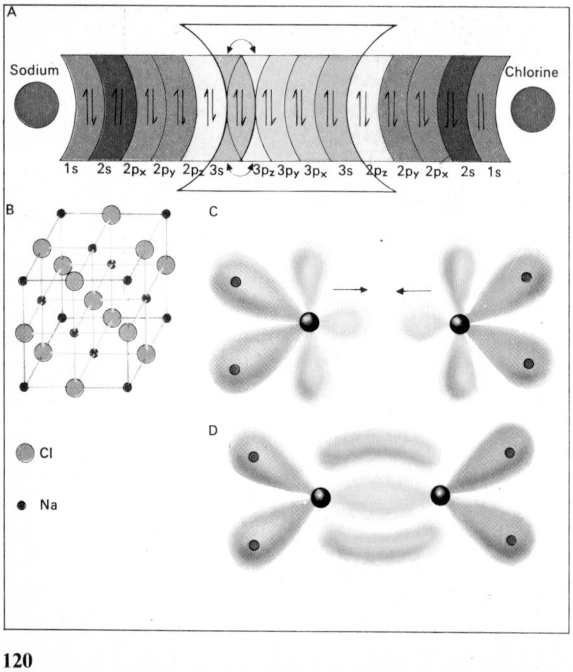
A
Sodium
Chlorine
1s 2s 2px 2py 2pz 3s 3pz 3py 3px 3s 3pz 2py 2px 2s 1s
B
C
D
Cl
Na

1 When a chemical bond forms the result is often a more stable configuration of atoms. In reaching such an arrangement, energy may be released. Hydrogen and oxygen can join together to form water molecules, liberating an enormous quantity of energy as they do so. This is why hydrogen is so inflammable and no longer used in airships, as it was in the *Hindenburg* which exploded in 1937.

2 The nucleus of any atom has its complement of electrons distributed in orbitals, or volumes of probability. For hydrogen's single electron the orbital is spherical [A] while the two available electrons of oxygen are each distributed in a pair of spherical probability regions [B]. The outer electrons of carbon can adopt a variety of distributions such as the two shown here [C].

3 In an ionic bond [A] electrons are transferred, eg from the 3s orbital of sodium (Na) to the 3p orbital of chlorine (Cl). Ionic compounds often have distinct geometries in which ionic charges balance [B]. But in a covalent bond two electrons in a molecular orbital are shared by both nuclei. Such orbitals have specific shapes as in the "double bond" (four electrons) linking the carbon atoms in ethylene [C, D]. The other carbon orbitals are bound to hydrogen.

4

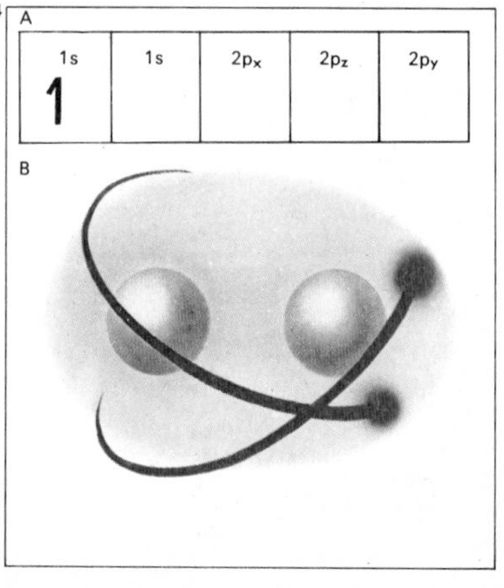
A
1s
1s
2px
2pz
2py
1
B

4 The simplest molecule, H_2, is made up of two covalently bonded hydrogen atoms. The two nuclei share each other's single 1s electrons [A]. As two hydrogen nuclei come together [B], and electron sharing commences, energy is released. The positively charged nuclei repel one another and partly counteract the binding force of the electrons. This keeps the nuclei a roughly constant distance apart – called the bond length. Such two-atom molecules are called diatomic.

electrons than others and completely gain or lose electrons to combine by means of an ionic bond. The resulting atoms are no longer electrically neutral; they carry a positive or negative electric charge (depending on whether they have lost or gained electrons) and are known as ions. Chlorine, for example, with seven electrons in its outer shell needs only one more to achieve the stability of a completely filled shell (with eight electrons). When it gains this electron it becomes a chloride ion (Cl^-) and carries a negative charge. Sodium, by contrast, has only one electron in its outer shell and as a result readily loses this to form a positively charged sodium ion (Na^+).

Sodium chloride, or common salt, is an example of a compound with an ionic bond. When it is dissolved in water the chloride ions each carry an extra electron borrowed completely – not shared – from the sodium ions.

The co-ordinate bond
A third possibility exists for joining atoms in a simple way. This is an extension of the sharing arrangement of covalent bonding.

But in this case both electrons in the bond, called a co-ordinate bond, come from a single atom and use a totally empty orbital in the second atom involved in the bond. Nitrogen, for example, has five electrons in its outermost shell. Three of these may be involved in covalent bonds with three hydrogen atoms, to form the compound ammonia, NH_3. Nitrogen now has shares in eight electrons – a complete outer octet. In a molecule of ammonia, however, there remains a pair of electrons in the nitrogen atom that have not formed covalent bonds with hydrogen atoms. These can be donated to an empty orbital of various metal atoms, such as copper, to form a third type of bond called a co-ordinate bond. The resulting compounds are known as complexes or co-ordination compounds.

When more than two atoms are involved in joining together, more complicated arrangements are possible. Molecular orbitals may spread out over more than two nuclei to give compounds in which the average number of electrons per bond is less than two, but in which the molecules nevertheless hold together.

Atoms join together to form molecules. Only since the discovery of the wave-nature of matter in the 1930s has it been possible to describe this bonding of atoms clearly. Before this time the way in which atoms held together was a mystery, often shown fancifully, as in this "model" of benzene. Today benzene is pictured as a hexagonal ring of six carbon atoms all linked together by equivalent bonds.

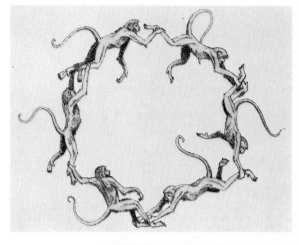

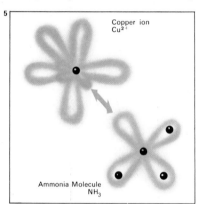

5 A co-ordinate bond involves the sharing of two electrons, both contributed by the same combining atom or molecule (hence the alternative name: dative covalency). Here a "lone pair" of electrons in an orbital of ammonia enter an empty orbital of a copper (cupric) ion to form such a bond with the required number of two electrons. The resulting compounds are called co-ordination compounds and often are brightly coloured.

5
Copper ion
Cu^{2+}

Ammonia Molecule
NH_3

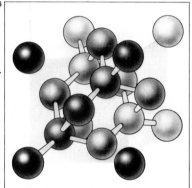

6 In a diamond any one carbon atom is co-valently bonded to four others, orientated at the corners of a tetrahedron. This strain-free co-valent configuration accounts for the diamond's hardness.

7 By mimicking the strain-free structure of diamonds chemists have been able to "engineer" even tougher compounds, such as the tungsten carbide on the tips of drills used in oil wells.

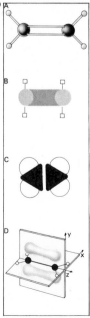

8 A sodium atom here appears as it would look seen from the nearest chlorine atom in a crystal of sodium chloride. One electron is shown moving from the sodium to the chlorine, resulting in an ionic bond between them. The dimensions of the sodium nucleus (made up of protons [red] and neutrons) and of the two complete atoms are given in femtometres – a unit equal to a million-millionth of a millimetre (10^{-15}m).

8
Sodium

100,000
180,000
280,000

Chlorine

9 When two atoms spontaneously form a bond the release of energy stabilizes the compound. The process may be reversed by supplying energy. Colourless silver salts used in automatically dimming sunglasses (A) and an astronaut's helmet (B) take the form of silver ions in a glass matrix. In sunlight the glass darkens because light energy breaks the ionic bonds and reconverts the silver into metallic atoms. Colourless ions re-form when the light is removed.

10 Chemical bonding can be illustrated in many ways. The four diagrams shown here depict the simple molecule ethylene, made up from two carbon atoms and four hydrogen atoms. As in the diamond structure, each carbon atom can form four bonds: two of these link the two carbons together and each carbon also has two hydrogens attached to it by single covalent bonds. The simple ball-and-stick model A shows the atoms and the number of bonds linking them. Model B gives similar information but is designed specially for biological molecules while models C and D reveal more about the actual molecular shape, and the distribution of orbitals, respectively.

Simple chemicals and their structures

Mankind's interest in chemistry derives from the useful information that the subject can provide about the properties of different substances. By understanding the structure of molecules and the way they interact with one another it is possible to invent new compounds that are useful, for example, as drugs, or building materials or fibres for clothing. It is also possible to acquire a better understanding of how the earth on which we live came to its present form and how it is still developing. Geochemistry (as this sub-branch of the subject is called) can lead to the discovery of new supplies of fuels and ores and new ways of processing them.

Structures of molecules

All substances are made up of molecules that, in turn, are composed of individual atoms. One of the basic aspects of chemical knowledge is an understanding of the structure of molecules. An atom is a relatively insubstantial entity: a small, hard nucleus surrounded by an electron occupying a volume of probability. Molecules composed of such atoms are similarly made up, in terms of volume, largely of electron orbitals (the areas in space occupied by the electrons). Nevertheless, despite the fact that an orbital can contain a maximum of only two electrons, they often have definite directions in space, so that molecules have particular shapes. In complex molecules such shapes may be crucial to the behaviour of the substance. This is particularly true of biological molecules, which contain thousands of individual atoms linked together, but even simple molecules have shapes that can determine their properties.

The structures of ionic compounds [1] depend on the electric charge of the ion and on its ionic volume. An ion of sodium, for example, can be regarded as a small sphere having a particular diameter. In general, provided ions of different elements have the same electric charge and similar radii, they can substitute for one another in different materials. As the earth settled down after its formation, rocks gradually solidified from molten material. Many of these original rocks contain crystalline compounds but the compounds are nearly always impure. For example, the common mineral potassium felspar, an ionic compound containing potassium, silicon and oxygen, is always contaminated with rubidium because rubidium forms a singly charged ion of approximately the same radius as potassium. Germanium forms a similarly charged, similarly sized ion to silicon so it is also a contaminant of felspars.

In covalent (non-ionic) compounds the bonds between the different atoms are separate. Covalent compounds can still form crystals, but this is because the molecules as a whole can arrange themselves in geometric arrays, whereas with ionic compounds it is the geometric arrangement of ions that leads to crystallinity. With a crystal of a covalently bonded compound each component molecule has its own characteristic shape.

Shapes of covalent compounds

The shape of a covalently bonded molecule [3] depends on the shapes of the orbitals occupied by the electrons – both those involved in chemical bonding and any others in the outermost shells of the individual atoms. A water molecule, for example, in which two hydrogen atoms are each singly

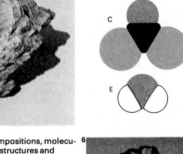

Sodium ion   Chloride ion

1 Sodium chloride, common salt, has a simple cubic crystal structure in which each sodium ion (Na$^+$) is surrounded by six chloride ions (Cl$^-$) and vice versa. Around each ion, the six ions of opposite electrical charge are situated at the corners of an imaginary octahedron. The main force holding the ions in place is the balanced electrical attraction of the neighbouring ions.

2 The shape of any crystalline, ionic solid depends on the size and the number of ions that make it up. However, different chemical substances may look alike, even though they have different compositions, molecular structures and chemical properties. Iron sulphide, shown here, is called "fools' gold" because of its resemblance to the much more valuable element, gold.

A Nitrogen dioxide NO$_2$
B Carbon dioxide CO$_2$
C Phosgene COCl$_2$
D Sulphur dioxide SO$_2$
E Water H$_2$O
F Ammonia NH$_3$

3 Covalently bonded molecules have individual molecular orbitals holding different atoms together, unlike the balanced geometric cluster of an ionic compound. Because of the forces of repulsion between the electron clouds surrounding adjacent nuclei, even small molecules have distinct shapes, which may differ quite markedly from one another as in the half-dozen common molecules here.

4 In hydrogen peroxide two hydrogen atoms and two oxygen atoms are joined in a single molecule. It readily releases an OH group whose oxygen can, for example, bleach hair (as here) or kill germs and act as a mild disinfectant.

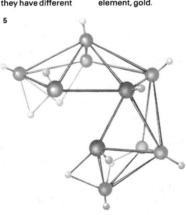

5 In most covalent bonds two electrons hold two nuclei together. By adopting tightly geometric patterns electron-deficient compounds, such as this decaborane, can hold together with a smaller number of electrons.

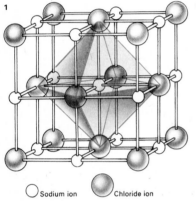

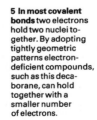

6 In addition to electron-deficient compounds, there are also compounds that seem to have too many electrons. For many years it was believed that the noble gases – helium, neon, xenon, krypton and radon – would not form any compounds because their outer electron shells had eight electrons in them already. However in 1963 Neil Bartlett discovered that xenon would react to form colourful crystalline compounds. An extension of chemical bonding theory has shown how the formation of such compounds does not violate any chemical law and since 1963 a large number of compounds of xenon (shown here) and krypton have been made in laboratories throughout the world.

bonded to a central oxygen atom, might be visualized as the three atoms joined in a straight line. Electrons, all being negatively charged, repel each other, so this in-line arrangement might seem best. It would mean that the volumes of electron probability around the two hydrogen atoms are as far apart from each other as they possibly could be, thus reducing repulsion to a minimum. But, in addition to the two electrons from the oxygen's outer shell, which are involved in bonding, there are four other electrons in this shell, situated as two "lone pairs" in filled orbitals. Their effect on neighbouring electron clouds has to be taken into account. When this is done it is found that a shape almost like that of one segment of a diamond [3E] is adopted. It is a tetrahedral structure in which the hydrogen atoms and the two pairs of oxygen electrons (not involved in bonding) all lie as far away from each other as possible.

Methane [8], in which one carbon atom is surrounded by four hydrogen atoms and all the outermost carbon electrons are involved in bonding, adopts a regular tetrahedral configuration. Intermediate in structure be-

tween methane and water is ammonia (NH_3), in which there are three nitrogen-hydrogen bonds and one filled orbital containing a lone pair of nitrogen electrons [3F].

Co-ordination compounds

The lone-pair electrons in water and ammonia molecules sometimes form bonds to metal atoms that have empty orbitals. Anhydrous copper sulphate, for example, is white. When water is present the molecule turns blue as a number of water molecules "co-ordinate" to empty copper orbitals through the unbonded oxygen lone pairs. Because the empty orbitals in such metals have definite shapes most "co-ordination compounds" generally have highly geometric structures [7].

Some atoms can form several bonds with other atoms, so it is often possible for a number of different molecules to be made up from the same mixture of atoms [10]. One of the major advances in chemistry since the 1940s has been the development of sophisticated instruments that analyse exactly how the atoms of a compound are linked together.

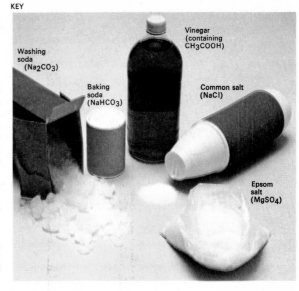

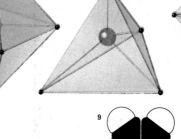

KEY

Washing soda (Na_2CO_3)

Baking soda ($NaHCO_3$)

Vinegar (containing CH_3COOH)

Common salt (NaCl)

Epsom salt ($MgSO_4$)

Everything around us is made up of chemicals, most of them complex mixtures. But these familiar substances from the kitchen are comparatively simple chemical compounds.

7 Where a central atom in a molecule can bond to a number of other atoms, or groups of atoms, a variety of different molecular geometries is possible. In the particular case of co-ordination compounds, in which the central atom is sharing electrons from other atoms and not contributing any of its own electrons to the bonding, the commonly found geometries are those shown here. Whether a compound made up of, say, a central cobalt atom and four outer atoms adopts a square planar or a tetrahedral form depends on the influence of non-bonding electrons associated with the different atoms involved.

7

Square planar

Octahedral

Tetrahedral

Tetragonal pyramidal

Trigonal bipyramidal

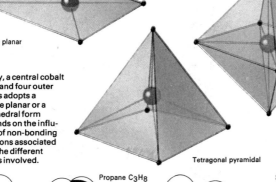

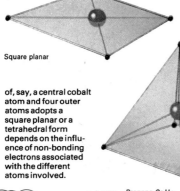

9

Ethylene C_2H_4

Acetylene C_2H_2

9 As well as forming chains joined by single bonds carbon atoms can be joined to one another by two or three molecular orbitals: ethylene and acetylene are, respectively, the doubly and triply bonded analogues of ethane, all of which contain two carbon atoms.

8

Methane CH_4

Ethane C_2H_6

Propane C_3H_8

Butane C_4H_{10}

8 Carbon atoms can combine covalently to form long chains. Consequently carbon compounds occur in series such as the alkanes (paraffins); the first four (commencing with methane) are shown here.

10

A

Carbon

Carbon

Oxygen

○○○
○○○ Six hydrogens

B

10 Where the same numbers of the same kinds of atoms are joined to one another in different ways the resultant compounds behave differently. Because the gross structures of the molecules are different they are called structural isomers; examples are dimethyl ether [A] and ethyl alcohol [B].

11 Some compounds such as cyclohexane, can exist in two forms differing only in the way their chemical bonds are arranged in space. This illustration shows the "chair" [A] and "boat" [B] forms of cyclohexane. Such compounds are known as conformations: they may "flip" from one form to the other, and a sample of the compound may contain both.

11

A

B

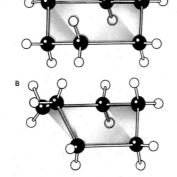

12 During the 20th century hundreds of thousands of carbon compounds hitherto unknown in nature have been synthesized in chemical laboratories. Some of the simplest such molecules of commercial significance are insecticides. De-

veloped mainly to protect food crops, they are also a help to the home gardener. The active ingredients in many insecticide sprays and powders – dichlorvos and BHC for example – are molecules containing only one or two dozen atoms.

12

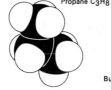

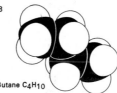

Complex chemicals and their structures

Carbon atoms have the ability to link together in large numbers to give an infinite variety of different substances [2]. Most complex chemicals are carbon-based although there are some important complex materials, such as glass, that contain no carbon.

At one time it was believed that most carbon compounds could be made only by living processes. For instance urea was discovered in the urine of mammals. Consequently, this and similar compounds were called organic chemicals, a name that has stuck. Then organic chemicals were synthesized in the laboratory – for example urea (organic) was made from ammonium cyanate (an inorganic compound). Today organic chemicals account for 50 per cent of the total output of the chemical industry.

The basis of an organic chemicals industry

The discoveries that led to the development of an organic chemicals industry came towards the end of the nineteenth century [3]. It was found that a wealth of useful substances could be obtained from coal tar, a by-product of the manufacture of domestic gas from coal. At that time many of the substances extracted from coal tar were too complex in structure to be made in the laboratory. Once purified, however, it was possible to use them as starting materials from which to produce a range of commercial substances. Dyes, aspirin, saccharin, and explosives such as TNT were all made before the end of the nineteenth century from coal-tar chemicals.

A basic constituent of many of the coal-tar products, and of many other complex organic chemicals, is the group formed of a ring of six carbon atoms joined together. As in other molecules, the chemical bonds between the carbon atoms take the form of electron-carrying orbitals. These orbitals are not located strictly between adjacent carbon nuclei but spread over all six, so that each carbon atom is effectively joined to the next by one-and-a-half bonds.

The simplest of such compounds, in which each carbon atom is also linked to a hydrogen atom (giving a formula C_6H_6), is benzene – originally a coal-tar product but now made mainly from petroleum [1]. In some compounds several benzene rings are fused together to give what are called polycyclic structures such as naphthalene (used in mothballs) benzpyrene (a cancer-inducing chemical) and the hallucinogenic drug LSD.

Many complex organic chemicals found in nature do not contain benzene-type rings. Instead, they are made up of long chains of carbon atoms, with other atoms attached. The other atoms nearly always include hydrogen and often oxygen and nitrogen as well. These compounds include useful natural products such as fats, waxes, sugars and proteins.

Synthetic polymers and their products

Organic molecules have been the basis of one of the major industrial developments of the twentieth century – the widespread manufacture and use of synthetic polymers as plastics, rubbers and fibres. Polymer is a general term for any large molecule that is made by repeatedly linking together the same small molecular unit, which is called the monomer.

Most organic polymers are formed either by addition reactions or by elimination reactions. In many examples of the first type the monomer molecule has a double bond and

1 The six-carbon benzene ring is one of the most important molecules in organic chemistry. Each carbon atom is attached to a single hydrogen atom, so it can form three other bonds with its two neighbouring carbon atoms. It was once thought that single and double bonds alternated around the benzene ring [A, B], although if this were so not all the carbon atoms would have the same chemical reactivity. It is now known that all the carbon-carbon bonds in the ring are equal, because the molecular orbitals (blue [C]) spread out over the whole ring. Below, [D] is a more convenient representation of the actual shape of the molecule.

2 In benzene other atomic groups can replace hydrogen atoms. In aniline [A] one hydrogen is replaced by an amino (—NH₂) group, while phenol [B] has a hydroxyl (—OH) group in place of one hydrogen. Styrene [C], from which polystyrene is made, has a small carbon chain attached to the benzene ring. More than one hydrogen can be replaced: catechol [D], for example, has two —OH groups, while aspirin [E] has two different groups attached to the ring. The shared orbital structure of benzene is sometimes retained even when carbon atoms are replaced, as in pyridine [F].

3 The English chemist William Perkin (1838–1907) tried to make quinine from aniline. Instead his experiments of 1856 accidentally produced the dye aniline purple. This was the first synthetic dye: until that time all dyes were natural compounds extracted from plants or animals.

4 Modern pigments brighten this train with contrasting colours, and paint makers are no longer dependent on natural substances for their products.

5 The chemical heart stimulant digitalin was first obtained by herbalists from leaves of the foxglove (*Digitalis purpurea*).

links with others by using electrons from the double bond. In the second type atoms at the ends of two monomer molecules are "eliminated" and a bond forms between the remaining parts of the monomer molecules.

Natural rubber appears to be an addition polymer, as are many of the man-made rubbers developed in the past few decades. Many synthetic fibres on the other hand are elimination polymers or condensation polymers (in which water is eliminated), as are their natural counterparts such as wool and cotton. A synthetic polymer can have characteristics built into it by the careful choice of starting materials. As a result, different synthetic fibres can have widely differing properties.

Plastics [6] can be fibrous, rubbery, clear, hard, opaque or flexible. The possibilities are almost endless, as the widespread use of synthetic polymers in everyday life confirms.

Linking silicon atoms

Silicon falls directly below carbon in the periodic table of the elements and so logically should have similar chemical properties. But because of their larger size silicon atoms cannot link to form long chains by themselves. Nevertheless, the important polymers called silicones are based on long chains of alternating atoms of silicon and oxygen. The commercially available silicones are often partly organic, and their forms range from plastics for replacement parts such as artificial heart valves in surgery, through greases and lubricating fluids, to insulating materials for electrical cables in submarines.

In silicones, carbon groups are linked to the silicon atoms and stick out on each side of the polymer chain. Like carbon, silicon can form four bonds, whereas oxygen forms only two. This means that, in a repeating —Si—O— chain, there must be other atoms joined to the silicon atoms. These do not have to be organic; each silicon atom can be bonded to four oxygen atoms. If each of these oxygens has two silicons attached, the result is a three-dimensional polymer matrix with the overall formula SiO_2. Sand and glass are composed largely of this inorganic polymer [7], which is often known as silica, and it is also used in ceramics and paint manufacture.

KEY

A modern chemist deals in hundreds of drugs. The old chemist, called an apothecary, displayed in his shop rows of glass jars filled with tinctures and essences extracted from botanical plants. Many balms and medicines made from the contents of such jars are still manufactured today, not from natural extracts but from substances that are produced in chemical plants. Increasing knowledge of the complex molecules found in nature has enabled man to copy and in some cases improve nature's own efforts. Synthetic drugs, rubber and pigments are only a few of the products that man's ingenuity has created to replace natural materials.

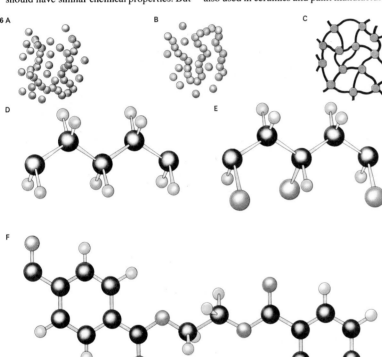

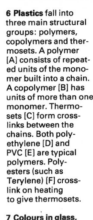

6 Plastics fall into three main structural groups: polymers, copolymers and thermosets. A polymer [A] consists of repeated units of the monomer built into a chain. A copolymer [B] has units of more than one monomer. Thermosets [C] form crosslinks between the chains. Both polyethylene [D] and PVC [E] are typical polymers. Polyesters (such as Terylene) [F] crosslink on heating to give thermosets.

7 Colours in glass, such as those in the windows of Coventry Cathedral, come from added metallic compounds. Cross-linked polymers are not all based on organic molecules and glass is probably the oldest synthetic polymer.

○ Oxygen
○ Carbon
○ Hydrogen

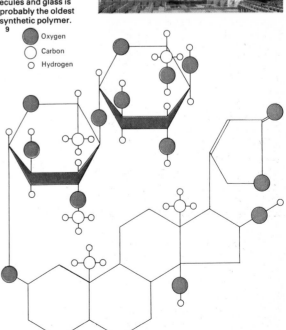

8 Modern plastics are replacing metals in many applications, such as the bodywork of motor vehicles.

9 Digitalin, one of the active ingredients derived from the foxglove (see illustration 5), is typical of biologically active complex compounds found in nature. The three-ring phenanthrene residue in the lower half of the molecule is common also to such compounds as steroids and hormones, cholesterol and the human male and female sex hormones, for example.

125

Chemicals in solution

Every day millions of people make solutions. Many start at breakfast, when they dissolve sugar in tea or coffee. So common is this action that it is taken for granted. But where does the sugar go when it dissolves? Why, if a spoonful of sand is stirred into hot liquid, does it not dissolve?

In chemical terms, a solution is a homogeneous mixture of different sorts of molecules. The criterion of homogeneity is that the two or more types of molecules involved are thoroughly mixed up with one another – as water and sand clearly are not.

Solutes and solvents

Solutions are usually thought of as solids dissolved in liquids – coffee in water, sugar in the coffee, salt in water in the sea [6], detergent in washing water, iodine in alcohol in tincture of iodine, and many more. But there are other kinds of solutions. Gases can dissolve in liquids, as in soda water. Many solutions are made by dissolving liquids in other liquids. Gases can also dissolve in some solids, and solutions of solids in solids are found in metal alloys, for example.

For a solution to form, there must be an interaction between the substance which dissolves (solute) and the material it dissolves in (solvent). Sugar, for example, usually occurs as crystalline arrays of sucrose molecules. To dissolve it, energy is needed to break apart the crystal lattice so that sucrose molecules can disperse evenly through the solvent. Where water is the solvent, the attraction for solute molecules comes from the "polar" character of the water molecule. The central oxygen atom in H_2O is electrically slightly negative, while the hydrogen atoms are slightly positive. Molecules of water tend to attract one another – which is why water is a liquid at room temperature whereas most such small molecules are gases [1]. Water molecules also tend to attract (ie dissolve) other "polar" compounds, such as sugar, with many OH groups in their molecules.

Molecules and compounds

For similar reasons, but via weaker attractive forces, non-polar molecules such as hydrocarbons will dissolve other non-polar compounds, such as fats. Modern detergents work by a compromise between both types of attraction: part of the molecule dissolves in grease, the other part dissolves in water, so that the detergent molecule acts as a bridge between them and disperses grease in water.

Some compounds, such as ethyl alcohol, dissolve completely in either water or hydrocarbons – substances that will not dissolve in one another. Other compounds may show a preference for polar or non-polar solvents, according to their chemical structures.

The attraction between individual molecules of different types can be seen easily where it results in a reduction of the overall volume of material. If, for example, equal parts of water and ethyl alcohol are mixed together, the total volume of solution is only about 97 per cent of the sum of the separate components.

When a substance will not dissolve, it is because the solvent does not overcome the intermolecular forces which hold the molecules together. With any substance, there are limits to solubility, which may vary with temperature – hot solvents dissolving more solute than cold solvents.

1 The atoms and molecules of all materials are in motion, the energy of this motion depending on the temperature. In a liquid, the motion prevents any permanent intermolecular structure from forming, but forces of attraction govern the overall volume. In water, there are many temporary linkages (shown blue) between the H_2O molecules; very small enclosed cavities [1] form and disappear continually.

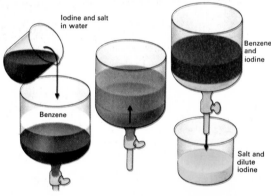

2 The slight positive charge on the hydrogen atoms and slight negative charge on the oxygen atoms of water make it particularly suitable for dissolving inorganic salts. Trichloroethylene, widely used in dry cleaning, and chloroform both dissolve many organic compounds. Acetone, with behaviour intermediate between water and trichloroethylene, is able to dissolve both organic and inorganic compounds.

Water Trichloroethylene Acetone Chloroform

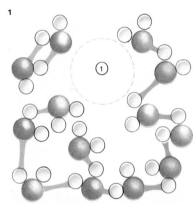

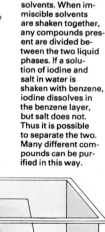

3 Ordinary washing removes water-soluble dirt and also non-soluble dirt that can be emulsified in water by the addition of detergents. (Milk is a typical example of an emulsion where one liquid mixed and joined with another does not separate.) In dry cleaning, an organic solvent is employed; most of those used commercially are small, halogen-containing molecules, such as trichloroethylene. These solvents dissolve grease; however, because their fumes are unpleasant they have to be used in special machines, as shown here. Similar compounds are also used in industrial degreasing operations, such as cleaning pieces of metal prior to machining, or in the manufacture of electronics components.

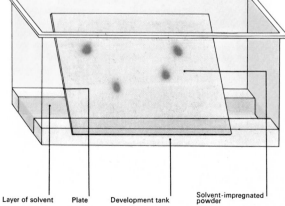

Iodine and salt in water

Benzene

Benzene and iodine

Salt and dilute iodine

4 The solubility of a substance is different in different solvents. When immiscible solvents are shaken together, any compounds present are divided between the two liquid phases. If a solution of iodine and salt in water is shaken with benzene, iodine dissolves in the benzene layer, but salt does not. Thus it is possible to separate the two. Many different compounds can be purified in this way.

5 Different compounds can also be separated by partitioning them between a solid and a liquid. In thin-layer chromatography, the process shown in this illustration, a spot of mixed compounds is placed on a plate coated with absorbent powder, which is put into a development tank containing a solvent (ensuring the tank is saturated with its vapour). As solvent ascends the plate, the mixture separates out into its component chemicals.

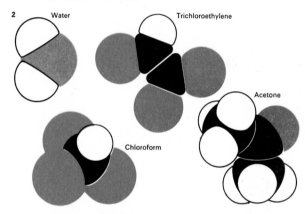

Layer of solvent   Plate   Development tank   Solvent-impregnated powder

126

A solution containing the maximum possible amount of solute (dissolved substance) is called saturated. A hot liquid generally has a greater capacity for holding solid in solution than a cold one (with gases in liquids, the reverse is true). Consequently, if as much solid as possible is dissolved in boiling water, some of it may crystallize out when the water cools. If it does not, the solution is said to be supersaturated. This is the basis of many experiments for growing giant crystals in school laboratories.

Dissolving a solid in a liquid affects the liquid in a variety of ways. For example, pure water freezes at 0°C (32°F) and boils at 100°C (212°F). The freezing-point of a solution of common salt, however, is lower than 0°C; thus, salt sprinkled on roads in winter prevents ice from forming.

Osmotic pressures

One of the more important properties of solutions is their ability to exert osmotic pressure. If a solution encased in certain types of membrane is brought into contact with pure solvent, the solvent molecules pass through the membrane into the solution, making it more dilute. The molecules of solute, on the other hand, are unable to pass through the membrane, which is called "semi-permeable" in consequence.

Osmosis is crucial to many living organisms. For example, the absorption of water by the root hairs of plants depends on it. If the concentration of dissolved matter in the plant cells is greater than in the water surrounding them, water is drawn in. On the other hand, if the reverse is true – in very salty soils, for example – water may be drawn out of the plants, so that they die.

Plants and animals are also responsible for producing complex substances that form so-called colloidal solutions. These are part way between a solution and a suspension. The jellies eaten by children are one type of colloidal solution, and non-drip paint is another. Jellies set on cooling and "melt" again on heating, but a non-drip paint becomes more liquid as it is stirred and more solid when it is left standing. These differences are accounted for by the different types of colloidal substances used.

Rivers and streams dissolve small quantities of minerals. Under certain conditions, these minerals can be precipitated from solution – sometimes in impressive forms, such as these stalactites and stalagmites formed over thousands of years in limestone caves in various parts of the world.

6 There is a limit to the amount of any particular compound that will dissolve in a solvent. When this limit is reached, the solution is said to be saturated. If solvent is evaporated, or if the temperature falls, the amount of compound that can be held in solution drops and solid precipitates. The Dead Sea is one of the most concentrated naturally occurring solutions of minerals, some of which crystallized out when the water level dropped in the past. Here Israeli industry evaporates large quantities of Dead Sea water in nearby "pans" to obtain important minerals for making various inorganic chemicals.

7 Although two-thirds of the earth's surface is covered with water, in many countries there is a lack of pure water for drinking. In this modern desalination plant, pure water is evaporated from solutions such as seawater and then condensed in large tanks. The concentrated brine left over from the process is usually returned to the sea, where it is diluted by tidal mixing.

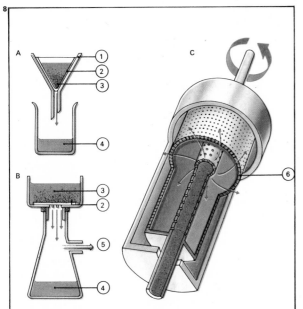

8 Filtration removes solid particles from solution. A mixture placed [A] in a filter funnel [1] drains through the filter paper [2] by gravity, leaving sediment [3] trapped while the filtrate [4] flows through. In the Buchner funnel [B], the same principle is enhanced by suction [5]. In the industrial rotary filter [C] the spinning action of the drum drives the mixture onto the fine mesh filter [6].

9 In a domestic water softener, water flows up a column [A] and ions of calcium and magnesium (which cause "hardness") are exchanged for sodium ions. In time all the sodium ions are used [B]. The column is regenerated using sodium chloride [C].

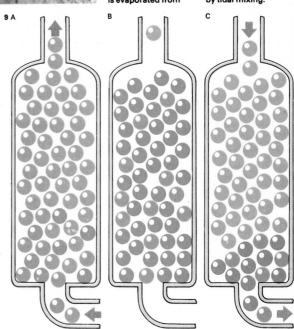

Key chemical reactions

In an enclosed space, a mixture of air and an organic vapour composed mainly of hydrocarbons are pressed together. The hydrocarbons consist of molecules in which several carbon atoms are chemically bonded to each other and to a number of hydrogen atoms. A spark is generated. In an instant, many of the bonds between carbon and hydrogen and between carbon and carbon are broken and replaced by chemical bonds that combine these atoms with oxygen from the air. An explosion results, and a chemical reaction has taken place. This particular reaction takes place millions of times each day in most parts of the world, wherever people use petrol-driven internal combustion engines in cars and other motor vehicles.

Molecular energy
Chemists are interested in how individual compounds react: how quickly they will react, what the products are and how much "persuasion" is needed to make a reaction take place.

Why, for example, is a spark needed before the hydrocarbons that compose petrol will react with oxygen? Why, however many sparks are provided, will exhaust gases such as carbon dioxide and steam not burn? Why does the spark cause an explosive reaction in a petrol/air mixture, whereas a spark landing on this page would probably only char a small portion of the paper; and, if the paper did catch fire, why would it burn steadily rather than explode?

The answers to all these questions are related to the energies of different molecules. The world is full of molecules, rather than unlinked atoms, because the formation of chemical bonds releases energy and makes the resultant product more stable. The same is true of molecular reactions. If a reaction occurs spontaneously, there is usually a release of energy and the production of more stable molecules.

It is theoretically possible to get water and carbon dioxide to react to form petrol and oxygen. But, because petrol and oxygen are less stable molecules, large quantities of energy would have to be put into the reactants (starting materials) to succeed. A better example is, perhaps, metallic corrosion.

Many metals are more stable as compounds, such as the oxide or sulphide, than as pure metal. Using processes that supply energy to metallic compounds, scientists can refine their ores to make metals for steel girders or silver teaspoons. But if unprotected, the metals gradually corrode – that is, spontaneously form compounds such as iron oxide (rust) or silver sulphide (tarnish) that are more stable than the pure metals.

Kinds of reactions
Whereas certain reactions may occur spontaneously, they do not necessarily do so. A petrol/air mixture needs the spark to set it off because, in between the reactants and the products, there is a transition state which is of higher energy. It is necessary to give many reactants an energy "lift" to help them over the activation barrier. The larger the amount of energy arising from a reaction, the more molecules can be lifted over the barrier. And if the reaction happens fast enough, the result is an explosion.

The energy to initiate a reaction can come from a variety of sources. Heat is commonly

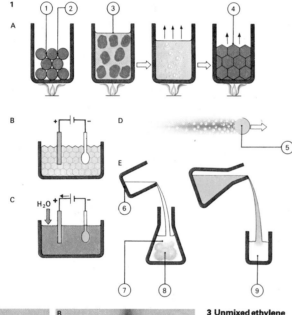

1 The application of heat [A] alone to aluminium sulphate [1] and potassium sulphate [2] produces no reaction, but they "combine" when dissolved in water [3]. If heating is continued to evaporation, alum [4] forms. Dry copper sulphate crystals [B] do not conduct current; but dissolve them in water [C] and electrolysis can proceed. Metals may react with a liquid [D]: a grain of sodium [5] dropped into a water bath melts, generating hydrogen. Solutions and other liquids react readily [E]. Phenolphthalein [6] added to a solution of alkali [7] produces a pink solution [8]. When this is added to an acid solution [9], the pink disappears.

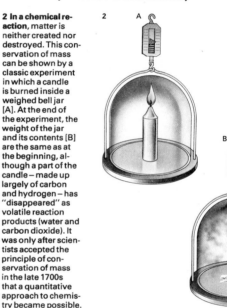

2 In a chemical reaction, matter is neither created nor destroyed. This conservation of mass can be shown by a classic experiment in which a candle is burned inside a weighed bell jar [A]. At the end of the experiment, the weight of the jar and its contents [B] are the same as at the beginning, although a part of the candle – made up largely of carbon and hydrogen – has "disappeared" as volatile reaction products (water and carbon dioxide). It was only after scientists accepted the principle of conservation of mass in the late 1700s that a quantitative approach to chemistry became possible.

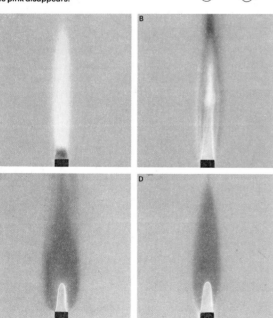

3 Unmixed ethylene burns with a luminous diffusion flame [A], reacting with oxygen drawn in from round the flame. If mixed with a little air, the ethylene gives a flame with three distinct layers – an inner cone of unburnt gas, a blue-green layer of reacting premixed gas and an outer cone where partially oxidized products of the premixed layer are burned by a diffusion flame [B]. Addition of nitric oxide to the mixture cuts down the amount of oxygen available for immediate combustion and the resultant flame [C] shows a complex series of reactions, as in B. But if more air is added to the gas mixture, the diffusion layer disappears [D].

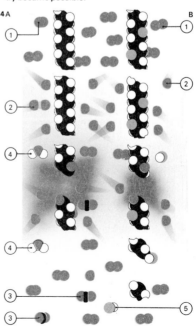

4 A hydrocarbon fuel [A] will burn more readily than similar molecules in which some of the hydrogen atoms have been replaced by chlorine [B]. When mixed with oxygen [1] and subjected to a spark, both types of molecules burn, but the chlorinated one burns more slowly. The spark breaks oxygen molecules into reactive oxygen atoms [2]. These combine with carbon and hydrogen in the hydrocarbon to give carbon dioxide [3] and water [4]. Sufficient heat is produced to keep the reaction going rapidly. With the chlorinated material, more complex reactions take place more slowly. These produce, in addition, hydrogen chloride [5] but generate less heat.

used by chemists to help reactions along. But other forms of energy, such as light, are sometimes enough to initiate reactions.

There are a great many types of reactions, but they can all be broken down into simple categories. There are reactions in which a single substance rearranges its chemical bonds to produce a different single substance (rearrangement); alternatively, it may break into two or more different parts (decomposition, fragmentation). Conversely two, or occasionally more, compounds can combine to form a single compound (addition). More often, there are a number of products.

Reaction requirements

When there is only one starting material, the activated state is achieved by molecules absorbing sufficient energy to initiate a change. For example, when the visual pigment rhodopsin in the retina of the eye absorbs light, one of its electrons is energized and the molecule is catapulted into a more energetic state. As a result, the molecule changes shape to form a different geometric isomer (substance whose molecules are made of the same numbers of the same atoms, but whose atoms are differently arranged).

When different starting materials are involved, not only must they have enough energy to form the activated intermediate state, but they must also collide physically before the rearrangement of bonds can be completed. This is why some reactions take place under high pressure, as in a car engine, because packing molecules more tightly together makes collisions more likely.

Another way to improve the chances of a successful collision is to provide a surface that has an appropriate geometry for bringing molecules together. Substances that provide such surfaces are among various types of catalysts. They speed up reactions by lowering the activation barrier. Other, negative, catalysts slow or even prevent reactions.

To follow reactions as they occur and identify the various products, modern chemists use a large range of different techniques [6, 7]. Some of them, such as nuclear spin resonance and Mossbauer spectroscopy, are based on physical phenomena discovered during the past 30 or 40 years.

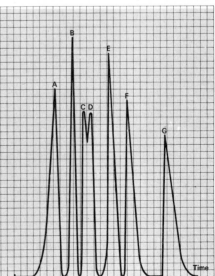

KEY

A reaction takes place as drops of alkali fall into a dilute solution of a copper salt. This is a precipitation reaction – one of many different kinds that can take place in chemistry. One of the chemist's major tasks lies in discovering how various materials react with each other.

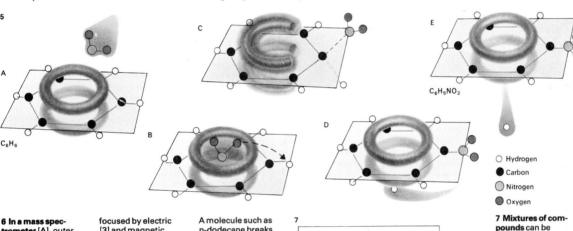

5

A
C_6H_6

B

C

D

E
$C_6H_5NO_2$

○ Hydrogen
● Carbon
○ Nitrogen
● Oxygen

5 The nitration of benzene produces a reaction that goes through several stages. Initially [A], the entering group approaches and associates weakly with the benzene ring [B]. Then, rearrangement produces an unstable high energy intermediate [C] which breaks down to a complex [D] in which the leaving group is weakly associated with the ring. It ends with the departure of the leaving group [E].

6 In a mass spectrometer [A], outer electrons of a compound are removed in an ionization chamber [1]. Positively charged ions pass into an adjacent chamber under vacuum [2] and are focused by electric [3] and magnetic [4] fields. The way they are deflected by these fields is characteristic for each ion, which can be identified by its position on a photographic plate [5]. A molecule such as n-dodecane breaks down into a number of fragments that produce various "peaks" on a graph [B]. From the position of these, the parent molecules can be precisely identified.

7 Mixtures of compounds can be separated by gas chromatography. Gaseous molecules travel down columns of liquid-impregnated solids at different rates. Special detectors reproduce on a graph the peaks produced by the molecules as they leave the column. Each can frequently be identified by the time it takes to go through the column – the "retention" time. The chromatogram shows the separation of hydrocarbons: isobutane [A], n-butane [B], n-butene [C], isobutene [D] trans-but-2-ene [E], cis-but-2-ene [F], cis-1-3-butadiene [G].

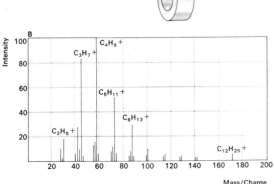

6

A

B

Intensity

$C_3H_7{}^+$
$C_4H_9{}^+$
$C_5H_{11}{}^+$
$C_6H_{13}{}^+$
$C_2H_5{}^+$
$C_{12}H_{25}{}^+$

Mass/Charge

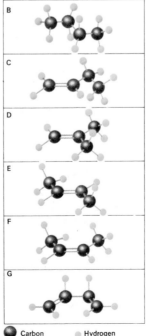

7

A
B
C
D
E
F
G

● Carbon   ○ Hydrogen

Electrochemistry

Electrons are negatively charged particles that form a part of every atom and it is with the interactions of electrons from different atoms that chemistry is mainly concerned. An electric current is no more than a flow of electrons. Consequently, it is not surprising that electricity and chemistry are connected.

Early research

Studies of electricity and chemistry went hand in hand long before anyone knew of the existence of electrons. During the eighteenth century, there was much interest in static electricity, leading to the development of the Leyden jar (for storing "electric fluid" generated by friction) and the lightning conductor. However, it was not until the Italian physiologist Luigi Galvani (1737–98) found, towards the end of that century, that frogs' legs would contract if different metals were applied to nerve and muscle that current electricity was discovered. In 1795, another Italian, the physicist Alessandro Volta (1745–1827) [1], showed that this "animal electricity" could be produced without living tissue. He separated two pieces of metal by a cloth moistened with salt solution and thus made the first electrical battery. Within five years, it was discovered in England that current from such a battery could decompose water into hydrogen and oxygen gases. Thus, the foundations of electrochemistry were laid. By a chemical reaction involving two metals, a flow of electrons can be produced; such flow can bring about other reactions.

Batteries soon became important equipment in every laboratory and led to many new discoveries, such as the isolation of the elements sodium and potassium in the first decade of the nineteenth century by Humphry Davy (1778–1829).

Chemical reactions

When a metal such as zinc forms compounds, it does so in many instances by losing two electrons to form a doubly positive zinc ion (Zn^{2+}). Metals differ in the ease with which they lose electrons, so that if a piece of zinc metal is placed in a solution of copper sulphate (which contains Cu^{2+} ions), the zinc gives up electrons to the copper. The net result is that zinc is converted to zinc sulphate, which contains Zn^{2+} ions, and copper ions become metallic copper.

When an element gains electrons to form a negatively charged ion, it is said to be reduced; if it loses electrons to form a positively charged ion, it is said to be oxidized. A reaction where reduction and oxidation cancel each other out, as in the zinc/copper sulphate case, is called a redox reaction. Redox reactions can be tapped to supply electric currents by preventing the reduction and oxidation from occurring at the same place. A battery can be made by suspending zinc in zinc sulphate and copper in copper sulphate and linking the two solutions by a porous partition and the metals with wire.

Each of the reactions in such an arrangement is called a "half cell". When two "half cells" are added together, a cell is completed and the voltage it produces depends on the particular half cells that make it up.

That different batteries produce different, but specific, voltages depending on their chemical composition is not surprising, in view of the differences in reactivity between different elements. The reverse also seems

1 Alessandro Volta,
professor of natural philosophy at the University of Pavia, Italy, constructed in 1800 an "artificial electrical organ", an apparatus he described as like the electrical organ of the electric eel. Made by piling alternate discs of copper and zinc, each pair separated by a piece of brine-soaked cloth, his electrical organ was one of the first scientific batteries ever made.

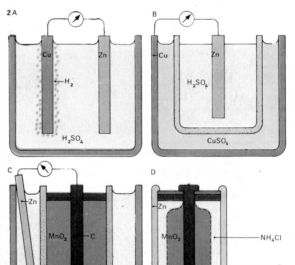

3 Heart pacemakers like the one shown here, and miniature hearing aids, can be powered by batteries. These are examples of primary cells. Secondary cells or storage batteries can be recharged. Early batteries all had metallic plates separated by solutions of salt-like chemicals. The dry, or Leclanché, cell replaced the liquid with a paste. Such batteries, which use zinc and carbon (with a manganese dioxide depolarizer) as electrodes, are the type used in transistor radios, torches, and many other everyday appliances. In recent years, battery technology has led to the production of very small but highly reliable batteries which also use zinc and a metal oxide, in this case mercury.

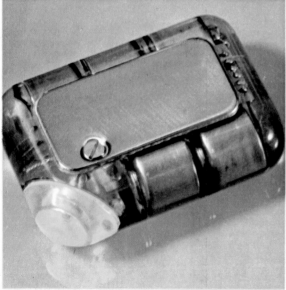

2 The voltaic cell [A] consists of a jar containing sulphuric acid (H_2SO_4) in which are suspended a copper (Cu) anode and a zinc (Zn) cathode. When the circuit is closed a current flows, zinc ions pass into the acid from the cathode and hydrogen (H_2) is deposited on the anode. Hydrogen eventually obstructs the reaction, but not so in the Daniell cell [B], in which the zinc cathode and sulphuric acid are encased in a porous pot surrounded by a solution of copper sulphate ($CuSO_4$). The copper case acts as the anode. The Leclanche [C] and dry cells [D] have carbon (C) anodes enclosed in manganese dioxide (MnO_2) in ammonium chloride (NH_4Cl); both types have zinc cathodes.

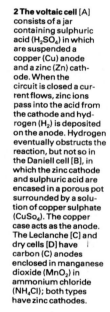

4 Elements which gain or lose electrons easily are often prepared from ionic compounds by electrolysis. Chlorine [1], for example, can be produced by electrolysis of a sodium chloride solution [2] at graphite anodes [3]. Hydrogen [4] from the electrolysis of water is released at the cathodes [5]. Left behind in solution are sodium and hydroxyl ions, giving a solution of sodium hydroxide [6]. In the practical cell a partition keeps the products (hydrogen and chlorine) apart to prevent them from reacting together to produce hydrogen chloride. Similarly a diaphragm keeps the hydroxyl ions away from the chlorine to prevent them from reacting to form sodium hypochlorite.

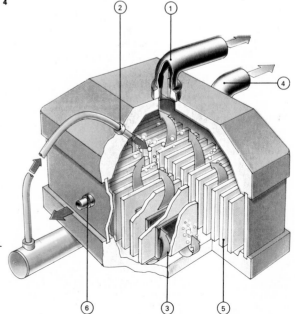

logical: that a particular quantity of electrons should produce a particular amount of change in a substance. The quantitative relationships between electricity and chemical reactions were stated during the nineteenth century by Michael Faraday [Key]. The extraction and electroplating of metals, and the production of reactive electronegative elements such as chlorine [4] and fluorine, are often done electrolytically.

Electrolysis

The products from electrolysis reactions [2] sometimes depend on the conditions used, as well as the amount of electricity. If fused (molten) sodium chloride is electrolyzed, sodium metal forms at one electrode and chlorine gas at the other. However, when a solution of sodium chloride is electrolyzed, using a graphite anode (positive electrode) and an iron cathode (negative electrode), chlorine and hydrogen gases are produced, leaving behind sodium hydroxide solution.

The ions of different elements may be positive (cations) or negative (anions). In a solution that is being electrolyzed, cations are attracted to the cathode and anions to the anode. If aluminium is made into an anode in an acid solution, a very thin layer of aluminium oxide forms on it. This anodization protects the aluminium from corrosion and is used on a wide range of articles.

Many oxidation reactions are used in everyday life: for example, the burning of petrol in a car is such a reaction. Instead of releasing the energy from such a reaction as heat, it can be converted into a flow of electrons in a "fuel cell". These cells are theoretically much more efficient energy converters than heat engines. However, difficulties in designing suitable fuel cells for everyday purposes have meant that their use has been limited largely to applications where cost is not an important factor.

The chief commercial application of electrochemistry is electroplating by means of electrolysis. For example, decorative metals such as gold and silver are electroplated onto articles of jewellery, whereas chromium is electroplated onto steel (preferably over base layers of copper and nickel) to provide resistance to corrosion.

As a youth, Michael Faraday (1791–1867) attended Humphry Davy's lectures at the Royal Institution in London. He copied these out and sent them to Davy with a request for employment. From Davy's assistant, he rose to become professor of chemistry at the Royal Institution, a post he held for more than 30 years. Most of Faraday's work was in physics – particularly in the field of electromagnetic induction. He also founded the science of electrochemistry through his discovery of the quantitative relationships between the amount of electricity passed through a solution and the amount of substances deposited as a result.

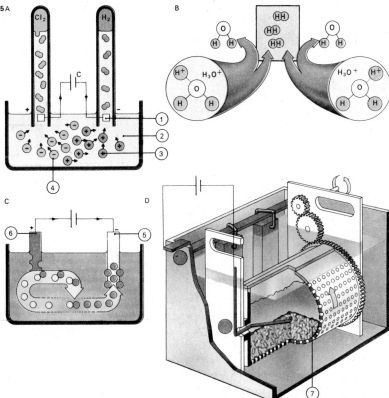

5 Electrolysis can easily be shown. A current is passed [A] between platinum electrodes [1] through a dilute hydrochloric acid electrolyte [2]. Positively charged cations [3] move towards the negative electrode (cathode) and anions [4] move to the positive electrode (anode). The hydrogen ions combine with water to form hydronium ions, H_3O^+; when two hydronium ions [B] reach the cathode, they each receive an electron, thus forming atoms of hydrogen which combine to form a molecule of gas. In copper plating [C], copper from the copper sulphate electrolyte is deposited onto the object to be plated [5], while copper from the anode [6] is drawn into solution. A modern barrel electroplating machine [D] can plate many small objects [7] simultaneously.

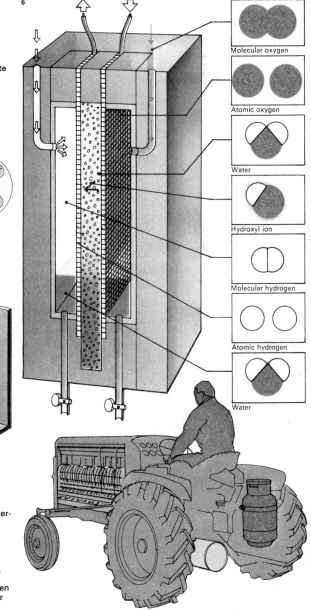

Molecular oxygen

Atomic oxygen

Water

Hydroxyl ion

Molecular hydrogen

Atomic hydrogen

Water

6 The fuel cell, like a battery, uses the energy generated during a chemical reaction to produce electrical power. One simple cell uses oxygen and hydrogen as "fuels" to produce electricity, the water formed being a by-product. The electrolyte in this case is located in a very thin, water-saturated membrane. This allows ions to pass through it, but does not allow the passage of atoms or molecules. The electrodes are of wire mesh, coated with platinum. Molecular hydrogen and oxygen are fed to them from gas chambers. The cathodic platinum converts oxygen to hydroxyl ions, which move across the membrane and react with hydrogen at the anode to form water. Electrons released by the hydrogen traverse the external circuit – as an electric current – to help form hydroxyl at the anode. A battery of such cells can power a tractor, with fuel tanks holding liquid oxygen and hydrogen either as a liquid or as a solid hydride.

Chemical analysis

One of the main branches of chemistry – chemical analysis – is concerned with determining the composition of a substance or a mixture of substances. Identifying the ingredients is termed qualitative analysis, whereas determining their precise proportions is called quantitative analysis. Organic chemicals (the large class of compounds containing the element carbon) and inorganic chemicals (all other compounds) require different analytical techniques in the laboratory.

Methods of inorganic analysis
Qualitative inorganic analysis is generally carried out on a semi-micro scale [1] using small quantities – much less than a gramme. Chemists make preliminary tests on a dry sample of a substance and these give general information about its composition. The effect of heat may cause a colour change, sublimation or the evolution of a gas. A reagent is added to a solution of the sample and the resulting mixture examined for the evolution of a gas, a precipitate or a coloration.

Metal ions are identified by a systematic separation into "groups". A variety of techniques exists, but metals are usually split into groups by adding a series of reagents and collecting any precipitate produced. Group precipitates are, in turn, separated and identified by characteristic reactions.

Quantitative inorganic analysis may be carried out using either volumetric or gravimetric methods. Volumetric analysis involves reacting a solution of known concentration, referred to as a "standard" solution, with a solution of the substance to be determined. After preparing the standard solution the chemist carries out a titration [Key] in which one solution is slowly added to the other. From the concentration and volume of the standard solution, the concentration of the "unknown" can be calculated.

Gravimetric analysis involves preparing a solution with a known mass of the sample. This solution is then reacted with a chosen reagent so that the desired component is completely separated, generally as a precipitate. The product, which must be pure, is isolated and weighed and the amount of the component calculated.

Merely identifying the elements present is insufficient to make a definite description of an organic compound. The ability of carbon compounds to exhibit isomerism (in which two different substances can contain the same chemical elements, in the same proportions, but combined in a different way) means that the arrangements of the elements present must also be analytically determined.

Methods of organic analysis
Identification of the elements in an organic component involves systematic elimination of all possible elements one by one. Carbon and hydrogen are always present and tests for them are rarely carried out. But tests are made to identify other elements. An example is the Lassaigne sodium fusion, which reveals the presence of nitrogen, the halogens (chlorine, bromine and iodine) and sulphur. A knowledge of the elements allows a chemist to allocate the compound to a main group. This is followed by the application, within the group, of classification tests for functional groups, which determines the types of organic compound present.

1 Analysis on a semi-micro scale saves time and money. Small test tubes are used for reactions and tapered tubes are used for the centrifuge. Solutions do not mix well in these small tubes, so a stirring rod is necessary. Solutions are handled in a teat-pipette and each reagent bottle should be fitted with its own "dropper". Solids require the use of a semi-micro spatula. To avoid the dangers of "bumping" during heating, solutions are heated indirectly in a metal block, although evaporation to dryness requires the use of a small crucible. Identification of gases is usually carried out with a bubble-cap fitted to a test tube.

2 The melting-point is a characteristic of an organic compound and can be measured, using this automatic apparatus, to help to identify it. A sample is first heated quickly to get an approximate value and then slowly melted to obtain a more accurate reading.

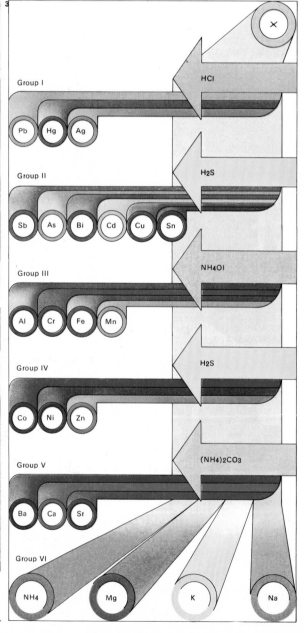

3 Metal ions can be detected in qualitative chemical analysis by a systematic separation into groups by means of a series of characteristic precipitation reactions. The chemist tries to dissolve a sample of the substance to be analysed in dilute hydrochloric acid. Metals with insoluble chlorides – lead, mercury and silver – constitute Group I. Next hydrogen sulphide is bubbled through the acid solution; a sulphide precipitate indicates one of Group II metals – antimony, arsenic, bismuth, cadmium, copper or tin. The addition of ammonia solution precipitates the hydroxides of the Group III metals – aluminium, chromium, iron or manganese. The Group IV metals have sulphides that are precipitated from alkaline solution by bubbling in hydrogen sulphide gas; they are cobalt, nickel and zinc. The addition of ammonium carbonate to the remaining solution at this stage of the analysis precipitates the carbonates of barium, calcium or strontium, the Group V metals. Group VI of the analysis table contains the metals magnesium, sodium and potassium as well as the "metallic" ion ammonium, left after eliminating all other possible metal ions. This analysis scheme can be carried out on the semi-micro scale and it can be enlarged to include some of the less common metals. It reveals only the presence of a metal and not its quantity.

Quantitative organic analysis also involves estimation of the elements present, followed by purification and a determination of molecular weight to give the empirical and molecular formulae. The amounts of carbon and hydrogen are found by completely oxidizing a known mass of the organic compound and weighing the carbon dioxide and water formed. Then any other elements are estimated by a variety of methods.

These results allow the chemist to calculate the percentage composition of the substance (the proportions of each element present) and to determine its empirical formula. The molecular formula is found by comparing the empirical formula with the molecular weight. Dissolving a sample of the substance in a solvent affects the physical properties of the solvent. The lowering of vapour pressure, the elevation of boiling point and the depression of freezing point are all proportional to the mole fraction (concentration in terms of molecular weight) of the dissolved substance present in the solution. The concentration also affects the osmotic pressure, viscosity and light-scattering properties of solutions. Careful measurement of one of these effects is then followed by a calculation of the molecular weight before the chemist has enough information to complete the analysis.

Modern instrumental analysis

Various forms of chromatography are based on the fact that different substances diffuse or are absorbed at different rates. Spectroscopy [7] makes use of the fact that each species of atom has a unique characteristic spectrum. A spectrum is produced when atoms, ions or molecules are excited by absorbing energy and may be observed by using a prism or, preferably, a diffraction grating.

In mass spectroscopy [5] a substance is bombarded with low-energy electrons and fragmentation produces a number of positive ions. Ions of the same mass/charge ratio are focused by magnetic or electrostatic fields and detected photographically or electronically. The highest mass/charge ratio can give the molecular weight. Investigation of the fragmentation pattern determines the molecular structure.

A titration is performed to estimate the unknown concentration of a solution by reacting it with a "standard" solution of known concentration. This is usually added from a burette to a fixed volume of the "unknown". The end-point of the reaction is shown either by a visible change in the reactants or by the addition of a chemical indicator. Acid/base indicators have different colours according to the hydrogen-ion concentration (pH) of the solution and change as the pH of the solution changes. The pH at which colour changes occur varies so an indicator can be selected that shows a colour change at a pH close to the end-point.

4 Molecular weight may be determined by the depression of freezing-point. When a substance is dissolved in a solvent the freezing-point is depressed. If dilute solutions are used then the depression is directly proportional to the number of molecules of the solute in unit mass of the solvent. The molecular depression constant of a solvent is the depression of freezing-point produced for one mole of solute in 100g (3.5oz) of solvent. Experimentally this quantity would need too high a concentration so dilute solutions are used and the constant calculated by proportion. The most convenient freezing agent is ice and water.

5 The masses of atoms can be compared with great accuracy using a mass spectrometer. A vaporized sample is ionized by electron bombardment and the beam of positive ions produced is accelerated to a constant speed. Application of a strong magnetic field deflects the beam – the lightest ions being deflected most and the heaviest least. The field is adjusted so that ions of a particular mass fall on to a detector, either a moving photographic plate or an electrometer. From an electrometer the signal is amplified and recorded on a graph. Further adjustment of the magnetic field allows ions of different mass to be recorded.

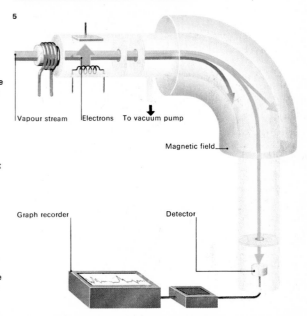

Vapour stream | Electrons | To vacuum pump

Magnetic field

Graph recorder | Detector

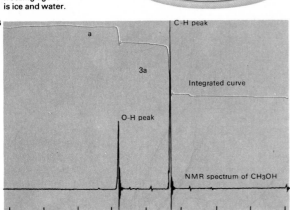

6 | C-H peak
a
3a
Integrated curve
O-H peak
NMR spectrum of CH₃OH

7 | Infra-red spectrum of CCl₄
100
90
80
70
60
50
40
30
20
10
0
Transmittance (%)
4,000 3,600 3,200 2,800 2,400 2,000 1,800 1,600 1,400 1,200 1,000 800
Frequency (cm⁻¹)
C-Cl peak

6 Nuclear magnetic resonance (NMR) spectroscopy of a substance with a molecular formula of CH₄O shows two peaks. The areas under the peaks are integrated automatically and indicated by the upper curve. This shows a ratio of one to three. The inference is that the four hydrogen atoms in the molecule are arranged so that three are in the same environment, and the other is different. The larger peak is produced by those in the O-CH₃ group and the smaller by that in the O-H group – indicating the structure CH₃OH: methanol. Normally a "standard" is added and all lines are measured relative to it. Tetramethylsilane or a sodium salt of 4,4-dimethyl,4,silapentanesulphonic acid is a suitable standard.

7 Infra-red radiation is absorbed by the chemical bonds in an organic compound and can cause vibrational effects in them. The frequency of the absorbed radiation is characteristic of the bond concerned, so that measuring these frequencies provides a means of determining the bonds present and analysing the compound. This is the basis of infra-red spectroscopy. The absorption frequencies are measured electronically and plotted as a series of peaks on a graph. In this example the main absorption peak at a frequency of 750cm⁻¹ is due to stretching of a carbon-chlorine bond, indicating that the substance producing it is probably tetrachloromethane (carbon tetrachloride, CCl₄). The minor peak at 1,550cm⁻¹ is probably a harmonic of the main one. The bending and rocking of chemical bonds after infra-red absorption also produce characteristic peaks on the spectrograph and aid the analysis.

Towards the chemistry of life

Only half a dozen of the 93 or more chemical elements that occur naturally on earth make up the bulk of living matter, and life's diversity is due largely to the combining properties of just one element: carbon. Carbon atoms can form chemical bonds with each other to produce an extensive range of basic structures. These can be modified by the addition of the atoms of other common elements of life – hydrogen, oxygen, nitrogen, phosphorus and sulphur – to produce the enormous diversity of chemical substances found throughout the living world.

Isomers and polymers

Many naturally occurring carbon compounds have another distinctive property. A single atom of carbon can form chemical bonds to four different atomic groupings. These groupings can be arranged to produce two different molecules that are as similar to and as different from each other as a pair of gloves [1]. They are called optical isomers and where two of these are possible, usually only one form occurs naturally.

Many key substances in living organisms are polymers – giant molecules containing thousands or even millions of individual atoms linked together. Carbohydrates, proteins and nucleic acids are all polymers. But they are all made by joining together small molecular building blocks rather than individual atoms.

Carbohydrates, for example, are all made from small molecules called sugars, or saccharides. Common table sugar is not one of the simplest: it is made by linking two smaller saccharides. Chemists call it a disaccharide. It is an ingredient of many proprietary foods, such as pickles and ketchup [3].

Like all carbohydrates, saccharides are composed of carbon, hydrogen and oxygen. These elements are generally linked together in such a way that a loop is formed between the ends of the molecule by an oxygen atom bridging two carbon atoms.

Sugars and fats

Sugars [2] not only supply living organisms with energy, but they also make up a broad range of polymeric substances, such as starch and cellulose. Starch, for example, is the chief carbohydrate in potatoes, rice and bread [3]. Human beings cannot digest cellulose, but the polymer can be broken down chemically to form molecules of glucose, which is an example of a simple sugar (monosaccharide). Sugar from beet or cane is sucrose.

Virtually all food has sugars or polysaccharides in it. Almost as common in food are the lipids, composed solely of carbon, hydrogen and oxygen. Lipid is a general term that includes oils, fats and waxes, all of which have similar chemical structures. In a simple lipid, the same sort of carbon-oxygen-carbon bond that holds a disaccharide together joins three fatty acids to a small molecule called glycerol (also known as glycerine) [4B]. The resultant triglyceride may be a liquid (oil) or solid (fat) at room temperature, depending on the structures of the fatty acids, which can all be the same (as in olive oil) or all different. All meats contain some fat [3].

The so-called unsaturated fatty acids contain carbon-carbon double bonds. In recent years, margarines containing them have been available in many countries because a link has been suggested between high consump-

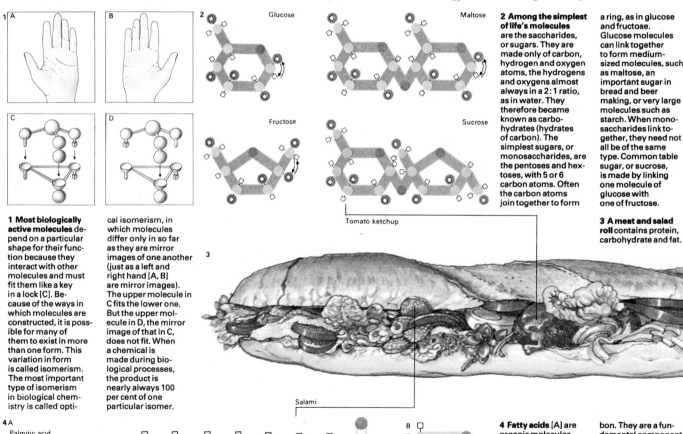

Glucose

Fructose

Maltose

Sucrose

Tomato ketchup

1 Most biologically active molecules depend on a particular shape for their function because they interact with other molecules and must fit them like a key in a lock [C]. Because of the ways in which molecules are constructed, it is possible for many of them to exist in more than one form. This variation in form is called isomerism. The most important type of isomerism in biological chemistry is called opti-cal isomerism, in which molecules differ only in so far as they are mirror images of one another (just as a left and right hand [A, B] are mirror images). The upper molecule in C fits the lower one. But the upper molecule in D, the mirror image of that in C, does not fit. When a chemical is made during biological processes, the product is nearly always 100 per cent of one particular isomer.

2 Among the simplest of life's molecules are the saccharides, or sugars. They are made only of carbon, hydrogen and oxygen atoms, the hydrogens and oxygens almost always in a 2:1 ratio, as in water. They therefore became known as carbohydrates (hydrates of carbon). The simplest sugars, or monosaccharides, are the pentoses and hexoses, with 5 or 6 carbon atoms. Often the carbon atoms join together to form a ring, as in glucose and fructose. Glucose molecules can link together to form medium-sized molecules, such as maltose, an important sugar in bread and beer making, or very large molecules such as starch. When monosaccharides link together, they need not all be of the same type. Common table sugar, or sucrose, is made by linking one molecule of glucose with one of fructose.

3 A meat and salad roll contains protein, carbohydrate and fat.

Salami

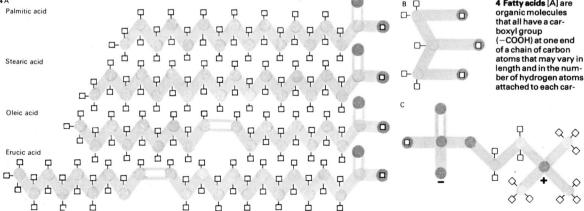

4 Fatty acids [A] are organic molecules that all have a carboxyl group (−COOH) at one end of a chain of carbon atoms that may vary in length and in the number of hydrogen atoms attached to each car-bon. They are a fundamental component of lipids, compounds found in materials as diverse as bacon fat and olive oil. In the most common lipids, three fatty acid molecules are linked chemically to one molecule of glycerol [B]. In some important biological molecules, one of the fatty acids may be replaced by a phosphorus-containing molecule, such as choline phosphate [C], to form a type of compound known as a phospholipid.

Palmitic acid

Stearic acid

Oleic acid

Erucic acid

tion of saturated fats (such as butter) and the incidence of heart disease. Lipids also provide energy for animal cells but, in more complex forms, they play other roles, such as "insulators" for nerve fibres.

Triglycerides are the simplest lipids. An important and more complicated example is cholesterol, widely found in dairy foods such as cream and cheese [3]. It is a major constituent of gall-stones and also implicated in heart disease. Cholesterol, with a complex chemical structure related to that of human sex hormones, is a type of molecule called a steroid. Steroids may be synthesized in living systems from a molecule called squalene, a kind of terpene. Some terpenes are made from only carbon and hydrogen, but others also contain oxygen and nitrogen. They include not only substances such as turpentine, vitamin A and cholesterol, but many flavours and fragrances as well.

Amino acids
From small groupings of carbon, oxygen, nitrogen, hydrogen and occasionally sulphur, all joined in a particular pattern, come the

amino acids [5], the building blocks for proteins. Proteins are major constituents of some of the most important foodstuffs, such as meat, fish and eggs. They are usually made from only 20 different amino acids and yet they have a wide range of valuable properties. In addition a number of other, less common amino acids are known. These can combine to form compounds such as the antibiotic valinomycin, which is made by linking together a small number of amino acids, and the extremely poisonous seven and eight amino-acid rings occurring naturally in toadstools of the genus *Amanita*, such as the death cap and fly agaric.

More complex than the amino acids are the nucleotides, the basic building blocks of the nucleic acids, which carry genetic information. Each nucleotide is made from one of the five types of base [7] which is joined to a sugar and this, in turn, is joined to a phosphate grouping. Some foods are very rich in nucleic acids and too much of them can cause an illness, such as gout, in which the mechanism that usually deals with the bases falters or fails completely from overwork.

Atmospheric carbon dioxide

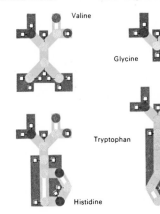

Carbon, the basic element of organic chemistry, undergoes a natural cycle in the environment. It exists in the form of carbon dioxide in the atmosphere.

From there it is absorbed by plants [1] to build carbohydrates in green leaves. When plants burn [2], and animals breathe out [3], carbon dioxide

passes back into the air. Also in decaying plant and animal remains [4], carbohydrates are broken down to release carbon dioxide into the atmosphere.

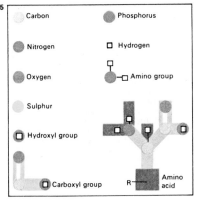

5 About 20 amino acids play essential roles in the structure and function of living organisms. All contain carbon, hydrogen, nitrogen and oxygen atoms; a few also contain sulphur. All except proline have a free unsubstituted amino group and a free carboxyl group. In addition, each amino acid has a characteristic "R" group attached to this carbon atom. This key applies to both of these pages.

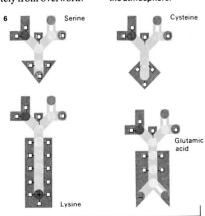

Meat

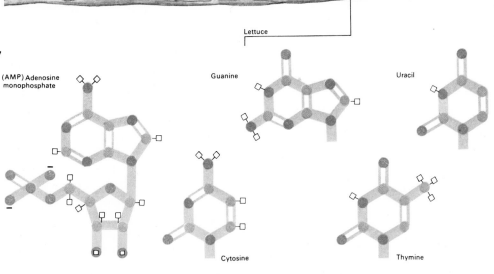

Lettuce

6 Amino acids usually occur in living organisms linked together in hundreds to form complex molecules. But monosodium glutamate, a simple derivative of glutamic acid, has been used as a food additive to enhance the flavour of meat. The "R" group attached to the central carbon atom in an amino acid can vary widely – from the simple hydrogen atom in glycine, to the complex groups found in the

other amino acids illustrated here. In proline, the end of the "R" group is linked also to the nitrogen atom of the amino group, so looping round on itself to form a ring structure.

7 All living matter, be it in the form of liver or lettuce, contains substances called nucleic acids. These are the giant molecules that ultimately are in control of all living processes. Protein made by bacteria, a possible source of synthetic food for man, is rich in nucleic acids. But an excess of these substances or foods containing them can produce unpleasant side-effects in human beings. They are formed by linking together large numbers of a few simpler molecules

called nucleotides. A single nucleotide is, in turn, made by linking together three even simpler chemical groupings: a phosphate, which is joined to a 5-carbon monosaccharide (either ribose or deoxyribose), to which a nitrogen-containing base is attached. Only five of these bases are common: adenosine (shown here linked to phosphate), cytosine, guanine, thymine and uracil. The nucleic acids DNA and RNA contain chains of four such bases linked through a sugar and phosphate.

Carbon
Nitrogen
Oxygen
Sulphur
Hydroxyl group
Carboxyl group

Phosphorus
Hydrogen
Amino group
R — Amino acid

Serine
Cysteine
Valine
Glycine
Glutamic acid
Tryptophan
Lysine
Histidine
Proline

(AMP) Adenosine monophosphate
Guanine
Uracil
Cytosine
Thymine

135

The chemistry of life: biochemistry

All living things – plants and animals – build up and break down different chemicals. These chemical processes ensure that an organism has an adequate supply of both the basic materials and the energy it needs for survival. A person eating a salad roll derives energy from it, which he may use up by running several kilometres; but there is no obvious, direct link between the salad roll and the exercise. Biochemistry, through interlocking reactions, provides that link.

Fundamentals of biochemistry

The complexities of biochemistry can be reduced to two fundamental processes. The first is the way in which living cells develop an energy currency. This, like ordinary money, can be used to exchange one vital commodity for another. The second is the use of substances called enzymes [2] as go-betweens to reduce the amount of energy needed to make many chemical reactions essential to life take place fast enough.

The "currency" used by living cells is a chemical called adenosine triphosphate (ATP) [1]. Closely related to one of the units from which nucleic acids are built, ATP can break down to form adenosine diphosphate (ADP) and phosphate. In doing so, it can supply energy for a biochemical reaction – either one in which simple molecules are built up into more complex ones, or one that controls an activity such as muscle contraction [Key]. On the other hand, where a biochemical reaction gives off energy, as in the breakdown of sugars, that energy can be used to re-form ATP. Consequently, an organism can balance energy inputs against energy outputs by recycling ATP.

Although some biochemical reactions ultimately give off energy and others use it, all need an energy push to get them started. The strength of this push can be decreased if the reacting molecules are close together and are lined up in the correct relationship to each other. Substances called catalysts introduce reacting molecules to one another more efficiently and so reduce the amount of energy needed to get the reaction moving. The overall effect is to make chemical reactions proceed much more quickly.

Life relies heavily on a special class of catalysts, the enzymes [4]. These are made mainly from protein, but they may also include metal atoms or small non-protein organic molecules called coenzymes. Many of the vitamins included in a balanced diet are used by the body as coenzymes.

The shape and activity of enzymes

Enzymes [3] are very large molecules whose activity is governed by their shape. By changing their shapes it is possible to inactivate them, and thus stop certain reactions from occurring at a noticeable rate. For example, the important protein-digesting enzyme chymotrypsin occurs in an inactive form called chymotrypsinogen. Only when a few of the amino acids that make up this protein are removed does it adopt the catalytic shape of chymotrypsin. This change is triggered by the presence of food in the digestive tract. If the chymotrypsin were active all the time it would rapidly digest the intestinal wall while waiting for food to arrive.

In many biochemical processes a molecule is passed from enzyme to enzyme before it becomes an end product. At each

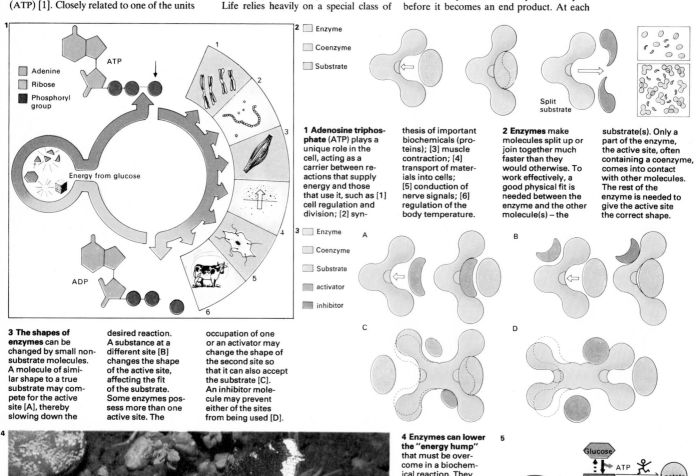

2 Enzyme / Coenzyme / Substrate

1 Adenosine triphosphate (ATP) plays a unique role in the cell, acting as a carrier between reactions that supply energy and those that use it, such as [1] cell regulation and division; [2] synthesis of important biochemicals (proteins); [3] muscle contraction; [4] transport of materials into cells; [5] conduction of nerve signals; [6] regulation of the body temperature.

2 Enzymes make molecules split up or join together much faster than they would otherwise. To work effectively, a good physical fit is needed between the enzyme and the other molecule(s) – the substrate(s). Only a part of the enzyme, the active site, often containing a coenzyme, comes into contact with other molecules. The rest of the enzyme is needed to give the active site the correct shape.

3 Enzyme / Coenzyme / Substrate / activator / inhibitor

A / B / C / D

3 The shapes of enzymes can be changed by small non-substrate molecules. A molecule of similar shape to a true substrate may compete for the active site [A], thereby slowing down the desired reaction. A substance at a different site [B] changes the shape of the active site, affecting the fit of the substrate. Some enzymes possess more than one active site. The occupation of one or an activator may change the shape of the second site so that it can also accept the substrate [C]. An inhibitor molecule may prevent either of the sites from being used [D].

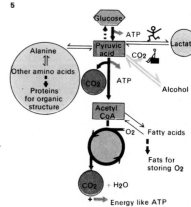

4 Enzymes can lower the "energy hump" that must be overcome in a biochemical reaction. They act as catalysts and are found in many common reactions, such as the rotting of fruit.

5 Pyruvic acid, a key biochemical, is formed during the breakdown of glucose and some amino acids. Further breakdown varies, depending on the biochemical system. In yeast, for example, the end product can be alcohol or gas to raise dough.

stage, an intermediate compound is formed. Sometimes the final product, or one of the intermediates, can combine with an enzyme farther back along the chain and switch it off. This feedback is like automation in a factory that ceases production when enough of a particular material has been made. Other small molecules may combine with an enzyme molecule to increase its activity.

Energy from combustion

The many-step processes involving enzymes are a necessary adaptation to circumstances. Most organic chemicals are combustible. Common sugar, for example, can be burnt completely to produce carbon dioxide, water and heat. But heat energy from total combustion is of no use to living cells. To use such energy a large temperature difference is needed, as in a car engine. Living organisms have roughly the same temperature throughout – the temperature of a healthy human being rarely deviates far from 37°C (98.6°F). Consequently, chemical energy is extracted from the "combustion" process by breaking it down into a large number of small

steps, to produce energy measurable (and removable) in one or two units of the cell's energy currency.

A molecule of glucose, which contains six carbon atoms, can be broken down into two three-carbon pyruvic acid molecules [5]. The process takes ten different steps, uses up two molecules of ATP and produces four new molecules of ATP. The net result of the process is therefore the production of two units of energy currency.

Pyruvic acid becomes involved in one of the key cycles of biochemistry, the citric acid (tricarboxylic acid) or Krebs cycle. It is converted into carbon dioxide and other chemicals [8]. At the same time, energy is transferred to another type of "currency" molecule, but this is soon exchanged for more ATP. Another example of energy-generation is photosynthesis, the primary process taking place in the leaves of green plants. Sunlight is absorbed by complex molecules, particularly chlorophyll, to produce "excited" molecules. These power chemical cycles that, after a number of steps, produce the ATP necessary to pay the biochemical cost of living.

The energy that a strong man uses to lift his weights comes ultimately from the sun. Plants use light to make energy-rich chemicals. Animals eat these and make even more complex substances. Human beings eat animals and plants as food, which is broken down by the digestive system into its component chemicals. These are reassembled to make various body tissues and chemicals for essential life processes. In this way, these biochemicals are employed to supply both the weightlifter's muscles and the energy necessary to flex them. The detailed study of these substances and their circuitous interactions is the science of biochemistry.

KEY

Oxygen
Carbon
Nitrogen
Hydrogen
A — Coenzyme
Iron
Magnesium

6 Every cell is the site of a complex series of chemical reactions that includes both synthesis (anabolism) and breakdown (catabolism). These processes are known collectively as metabolism. Pathways that are basically catabolic are shown in blue, those basically anabolic in green. Paths directly concerned with energy production and use are in brown. Many thousands of separate chemical reactions are involved, each controlled by a different enzyme. Overall balance and control is ultimately maintained by the genetic material of the cell, which governs the production of enzymes.

7 Nature's wide diversity is achieved with much chemical economy. Large molecules are built from a small range of simple ones. Also certain key structures can have widely different functions. Both haemoglobin [6], which transports oxygen in the bloodstream, and chlorophyll [7], with which plants trap the energy of sunlight, need metal atoms in order to function. In haemoglobin iron is used; in chlorophyll, magnesium. In both cases the metals are attached to an organic molecule called a porphyrin [4], made from a compound such as δ-aminolaevulinic acid [3] which is made from glycine [1] and succinyl coenzyme A [2]. Thus the red pigment haem [5] and the green pigment chlorophyll are synthesized from the same smaller molecules, although one of them occurs in animals and the other in plants. Similar compounds play key roles in other biochemical processes. Vitamin B_{12}, a porphyrin-like compound with a cobalt atom at its centre, is needed to prevent pernicious anaemia.

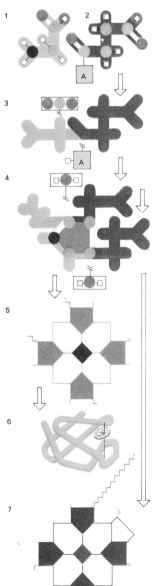

8 All cycles interlink so that the energy from breaking down one type of chemical can be used to make another. If a man overeats, he will put on excess weight – in other words he becomes fat. Yet as the dieter is frequently warned, it is carbohydrates such as sugar, more than fats, that increase weight. Pyruvic acid is the key to this apparent paradox. When it is broken down, in addition to carbon dioxide, a substance called acetyl coenzyme A can be formed. The acetyl part (the triangles) is the basic building block for the fatty acids which, together with glycerol (E-shape), make up oils and fats such as the one pictured at the bottom.

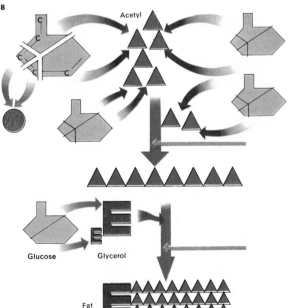

6
Hexose
Derived monophosphate
O_2
H_2O
ADP
ATP
Glycolysis
Reduced coenzymes
Electron transport
Acetyl CoA
Fatty acids
Fats
Pyruvic acid
Glucose
Glycogen
Cycle of tricarboxylic acid
CO_2
Cycle of urea
Urea
Ammonia
Amino acids
Nucleic acids
Nucleotides
Proteins

8
Acetyl
C
Glucose
Glycerol
Fat

Polymers: giant molecules

The metals that make up a car's body and engine are chemically quite different from the oil products that power and lubricate them. Nature is more economical; the same few elements used to build living organisms are also those that trap and transport the energy, all originating from sunlight.

Proteins: polymers of amino acids

The important structural molecules of plants and animals are polymers, very large molecules known as macromolecules, made by joining together a succession of simple chemical building blocks. Proteins, for example, are polymers of amino acids which are small molecules, each containing an amino group and a carboxylic acid group. These two groups can react with one another to form a chemical bond. As a result, different amino acids can be linked through these groups in very large numbers. A small protein, such as insulin [1], may be made up of only 50 or so amino acids, but on the other hand many proteins contain hundreds of individual amino-acid units.

Animals employ proteins [2] both to build tissues and in the biochemical processes which take place in them. Collagen, for example, is a common structural protein. One of its jobs is to provide materials for tendons, which are essential to movement. A tendon "rope" of intertwined collagen molecules can have the strength of light steel wire. Another structural protein, keratin [8], occurs in hoof, hair, horn and feathers, and actin and myosin are important constituents of muscle. Proteins also supply the major (in some cases the sole) component of enzymes, the cell's catalysts which speed up specific biochemical reactions, and the antibodies which fight infective micro-organisms.

Essential to these differing roles are the various physical structures of proteins. When amino acids link together, they do not just form long chains. According to the shapes and the chemical properties of the side-chains of the individual amino acids used in a protein's make-up, it can be long and thin, or compact and globular. The structures contain electrically charged groups and, in addition, sulphur atoms can form bridges between amino acids. In insulin, sulphur atoms bridge adjacent chains of amino acids. In cytochrome C, a sulphur atom attaches a non-protein organic molecule (in this case haem) to a protein molecule.

Polysaccharides: polymers of sugars

The essential structural components of plants are polysaccharides, polymers of the small sugar molecules which provide most of the energy for cells. Not surprisingly, some polysaccharides are also used as a convenient means of storing energy.

It has been estimated that up to 50 per cent of the carbon atoms incorporated in plant tissues are in molecules of cellulose, a structural glucose polymer. In some forms cellulose has commercial value; cotton, for example, is 98 per cent cellulose.

The main energy reserve polymer of plants is starch, which is composed of two polymers – amylose and amylopectin. Like cellulose, amylose is a straight-chain polymer of glucose. The only difference between the two molecules is in the shape of the chemical bond that links the units together. This single difference is enough to make starch a readily

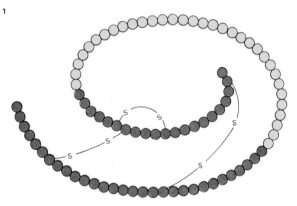

1 Insulin is formed by the removal of 33 amino acid units (yellow) from the protein proinsulin. The two chains of the insulin molecule are bound covalently by sulphur-sulphur bridges.

2 In all proteins, amino acids made of carbon (black), nitrogen (blue), hydrogen (white) and oxygen (red), join to form chains. Hydrogen bonds (red) can hold chains together – as in this pleated β-sheet structure of silk.

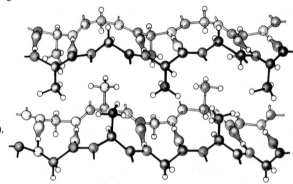

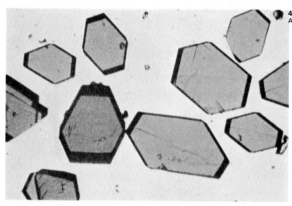

3 Some proteins can be purified sufficiently to form crystals. Once the crystals have grown large enough, their molecular structure can be determined by X-ray crystallography. Myoglobin, a protein which is involved in the carrying of oxygen in muscles, occurs in many species, including sperm whales from which the crystals illustrated here (enlarged 40 times) were obtained.

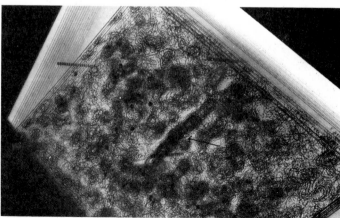

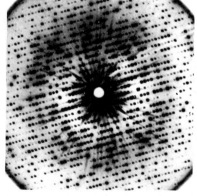

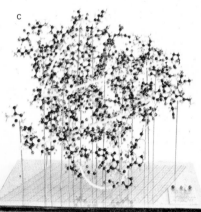

4 The diffraction pattern produced when a beam of X-rays is diffracted (scattered in a periodic manner) by a single crystal can be detected on photographic film [A]. The position and intensity of each spot is measured. Thousands of diffraction spots, from several films, may have to be analysed with the aid of a computer. This provides information from which electron density maps can be drawn. Made from sheets of perspex stacked on top of one another, these maps show where particular atoms in the protein molecules are located [B]. It is then possible to construct an accurate 3-dimensional model [C]. From the structure of myoglobin much can be learnt about its function. The white tube traces the path of the "Backbone chain" of the amino acid polymer. It folds around a raft-like "heme-group" containing an iron atom (large red ball) at its centre. This binds and releases oxygen in response to its environment.

digestible dietary ingredient and cellulose completely indigestible to human beings. In amylopectin, there are chemical links at more than one point on some of the glucose units, so that a branched-chain polymer is produced. The same sort of structure occurs in glycogen (animal starch), the glucose polymer used by animals for energy storage.

Many other sugars, apart from glucose, can form polysaccharides. Chitin, the hard shell material of insects, crabs and lobsters, is a polymeric aminosugar. Alginates, important food additives which keep the head on beer and give dehydrated soups their thickness, are polysaccharides from seaweed, while the pectins, which are widely used in jam-making, occur notably in apples. Natural adhesives, such as gum arabic, are polysaccharides, as is heparin, an important substance that prevents blood clots; it is often used in the treatment of thrombosis.

Nucleic acids
Although not present in such large quantities in most cells as proteins and polysaccharides, the most important macromolecules are the nucleic acids [7]. These make up the genetic material which controls each cell, making it not only a man-cell or a mouse-cell, but a man-liver-cell or a mouse-tail-cell. Nucleic acid polymers are able to reproduce themselves accurately, therefore allowing any species to produce more of its own kind. They also control the chemical building of proteins. As the latter effect includes production of various enzymes, nucleic acids control all other chemical building up and breaking down in living tissues.

Nucleic acid polymers [7] can be thousands of units long. The basic repeating unit is made up from a nitrogen-containing base and a phosphate group. Both of these are attached to one of two types of sugar: ribose (in RNA) or deoxyribose (in DNA). Because of the chemical properties of the bases, particularly those in DNA, it is possible for two strands of nucleic acids to fit together readily to form the "double helix".

Synthetic rubber and plastics are also polymers – often man-made copies of natural molecules. Glass and similar substances are inorganic polymers.

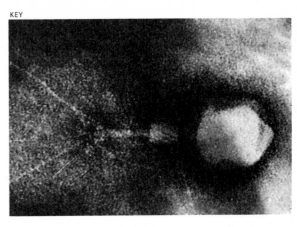

On the margin of life lie the viruses, each made up of a few macromolecules, all of which can be defined in purely chemical terms. Yet, when placed in a living cell, a virus is able to take over that cell's biochemical machinery and make it reproduce virus components. This electron micrograph of a bacteriophage – a virus that attacks bacteria – shows the shape of its protein molecules: inside the diamond-shaped head is the bacteriophage's nucleic acid which directs the build-up of further examples of both itself and the protein components after it has infected a cell.

5 Polysaccharides, proteins and polynucleotides are the basic polymers of life. They are not, however, the only ones. Natural rubber, for example, is a polymer made up mainly of repeating units of the unsaturated hydrocarbon isoprene. From 1,000 to 5,000 such units join together in a single molecule of rubber. The cell walls of some bacteria are made from a combination of sugar and amino acid molecules, to form a mixed polymer. This photograph, taken at a magnification of 280,000 times with the aid of an electron microscope, shows part of the outer cell wall of the bacterium *Clostridium thermohydrosulfuricum*. At this magnification it is possible to see the individual subunits, arranged in regular rows, that make up the surface of the bacterium's cellular wall.

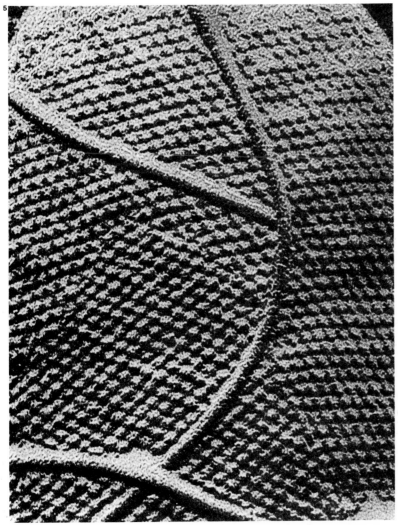

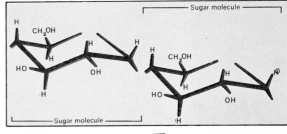

6 Monosaccharides, the simplest of the sugar molecules, can join together to form very large molecules such as starch. According to where the links form, the macromolecule may be a single chain (as shown) or branched.

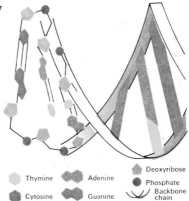

Thymine Adenine Deoxyribose
Cytosine Guanine Phosphate Backbone chain

7 Deoxyribonucleic acid (DNA) is the master molecule of life. It occurs as a double helix in which two complementary strands of polymer are held together by hydrogen bonding. This bonding occurs between the nitrogen-containing bases which form part of the nucleic acid unit.

8 Hair is composed mainly of the protein keratin, which also occurs in feathers and skin. Although these hairs are magnified many times, it is still not enough to make individual keratin molecules visible. Whether a person's hair is straight or curly depends on the tertiary structure of the keratin molecules.

INDEX

Bibliography

The Growth of Science
Asimov, I.; *Guide to Science*; Penguin, 1975
Lloyd, G. E. R.; *Early Greek Science*; Chatto, 1970
Bronowski, J.; *Ascent of Man*; B.B.C., 1973
Boas, M.; *The Scientific Renaissance 1450–1630*; Collins, 1962
Burland, C. A.; *Arts of the Alchemists*; Weidenfeld & Nicolson, 1967
Mathematics
Kramer, E. E.; *Main Stream of Mathematics*; Oxford U.P., 1951
Bell, E. T.; *Development of Mathematics*; McGraw-Hill, 1945
Courant, R. & H. Robbins; *What is Mathematics?* Oxford U.P., 1941
Gardner, K. L.; *Discovering Modern Algebra*; Oxford U.P., 1966
Lockwood, E. H.; *Book of Curves*; Cambridge U.P., 1961
Campbell, H.; *Using Logarithms*; Stillit, 1966
Kuratowski, K.; *Introduction to Set Theory and Topology*; Pergamon, 1972
Thompson, S. P.; *Calculus Made Easy*; Macmillan, 1965
Selby, P. H., *Geometry and Trigonometry for Calculus*; Wiley, 1975
Lunt, W. J.; *Basic Mathematics for Technical College Students*; McGraw-Hill, 1969
Cundy, H. M. & A. P. Rollett; *Mathematical Models*; Oxford U.P., 1973
Griffiths, H. B.; *Surfaces*; Cambridge U.P., 1976
Stephenson, G.; *Introduction to Matrices, Sets and Groups*; Longman, 1965
Moroney, M. J.; *Facts from Figures*; Penguin, 1969
Weaver, W.; *Lady Luck: Theory of Probability*; Penguin, 1977
Adler, I.; *Probability and Statistics for Everyman*; Dobson, 1963
Atomic Theory
Matthews, P. T.; *The Nuclear Apple*; Chatto, 1971
Jungk, H.; *Brighter Than a Thousand Suns*; Penguin, 1960
Statics and Dynamics
Jardine, J.; *Physics is Fun*; Heinemann Educ., 1964–67
Abbot, A. F. & M. Nelkon; *Elementary Physics*; Heinemann Educ., 1971
Heat, Light and Sound
Starling, S. G. & A. Woodall; *Physics*; Longman, 1957

McKenzie, A. E. E.; *A Second Course of Light*; Cambridge U.P., 1956
Jenkins, F. A.; *Fundamentals of Optics*; McGraw-Hill, 1976
Adler, R.; *Introduction to General Relativity*; McGraw-Hill, 1965
Katz, R.; *Introduction to the Special Theory of Relativity*; Van Nost, Reinhold, 1964
Marks, J.; *Relativity: Elementary Non-Mathematical Introduction (Classical, General and Special)*; Chapman, 1972
Sapriel, J.; *Acousto-optics*; Wiley, 1979
Taylor, C. A.; *Physics of Musical Sound*; Eng. U.P., 1965
Matter
Walshaw, A. C.; *Mechanics of Fluids*; Longman, 1972
Kittel, C.; *Introduction to Solid-State Physics*; Wiley, 1976
Electricity and Magnetism
Bleaney, B. I. & B. Bleaney; *Electricity and Magnetism*; Oxford U.P., 1976
Solymar, L.; *Lectures on Electromagnetic Theory*; Oxford U.P., 1976
McKenzie, A. E. E.; *A Second Course of Electricity*; Cambridge U.P., 1973
Jurek, S. F.; *Electrical Machines for Technicians and Technician Engineers*; Longman, 1974
Smith, R. J.; *Circuits, Devices and Systems*; Wiley, 1976
Ahmed, H. & P. J. Spreadbury; *Electronics for Engineers*; Cambridge U.P., 1973
Chemistry
Rossotti, H.; *Introducing Chemistry*; Penguin, 1975
Puddephat, R. J.; *Periodic Table of the Elements*; Oxford U.P., 1972
Brown, G. I.; *Introduction to Inorganic Chemistry*; Longman, 1974
Holden, A.; *Bonds between Atoms*; Oxford U.P., 1971
Parker, D. B. V.; *Polymer Chemistry*; Applied Science, 1974
Thomas, R. W.; *Inorganic Reactions and Volumetric Analysis*; Pitman, 1967
Whitfield, R. C.; *Guide to Understanding Basic Organic Reactions*; Longman, 1974
Denaro, A. R.; *Elementary Electrochemistry*; Butterworth, 1971
Robbins, J.; *Ions in Solution: Introduction to Electrochemistry*; Oxford U.P., 1972
Skoog, D. A. & D. M. West; *Fundamentals of Analytical Chemistry*; Holt, 1969
Irving, H. M. N. H.; *Techniques of Analytical Chemistry*; HMSO, 1974
Rose, S.; *Chemistry of Life*; Penguin, 1970

Major contributors and advisers to The Joy of Knowledge

Fabian Acker CEng, MIEE, MIMarE; Professor Leslie Alcock; Professor H. C. Allen MC; Leonard Amey OBE; Neil Ardley BSc; Professor H. R. V. Arnstein DSc, PhD, FIBiol; Russell Ash BA (Dunelm), FRAI; Norman Ashford PhD, CEng, MICE, MASCE, MCIT; Professor Robert Ashton; B. W. Atkinson BSc, PhD; Anthony Atmore BA; Professor Philip S. Bagwell BSc(Econ), PhD; Peter Ball MA; Edwin Banks MIOP; Professor Michael Banton; Dulan Barber; Harry Barrett; Professor J. P. Barron MA, DPhil, FSA; Professor W. G. Beasley FBA; Alan Bender PhD, MSc, DIC, ARCS; Lionel Bender BSc; Israel Berkovitch PhD, FRIC, MIChemE; David Berry MA; M. L. Bierbrier PhD; A. T. E. Binsted FBBI (Dipl); David Black; Maurice E. F. Block BA, PhD(Cantab); Richard H. Bomback BSc (London), FRPS; Basil Booth BSc (Hons), PhD, FGS, FRGS; J. Harry Bowen MA(Cantab), PhD(London); Mary Briggs MPS, FLS; John Brodrick BSc(Econ); J. M. Bruce ISO, MA, FRHistS, MRAeS; Professor D. A. Bullough MA, FSA, FRHistS; Tony Buzan BA(Hons) UBC; Dr Alan R. Cane; Dr J. G. de Casparis; Dr Jeremy Catto MA; Denis Chamberlain; E. W. Chanter MA; Professor Colin Cherry DSc(Eng), MIEE, late FRAI; Stella Christie MA, FRAI, FRAS; Dr Anthony W. Clare MPhil(London), MB, BCh, MRCPI, MRCPsych; Professor Aidan Clarke MA, PhD, FTCD; Sonia Cole; John R. Collis MA, PhD; Professor Gordon Connell-Smith BA, PhD, FRHistS; Dr A. H. Cook FRS; Professor A. H. Cook FRS; J. A. L. Cooke MA, DPhil; R. W. Cooke BSc, CEng, MICE; B. K. Cooper; Penelope J. Corfield MA; Robin Cormack MA, PhD, FSA; Nona Coxhead; Patricia Crone BA, PhD; Geoffrey P. Crow BSc(Eng), MICE, MIMunE, MInstHE, DIPTE; J. G. Crowther; Professor R. B. Cundall FRIC; Noel Currer-Briggs MA, FSG; Christopher Cviic BA(Zagreb), BSc(Econ, London); Gordon Daniels BSc(Econ, London), DPhil(Oxon); George Darby BA; G. J. Darwin; Dr David Delvin; Robin Denselow BA; Professor Bernard L. Diamond; John Dickson; Paul Dinnage MA; M. L. Dockrill BSc(Econ), MA, PhD; Patricia Dodd BA; James Dowdall; Anne Dowson MA(Cantab); Peter M. Driver BSc, PhD, MIBiol; Rev Professor C.

W. Dugmore DD; Herbert L. Edlin BSc, Dip in Forestry; Pamela Egan MA(Oxon); Major S. R. Elliot CD, BComm; Professor H. J. Eysenck PhD, DSc; Dr Peter Fenwick BA, MB, BChir, DPM, MRCPsych; Jim Flegg BSc, PhD, ARCS, MBOU; Andrew M. Fleming MA; Professor Antony Flew MA(Oxon), DLitt (Keele); Wyn K. Ford FRHistS; Paul Freeman DSc(London); G. S. P. Freeman-Grenville DPhil, FSA, FRAS, G. E. Fussell DLitt, FRHistS; Kenneth W. Gatland FRAS, FBIS; Norman Gelb BA; John Gilbert BA(Hons, London); Professor A. C. Gimson; John Glaves-Smith BA; David Glen; Professor S. J. Goldsack BSc, PhD, FInstP, FBCS; Richard Gombrich MA, DPhil; A. F. Gomm; Professor A. Goodwin MA; William Gould BA(Wales); Professor J. R. Gray; Christopher Green PhD; Bill Gunston; Professor A. Rupert Hall DLitt; Richard Halsey BA(Hons, UEA); Lynette K. Hamblin BSc; Norman Hammond; Peter Harbison MA, DPhil; Professor Thomas G. Harding PhD; Professor D. W. Harkness; Richard Harris; Dr Randall P. Harrison; Cyril Hart MA, PhD, FRICS, FIFor; Anthony P. Harvey; Nigel Hawkes BA(Oxon); F. P. Heath; Peter Hebblethwaite MA (Oxon), LicTheol; Frances Mary Heidensohn BA; Dr Alan Hill MC, FRCP; Robert Hillenbrand MA, DPhil; Catherine Hills PhD; Professor F. H. Hinsley; Dr Richard Hitchcock; Dorothy Hollingsworth OBE, BSc, FRIC, FIBiol, FIFST, SRD; H. P. Hope BSc(Hons, Agric); Antony Hopkins CBE, FRCM, LRAM, FRSA; Brian Hook; Peter Howell BPhil, MA(Oxon); Brigadier K. Hunt; Peter Hurst BDS, FDS, LDS, RSCEd, MSc(London); Anthony Hyman MA, PhD; Professor R. S. Illingworth MD, FRCP, DPH, DCH; Oliver Impey MA, DPhil; D. E. G. Irvine PhD; L. M. Irvine BSc; E. W. Ives BA, PhD; Anne Jamieson cand mag(Copenhagen), MSc (London); Michael A. Janson BSc; G. H. Jenkins PhD; Professor P. A. Jewell BSc (Agric), MA, PhD, FIBiol; Hugh Johnson; Commander I. E. Johnston RN; I. P. Jolliffe BSc, MSc, PhD, ComplCE, FGS; Dr D. E. H. Jones ARCS, FCS; R. H. Jones PhD, BSc, CEng, MICE, FGS, MASCE, Hugh Kay; Dr Janet Kear; Sam Keen; D. R. C. Kempe BSc, DPhil, FGS; Alan

Kendall MA(Cantab); Michael Kenward; John R. King BSc(Eng), DIC, CEng, MIProdE; D. G. King-Hele FRS; Professor J. F. Kirkaldy DSc; Malcolm Kitch; Michael Kitson MA; B. C. Lamb BSc, PhD; Nick Landon; Major J. C. Larminie QDG, Retd; Diana Leat BSc(Econ), PhD; Roger Lewin BSc, PhD; Harold K. Lipset; Norman Longmate MA(Oxon); John Lowry; Kenneth E. Lowther MA; Diana Lucas BA(Hons); Keith Lye BA, FRGS; Dr Peter Lyon; Dr Martin McCauley; Sean McConville BSc; D. F. M. McGregor BSc, PhD(Edin); Jean Macqueen PhD; William Baird MacQuitty MA(Hons), FRGS, FRPS; Professor Rev F. X. Martin OSA; Jonathan Martin MA; Rev Cannon E. L. Mascall DD; Christopher Maynard MSc, DTh; Professor A. J. Meadows; Dr T. B. Millar; John Miller MA, PhD; J. S. G. Miller MA, DPhil, BM, BCh; Alaric Millington BSc, DipEd, FIMA; Rosalind Mitchison MA, FRHistS; Peter L. Moldon; Patrick Moore OBE; Robin Mowat MA, DPhil; J. Michael Mullin BSc; Alistair Munroe BSc, ARCS; Professor Jacob Needleman, John Newman MA, FSA; Professor Donald M. Nicol MA PhD; Gerald Norris; Professor F. S. Northedge PhD; Caroline E. Oakman BA(Hons, Chinese); S. O'Connell MA(Cantab), MInstP; Dr Robert Orr; Michael Overman; Di Owen BSc; A. R. D. Pagden MA, FRHistS; Professor E. J. Pagel PhD; Liam de Paor MA; Carol Parker BA(Econ), MA (Internat. Aff.); Derek Parker; Julia Parker DFAstrolS; Dr Stanley Parker; Dr Colin Murray Parkes MD, FRC(Psych), DPM; Professor Geoffrey Parrinder MA, PhD, DD(London), DLitt(Lancaster); Moira Paterson; Walter C. Patterson MSc; Sir John H. Peel KVCO, MA, DM, FRCP, FRCS, FRCOG; D. J. Penn; Basil Peters MA, MInstP, FBIS; D. L. Phillips FRCR, MRCOG; B. T. Pickering PhD, DSc; John Picton; Susan Pinkus; Dr C. S. Pitcher MA, DM, FRCPath; Alfred Plaut FRCPsych; A. S. Playfair MRCS, LRCP, DObst, RCOG; Dr Antony Polonsky; Joyce Pope BA; B. L. Potter NDA, MRAC, CertEd; Paulette Pratt; Antony Preston; Frank J. Pycroft; Margaret Quass; Dr John Reckless; Trevor Reese BA, PhD, FRHistS; M. M. Reese MA (Oxon); Derek A. Reid BSc, PhD; Clyde Reynolds BSc; John

Rivers; Peter Roberts; Colin A. Ronan MSc, FRAS; Professor Richard Rose BA(Johns Hopkins), DPhil (Oxon); Harold Rosenthal; T. G. Rosenthal MA(Cantab); Anne Ross MA, MA(Hons, Celtic Studies), PhD, (Archaeol and Celtic Studies, Edin); Georgina Russell MA; Dr Charles Rycroft BA (Cantab), MB(London), FRCPsych; Susan Saunders MSc(Econ); Robert Schell PhD; Anil Seal MA, PhD(Cantab); Michael Sedgwick MA(Oxon); Martin Seymour-Smith BA(Oxon), MA(Oxon); Professor John Shearman; Dr Martin Sherwood; A. C. Simpson BSc; Nigel Sitwell; Dr Alan Sked; Julie and Kenneth Slavin FRGS, FRAI; Professor T. C. Smout; Alec Xavier Snobel BSc(Econ); Terry Snow BA, ATCL; Rodney Steel; Charles S. Steinger MA, PhD; Geoffrey Stern BSc(Econ); Maryanne Stevens BA(Cantab), MA(London); John Stevenson DPhil, MA; J. Sidworthy MA; D. Michael Stoddart BSc, PhD; Bernard Stonehouse DPhil, MA, BSc, MInst Biol; Anthony Storr FRCP, FRCPsych; Richard Storry; Charles Stuart-Jervis; Professor John Taylor; John W. R. Taylor FRHistS, MRAeS, FSLAET; R. B. Taylor BSc(Hons, Microbiol); J. David Thomas MA, PhD; D. Thompson BSc(Econ); Harvey Tilker PhD; Don Tills PhD, MPhil, MIBiol, FIMLS; Jon Tinker; M. Tregear MA; R. W. Trender; David Trump MA, PhD, FSA; M. F. Tuke PhD; Christopher Tunney MA; Laurence Urdang Associates (authentication and fact check); Sally Walters BSc; Christopher Wardle; Dr D. Washbrook; David Watkins; George Watkins MSc; J. W. N. Watkins; Anthony J. Watts; Dr Geoff Watts; Melvyn Westlake; Anthony White MA(Oxon), MAPhil(Columbia); Dr Ruth D. Whitehouse; P. J. S. Whitmore MBE, PhD; Professor G. R. Wilkinson; Rev H. A. Williams CR; Christopher Wilson BA; Professor David M. Wilson; John B. Wilson BSc, PhD, FGS, FLS; Philip Windsor BA, DPhil(Oxon), Roy Wolfe BSc(Econ), MSc; Donald Wood MA PhD; Dr David Woodings MA, MRCP, MRCPath; Bernard Yallop PhD, BSc, ARCS, FRAS Professor John Yudkin MA, MD, PhD(Cantab), FRIC, FIBiol, FRCP.